The Passionate Mind of Max

Dedication:
For Maxine Greene

Note:
All royalties from this collection go to
Center for the Arts, Social Imagination, and Education
founded by Maxine Greene
at Teachers College, Columbia University.

The Passionate Mind of Maxine Greene:
'I Am . . . Not Yet'

Edited by

William F. Pinar

FALMER PRESS
Taylor & Francis Group

UK	Falmer Press, 1 Gunpowder Square, London, EC4A 3DE
USA	Falmer Press, Taylor & Francis Inc., 1900 Frost Road, Suite 101, Bristol, PA 19007

First published in 1998

A catalogue record for this book is available from the British Library

ISBN 0 7507 0812 3 cased
ISBN 0 7507 0878 6 paper

Library of Congress Cataloging-in-Publication Data are available on request

Cover design by Caroline Archer

Cover printed in Great Britain by Flexiprint Ltd., Lancing, East Sussex.

Typeset in 10/11.5pt Times by
Graphicraft Ltd., Hong Kong

Printed in Great Britain by T.J. International, Ltd., Padstow on paper which has a specified pH value on final paper manufacture of not less than 7.5 and is therefore 'acid free'.

Every effort has been made to contact copyright holders for their permission to reprint material in this book. The publishers would be grateful to hear from any copyright holder who is not here acknowledged and will undertake to rectify any errors or omissions in future editions of this book.

Contents

Introduction   1
William F. Pinar

1   An Autobiographical Remembrance   9
Maxine Greene

Section One   Four Books

2   'And he pretended to be a stranger to them . . .'
Maxine Greene and *Teacher as Stranger*   14
Alan A. Block

3   Views across the Expanse: Maxine Greene's *Landscapes of Learning*   30
Anne E. Pautz

4   *The Dialectic of Freedom*   39
Jon Davies

5   *Releasing the Imagination* and the 1990s   46
Patrick Slattery and David M. Dees

Section Two   Themes

6   The Passion of the Possible: Maxine Greene, Democratic Community,
and Education   60
Jesse Goodman and Julie Teel

7   From Both Sides of the Looking Glass: Visions of Imagination, the Arts,
and Possibility   76
Carol S. Jeffers

8   Confinement, Connection and Women Who Dare: Maxine Greene's
Shifting Landscapes of Teaching   81
Mary-Ellen Jacobs

9   Signifying Self: Re-presentations of the Double-consciousness
in the Work of Maxine Greene   89
Denise M. Taliaferro

10   Maxine Greene and the Project of 'Making the Strange Liberty of
Creation Possible'   99
Paula M. Salvio

Section Three   Influences on Greene's Thought

11   Existential and Phenomenological Influences on Maxine Greene   124
Marla Morris

Contents

12 Maxine Greene: Literary Influences   137
    Thomas Barone

13 The Slow Fuse of Aesthetic Practice   148
    Rebecca Luce-Kapler

14 What Are the Arts For? Maxine Greene, the Studio and Performing Arts,
    and Education   160
    Donald Blumenfeld-Jones

15 Maxine Greene: The Literary Imagination and the Sources of
    a Public Education   174
    James M. Giarelli

Section Four   Greene's Influence on Educational Theory

16 A Situated Philosopher   180
    Wendy Kohli

17 Maxine Greene and the Current/Future Democratization of Curriculum
    Studies   190
    James G. Henderson, Janice Hutchison, and Charlene Newman

18 Of Friends and Journeys: Maxine Greene and English Education   213
    Robert J. Graham

19 Maxine Greene and Arts Education   222
    Susan W. Stinson

20 Maxine Greene: A Religious Educator's Religious Educator   230
    Kathleen O'Gorman

21 Feeling the Teacher: A Phenomenological Reflection on
    Maxine Greene's Pedagogy   238
    Nancy Lesko

22 Thinking about Thinking: Maxine Greene on Cognition   247
    Brent Davis and Dennis J. Sumara

Section Five   Conclusion

Towards Beginnings   256
Maxine Greene

Notes on Contributors   258

Index   263

Introduction

William F. Pinar

The last time I saw Maxine was Thursday 27 June 1996. That morning she spoke at LSU (not for the first time), to an overflow crowd packed into the old Hill Memorial Library. She had been invited to speak about her 'present passions.' What were they, as she faced her 80th year? 'I ask myself,' she seemed to confide to us, as if there were two not one hundred people in the room, 'what is the meaning of what I have done?' Surveying the current scene, she is, she says, somber. In a time characterized by the continued deterioration of the nation's schools, the degradation of the public sphere generally, when the progressive project itself seems a memory. 'What,' she asked herself, looking at us, 'has my work meant?' There was no hint of self-pity: only the feeling-filled, engaged voice of a serious intellectual.

It was then clear to us that morning, listening to her, that the past does not hold her attention for long. It is the future that draws her, the future that calls to her. She is rewriting, she tells us, her first book, *The Public School and the Private Vision* (and asked me not to include discussion of the original version in this book). She continues a rigorous schedule of public speeches and professional obligations, including teaching. It is late morning now, and she has been speaking for an hour. As she draws near to what feels like the end of the speech, she pauses and looks at us. 'Who am I?' she poses, partly to us, partly to herself. She answers: 'I am who I am not yet.' 'Not yet' . . . the phrase still hangs in the air around me. Maxine Greene **is** . . . **not yet**. Her own sense of incompletion, of what is not yet but can be, inspires us to work for a future we can only imagine now. You will see that inspiration at work in the essays collected here.

The intimacy of our relationship to Maxine — an intimacy shared of course by others who have heard and read her — will be evident in these essays also. To introduce them I want to say something about Maxine in a more public sense. Yes, she is a distinguished philosopher of education, probably the most important of her generation. Her work is very widely known, her name — along with Paulo Freire's — among the most recognized worldwide by those interested in education. She is a former president of the American Research Association, the first woman so honored in 31 years. Within philosophy of education (see Kohli, 1995) she has triumphed despite 'paradigm wars' and gender trials. Her victories there and at Teachers College have not always come automatically. But this is not an occasion to speak to the internal history of her career.

I hope to contribute to our reflection upon her public accomplishment by going outside the field of education for a moment. I note first of all that she is an intellectual, a serious intellectual; it was to this fact I spoke in the Ayers/Miller collection (Pinar, 1998). In this volume I wish to suggest a related characterization, still as intellectual, but more specifically as a New York public intellectual. To do that, I will speak a bit about Susan Sontag, one of the most important and accomplished public intellectuals in the New York tradition.

There are risks, of course: the two figures are quite different in many respects. There are, however, certain resonances between aspects of Sontag's work — particularly her sense of herself as a public intellectual — and Greene's. My aim is not to make a comparative argument, but rather to help us see Maxine Greene more vividly, outside our private feelings for her, by focusing on Susan Sontag. Because Maxine Greene is unique — no one can copy her singular, virtuoso interweaving of philosophy, literature, and social theory — we lack a suitable context from within the field of education to characterize her, to appreciate her, to grasp her achievement. I want the juxtaposition to point directly at that final element, as Greene's achievement is great.

Susan Sontag

Like Maxine Greene, Susan Sontag arrived on the New York intellectual scene in the early 1960s. It was the end-time for a certain form of American intellectual culture and the figure — what has been termed the public intellectual — it supported. Sontag's early essays, collected in *Against Interpretation* (1966a), argued on behalf of avant-garde tastes, criticized what she took to be the parochialism of American arts and criticism, and demanded a new intellectual agenda. Calling for a 'new sensibility,' Sontag seemed to express and even lead much of what would later be dismissed as 'the Sixties.' In the 1960s, Sontag achieved a media exposure hitherto rare in American intellectual life. In a decade of rapid cultural shifts as well as political, gender, and racial radicalization, Susan Sontag assumed an iconic significance (Kennedy, 1995). Stanley Aronowitz (1982) declared that Sontag 'has become the major American example of the Critic as Star' (p. 13). While her reputation is no longer that of the avant-garde radical, the aura of the *enfant terrible* remains, as she remains 'one of the last of a kind, and no less a legend' (Kennedy, 1995, p. 2).

The intellectual role Sontag has often self-consciously performed is that of the generalist or 'writer–intellectual' (Beyer, 1980, p. 43). Her studies of thought and culture — wide-ranging, marked by changing personal taste and interest — include essays on historical events, 'camp', science-fiction, pornographic literature, photography, fascist aesthetics, cancer, and AIDS. She has explicitly endorsed the generalist figure of the intellectual, acknowledging both Americans (Paul Goodman and Harold Rosenberg) and Europeans (Walter Benjamin and Roland Barthes) as models. Introducing the 1966 American edition of Barthes's *Writing Degree Zero*, she was discussing herself as well as Barthes when she wrote: 'Only if the ideal of criticism is enlarged to take in a wide variety of discourse, both theoretical and descriptive, about culture, language and contemporary consciousness, can Barthes plausibly be called a critic' (Sontag, 1966b, p. xi). For Sontag, the work of the contemporary intellectual requires this expanded concept of 'criticism' (Kennedy, 1995).

'The deepest structure in the culture and ideology of intellectuals,' Alvin Gouldner (1979) once observed, 'is their pride in their own autonomy' (p. 33). Sontag exhibited such a pride as an independent thinker and champion of critical intelligence. It is a role she sometimes imagined — as has Edward Said (1996) — as a condition of intellectual 'exile.' Anticipating Said (1996), Sontag saw the intellectual as a kind of 'amateur' unrestricted by disciplinary and professional allegiances. This formulation of her intellectual self-image, Kennedy (1995) insists, is crucial to an understanding of her work: 'I think of myself as self-created, that's my working illusion' (quoted in Cott, 1979, p. 53). This longheld 'illusion' — as Kennedy (1995, p. 4) characterizes it — is one that might have been born during what she has described as her 'very solitary and very bookish childhood' (quoted in Kennedy, 1995, p. 4). It may have to do as well with the struggles of a woman in a predominantly male intellectual world (Kennedy, 1995).

New York intellectual culture at mid-century was typified by intellectual generalists: Edmund Wilson, Paul Goodman, and Harold Rosenberg. There were as well important literary critics, such as Lionel Trilling, Irving Howe, Mary McCarthy, and Philip Rahv, who shared with the generalists an interest in exploring diverse contemporary topics in their writings. These were critics who, in Howe's words, 'found a way to pay attention to a particular text and also comment on the the larger cultural context in which these texts had appeared' (Cain, 1989, p. 561). Many wrote to express the moment, an ambition deriving, for some, from 1930s leftist political movements as well as from the practical demands of small-journal publication. Stylistically, they exhibited a preference for the essay, 'develop[ing] a characteristic style of exposition and polemic . . . The kind of essay they wrote was likely to be wide-ranging in reference, melding notions of about literature and politics . . . It is a kind of writing highly self-conscious in mode, with an unashamed bravura and display' (Howe, 1971, pp. 240–1).

New York intellectuals had a strong sense of European cultural models, and not only due to ethnic inheritance (several were or were children of Jewish immigrants). Himself a New York intellectual, Daniel Bell (1989) described these individuals as 'self-invented,' keen to play down family origins and stimulated by a 'hunger for culture' (p. 131). This cosmopolitan sense of culture — typically New York — might be characterized as 'an admixture of Marxism and modernism . . . though by the 1950s Freud show[ed] more influence than Marx' (Kennedy, 1995, pp. 8–9).

New York intellectuals tended to associate intellectuality with critical inquiry as an activity as well as the general breath of the cultural critic's interests. Intellectual labor was construed as 'critical contention and interventionism' which seeks 'an immediate relation to public issues' (Kennedy, 1995, p. 9). Harold Rosenberg (1970) explained: 'If criticism . . . waits for aesthetics and history to reassert themselves, it avoids the adventure of playing a part in events' (p. 10).

Sontag owes much, Kennedy (1995) points out, to this New York model of engaged intellectuality; it has, in part, formed her commitments to intellectual generalism and cultural criticism, her insistence upon critical autonomy, and her reliance upon the essay form. However, while very much influenced by the critical and ideological commitments of the postwar generation, Sontag has also challenged these. In so doing she exhibited a strong sensitivity to cultural and political shifts of the 1960s. But this sensitivity did not detach her from those earlier preoccupations associated with high modernism important earlier in the century.

The 'mind as passion' and the 'body in pain' are key motifs in Sontag's work. These themes emerge from certain ideas associated with high modernism: the negative, the transcendent, the transgressive, the authentic, the difficult, the silent. 'The ethical task of the modern writer,' she writes, 'is not to be a creator but a destroyer — a destroyer of shallow inwardness, the consoling notion of the universally human, dilettantish creativity, and empty phrases' (1983, p. 131). She accepts this task as morally serious, as a correlative of the principle of negation she admires in modernist thinking. 'All possibility of understanding,' she states, 'is rooted in the ability to say no' (Sontag, 1979, p. 23). The necessity of negation informs both the style and the content of her own writings. As Kennedy (1995) observes: 'Her remarkably self-reflexive prose dramatizes the activity of mind as an antinomian or dialectical play of ideas and valorizes the restlessness of the self-critical intellect' (p. 10). 'In the passion play of thought,' Sontag (1987) wrote, 'the thinker plays the roles of both protagonist and antagonist' (p. 80). Sontag self-consciously manipulates the essay form, especially its performative features, enabling her to experiment with ideas. As Kennedy (1995) notes, Sontag favors disjunctive forms of argument; aphoristic and epigrammatic modes of critical expression are evident throughout her writing.

Sontag's role as a New York public intellectual has come to seem somewhat dated in recent years. The ideals of autonomy and responsibility which support the figure of the free-floating public intellectual are now frequently questioned, especially by academic cultural critics (see, for instance, Leitch, 1992). Independent intellectual activity is widely viewed as being in terminal decline, overwhelmed by the pressure of professionalization and institutionalization which have given rise to a 'new class' of intellectual specialists — technical experts, policy advisers, and academic theoreticians (Gouldner, 1979; Jacoby, 1987; Ross, 1989; Said, 1996; Wexler, 1997). There has been a fundamental restructuring of the intellectual terrain; the role of the public intellectual has faded. The New York intellectual, characterized by a general and contestatory critique of culture and politics, has not completely disappeared, but this figure has been increasingly difficult to imagine within a public sphere which has become increasingly polycentric (Kennedy, 1995).

In the 1990s Sontag is regarded as something of an eccentric in American intellectual life, as one of 'the last intellectuals' (Jacoby, 1987) in the New York tradition. Her commitment to the generalist role and her sense of a common culture that is responsive to rational thought and argument seems to many anachronistic given the fragmentation of the public sphere in the United States over the last 30 years. Thomas Bender (1993) argues that such an intellectual can no longer assume a public:

> [A] plurality of audiences [exists] within a public culture that is essentially cosmopolitan and contested. In the past a fragment of the public, the educated middle-class audience . . . was able to pose with success as the whole. Today, the public is at once increasingly representative, and more fragmented, making it harder to find, to reach, and to define. The intellectual no longer has an unselfconscious 'we' relationship to the public. (p. 144)

In place of a common culture there is a plurality of cultures and tastes, and the generalist can assume no sure constituency under such conditions. Todd Gitlin (1990) observed that 'general thought is so distinctive a taste, now, as to qualify as a special interest alongside personal computing, running, and so on at the serious newstand' (p. 222). As the public sphere becomes increasingly polycentric, intellectuals will probably limit their thinking to localized and specialized problems and communities. However, as Liam Kennedy concludes:

> the universalizing public intellectual has not disappeared and many continue to find a large, differentiated audience. Sontag stands as a singular if not sole example. She is not the last intellectual, but an intellectual who has made public her own ambivalent, speculative, and provocative thoughts on the decline of the new. (1995, p. 129)

An extraordinary American intellectual, Susan Sontag brings to mind another.

Maxine Greene

Like Sontag, Maxine Greene has presented a new sensibility in the broad field of education, our own equivalent of the 'public sphere,' fragmented as it is into specialized even balkanized terrains. Not content to remain within philosophy of education (see Wendy Kohli's essay in this collection), she has assumed a 'generalist' or 'writer–intellectual' identity, emphasizing the genre of the essay. Like Sontag, Greene has engaged many of the major intellectual influences of the twentieth century in the West, as Marla Morris, for instance, explains. Like Sontag, Maxine's aesthetic sense is highly developed. Her commitment to the arts is complete, witness the essays by Donald Blumenfeld-Jones, Mary-Ellen Jacobs, Carol Jeffers, Rebecca Luce-Kapler, Patrick Slattery/David Dees, and Susan Stinson in this volume. There seems to be a strong, if submerged, autobiographical element in Greene's work too, and this becomes somewhat discernible when we place her autobiographical statement (Chapter 1) next to her texts. Maxine's scholarship also stimulates autobiographical reflection, witness the essays by Robert Graham, Wendy Kohli, Nancy Lesko, Kathleen O'Gorman, Anne Pautz, Susan Stinson, and Denise Taliaferro in this volume. Just as Sontag experimented with an expanded notion of 'criticism,' Maxine Greene has performed an expanded idea of scholarship, as the Tom Barone, Alan Block, Brent Davis/Dennis Sumara, and Paula Salvio pieces testify. Her virtuoso performances — composed from literature, philosophy and theory (social, feminist, racial) — dissolve traditional disciplinary boundaries, showing not only extraordinary depth but a breathtaking intellectual range as well. Like the New York intellectuals, and Susan Sontag in particular, Maxine also seems to conceive of intellectuality as very much a matter of political engagement, critical inquiry, and cultural criticism, as the Jon Davies, Jesse Goodman/Julie Teel, James Giarelli, James Henderson/Janice Hutchison/Charlene Newman, and Nancy Lesko essays testify. And Greene too has relied upon the essay as the vehicle through which to convey her passionate mind (Greene, 1995, p. 20). Finally, like Sontag, Maxine seems to many of us 'the last intellectual' in the broad field of education. After all, to whom would we point as a successor? Like Sontag, Maxine Greene is a legend.

Organization of the Book

Because Maxine is so vivid for us, such an embodied presence (Mary-Ellen Jacobs, Nancy Lesko, Susan Stinson, among others, speak to this point), I wanted to start the book with her own autobiographical voice. From her autobiographical voice I wanted us to return to the texts; they are gifts from her to us. Through four books Maxine has inspired an entire generation of scholars to think in politically engaged and powerfully interdisciplinary ways, as these essays make clear. As indebted as we are to her, as fond of her as we are, we must remember, however, that we do not know her in any definitive or final fashion, that she — as an intellectual, as a scholar, as an individual — is not finished. As she said in June 1996, 'I am . . . not yet.' To emphasize this sense of her singularity, of her temporality as an intellectual, as a woman, as a singular individual, to underline her autobiographical as well as public intellectual voice, I choose that phrase to subtitle this collection of gifts from us to you, Maxine.

To make these essays a gift to you is not only to admire you in public, but to reflect in sometimes concrete sometimes abstract ways about your work: the four books, the themes we see laced throughout your work, the influences of others we see in your texts, and finally what we discern as your influence on the series of specialized areas which comprise, in part, the broad field of education. And so I invited the contributors to make statements on these four topics. They have done their job well.

If we have succeeded in this endeavor, that success will not be indicated by your personal pleasure — although of course we want that — but by an intensification of public interest in your work. We want even more readers to know what you have done, know your intellectual leadership, your educational vision. If more of us teach your books, if more prospective and practicing teachers know their 'landscapes of learning,' how to 'release their imagination,' know what freedom is, then we will be gratified indeed. We realize that the task of intensifying interest in your work is not finished with this volume and with the Ayers/Miller volume (Pinar, 1998) which preceded it. I hope there appear a dozen books on your contribution during the next few years. What a hopeful sign that would be for the twenty-first century, for those of us who, like you, are not yet.

Acknowledgments

I wish to thank Philip Wexler for the invitation to edit this book and for his unwavering support during the process. Thanks to Craig Kridel and Alan Wieder for providing the photograph, to Toby Daspit for general assistance, to Wendy Kohli for her helpful editorial advice, and most especially to Maxine Greene, who generously conferred with me from the project's inception.

William F. Pinar
January 1998

References

ARONOWITZ, S. (1982) 'Opposites detract: Sontag versus Barthes for Barthes' sake,' *The Village Voice Literary Supplement*, pp. 13–14, November.

BELL, D. (1989) 'The intelligentsia in American society,' *The Winding Passage: Essays and Sociological Journeys 1960–1980* (pp. 119–37), Cambridge, MA: Abt Books.

BENDER, T. (1993) *Intellect and Public Life: Essays on the Social History of Academic Intellectuals in the United States*, Baltimore: Johns Hopkins University Press.

BEYER, M. (1980) 'A life style is not a life: An interview with Susan Sontag,' *Polish Perspectives*, **XXIII**, IX, pp. 42–6.

CAIN, W. (1989) 'An interview with Irving Howe,' *American Literary History*, **1**, 3, pp. 554–64, autumn.

COTT, J. (1979) 'Susan Sontag: The Rolling Stone Interview,' *Rolling Stone*, pp. 46–53, 4 October.

GITLIN, T. (1990) 'Sociology for whom? Criticism for whom?' in GANS, H.J. (ed.) *Sociology in America* (pp. 214–26), Newbury Park, CA: Sage Publications.

GOULDNER, A. (1979) *The Future of Intellectuals and the Rise of the New Class*, New York: Seabury Press.

GREENE, M. (1995) 'What counts as philosophy of education?' in KOHLI, W. (ed.) *Critical Conversations in Philosophy of Education* (pp. 3–23), New York: Routledge.

HOWE, I. (1971) *Decline of the New*, London: V. Gollancz.

JACOBY, R. (1987) *The Last Intellectuals*, New York: Basic Books.

KENNEDY, L. (1995) *Susan Sontag: Mind as Passion*, Manchester: Manchester University Press.

KOHLI, W. (1995) 'Contextualizing the conversation,' in KOHLI, W. (ed.) *Critical Conversations in Philosophy of Education* (pp. xiii–xvi), New York: Routledge.

LEITCH, V.B. (1992) *Cultural Criticism, Literary Theory, Poststructuralism*, New York: Columbia University Press.

PINAR, W.F. (1998) 'Notes on the intellectual: In praise of Maxine Greene,' in AYERS, W. and MILLER, J.L. (eds) *A Light in Dark Times: Maxine Greene and the Unfinished Conversation*, New York: Teachers College Press.

ROSENBERG, H. (1970) *The Tradition of the New*, London: Paladin.

ROSS, A. (1989) *No Respect: Intellectuals and Popular Culture*, New York: Routledge.

SAID, E.W. (1996) *Representations of the Intellectual: The 1993 Reith Lectures*, New York: Vintage.

SONTAG, S. (1966a) *Against Interpretation*, New York: Farrar, Straus & Giroux.

SONTAG, S. (1966b) 'Preface to Roland Barthes,' *Writing Degree Zero*, New York: Hill & Wang.

SONTAG, S. (1979) *On Photography*, Harmondsworth, UK: Penguin.

SONTAG, S. (1983) *Under the Sign of Saturn*, London: Writers and Readers.

SONTAG, S. (1987) *Styles of Radical Will*, New York: Farrar, Straus & Giroux. Originally Published 1969.

WEXLER, P. (1997) 'Lasch: From nihilism to being in the new age,' Paper presented to the American Educational Research Association, Chicago.

1   An Autobiographical Remembrance

Maxine Greene

I grew up in a family that discouraged intellectual adventure and risk. To me, the opera and the Sunday concerts in the Brooklyn Museum Sculpture Court and the outdoor concerts in the summer were rebellions, breakthroughs, secret gardens. Since the age of 7, of course, I was writing — mostly stories in hard-covered notebooks to give to my father, because I knew no way of communicating with him. I think it was a sublimation; and I wrote so much — in journals, on the backs of old compositions, on flyleaves — I developed a kind of facility. Later, I wrote out all my pain and guilt and embarrassment and loss in journals and notebooks, while I was trying to write novels when I graduated from college. Some years later, when I entered therapy, I realized that I was using the notebooks as a way of ridding myself of my perplexities and confusions, instead of really dealing with them. Also, I let a lot of my passion find its way into that kind of private writing — and that may have caused a writing block in other domains. Anyway, I have not used journals since those first days of therapy — although I sometimes write down descriptions of things or feelings, and I sometimes write lines of poetry or metaphors or something, but it is different; and I now try to tap the subjectivity I was releasing into those notebooks when I write other things, even philosophy.

My occupational history is not interesting. I married a doctor when I was quite young, had a child, took care of the medical office, entered politics in a way, later became Legislative Director of the American Labor Party in Brooklyn, where I edited a newspaper and learned how to make speeches on price controls and the United Nations and things I scarcely think about now.

I forgot to say that the roots of all that were probably in a trip I took to Europe in my late teens where I got involved with people going to fight in Spain and then worked for the Loyalists in Paris and had to be forced to come home and finish school. That got me into activity for Republican Spain, speech making, writing, stuff; and it made me very, very antifascist (prematurely, as they used to say). Anyhow, while married to my doctor I wrote two and a half novels, the first two 'almosts,' but finally failures. And I wrote many rejected articles and things and published a little — once (to my great delight) in *Mademoiselle*. And I had odd jobs, none glorious, some lowly, some hard. And then — after the big war — I was divorced, remarried, and decided to go back to school for an MA — after quite a few years out of Barnard, where I had majored in history and minored in philosophy.

I went to NYU quite accidentally, because it was the only place where I could be a special student on my own time (when my daughter was in school). The most convenient class met two afternoons a week; it was history and philosophy of education, taught by Adolphe Meyer, George Axtelle, and Theodore Brameld in a kind of troika. I had never thought about education before, had never heard of Dewey (partly because Marx and Freud at that time dominated my thinking, or some of my thinking). I think I stumbled on Albert Camus myself at that time, treated *The Myth of Sisyphus* and *The Rebel* as new secret gardens, all mine. Anyway, I was a hard-working student in the class, was asked to assist the next time around, and suddenly I was hooked. I got an MA in philosophy of education. I made up one called philosophy and literature, and another on the individual while I was writing my dissertation. I wrote a dissertation on the eighteenth century, because I never really cared for the eighteenth century, and I thought I would do better with a subject I could distance. I did a whole intricate, interdisciplinary thing called 'Naturalist-Humanism in 18th Century England: An Essay in the Sociology of Knowledge,' partly because my sponsor, George Axtelle, wanted me to do something on humanism. I think. I made a mural, sort of; and I supposed some of it was all right, because they liked it at NYU; but I have never looked at it since. In the course of doing that, I took a seminar with Brameld — half on existentialism (mostly Kierkegaard and Sartre) and half on positivism; I remain grateful to Brameld for that. I even helped write — did write — an article for *Educational Theory* under his name and some fellow-students'. I started teaching off-campus courses, because I was only part-time, things like perspectives on world literature, East and West, and I learned. I even taught American literature. I needed to publish; asked William Brickman, editor of *School and Society*, if I could do profiles for him, proceeded to do some on Robert Maynard Hutchins, the president of Harvard, the president of MIT, Dean Francis Keppel at the Harvard Graduate School (no, the last was for the *Saturday Review* later on, along with one on John Gardner, and some others).

A new chairman took over our department at NYU, and he was one of Rudolph Carnap's students and did not like me, and suddenly I was teaching in the English department — quite unprepared but excited enough. Having published, then, and with a PhD, I got a job as assistant professor of English at Montclair State College in New Jersey. I traveled there from Queens every day, had a little boy at home then, could only manage the commute for a year. But I learned a lot about world literature, from the Illiad to Shakespeare, and I am glad I had the opportunity. Back to NYU to teach English and some educational theory, finally became an associate professor there, published more — an article on tragedy, that was a lead article in the Saturday Review in 1959, and that got me invited to give a public lecture at the University of Hawaii and to teach a summer session there (which I did in 1960 and 1962). Then I was asked to Brooklyn College, where I could teach philosophy of education again. And I started doing *The Public School and the Private Vision* because of a seminar I gave in Hawaii and my desire to pull my various fields (literature, history, educational theory) together.

Also, I started getting papers accepted at the Philosophy of Education Society and actually got invited to give a main session paper in 1963, I think. I was very much into multiple ways of knowing and the problem of the 'pseudo-question' and 'the uses of literature' and so on. At length, I was a program chairman and, a few years later, president of the Philosophy of Education Society and the regional one (something still hard to believe). And I was lucky enough to publish in a few journals, to write prefaces to paperback novels (by Conrad and George Eliot), to review lots of books, to speak in quite a few places.

In 1965, I was asked to come to TC to edit the *Teachers College Record*; and for about seven years I was based in the English department, teaching half my courses in philosophy and the social sciences (where I became full-time in 1973, I guess). I was editor — meaning full responsibility and an editorial eight times a year for the first four years of my tenure (four in the fifth year, when the journal became a quarterly) — until I really wanted to do other things more. I taught philosophy of literature; the arts and American education; philosophy, literature and the visual arts; criticism and contemporary art forms, other things. In time, I began teaching social philosophy (including critical theory, as time went on), modern philosophies of education, a colloquium in existentialism and philosophy, aesthetics and education. When I chose to do philosophy of literature while still in the English department, I did not quite realize that that was opening the doors to the complexities of aesthetics; but it meant an involvement with that complicated and many faceted literature, and I like to think it expanded my philosophical and pedagogical reach. In 1967, I wrote *Existential Encounters for Teachers* in about six weeks or so. And I did lots of chapters in people's books on aesthetics, mostly, literature, etc.

In the early 1970s, I published *Teacher as Stranger*, which seems to be remembered by most of those who have heard of me; and I gave more and more papers on the arts as well as social issues, youth issues, curriculum. Some of those were gathered in *Landscapes of Learning*, which appeared in 1978. Maybe the best thing that happened, however, in the 1970s was the foundation of the Lincoln Center Institute for the Arts in Education, whose philosophy I have always had something to do with, even from the beginning. It is an institute for teachers that has been going on for three weeks every July at the Juilliard School. Public school teachers come to work in workshops with professional artists: musicians, theatre people, painters and sculptors, dancers. They attend performances, hear lectures by me ('philosopher-in-residence') on approaches to aesthetics, art experiences, perception, imagination, etc. . . . Now and then there will be other lectures. During the school term, artists will go to schools to work with teachers who attended in the summer, and with school children, and there will be performances. My idea, you see, was (is) that to engage with works of art, we ought to have some immediate experience with the medium of that work — the body in motion, language, gesture, musical sounds, paint, clay, and so on. We are more likely, with such experiences, to make the work at hand an object of our experience, to let our energy pour into it, to bring it to life. As is obvious, I have been much influenced by Dewey's *Art As Experience* and by a number of existential and phenomenological works — Sartre's, Dufrenne's, Heidegger's. Contact with the history, the questions, the artists, the teachers has been enormously meaningful to me, and I am still teaching at the Institute. For the last ten years I have had a week-long work-shop in the summers at the Institute, in 'literature as art,' which has also been meaningful; and I have worked with other artists in bringing novels, short stories, poetry to life in the course of a number of summers. This has had considerable influence on my doing of philosophy, my thinking about social justice and about the haunting problem of 'multiple realities.'

The most startling event, I suppose, in my professional life was my election to the presidency of AERA (American Educational Research Association) in 1984. There had been no woman president for 31 years, when the organization was far smaller; and I can only attribute it to my many appearances on panels, etc., the papers I gave, and the familiarity of my name because of my editorial posts, and so on. It was, I must say, a difficult time. Reagan was president; it took considerable effort to keep support for educational research flowing. Given my humanities concern, my existentialist orientation, it was not always easy to argue for and to consort with the empiricists, certain ones of whom were positivists, technicists, and so on. But I had a chance to insert my views on multiple literacies into *Educational Researcher* once a month, to talk philosophy when openings appeared, and (I am sure) to advance the feminist cause at the Council and at larger meetings. Since, of course, women have taken increasingly prominent roles in AERA; there have been five women presidents since my term. Actually, I attribute my election and the emergence of women as much to the tides of change as I do to any particular activity of mine or my colleagues. It is interesting to see the rise of interest in qualitative research, in narrative, in story-telling, in new modes of representation. At 'my' annual meeting, we did a lot on art and the aesthetic; we had a special session for Louise Rosenblatt and 'reader response' theory in literature; we even arranged to have an enactment of a David Mamet play, *Duck Variations*, during the meeting. Then it was unusual, and some of the serious quantifiers felt it to be somewhat unbecoming. Today, what with 'reader theatre,' various modes of performance, etc., there is evidence that times have changed. It is odd to contemplate it in these desolate days of preoccupations with standards, performance, the measurable, and the rest.

I have remained active in AERA, and have been able to explore and present papers on pluralism, imagination, literature, the arts. I worry about being obsessive, of pushing too much; but I generally retain a sense of absurdity — and I know how hard it is to perceive all these activities as meaningful. The loss of my daughter in 1986 from cancer; the recent loss of my younger sister from the same disease; the loss of my stepson from a nameless neurological deterioration; and, of course, the predictable loss of friends as old or not as old as I am all reinforced my sense of the tragic, the unpredictable. I want to choose myself, as Sartre said, 'as indispensable,' even though I well know that no one is indispensable. I have written *The Dialectic of Freedom* (which was the Dewey Lecture some years ago) and *Releasing the Imagination*; and, of course, there are great fulfillments when someone responds, writes me about one of them. There is an even greater fulfillment when a student who remembers a class with me in time past will stop me and tell me that I made a difference. (Sometimes I am lucky enough to have someone say I changed his/her life; and I hope against hope that means he/she awakened a bit more, chose himself/herself with more passion and insight, developed more courage to be. And I also hope he/she sees more movies than before, takes the risks of new theatre and painting and music, returns to what he/she has learned to love.)

Technically retired, I have found it hard to stop — and may even be teaching aesthetics again next spring. I founded and have been conducting a Center for Social Imagination, the Arts, and Education, which has thus far held two rather remarkable conferences, bringing together the multiple realities of philosophers, college presidents, educational activists, child playwrights, musicians, actors, jazz players, rappers, classroom teachers, poets in workshops and plenary sessions and small discussion groups. We are planning another this December; and I hope for more philosophers, more children, more sound, more imagery, more questions.

Meanwhile, under the rubric of the Center (now part of Teachers College's Educational Outreach and Innovation Center), I have been holding what we call 'educational salons' at my home once a month. Teachers come from various parts of the city for discussion with each other and visitors like Lisa Delpit (who came to talk about relations between imagination and teaching 'other people's children'), Valerie Polakow, author of *Lives at the Edge* (about single mothers in Detroit), Wesley Brown (novelist and playwright) along with me and two colleagues in philosophy (Rene Arcilla and Wendy Kohli) talking about the canon and the curriculum. Another time we went to the Studio Museum in Harlem for our salon, for a remarkable discussion of the blank spaces where African-American painters must be discovered and named at last. We have had good personal discussions about art, imagination, teaching on various levels; and I find that, when a space is provided (and people can sit on the floor, drink coffee, take their time) something rather wonderful can happen. So I keep trying, in order to stay alive and keep alive the sense of possibility, knowing well that there are no guarantees.

Section One

Four Books

2 'And he pretended to be a stranger to them . . .'
Maxine Greene and *Teacher as Stranger*

Alan A. Block

It has come time for the confession: I am a teacher.[1] For my entire professional life I have never been anything but a teacher. I have stood in thousands of classrooms during my 25 years in the profession. I have gazed upon the faces and been gazed upon by the faces of thousands of students. I stand several times daily with my hand on the doorknob to a classroom, and several times daily I experience terror. Standing at the entrance way ('Abandon home all Ye who enter here' Dante posts above the gate of hell) I think of J. Alfred Prufrock who declared that 'there will be time/To prepare a face to meet the faces that you meet;/There will be time to murder and create . . .' I, to the contrary, have never had enough time, though I do ponder with Prufrock, 'And should I then presume?/And how should I begin?' Yet despite the fact that, unlike Prufrock, I *have* heard the mermaids singing even to me, and unlike the reserved Prufrock, I am at home in school, I acknowledge that I have rarely engaged in a classroom as a teacher in which I did not feel first very frightened and in which I did not experience a radical estrangement. Even now, after all these years, I stand at the door of the classroom and as I enter the room I sense my breathing unnaturally quicken and my heart beat rather wildly. In such moments I cannot but be reminded of Edgar Allen Poe's (1967) horror tale *The Tell-Tale Heart*. Believing he has rid himself of the old man's gaze by stilling his heart, the story's narrator, experiencing the growing terror at the perceptible beating of the heart but trying desperately to deny its sound, remarks, 'No doubt I now grew *very* pale; — but I talked more fluently, and with a heightened voice. Yet the sound increased — and what could I do? . . . I gasped for breath' (1967, p. 448). Hiding his terror behind a facade of rationalism, the narrator vainly attempts to mislead the investigators. I push open the door to my classroom and I, too, reveal the tell-tale heart. Like the unnamed protagonist in the story I, too, must ultimately acknowledge my humanity.

I stand before a class and I am unnerved by their beating hearts. On the one hand I know that the students look to me as the one who knows; after all, so much of the architecture of the room speaks in this tone: I stand at the front and they face me; I am socratically peripatetic and they remain fixed; I question them in their seats and they await my approval for their response. Or worse, they sit silently unwilling to risk any disapproval for a wrong answer and I stalk the room desperate for conversation. They are terrified of my power. I am terrified of my power. I am frightened that all of my knowledge is inadequate to the task that abides in the classroom. I am terrified that I have nothing to teach these students. I am terrified that I will not know what to teach these students. I am terrified that I am alone in this classroom. Truly, I wonder, what exactly is my task as I stand in front of this classroom and how will I judge the accomplishments of the students and of myself from my position at the front? I know there are people who attempt to answer that question for me: Diane Ravitch (1995) writes that 'curriculum standards describe what teachers are supposed to teach and students are expected to learn ... Performance standards describe what kind of performance represents inadequate, acceptable, or outstanding accomplishment' (p. 12). I am envious of her certainty; doubtful of her claim. Oh, I know to what she refers; like Bartleby imprisoned I can say 'I know where I am.' But like Bartleby I must say 'I prefer not to.'

Teacher as Stranger

Maxine Greene (1973), unlike Ravitch, gives me comfort but offers me no easy answer. Maxine Greene argues that the teacher must continually interrogate the very purpose of education, her very presence in the classroom. Everything is always suspect. Her charge to the teacher is to remain in doubt. Maxine Greene urges the teacher to be a stranger. No wonder, then, that the heart beats so tellingly.

> We simply suggest that he [the teacher] struggle against unthinking submergence in the social reality that prevails. If he wishes to present himself as a person actively engaged in critical thinking and authentic choosing, he cannot accept any 'ready-made standardized scheme' at face-value. He cannot even take for granted the value of intelligence, rationality, or education. Why, after all *should* a human being act intelligently or rationally? How *does* a teacher justify the educational policies he is assigned to carry out within his school? If the teacher does not pose such questions to himself, he cannot expect his students to pose the kinds of questions about experience which will involve them in self-inquiry. (1973, p. 269)

It is the process of inquiry — the production of doubt — that creates the educational environment. The rest is silence. In the Talmud is a story of Rabbi Johanan who has had an argument with his student and brother-in-law, Resh Lakish, and feels affronted and hurt. Now, Resh Lakish is actually a good student and because Lakish lives in such respect for his teacher and because he feels that he has insulted him, he actually falls ill at the consideration of the possible insult to this beloved teacher. Johanan's sister, who is also Lakish's wife, comes to her brother, Johanan, to beg him to forgive Lakish that he might become well. Johanan refuses to do so and, quoting Scripture, assures his sister that he will be sufficient to care for her should her husband actually die. In short time, indeed, Lakish expires and Johanan grieves deeply. To draw him out of his grief, Rabbi Eleazar ben Pedath 'whose disquisitions are very subtle' is sent to study with Johanan in hope that the conversation will enliven the scholar. But Johanan is displeased because Eleazar only agrees with the teacher rather than interrogate him. Johanan chastizes Eleazar: '... when I stated a law, the son of Lakisha used to raise twenty-four objections, to which I gave twenty-four answers, which consequently led to a fuller comprehension of the law; whilst you say, "A baraitha[2] has been taught which supports you:" do I not know that my dicta are right?' Then Johanan went on grieving and mourning, crying out 'Where are you O son of Lakisha, where are you O son of Lakisha.' And his grief at the loss of his student drove Johanan mad and he died. The teacher who is not challenged cannot learn; the student who will not challenge needs no teacher. In a classroom in which all is prescribed and known — in which it is declared what a teacher should teach and a student should learn — there can be no teachers and no students. In such a place we would be not strangers but unseen.

Of course, it is not just the architecture of the room; it is the entire structure of American education that isolates me at the front of the room and quickens my breath and causes my heart to tell the tale. Franklin Bobbitt (1918, p. 42), who claims to have written the first book on curriculum in America and whose work remains a primary influence on American education, tells us that the curriculum ought to be means to an end. The curriculum is 'that series of experiences which children and youth must do and experience by way of developing abilities to do the things well that make up the affairs of adult life; and to be in all respects what adults should be.' School is a training ground for adult life, and the school must create educational objectives that will permit attainment of those adult behaviors that are not already learned from general experience or that are learned imperfectly. It is our job as educational workers to find the disease and cure it. '*The curriculum of the directed training,*' Bobbitt (1918) writes, '*is to be discovered in the shortcomings of individuals after they have had all that can be given by the undirected training*' (p. 45, italics added). I am unnerved by this task. How can I discover imperfection? Who made me so perfect? Diane Ravitch (1995) says that 'Teachers who know what the students' preconceptions are can help them understand new ideas and replace misconceptions' (p. 103). This remarkable sentence follows her acknowledgment that knowledge is actually constructed, is based on previous knowledge, experience, and understanding; yet here she advocates the mere excision of old knowledge and the implanting of new by the teacher. Would teaching were so easy as removing an appendix and inserting, say, a new stomach. Maxine Greene, on the other hand, writes in *Teacher as Stranger* (1973) that 'the existential teacher must confront his [sic] freedom along with the alien freedoms of his students; and because he is bound to attend to so much more than performance, speech, and observable instances of mastery, he can never be sure of what he or they achieve' (p. 287). I am to look for learning in both my students and myself; for each and every individual this learning will take on different characteristics and appear differently. 'And how should I presume?'

E.D. Hirsch argues that everyone should have the same knowledge. So, too, do the advocates of national standards. Ravitch (1995) writes that 'Standards can improve achievement by clearly defining what is to be taught and what kind of performance is expected. They define what teachers and schools should be trying to accomplish' (p. 25). But in the national standards movement of the 1990s, it is claimed that our educational ills have sickened all of society.[3] In an article in *The New York Times Magazine,* Sara Mosle (1996) argues that the answer to our educational ills (who is 'our?') is national standards. She writes: 'Whoever takes the oath of office as President on January 20, 1997,[4] would be wise to seize the moment and advocate the creation of a national curriculum with high-stakes assessments and the means to help students meet them' (p. 68). In this view, curriculum is a reparative process for a sick society. Our nation's ills may be traced back to the schools and the curriculum.[5] The cure is the establishment of clear and defined standards and a strict system of assessment. Diane Ravitch (1995) writes that '"Education" means to lead forth, but it is impossible to lead anyone anywhere without knowing where you want to go. If you do not know what you are trying to accomplish, you will not accomplish much' (p. 25). I am reminded of the Grateful Dead (Garcia and Hunter, 1970) lyric, '*If* I knew the way, I would take you home.' My tell-tale heart discloses my doubts and fears. For Ravitch and others in the standards movement, the establishment of content standards would clearly define what is to be taught and what kind of performance to expect. They always seem to know where they are and where they are going. They are never strangers. 'And how should I presume.' 'If I knew the way, I would take you home.'

Maxine Greene's wonderful book *Teacher as Stranger* comforts me in these terrible moments. She reminds me that the terror I experience in the classroom is the experience of freedom and not of inadequacy; she offers me support in my conviction that I cannot presume: 'The problems are inescapable, wherever the teacher is assigned to teach, because he is asked to function as a self-conscious, autonomous, and authentic person in a public space where the pressures multiply . . . The teacher's responsibilities become more and more complex; and he is required every day to reinterpret, to make his own sense of modern life' (1973, p. 290).[6] Maxine Greene supports the contention that the conditions of society are not to be cured in and by the schools; indeed, within the classroom the effects of social disease are clearly evident. Schools are not autonomous institutions of society but are rather products of and influences upon that very society. The relationship is intricate and not causal. The complexities of contemporary life are such that it must be the teacher's function to introduce ways of thought to students so that they might recognize and act on options available to them. They must learn to interrogate those options and the condition in which they arise. The teacher 'must sensitize [students] to inhumanity, vulgarity, and hypocrisy; he must help them seek equivalents for violence and war. And at some level, he must enable them to comprehend their society's professed ideals: freedom, equality, regard for the individual' (1973, p. 290). Perhaps education should have always been so directed; but then, it is only in the twentieth century that school populations included the once-silenced voices in the American system. It is only in the twentieth century that the school schooled children who were not the inheritors of these professed ideas. The teacher has been during this century constrained to maintain the status quo because schools were in large part established to do so; indeed, it is the status quo that pays the teacher's salary. Maxine Greene advocates that the teacher as stranger look awry at the basic assumptions of even his own salaried position. Maxine Greene offers the terrifying freedom of the potentially exhilarating classroom.

Too often, however, teachers are not asked to so function, in which case they become passive promoters of the status quo and the present unjust situation is perpetuated. Too often students demand to be simply told what to do rather than be plagued with thinking about what they already do and what must yet be done. They do not desire to question but merely to answer. Too often program directors complain that their students don't see the relevance in theory; they just want something practical and hands-on that they can take with them from the classroom into the classroom, a barrier that will distinguish and separate between the knower and the unknowing, between the teacher and the student, and between the well and the sick. I do not think it odd that a book Maxine Greene keeps returning to — not just in *Teacher as Stranger* but throughout her life's work — is Albert Camus' *The Plague* (1972). Camus' story concerns a city that is ravaged by the plague; the novel follows the reactions of people — some heroic and others passive — to the deadly afflictions. It is this pandemic that arouses action in the city, turning some people into victims of the plague and others into fighters against it. This plague, a deadly affliction that robs people of their hopes, their powers, and even their lives, can be either accepted and succumbed to or it can be resisted. Which course of action one chooses rests with the individual; as Maxine Greene acknowledges (1973, p. 281), the distinction between the reactions is important and says a great deal about the type of existence of the individual. Because finally, Maxine Greene says, there is no 'good reason' to fight the plague. Contrary to Bobbitt's and Ravitch's prescription that schools cure social ills, Maxine Greene (Camus, 1972) acknowledges that though people may gain a temporary respite from its ravagings, 'the plague bacillus never dies or disappears for good; that it can lie dormant for years and years in furniture and linen-chests; that it bides its time in bedrooms, cellars, trunks, and bookshelves; and that perhaps the day would come when, for the bane and the enlightening of men, it would rouse up its rats again and send them forth to die in a happy city' (p. 287). Therefore, since no one knows how to ultimately stop the plague or heal the illness, the decision to choose to fight it becomes a personal decision. Indeed, it is the reaction of each person to the plague — as it is the reaction of each teacher to the classroom — that ultimately defines that person. The decision to be a fighter means that the Doctor and other volunteers like him refuse to accede to the way things are — to the presence of the plague or the architecture of the world or the educational institutions. As Tarrou says, 'All I maintain is that on this earth there are pestilences and there are victims, and it's up to us, so far as possible, not to join forces with the pestilences' (in Greene, 1973, p. 236). The fighters acknowledge that they cannot cure the plague: but that is not the point. Maxine Greene (1973) writes that 'Doctor Rieux keeps struggling because it is his job, it is only "logical," and because "a fight must be put up, in this way or that, and there must be no bowing down." Tarrou is committed to becoming 'a saint without God.' And they remain 'whole persons (out of "common decency"); they show compassion and refuse to become merely passive victims, at the mercy of the inhuman plague. *They do not act on predetermined principle*' (in Greene, 1973, p. 281, emphasis added). That is, they act not because they mean to cure but because they care. Their actions are not premised on pre-discovered objectives but rather on the exigencies of the moment and the needs of the plague-ridden populace. They accept that the plague cannot be cured but only relieved. Dr Rieux's chronicle is that the novel was compiled 'so that he should not be one of those who hold their peace . . . but should bear witness in favor of those plague-stricken people; so that some memorial of the injustice and outrage done them might endure; and to state quite simply what we learn in time of pestilence: that there are more things to admire in men than to despise' (1973, pp. 286–7). Unlike Bobbitt's curriculum worker, these fighters discover their purpose in the needs of those afflicted, and they acknowledge that we are all — or soon will be — afflicted. What we cure today cannot prevent another problem from arising tomorrow. How can there be standards when we don't even know the situation to which those standards must answer? I read that 60 per cent of the jobs that will exist in the first decade of the twenty-first century have not yet been invented. For what am I preparing whom? As Lenin so defiantly asked, 'What is to be done?'

'This book,' Maxine Greene (1973) writes in the 'Preface' to her book *Teacher as Stranger*, 'is specifically addressed to the teacher or teacher-to-be who is in the process of choosing as his "fundamental project" the activity of teaching in the classroom.' She argues, with Tarrou, that teachers be plague fighters, because the alternative is to be plague victims. And to be a plague fighter is to be, inevitably, a stranger: Tarrou says 'I have realized that we all have plague, and I have lost my peace. And today I am still trying to find it . . . This and only this can bring relief to men, and, if not save them, at least do them the least harm possible and even, sometimes, a little good. So that is why I have resolved to have no truck with anything which, directly or indirectly, for good reasons or for bad, brings death to anyone or justifies others' putting him to death' (Camus, 1972, p. 235). In fact, Maxine Greene offers strong but precarious advocacy. Why after all these years do I still experience the terror outside the classroom? Why do I still feel the beating of the tell-tale heart? Maxine Greene teaches me that it is endemic to the role of the teacher to be a stranger. And so the terror that I experience outside each and every classroom has material cause. It is my intentional position to make myself dissonant to the traditional classroom atmosphere, to call into question the assumptions of myself and my students, and to invite not quiet disquisitions but intense examination of the very bases of our work and intentions. *Teacher as Stranger* is subtitled "Educational Philosophy for the Modern Age.' Its intent is to advocate for a critical consciousness by calling into question many of the assumptions on which American education has been based in at least the twentieth century.

What Maxine Greene (1973) speaks of as the '"crisis" of belief which has affected ways of thinking about human nature, knowledge getting and knowledge claims, moral decisions and moral standards,' we have come to understand as evidences of the postmodern. She shows the postmodern as the expected result of doubt. But unlike the postmodern, Maxine Greene does not foresee the future as more of the present — the teacher as stranger will produce thinkers who will then decide the future rather than be trained to accept it. Thus the book is divided into sections that address the nature of the human being (Chapters 1–3), the question of knowledge (Chapters 4–7), and the subject of values (Chapters 8–10). That is, the book demands that we interrogate what our assumptions about the nature of the human being mean for the way we understand education; what do our understandings and theorizations about knowledge mean for the construction and organization of our curricula. Maxine Greene demands that we do philosophy. And if, as Mordecai Kaplan (1994) writes, 'The worth of a civilization depends not only upon the ideals and values it professes, but upon its ability to energize them' (p. 460), then Maxine Greene's book demands that we wonder upon what value system our educational system rests and what values does it interrogate and actualize? What does our educational system say about our civilization? Maxine Greene's book is a challenge to teachers or teachers-to-be to challenge what they know about what they mean to do, and therefore to challenge (and hopefully produce) who they are and what they will be — teacher-educators. Her final chapter, 'Teacher As Stranger,' is an advocacy for the notion of the teacher as intentional outsider.

From the stranger's position, the teacher may view society awry and interrogate its foundations and practices. 'To take a stranger's point of view on everyday reality is to look inquiringly and wonderingly on the world in which one lives. It is like returning home from a long stay in some other place' (1973, p. 267). That is, as the stranger, one sees things in the mundane that the residents cannot see. 'The homecomer notices details and patterns in his environment he never saw before. He finds that he has to think about local rituals and customs to make sense of them once more. For a time he feels quite separate from the person who is wholly at home in his ingroup and takes the familiar world for granted' (p. 268). That is, a stranger is someone who has returned from some other place and some other experience such that it is impossible to see the world again in the same way. The stranger is one who has become willfully estranged. Tarrou (Camus, 1972) argues that once he refused to accede to the plague, the only release is in death; until that time 'I have no place in the world of today; once I'd definitely refused to kill, I doomed myself to an exile that can never end' (p. 236). In another context Henry David Thoreau (1980) says: 'If you are ready to leave father and mother, and brother and sister, and wife and child and friends, and never see them again, — if you have paid your debts, and made your will, and settled all your affairs, and are a free man, then you are ready for a walk' (p. 94). That is, to engage in an educational experience is to make of yourself a stranger not because you never will return home again but because returning home again unchanged is impossible. That is why, Thoreau cautions, one must be free to first engage in the walk. The teacher must be an active walker. Maxine Greene's (1973) teacher-as-stranger too must be free not necessarily of entanglement — it is the nature of living to be caught in the contradictory aspects of existence — but of being entangled and incapable of wresting free. It is in this capacity that the category of stranger serves the teacher for it is in this looking awry that permits a critical glance even at one's own ideological stances. 'If . . . he is willing to take the view of the homecomer and create a new perspective on what he has habitually considered real, his teaching may become the project of a person vitally open to his students and the world . . . He will be continuously engaged in interpreting a reality forever new; he will feel more alive than he ever has before' (p. 270). In that process he will educate students to do the same.

Of course, Maxine Greene's book *Teacher as Stranger* serves this function for the reader. Exploring the Western philosophical tradition, Maxine Greene forces the reader to look as might a stranger at the assumptions on which the reader's view of education and of the teacher is based. She displaces the reader from the comfortable stance traditionally promulgated in the United States ('If the teacher agrees to submerge himself into the system, if he consents to being defined by others' views of what he is supposed to be, he gives up his freedom "to see, to understand and to signify for himself"') and demands that the teacher be engaged in 'transmuting and illuminating material to the end of helping others see afresh. If he is able to think what he is doing while he is vitally present as a person, he may arouse others to act on their own freedom. Learning to learn, some of those persons may move beyond the sheltered places until they stand by their own choice in the high wind of thought' (1973, p. 298). Of course, the teacher as stranger in the teacher education program will create teachers who will desire to be strangers. Then perhaps we might all live together in peace.

Choosing What?

As a Jew, I find that the designation of stranger has never been strange. Indeed, the Torah consistently reminds me that 'you were strangers in the land of Egypt' (Leviticus, 19:33–34). The revelation at Sinai that confers the status of a people on the Hebrews is predicated on our having once been strangers in the land. For the Jew, there is no need to become a stranger; it is a designation conferred and usually with opprobrium. The status of stranger has, as a condition, always come with the territory, and I understand that now it has become my effort to understand those structures and to work within them. Though Jews now figure prominently in the mainstream of American society, this position has come about not out of an 'educational epiphany' but as the result of what Karen Sacks (1994) acknowledges as the 'biggest and best affirmative action program in the history of our nation' (p. 79). Nor has this social position always been available: Karen Sacks writes that 'Anti-immigrant racist and anti-Semitic barriers kept the Jewish middle class confined to a small number of occupations. Jews were excluded from mainstream corporate management and corporately employed professions, except in the garment and movie industries, which they built. Jews were almost totally excluded from university faculties (and the few that made it had powerful patrons). Jews were concentrated in small businesses, and in professions where they served a largely Jewish clientele' (1994, p. 84).

Maxine Greene suggests that the teacher must choose the status of stranger in order to teach, but I am increasingly conscious of what I have forever understood — as a Jew I teach from the position of stranger not by choice but by historical necessity. If as Marx (1984, p. 15) says that 'Men make their own history, but they do not make it just as they please; they do not make it under circumstances chosen by themselves, but under circumstances directly encountered, given and transmitted from the past,' then as Jew I have always occupied the position of stranger and spoken from this locus of estrangement. Mordecai Kaplan (1994) writes that 'The Gentile populations treated [the Jew] at all times as an alien, and often as an outlaw. If they allowed him to live among them, it was only because they need him for such uses as money-lending, itinerant trading, or at best, tax farming — occupations which only served to render the Jew even more odious. There was no ground where Jew and Gentile could meet on a footing of equality' (p. 11). Given this situation, one searches, as Marx suggests, for advantages to strangerdom; unlike

Greene's charge that the teacher become a stranger, it appears to me now that the Jews' task has been to learn how to use the assigned designation of stranger for good. E.M. Cioran (in Bauman, 1995, p. 211) offers perhaps the ironic final benefit of being the stranger: to owe no allegiances and be bound by no obligatory loyalties. Cioran asserts that the Jew, 'emancipated from the tyranny of local commitment, from the stupidities of *enracinement*, without attachments, acosmic, is the man [sic] who will never be *from here*, the man from somewhere else, the stranger *as such* who cannot unambiguously speak in the name of the natives, *of all . . .*' In this sense, the Jew becomes the quint-essential postmodern. Hannah Arendt (1978) argues that the reality of the Diaspora made dissociation psychologically and physically essential for the Jew; thus, the Jews came to conceive of their existence as almost totally separate and independent from the rest of the world. The Jews were forced to conceive of themselves as strangers because the world enforced this distinction physically and psychologically upon them; the Jews' response was to accept the role.

That the Jew was to be a stranger seemed given; it was what to do with this status that concerned most Jews. Often, perhaps, the Jew was able, ironically, to rationalize this sense of strangerhood as an avenue to belonging and assimilating; in the Diaspora, the Jew, allied to *no* nation, could consider him/herself allied to *any* nation. Being Jewish facilitated assimilation because to be Jewish represented a religious affiliation and not a national one. The Jews could then circumvent strangerhood because they could be at home anywhere despite the exigencies of exile and persecution. Or the Jew would accept the notion of the stranger as a self-willed condition and assume the responsibilities personally of isolation. Often feeling the sense of estrangement, I assumed that it derived from my own character and I endeavored to end what I considered self-exile. Therapy — the Jewish science — would help me end my experience of isolation. Bernard Berenson, would write that 'I have not yet learned to like myself as I am. I still . . . look for flashes of hope that I am not so worthless as I often feel' (in Rubin, 1995, p. 75). Born strangers, many Jews when emancipated desired desperately to belong; but that sense of belonging often came at a high price: to become a stranger even to one's self. Berenson writes that 'it has been an effort . . . to act as if one were a mere Englishman or Frenchman or American' (in Rubin, 1995, p. 75). Assimilation meant the concerted attempt to be like the Northern European white males who defined the order. Barry Rubin writes that 'The response to oppression and feelings of inferiority as Jews was not self-assertion but concealment and flight' (1995, p. 69). American Jews tried desperately to cease being noticed as Jews: the education of Hyman Kaplan is the humorous story of one man's attempts to be an American; Philip Roth's *Goodbye Columbus* is another. 'The flight of American Jews from poverty and foreignness had resulted in an Americanization largely defined as the removal of any Jewish stigma . . . To become accepted, wealthy, famous, and successful was to stand astride the stage as "American" and "humanist," shorn of any other label' (Rubin, 1995, p. 85). Is it so strange, then, that in education the Western intellectual tradition has held sway and excluded almost all Jewish sources of culture and wisdom? As I have argued elsewhere (Block, forthcoming), Jewish voices in educational discourses have been silenced and suppressed except insofar as they have reinforced the dominant normative cultures. And so Maxine Greene's urging that the teacher might *become* a stranger might be perplexing to the Jew who was already a stranger and abhorred that condition. As a Jew I have been cast by history in the position of stranger, but the desires and pressures of assimilation into American society — indeed, the entire movement of Jewish history as a series of forced exile and wandering — have led to the repression of the ontological notion of the Jew as stranger. Greene's call for the teacher to be stranger is an ironic cry for the Jew to return to him/herself. Sergeant Marx, the assimilated Jew, says to Grossbart (Roth, 1969, p. 135) who wishes to practice as a Jew, 'This is a war, Grossbart. For the time be the same.' 'I can't,' says Grossbart. 'I refuse. I can't stop being me, that's all there is to it. Indeed,' says Grossbart, 'It's a hard thing to be a Jew. But . . . it's a harder thing to stay one.' The cost of being a stranger has been heavily paid by Jews; the pain and suffering that attends the designation has been obscene; assimilation promised an end to persecution and difference, an end to strangerdom. And yet, assimilation has not come without its attendant costs.

The pressures of and the desires for assimilation demanded and promised the end of strangerhood. It was for many a consummation devoutly to be wished, though it was inevitably a flawed path. Theodore Herzl would write in the 1880s that during those years it was 'not customary, not proper, and not desirable to emphasize one's Jewishness' (in Rubin, 1995, p. 4). And, if with the emancipation it became possible to finally belong to a national entity by having to deny cultural aspects of Judaism, it was a small price to pay. In the effort to assimilate, the Jew has even gone so far as to deny the existence of Jewishness: the Reform movement removed the title *Jewish* from its name and replaced it with the word Hebrew. The remembrance and reality of being cast the stranger strongly influenced the behavior of Jews. Hannah Arendt (1978) writes that history has offered the Jew two positions based on the designation of the Jew as stranger: the pariah and the *schlemihl*. Both categories are attempts to deal with the assignation as stranger. The *schlemihl* is the assimilated Jew, 'those who live in the ordered ranks of society and who have exchanged the generous gifts of nature for the idols of social privilege and preju-dice' (p. 72). The *schlemihl* is one who tries to pass — Gregor Samsa, in Kafka's *Metamorphosis*, say, trying not to acknowledge that he is actually a large bug but rather desperately seeking means to fool his family and his boss into thinking that he is yet like them. Gregor Samsa would not be a stranger even to himself; despite his condition he continues to think that nothing untoward has occurred. Not being a stranger was the desperate hope of the emancipated Jew. It was to accept the discourses of Western society and to eschew those of the exiled cultures. Specifically for my purposes here, it is clear that the Western educational tradition excludes Jewish thought and wisdom; as education is an introduction into the culture that culture was obviously not Jewish. The cultured American eschewed Jewish history and wisdom; the cultured American was excluded from Jewish history and wisdom except where it served the interests of the dominant classes to include it — as in the promulgation of the idea that Chris-tianity represented an unbroken chain of development from Judaism — as in the *Judeo-Christian* culture — and that American civilization represented the epitome of that tradition. Assimilation seemed to be the means to cease being the stranger.

But assimilation for the Jew — the loss of strangerhood — was an absolute failure. Zygmunt Bauman (1995, 1991) offers a frightening perspective on the failure of assimi-lation for the Jew and on the real danger of strangerhood. Bauman defines modernity as the rage for order and classification; the stranger, being neither friend nor enemy resists classification and must be eliminated for the good of the order. Strangerhood was a threat not only to social order and progress but to the very social structure. It was necessary to eliminate the stranger; the Nazi extermination camps are presented as merely the logical outcome of such modernist thinking. There were those who could not tolerate the idea that Jews might blend inconspicuously into the general population. Frederick Ruhs would write in 1816 (in Bauman, 1995, p. 209) that the Jews possess their own inimitable *Volkseigentumlichkeit*[7] of such a kind that "they should be proud of their distinctions, and even wear a special ribbon to distinguish themselves — as a sign of honour.' The yellow star of the Nazi horror became the sinister image of this dubious distinction. Second, the characteristics that were to be acquired in assimilation were defined by the polite society;

there were, therefore, a whole range of behaviors that the Jew practiced and that remained unaddressed and, therefore, clearly obvious. Assimilation was inevitably a failure. Ultimately the assimilated Jew would be always suspect for his/her behaviors because the dominant society knew that these behaviors were learned and would always be understood as a type of mask. The stranger could not, after all, be trusted. Thus, for the Jew the designation of stranger was imposed and not adopted. The Jew did not need to learn how to be a stranger: from the beginning the Jew was designated the stranger and worked desperately to end this social estrangement and to belong. And yet there seemed no escape from this designation.

Being a stranger for the Jew was anathema and extremely dangerous. It was also inevitable. Strategies had to be considered to deal with the situation. Ashkenazic Jews simply rejected the truths of the world and chose to remain apart and neither felt the pressure of assimilation nor strangerdom; they desired only to be left to their own truths and the lives these inspired. Theodore Herzl who lived through the virulent anti-Semitism of the Dreyfus affair, a natural result of the emancipation of the Jew and yet the acknowledgment of Jew's ultimate status as stranger, realized the impossibility of assimilation: 'The Jews have three roads before them: One is apathetic submission to insult and poverty; another is revolt, out-spoken hostility to an unjust social system' (in Rubin, 1995, p. 31). The third was to organize themselves, proclaim their heritage, and build a future of their making. This led to the Zionist movement. It is, of course, with the first two options with which I want to address myself here, for both concern the experience of being the stranger. Herzl acknowledges the position of the Jew as stranger but offers alternative means to deal with this status. The first option is that of the assimilationist dealt with above. The latter seems akin to Maxine Greene's notion of the teacher as stranger; the teacher as Jew however need not choose this status — it is an imposed condition. Thus the Jew chooses not the status of strangerhood but of social pariah. From that chosen position, the Jew assumes the role of social critic.

Arendt's (1978, p. 71) notion of 'the pariah' represents the alternative to impossible assimilation and brings us closer to Maxine Greene's significance of the teacher as stranger. The pariah refuses the attractions of assimilation and chooses to remain outside society. Arendt writes that 'For the pariah, excluded from formal society and with no desire to be embraced within it, turns naturally to that which entertains and delights the common people. Sharing their social ostracism, he also shares their joys and sorrows, their pleasures and their tribulations' (Arendt, 1978, p. 71). Of course we hear in Arendt's description Maxine Greene's notion of the teacher as stranger — the teacher as artist. The conscious pariah is a conscious rebel: 'to awake to an awareness of his position and, conscious of it, become a rebel against it — the champion of an oppressed people' (Arendt, 1978, p. 76). Maxine Greene (1973) argues similarly: 'The teacher, too, must raise his shadowy trees and let them ripen. Stranger and homecomer, questioner and goad to others, he can become visible to himself by doing philosophy. There are countless lives to be changed, worlds to be remade' (p. 298). In this sense the teacher as stranger is really the teacher as Jew. It is perhaps possible to look within the Jewish tradition to discover the creative and even prophetic uses of strangerhood; for the Jew this has been an ontological position: for we were strangers in the land of Egypt.

Teacher as Jew

And so as the stranger I would like to interrogate Maxine Greene's notion of teacher as stranger. I would like to understand from the position *as* stranger what it might mean —

what it has meant — *to be* the stranger in the classroom. Maxine Greene (1973) argues that the teacher must think her way into strangerdom — 'to do philosophy, to take the risk of thinking about what he is doing when he teaches, what he means when he talks of enabling others to learn. He is asked to become more self-conscious about the choices he makes and the commitments he defines in the several dimensions of his professional life. He is asked to look, if he can, at his presuppositions, to examine critically the principles underlying what he thinks and what he says' (Preface). To do philosophy is to self-consciously consider what it means to be and why to choose to be that way. I am not uneasy with Maxine Greene's urging that the teacher be stranger, but not having ever had to choose to become a stranger, rather, being ontologically situated as one, I contemplate now where that knowledge and wisdom within the tradition and from this position would help me understand who I have been and yet still am and might be in the classroom. Having been cast as the stranger and therefore by necessity self-conscious, I now consider how from that position I may have already spoken. The teacher as stranger and the teacher as Jew coalesce here and I look within the Jewish tradition for some insight into the experience.

For Maxine Greene the stranger is s/he who once was at home in the world and now has lost that sense of comfort. Maxine Greene suggests throughout her books that this movement is a willed action and must necessarily produce an 'experience of consciousness.' Meursault, in *The Stranger* or Hester Prynne in *The Scarlet Letter*, Maxine Greene suggests, are prototypical strangers: suddenly thrust outside the community and therefore able to see it anew: 'Both are ready to wonder and question; and it is in wonder and questioning that learning begins' (1973, p. 268). Both Hester and Meursault, however, must first commit some act to distinguish themselves and be, thus, cast as stranger: Hester Prynne has a child out of wedlock, and Meursault commits a seemingly senseless murder. But the Jew has simply *to be* to be cast in the role of stranger; the Jew has rarely if ever belonged to the community anonymously and cannot experience the luxury of suddenly seeing it anew from the perspective of the stranger. Indeed, for the Jew, that perspective is at the origin of his/her relation to society. Within Jewish history and tradition, the literature of the stranger and of exile is plentiful. The Jew as stranger is central to the story. Indeed, one of the first stories in the Torah concerns the exile of Abraham: 'YHWH said to Avram, Go-you-forth from your land, from your kindred, from your father's house, to the land that I will let you see' (Genesis, 12:1). It is from this exile that God promises Avram a great nation will arise. Avram, who will even be renamed Abraham, must leave home and become a stranger wandering in the land so that God might make of and from him a great nation. Jacob is always traveling; away from his home and his brother, Esau, whom he has callously tricked into giving up his birthright; away from his home in Shechem to Bet-El; away from there to Egypt and then finally, at his death to be returned to Hebron and the Cave of Machpelach. Remarkably enough, Rachel, the wife whom Jacob dearly loved dies enroute and must be buried on the way to Efrat; she is buried along the traveler's way, on the road, not at home. Rachel, we are told, may be heard weeping by the side of the road mourning for the suffering of the Jewish people who must pass by her into exile. The Jew as stranger seems to be at the center of the tradition; even Adam and Eve were cast out of Eden! Unlike Maxine Greene's idea of the teacher as stranger, the teacher as Jew need not think his way into the position of stranger; existence exists from that position. The position of stranger for the Jew is ontological and not pathological; strangerdom is not a disease to be unsuccessfully fought — albeit heroically — but a condition to be creatively used. Identified as the stranger, the teacher as Jew ontologically does not choose the ethics of behavior as do Tarrou and Rieux in Camus' *The Plague* but rather, the Jew is those ethics. Ethics is being.

The Haggadah (Levy, 1989, p. 60) — the story and service celebrating the Exodus from slavery in Egypt — demands that 'In every single generation every single one of us is obligated to view ourselves as though we had gone forth from Mitzrayim.'[8] That is, the Jew seems to be ontologically situated as the stranger and obliged to think and act like the stranger. This telling statement reminds me of Maxine Greene's use of Camus' *The Plague* (1972) in describing the human condition and the possible responses to it. She, too, accedes that we are all victims of the plague — either now or in the future; it is a ubiquitous eternal presence; it determines the conditions in which the human can act. Dr Rieux's chronicle bears witness 'in favor of those plague-stricken people; so that some memorial of the injustice and outrage done them might endure; and to state quite simply what we learn in time of pestilence; that there are more things to admire in men than to despise.' And to paraphrase slightly, the teacher, while unable to be a saint in these conditions, may yet be a healer. Maxine Greene's teacher as stranger, in consciously choosing to rage against the order, attains the position of stranger and may then 'see through his own eyes' (1973, Preface) and not through those of the assimilated. But the Jewish tradition offers an alternative perspective on the stranger. The Haggadah demands that we constantly remember that we were once slaves in the land of Egypt: once we were strangers in the land. It is from that position that we might continue to understand our freedom. The Passover Seder reminds us that though we are no longer slaves — the celebration of the Passover Seder is proof of our freedom — yet the memory of that experience must govern our relations in the world. Despite our celebration of the exodus, the Jew says 'Now we are still in bonds. Next year may we all be free' (Levy, 1989, p. 99). The Haggadah acknowledges not the movement toward being a stranger as evidence of freedom. Rather, the Haggadah insists that it is desire for freedom from slavery that defines the stranger. Embedded in Pesach, this celebration of freedom, is the memory of slavery: memory, Yerushalmi (1996) says, is that which is essentially unbroken, continuous. The conclusion that the Haggadah offers the Jew is that redemption is never complete: 'This year we are slaves/In the coming year may we all be free.' This is the unbroken tradition. We are yet strangers: freedom comes not from the position of stranger but from freedom from that slavery. It is this freedom that is to be celebrated and considered: 'Whoever searches deeply into the meaning of the Exodus from Egypt is considered praiseworthy' (Bronstein, 1984, p. 34). The action desired is not to think oneself into strangerdom but to effect a freedom from that slavery. It is the interrogation of the meaning of deliverance from slavery that is essential since we are always strangers. The still empty open door at the Seder through which Elijah the Prophet — should he come — will announce the coming of the heir of King David tells us that 'We have failed the test of the open door — yet in our failure lies our hope as human beings' (The Shalom Seders, 1984). As long as all are not free then none are free, and the Seder reminds us that it is from the position of stranger that we must act. 'Just as it was we, not our forebears only, who were liberated in Egypt, so it is we, not our forebears only, who live in slavery' (The Shalom Seders, 1984, p. 33). It is not thinking our way into the position of stranger that is central in the Haggadah but the insistence on the memory that we were strangers — and in that memory we identify with all those who may yet be slaves and strangers. It is a central pedagogical and active position to be the stranger. To have memory of this is to make the decision not to forget! We have met the stranger and she is us.

Maxine Greene's idea of the teacher as stranger draws its imagery from Camus' myth of Sisyphus. The teacher as stranger is also the teacher as modern but absurd hero. Camus writes (1955) that 'Sisyphus is the absurd hero. . . . His scorn of the gods, his hatred of death, and his passion for life won him that unspeakable penalty to which the whole being is exerted toward accomplishing nothing. This is the price that must be paid for the passions of this earth' (p. 89). Sisyphus chooses to estrange himself from his comfort and to dedicate his passion to the impossibility of human perfection. 'The teacher,' Maxine Greene writes (1973), 'who is familiar with anguish and absurdity can hardly feel sanguine in his ordinary life' (p. 258). By doing philosophy, the teacher becomes like Sisyphus, the absurd hero, understanding the injustices and difficulties of existence — indeed, its absurdities.[9] By doing philosophy the teacher becomes the stranger who might question the very structures that define the world. But the Jew as stranger has known no ordinary life and so absurdity is not an issue. Rather, it has been the effort of the Jew to accept the position of stranger and use it as a method to achieve freedom; the effort of the Jew has been not to accept this position but to live with it and to wrest from it the knowledge and healing that dialectically exist within it. Thus the position of the stranger has produced a remarkable body of literature and belief that situates creation as endemic to the position of the stranger.

The reality of strangerdom was dramatically made crystal clear with the traumatic expulsion of the Jews from Spain in 1492. Of course, this was not the first time that Jews had been cast out of their home, but in Spain the Jews had lived in relative ease and prosperity. They had even participated in the exercise of government. Suddenly they were ordered to abandon not merely their homes but their homelands. The whole sense of reality that the Jews in Spain had accepted was rent by this expulsion; finally, this expulsion emptied Western Europe of Jews. One response of the Jewish community was to a new interest in history that Yosef Yerushalmi (1996) says is a recognition that 'the [contemporary] events . . . have a meaning for the present and the future which cannot be grasped merely by focusing attention on ancient times . . .' (p. 62). The rhythms of Jewish history became written. Order might be achieved in the historiography.

But another response saw in the exile the paradigm of creation. Of course, redemption and apocalyptic dialects had always been part of the Jewish tradition, but the exile gave new expression to a 'vigorous insistence upon the fragmentary character of Jewish existence, and in mystical views and dogmas to explain this fragmentariness with its paradoxes and tensions' (Scholem, 1995, p. 249). Camus employed the myth of Sisyphus to help define our times; Maxine Greene draws heavily upon this myth to urge, define, and comfort the teacher as stranger. The Kabbalists of the fifteenth century found in the dialectic between exile and creation their sustaining myth. From their experience of exile, they understood that exile was intrinsic to creation and, therefore, central and essential to it. In the tradition of Jewish mysticism, in the Lurianic Kabbalah, that form of Jewish mysticism which derives from the Spanish outcasts who fled to Palestine, exile and strangerdom are the essence of existence. 'Life was conceived as Existence in Exile and in self-contradiction, and the sufferings of Exile were linked up with the central Kabbalistic doctrines about God and man' (Scholem, 1995, p. 249). What the Jew as stranger knew was that at the center of all life is exile but that creation resides in dialectical relation to that exile: we are all ontologically exiled but it is that sense of exile which makes space for creation. 'Reality for Luria is always a triple rhythm of contraction, breaking apart, and mending, a rhythm continuously present in time even as it first punctuated eternity' (Bloom, 1975, p. 39). Maxine Greene's stranger thus seems to have its ontological roots in the Kabbalic tradition of Tzimtsum, contraction or exile.

From the experience of exile these thinkers wondered: if, as is commonly known and taught, God is everywhere, if God is 'all in all' then how can there be things that are not God? That is, if as the Torah suggests God created the world out of nothing, how could there be nothing if God was everywhere and there was no nothing? And Isaac Luria responded by suggesting that before creation could occur, God had first to withdraw from

God's space. What is referred to as *Tzimtsum* — the exile of God from God's own self — a space is made for creation. 'According to Luria, God was compelled to make room for the world by, as it were, abandoning a region within Himself, a kind of mystical primordial space from which He withdrew in order to return to it in the act of creation and revelation' (Scholem, 1995, p. 261). That is, creation begins first with an act of exile; if God had not done so the world could not have come to being. And that exile might also be understood as a setting of limits: after all, God must set limits on God's self in order to create. Lurianic Kabbalah, then, understands the very basis of creation to be embedded in exile. Having withdrawn, God creates space for the creation of the world. The position of stranger makes possible the world and all of creation. What a pedagogy is there!

Maxine Greene counsels that the object of 'doing philosophy' is to help the teacher decide what makes sense for him or her, 'to find apertures in the wall of what is taken for granted; to pierce the webs of obscurity; to see and then to choose . . . He must think about what he is doing, take responsibility for his choices, *care* about the actions he undertakes to free his students and make himself the kind of teacher he wills himself to be' (1973, p. 263). To do philosophy is to become the stranger and the teacher as stranger. But the ontological situation of the Jew as stranger has already placed the Jew in the pedagogical position. We are told that when Joseph's brothers, who had cruelly earlier sold him into slavery, came to Egypt to buy food to sustain them in the famine, they came before their now highly placed brother and did not recognize him. The Torah tells us that 'When Joseph saw his brothers, he recognized them, but he *pretended to be a stranger* to them and spoke harshly with them' (Genesis, 42:7, emphasis added). At their hands he has experienced horrible cruelty and as the stranger he would know what, if anything, they have learned. They have yet a younger brother who is beloved, as Joseph was loved, by their father, Jacob. Joseph demands of his brothers that they bring to him their youngest brother who had remained behind with their father. He would know what value they place on the life of their brethren. Whom would they sacrifice for their own comforts? 'Then bring your youngest brother back to me, so that your words will be proven truthful, and you will not die.' Suddenly the brothers are reminded of the danger that they had inflicted many years ago on their brother Joseph when they cast him in the pit and sold him for slavery. They are reminded by the stranger of their cruelties: 'But they said, each man to his brother: Truly we are guilty: concerning our brother! that we saw his hearts' distress when he implored us, and we did not listen.' They consider that affliction and that 'for his blood — now, (satisfaction) is demanded.' But for the teacher as stranger this is not the moment of triumph: Joseph, their brother, against whom they had committed this great wrong stands now before them, a stranger to them and 'turned away from them and wept.' Joseph experiences their pain — is himself pained — but he must know that they have learned, must know what they have learned. The position of the stranger is not an easy one; from it learning derives.

Moses (Exodus, 2:22) says of himself, 'A sojourner have I become in a foreign land.' He has fled what he believes to be his natural home in Egypt, but where, in fact, he has been the stranger in the Pharaoh's house. By the murder of the Egyptian overseer, Moses has become not only a stranger to the courts of Pharaoh but to the Israelites whom he must help free. He is describing himself as the stranger now in exile from his homeland; remarkably though unknowingly he has been always the stranger, a Jew disguised and raised in Pharaoh's court. And from the land of Midyan to which he has fled and in which he now resides, Moses must return to Egypt where he was originally and will be yet a stranger to 'bring the Children of Israel out of Egypt.' This central event of the exodus will make of the Children of Israel a nation with the revelation at Sinai. Creation begins with exile. Only having been the stranger might the stranger know and teach freedom. Being depends on the memory of having been the stranger. Hillel asks, 'If I am not for myself, who will be? If I am only for myself, what am I? And if not now, when?'

I take a deep breath and as the stranger open the door to the classroom.

Notes

1   Where I come from that statement has been consistently followed by 'Oh, my sister (or my daughter or my wife) is a teacher.' The intent was always one of condescension.
2   A *baraitha* is part of the material in the law code but is not included in the official collection.
3   As I write this Newt Gingrich has admitted violations of ethics and been nonetheless overwhelmingly voted Speaker of the House of Representatives by his colleagues. I suppose it is his teachers (their teachers) who must be chastized for his (for their) lack of learning. Or indeed, were they not teaching him (them) ethics for their emphasis on reading, writing, and arithmetic? 'And how shall I presume?'
4   And though we now know the name of this person we have yet to wonder who he is that will take the oath of office!
5   It interests me to consider that George Counts' challenge *Dare the Schools Create a New Social Order* is now mirrored in Ravitch's and Mosle's insistence that the schools change to heal society.
6   Needless to say though I am compelled to say it, the teacher is not always required to serve these functions.
7   To be loosely translated as 'a people's peculiarity.'
8   Mitzrayim is the Hebrew word for Egypt; literally it means 'the narrow place.'
9   We are reminded of the opening of *Waiting for Godot:*

> *Estragon:* Nothing to be done.
> *Vladimir:* I'm beginning to come round to that opinion.

Of course that doesn't stop them from waiting for Godot.

References

THE SHALOM SEDERS (1984) New York: Adama Books.

LEVY, R.N. (ed.) (1989) *On Wings of Freedom: The Hillel Haggadah for the Nights of Passover* (R.N. Levy, trans.), Hoboken, New Jersey: Klav Publishing House, Inc.

BRONSTEIN, H. (ed.) (1975) *A Passover Haggadah*, New York: Penguin Books.

ARENDT, H. (1978) *The Jew As Pariah* (R.H. Feldman, ed.), New York: Grove Press, Inc.

BAUMAN, Z. (1991) *Modernity and Ambivalence*, Ithaca: Cornell University Press.

BAUMAN, Z. (1995) *Life in Fragments*, Cambridge, Mass.: Basil Blackwell Publishers.

BLOCK, A.A. (forthcoming) 'On singing the Lord's Song in a foreign land', in SHAPRIO, S. *Strangers in the Land: Modernity, Pedagogy and Jewish Experience*, New York: Peter Lang Publishing.

BLOOM, H. (1975) *Kabbalah and Criticism*, New York: Seabury Press.

BOBBIT, F. (1918) *Curriculum*, New York: Houghton Mifflin.

CAMUS, A. (1972) *The Plague* (S. Gilbert, trans.), New York: Vintage Books.

CAMUS, A. (1955) *The Myth of Sisyphus and Other Essays* (Justin O'Brien, trans.), New York: Vintage Books.

GARCIA, J. and HUNTER, R. (1970) 'Ripple' on *American Beauty*, New York: Warner Records.

GREENE, M. (1973) *Teacher As Stranger*, Belmont, California: Wadsworth Publishing Co., Inc.

KAPLAN, M. (1934/1994) *Judaism as a Civilization*, Philadelphia: Jewish Publication Society. Originally published in 1934.

MARX, K. (1984) *The 18th Brumaire of Louis Bonaparte*, New York: New World Paperbacks.

MOSLE, S. (1996) 'The answer is national standards,' *The New York Times Magazine*, 27 October.

POE, E.A. (1967) 'The Tell-Tale Heart,' in QUINN, A.H. and O'NEILL, E.H. (ed.) *The Complete Poems and Stories of Edgar Allen Poe*, New York: Alfred P. Knopf.

RAVITCH, D. (1995) *National Standards in American Education*, Washington DC: The Brookings Institution.

ROTH, P. (1969) *Goodbye, Columbus*, New York: Bantam Books.

RUBIN, B. (1995) *Assimilation and Its Discontents*, New York: Random House.

SACKS, K.B. (1994) 'How did Jews become white folks,' in GREGORY, S. and SANJEK, R. (eds) *Race*, New Brunswick, New Jersey: Rutger's University Press.

SCHOLEM, G. (1995) *Major Trends in Jewish Mysticism*, New York: Schocken Books.

THOREAU, H.D. (1980) *The Natural History Essays*, Salt Lake City, Utah: Perigrine Smith, Inc.

YERUSHALMI, Y.H. (1996) *Zakhor*, Seattle: University of Washington Press. Originally published in 1982.

3   Views across the Expanse:
Maxine Greene's *Landscapes of Learning*

Anne E. Pautz

To be in touch with our landscapes is to be conscious of our evolving experiences, to be aware of the ways in which we encounter our world. (Maxine Greene, 1978, p. 2)

Landscapes of Learning

We live within landscapes — landscapes which surround us and landscapes which mark our interior worlds of consciousness and unconsciousness — which integrate to form the ways we interact with those around us. Yet much of modern life mitigates against a full awareness of these landscapes. The constant consumption of information, experiences, and products leaves little space for reflection. Experience builds upon experience, at times in a seemingly haphazard way. In the rush it is easy to remain unaware of our landscapes within and against which we live, work, and learn.

The appearance of Maxine Greene's *Landscapes of Learning* in 1978 coincided with my first year of teaching in a vocational high school in rural South Carolina. Newly graduated from Clemson University, I was steeped in behavioral objectives, the bell curve, and a standardized curriculum. I still recall a professor looking forward to the not-too-distant day when the goal of standardization would be achieved and every student in the seventh grade would be on the same lesson, even the same page, at the same time. Much of my education in the 1960s and 1970s focused on information and facts which were presented as definitive knowledge. The acquisition of this information was promoted as prerequisite to attaining one's goals in life. The call for 'back to basics' became strident. Behavioral objectives were promoted as the most efficient way to present information to students and assess their learning. I was not comfortable with these concepts, but I lacked the language to articulate my feelings. Nor did I have a way to articulate the ways I was affected by a system of education which treated me as a passive, disembodied recipient of expert information.

The intervening years have seen the demand persist for the schools to get 'back to basics.' This has led to a focus on the minutiae of subject content areas rather than broad issues of significance across the subject fields, issues such as Maxine Greene elucidates in *Landscapes of Learning*. Instead, professional organizations such as the National Council of Teachers of Mathematics (1991) and the National Research Council (1996) have labored to establish national standards. Such bureaucratic reforms always seem to disappoint. Could it be that by focusing on subject-matter competencies that the urgent and complex issues are obscured, issues associated with the fact that students and teachers live within complex, unjust social systems? National standards reiterate the belief that student — and national — success can be defined by success on standardized tests.

Systemic social injustice is treated as a minor inconvenience which the individual — if he would only try — can overcome. The complex relationships among individual differences, cultural history, and social systems are ignored. The dichotomies created between experience and what is taught are inculcated year after year until the only way to deal with the cognitive dissonance is simply to become unaware. It is to such alienation from self and experience created in schools that Maxine Greene speaks so eloquently and insightfully in *Landscapes of Learning*.

Discovering Landscapes

While *Landscapes of Learning* consists of essays explicating concepts such as praxis, aesthetics, justice, equality, and mystification in education, the unifying theme is the need to be 'wide-awake,' present to ourselves and others in this world we inhabit together. Greene (1978) approaches wide-awakeness from philosophy, especially existentialism, drawing upon such philosophers as Kierkegaard, Nietzsche, Schutz, Sartre. Alfred Schutz (1962) defined 'wide-awakeness' as 'a plane of consciousness . . . originating in an attitude of full attention to life and its requirements. Only the performing and especially the working self is fully interested in life and, hence, wide-awake. This attention is an active, not a passive one' (p. 213).

It is just this active attention which Greene (1978) inspires as she examines the different landscapes, both internal and external, in which people live and learn. With its hierarchical structure and focus on disciplined students acquiring the teacher's authorized knowledge, the classroom begs for wide-awakeness. Students and teachers alike are often required to ignore the meanings they have made of their own lives in favor of the 'official' knowledge. This instills a mentally passive attitude in students and teachers alike, and as Schutz (1962) points out, '[p]assive attention is the opposite to full awakeness' (p. 213).

Perhaps the most important aspect of full awareness is that it is an active process. It requires not only the individual but the institution to be alive and attentive. Discussing the lack of passion and engagement during her public school teaching experience, Natalie Goldberg (1993) put it this way: 'Only something alive can die. The public schools go on year after year. They don't die because they are not alive' (p. 84). To be alive requires risk — the risk of knowing oneself, including the risk of seeing beyond one's biases and categories to know others and their situations. It requires being wholly in the present, rather than self-dissociated, one's mind in different places or times.

To be present to oneself, to be aware of oneself, does not simply mean occasionally stopping and assessing what is going on. It is a process of awareness of one's whole experience: of sights, sounds, scents, indeed, the sensuality of life. It calls for an awareness of the process of living in which we are all involved, which emphasizes our interconnectedness, and those processes of alienation which occur constantly in a society that consumes everything, including its people. Greene does not simply talk about the process of being present. She lives it, and she encourages her students to do likewise. Reflecting on his experience as a student of Greene at Teachers College, William Ayers (1996) remembers how she challenged her students 'to join her in "doing philosophy": becoming more intentional and aware, confronting issues as they emerged in our own consciousness and our lives, integrating our situations carefully, and responding thoughtfully to what we uncovered and discovered' (p. 119). The active process of following through on issues as they emerge requires a fortitude not apparent at first, including awareness of the frightening and appalling aspects of our lives and the lives around us.

Greene's (1978) focus on being present takes pedagogical forms within the classroom. The dilemmas and struggles of self faced by both teachers and students are not incidental issues to be disregarded in favor of content. They are to be faced directly, in depth, with creativity and originality. Difficult issues surrounding race, class, gender, and other sources and consequences of social objectification are key topics for classroom discussion, problems to be struggled with, not minimized or ignored. Democracy is not just a concept; it is a process to be practiced in the classroom. Praxis is an important concept for Greene; she stresses the need of the teacher and the school to critically examine what they believe, and how those beliefs impact the social and cultural lives of children.

Greene hopes for the transcendence of present situations, including those habits of the mind which foster an insensitivity to others. This is not transcendence in any degraded form, i.e. blind faith or behavioral manipulation. Rather, transcendence is an active and difficult willingness, indeed courage, to choose, grounded in individual history and experience, and it must be renewed continually. Greene (1978) explains:

> Transcendence has to be chosen; it can be neither given or imposed . . . [P]ersons are more likely to ask their own questions and seek their own transcendence when they feel themselves to be grounded in their personal histories, their lived lives. That is what I mean by 'landscapes'. (p. 2)

Thus the landscapes of experience form the basis for growth and change in the individual as social. Greene emphasizes the need for transcendence of situations in order to develop a sensitivity to others and she links the process of transcendence to the moral life. She sees the growing sense of powerlessness as a source of a numbness to moral and ethical issues. To lead a moral life is to overcome this numbness, to become aware and awake.

Drawing on Henry Thoreau and Alfred Schutz, Greene (1978) defines moral awareness as 'attentiveness . . . interest in things . . . the direct opposite of the attitude of bland conventionality and indifference so characteristic of our time' (p. 42). What needs to be transcended is the taken-for-grantedness which is embedded in each of us. Morality in a culture is defined within a 'matrix,' culturally comprised of the guiding principles, rules of right and wrong, some codified in law, some not, which denote what is acceptable and what is not. Greene (1978) explains, 'to be moral involves taking a position towards that matrix, thinking critically about what is taken for granted' (p. 49). Morality, then, involves choices by which to live, and principles one understands and chooses to inform the praxis of one's life. This involves taking responsibility for one's life within the wider, interconnected set of communities in which one lives. Confronting one's biases toward these wider communities is an important part of this stance. It calls for an awareness of one's indifference and callousness, for, as Ayers (1996) notes, '[t]he opposite of "moral" in our lives is not "immoral," but is, more typically, "indifferent," "thoughtless," and "careless"' (p. 122). Indifference or intolerance toward the lives of others is perhaps the most damaging and reprehensible stance we can take and adopt.

Greene (1978) knows schools must resist the temptation to concentrate on superficial teaching of right and wrong. Nor should schools promote the teaching of conventional ideas of morality for their own sake, especially any dogma of intolerance in the self-righteous name of morality. Teachers and the students they teach have the choice of developing tolerant or intolerant attitudes towards race, gender, and other differences. Herbert Kohl (1994) refers to this type of choice as a type of 'not-learning' which he describes as 'the conscious decision not to learn something that you could learn . . . for example . . . refusing to . . . yield to community pressure to become a racist or sexist . . .

choosing not to learn something you find morally offensive or personally noxious' (p. xiii). Such choice encourages a level of freedom in the classroom which is not often encountered. The teacher relinquishes the illusion of control, acknowledging that the choices often rest with the students.

A paradox arises when a student chooses not to learn what a teacher has chosen to teach. This may not be a failure to learn, but a conscious choice not to learn. This choice can be complex, at times involving aspects of identity and the preservation of native culture. A teacher's awareness of this requires confronting the assumption that education is unquestionably student-affirmative. Kohl (1994) describes a child in his first grade class who refused to learn to read. Far from being a 'slow' student in need of remediation, Kohl recognized that this student's construction of identity and power rested upon his refusal of the institution's ready and compulsory identity of a compliant learner. Remembering his own decision as a child not to learn Yiddish, Kohl found a way for the child to maintain a sense of identity and power while learning to read.

While it is easy to speak of democratic classrooms and the concept of freedom, these concepts are not easy to establish within the institution of school. Children have the choice to learn, to refuse to learn, to see the school as other than a benevolent institution. Students make these choices and judgments whether teachers or schools acknowledge them or not. If democracy and freedom are to achieve actuality, it is in schools where they must first be nurtured. This requires teachers to be aware of attitudes and practices which contribute to the treatment of children as objects. Rather, what is needed is the realization that schools are comprised of unique individuals, both teachers and students, in complex relationships within communities. Ayers (1996) notes that Greene's notion of freedom constitutes 'a refusal of the fixed, a reaching for possibility, an engagement with obstacles and barriers and a resistant world, an achievement to be sought in a web of relationships, an intersubjective reality' (p. 122). This concept of freedom requires an engagement with the world as it is found. Greene urges us to become passionately engaged with all spheres of the social, especially the schools. For her, this engagement is exemplified by the arts and is evident in an aesthetic orientation to the world.

Greene advocates the educational use of the arts to combat that numbing objectification which characterizes contemporary society. The arts, especially literature, provide alternative means to critically engage the world. As she explains:

> Works of art are, visibly and palpably, human achievements, renderings of the ways in which aspects of reality have impinged upon human consciousness . . . [A]ll art forms must be encountered as achievements that can only be brought to significant life when human beings engage with them imaginatively. (Greene, 1978, p. 163)

Thus, Gabriel Garcia Márquez's (1991) novel *One Hundred Years of Solitude* or Toni Morrison's (1992) novel, *Jazz*, provide lenses through which to make visible the workings of racism, sexism, classism, and colonialism in the lives of specific fictional characters. Literature provides a ground from which to understand that which may be too volatile to view clearly from personal experience only. Engagement with literature, as well as other art forms, transports the reader to another reality from which to look at the present moment and lived experience. Just as importantly, literature can provide access to the experiences and realities of others. In the work of Morrison or Márquez, non-Hispanic American or non-African American readers can begin to explore the experiences of the authors and their own (the reader's) situatedness in a world which might allow them to understand 'difference' — not as exotic 'other' — but as intelligible reality. Literature serves as a powerful and critical exploration of compelling historical and social issues.

Greene (1978) finds this aesthetic approach to education involves being present, aware, awake to the world. It requires the honesty of not hiding from political and social problems, not painting over them with rosy statistics or burying them in the grave dug by low test scores. Aesthetic awareness is a process of becoming aware of the historicity of the world, the technologies of culture, and the political and cultural issues which are present in all lives. It is to see the world with the awareness of an artist, to see a colored world, not a simplistic one of black and white, with an occasional gray added for the sake of 'balance.' This is an awareness which values difference, not an attempt to be color blind, or gender neutral, or to behave 'as if' the differences in cultures were equal and the same. Rather, difference is to be respected and valued through vision, through welcoming the colors, hearing the cacophony, the variety and particularities of each child, each teacher, each school.

Greene once said, 'My field of study is lived situations' (Greene quoted in Ayers, 1996, p. 121). Ayers (1996) comments:

> This involves refusing artificial divisions and 'blurring genres — philosophy, anthropology, literature, psychology, science, the arts — knocking down barriers, insisting on [the] right to use everything — any discipline, any curriculum, any encounter — as nourishment, as a source to pose our own fates.' (p. 121)

The most important function of school is to provide an environment in which students can explore choices, raise questions and reach for alternatives in the situatedness of their lives.

School Landscapes

The industrial model of education, employing the 'scientific' method to efficiently transfer information from the teacher to the student, places little curricular emphasis on the student as a unique, complex person. There are few opportunities in the school environment for the student to imagine. Greene (1978) proposes that this concept of education be changed to emphasize the child's experience — within the school and out. If meaningful learning is to occur, the child's life outside of the school must be taken into account. This is a move toward a different perspective of teaching — 'teaching as dialogue, teaching as resistance, teaching as action toward freedom' (Ayers, 1996, p. 122).

Many myths regarding education and teaching must be confronted in order to appreciate such a perspective. The mystification of expert knowledge, science, and of those power relations which structure society leaves us blind to oppression and political realities (Greene, 1978). Students are encouraged not to criticize or critique social institutions such as the school. For example, the myth that capitalism is a nearly perfect economic system is uncritically, patriotically advanced in more than a few schools. Those without an official voice — minorities, working-class women and men, poor children — are seen as the sources of problems rather than victims of capitalism.

Perhaps the most powerful myth which Greene (1978) identifies is that education alone can solve the myriad of social ills which surround us. Perhaps the second is that the uncertainty of the present can be remedied by somehow returning education to its past — by getting 'back to basics,' to a time when truth and procedure seemed simple, self-evident. This yearning for a past that never was is itself a flagrant disregard of the reality of the present and the past. It functions as a stumbling block to being present and aware of both the present and past.

Required subject matter as well as methods of learning and teaching tend to be outside the students' everyday experiences. The home, stressing verbal (and often non-linear) rather then written communication, tends to be vastly different from that of the school. As John Dewey (1990) noted, 'the child's life is an integral, a total one. He [sic] passes quickly and readily from one topic to another, as from one spot to another, but is not conscious of transition or break' (p. 183). Compounding the problem for many children is a home life with profound cultural, racial, and class differences from the bureaucratic model common to many schools. Additionally, our imagistic or semiotic society, in its consumption and objectification of others and self, seduces students and teachers into believing the mystifications of the material and political world.

Mystification can be resisted through political awareness which includes being present to oneself. The act of being present awakens one to the passage of time. It can slow the frenetic consumption — consumption of goods, consumption of resources, consumption of people. The proliferation of technologies — think of the internet — promotes the consumption of ever-increasing amounts of information. Awareness and presence to situations allows an adagio pace, permitting one to adopt a more critical and self-reflective stance to information and ideas which otherwise remain mystified. Greene (1978) identifies the need to demystify experts and expert knowledge as crucial to correcting the sense of powerlessness which is prevalent in the face of injustice within scientific, economic and political communities. Greene (1978) notes: 'educators ought to work to combat the sense of ineffectuality and powerlessness that comes when persons feel themselves to be victims beyond their control, in fact beyond any human control' (p. 64). In this process, the teacher herself must demystify her position with students.

Making Meaning, Making Culture

Discussing the themes which run through Greene's teaching, William Ayers (1996) points to Greene's focus on the way '[p]eople are, in her words, "condemned to meaning" — sentenced to create lives as meaningful in the face of disorder and inhumanity, to read our lived worlds and to name ourselves, again in her words, "in our dreadful freedom"' (p. 122). These meanings to which we are condemned are bound up with Western culture which permeates all we do and say, how we interpret and make meaning. Much of this culture is unconscious, unavailable for examination, yet the meanings we make out of our environment are often constrained by the culture, or rather the cultures, in which we live. Thus, as Greene (1991) points out, 'the meanings of the so-called "objective" world are contingent on subjective interpretation, on vantage point, on location . . . official definitions and interpretations [are] susceptible to challenge and critique by those whose voices [have] rarely been heard before' (p. 202). As the voices of those who have been excluded grow in volume, society will have to listen. On the individual level, people cannot reduce the pervasiveness of cultural influence, but they can work to be aware of the effects of culture and incorporate the cultural knowledge of others. Teachers play vital roles in creating cultural tolerance not only through their participation in socialization but also in the ways they encourage imagination and the exploration of difference.

Teachers must understand how their own culture is enacted, as well as be aware how their own culture — in generational as well as in racial terms — differs from that of their students. This awareness is gained by making tacit, taken-for-granted cultural knowledge explicit, open for discussion. Because culture is encoded in the language, the language which students acquire in the classroom is vital to their understanding of their own culture as well as that of their peers. Bowers and Flinders (1990) note that explicitly expressed culture 'when combined with a historical perspective . . . vocabulary, and theoretical framework that enables students to represent conceptually the complexity of the issues that are being dealt with, provides the conceptual basis for the . . . communication necessary for democratic decision making' (p. 25).

As we, especially the marginalized, become aware of the importance of their/our own histories, their/our own ancestral cultures, and the politics of contemporary culture formation, schools can more adequately grapple with both embedded (or hidden) and surfacing multicultural issues. Teachers can help children in the dominant culture understand other cultures while helping students from non-Western cultures gain access to dominant cultural capital (while appreciating and affirming their own uniqueness). 'For students who must increasingly interact with others who are not grounded in a Western-Anglo worldview, recognizing the deep underpinnings of the dominant culture as well as the deep patterns of others seems essential to . . . a multicultural society' (Bowers and Flinders, 1990, p. 124). This applies to teachers as well. Creative, critical questions and ideas are needed to reach toward such understanding.

Greene situates these issues and problems of freedom, justice, and equality in the schools. She examines, for example, the way teachers objectify students whose lives they seek to improve:

> There is . . . the matter of well-intentioned middle-class professionals who have no real faith in the capacities of the students . . . with whom they work, but who are nonetheless committed to transforming an unjust social order in their behalf . . . Not trusting the people, incapable of entering into communion with them . . . (although they believe they are doing something liberating) [they] do their part in denying freedom — and in treating those with whom they work as . . . little more than objects or things. (1978, pp. 96–7)

It is just such naive and paternalistic attitudes which must be examined and reworked. Ill-founded, non-professional beliefs about the race, class, gender, economic status, physical and mental ability ought not — cannot — be disguised. Failure to acknowledge the capability of certain children is not necessarily expressed as an overt act of oppression, of course. Indeed, such beliefs are reflected in many everyday school practices. The very subtlety of many teachers' professional poses, masked by detachment and 'objectivity,' makes attitudes about children difficult to confront or change. Critical questioning of both beliefs about children and beliefs about oneself in relationship to others who are different is needed to begin the shift of non-professional beliefs and miseducative practices.

Conclusion

In *Landscapes of Learning*, Maxine Greene warns us that it is just as possible to imagine the oppression of others as it is to imagine their freedom and emancipation. The bombers of the Federal Building in Oklahoma City imagined both the world they wanted to create and the means to achieve it. They made 'rational' choices based on their paranoid fantasies regarding government terrorism. While the world they wanted to create *was* a maniacal fantasy, it required imagination, a sense of the possible. If imagination is to avoid becoming entangled with destructive and fanatical dreams of power, it requires a vivid, lived and reasoned link to morality and ethics.

Conflict and controversy are essential if students are to begin to think critically about the issues they must resolve within themselves as well as in society. But only in a classroom atmosphere of tolerance and openness, with an emphasis on exploring and examining different beliefs, can creative solutions to controversial dilemmas emerge. Greene (1978) notes:

> Human *subjects* have to be attended to; human *consciousness* must be taken into account, if domination is to be in any way reduced. This is one reason for the central importance of pedagogy in these days: once pedagogy becomes crucial, the splits and deformation in those who teach or treat or administer or organize take on a political significance never confronted in time past. (p. 96, emphasis in original)

Being present to one's self and others and the understanding this awakens can create the classroom climate where a pedagogy of justice and difference can be performed. This understanding is not one of assimilating difference. It is an awareness which recognizes and honors the vastness and vitality of difference. It is a self-awareness which supports a transcendence through being present to difference.

Landscapes of our interior worlds flow and merge into the landscapes of the exterior world. We as individuals and groups may be separated within the world — through class, through gender, through disability, and so on. Awareness of these conditions, not as occasions for social hierarchies but as intellectual problems and conditions of the lived experience of others, can stimulate much needed educational change. Twenty years after Maxine Greene published *Landscapes of Learning*, the need for social justice has not diminished nor has the importance of being conscious, fully awake and aware decreased. There remain many landscapes to explore. Greene's (1978) book inspires us still:

> Consciousness thrusts toward the world . . . It is through acts of consciousness that aspects of the world present themselves to living beings. Alone or in collaboration, they bring individuals in touch with objects, events, and other human beings; they make it possible for individuals to . . . constitute a world. (p. 14)

References

AYERS, W. (1996) 'Doing philosophy: Maxine Greene and the pedagogy of possibility,' in KRIDEL, C., BULLOUGH, R. and SHAKER, P. (eds) *Teachers and Mentors: Profiles of Distinguished Twentieth-century Professors of Education*, New York: Garland Publishing.

BOWERS, C.A. and FLINDERS, D.J. (1990) *Responsive Teaching: An Ecological Approach to Classroom Patterns of Language, Culture, and Thought*, New York: Teachers College Press.

DEWEY, J. (1990) 'The child and the curriculum,' in DEWEY, J. *The School and Society / The Child and the Curriculum* (P. Jackson, ed.), Chicago: University of Chicago Press. Originally published in 1902.

GOLDBERG, N. (1993) *Long Quiet Highway: Waking Up in America*, New York: Bantam Books.

GREENE, M. (1978) *Landscapes of Learning*, New York: Teachers College Press.

GREENE, M. (1991) 'The educational philosopher's quest,' in BURLESON, D. (ed.) *Reflections: Personal Essays by 33 Distinguished Educators*, Bloomington, IN: Phi Delta Kappa Educational Foundation.

KOHL, H. (1994) *'I won't learn from you' and other thoughts on creative maladjustment*, New York: New Press.

MÁRQUEZ, G. (1991) *One Hundred Years of Solitude*, New York: HarperPerennial. Originally published in 1970.

Anne E. Pautz

MORRISON, T. (1992) *Jazz*, New York: Plume.
NATIONAL COUNCIL OF TEACHERS OF MATHEMATICS (NCTM) (1991) *Professional Standards for Teaching Mathematics*, Reston, VA: NCTM.
NATIONAL RESEARCH COUNCIL (1996) *National Science Education Standards*, Washington DC: National Academy Press.
SCHUTZ, A. (1962) 'On multiple realities,' in SCHUTZ, A. *Collected Papers Vol. 1: The Problem of Social Reality* (M. Natanson, ed.), Netherlands: The Hague.

4   *The Dialectic of Freedom*

Jon Davies

Introduction: 3 July 1997

It is particularly appropriate, if not ironic, to address *The Dialectic of Freedom* (Greene, 1988) on the eve of Independence Day in the United States. The ritual of an Independence Day celebration enacts Maxine Greene's critique of how most people conceptualize freedom in contemporary society. Greene points out that 'freedom is still taken to be a given in this country: to be an American is to be endowed with freedom, whether or not one acts on it or fights for it or does anything with it' (1988, p. 26). In this vein, each year in early July civic cultural images of freedom saturate the national landscape and pervade the media.

In St. Francisville, Louisiana, on the Mississippi River where I live with my family 30 miles north of Baton Rouge, a patriotically colored banner (dark blue letters, two red Coca Cola trademarks, and a white background) suspended above Highway 61 announces: 'St. Francisville, Louisiana Celebrates an Old-Fashioned Fourth of July.' Antebellum and late nineteenth-century wood-framed buildings, which now serve as antique shops, restaurants, and homes, line Ferdinand Street, the main thoroughfare through town, which connects Highway 61 to the New Roads ferry crossing and the west bank of the Mississippi River. During the Independence Day celebration, American flags and red, white, and blue bunting drape from Ferdinand Street's light posts and hang above the doors of its buildings. Perhaps the civic leaders in St. Francisville intend by the term 'old-fashioned' to conjure up images of bands in the park, ice-cream socials, and leisurely strolling, contented families. Economically, the St. Francisville Chamber of Commerce promotes the town as a tourist attraction by evoking such a tranquil fiction of bygone years. The Independence Day holiday is one of many commercial opportunities to capitalize on nostalgic appeal.

However, a conjuring up of the past is not without its potential discomfort and difficulty. Whose version of the past should St. Francisville resurrect? For example, until the end of the antebellum period, white plantation owners in St. Francisville owned black slaves. The effects of enslavement and the period of reconstruction following the end of the Civil War are evident today in the continued economic disparity and social division between whites and blacks in St. Francisville and the surrounding communities in West Feliciana Parish, and in the *de facto* segregation in the public institutions. Students at West Feliciana High School, 43 years after the US Supreme Court decided in *Brown v. Board of Education* (1954) to end segregated public schooling practices, attend black and white proms, a practice more reminiscent of the separate but equal spirit of an earlier Supreme Court decision, *Plessy v. Ferguson* (1896), that the *Brown* ruling overturned. Greene (1988) explains that entrenched social practices such as these endure because

when oppression or exploitation or segregation or neglect is perceived as 'natural'
or a 'given,' there is little stirring in the name of freedom . . . When people cannot
name alternatives, imagine a better state of things, share with others a project of
change, they are likely to remain anchored or submerged, even as they proudly
assert their autonomy. (p. 9)

In response to his teacher's social studies assignment to examine some aspect of the
local architecture in the parish, my son Jared chose the slave quarters on the plantations
— plantations that now attract visitors from all parts of the world. He contacted plantation proprietors to arrange to photograph the slave quarters only to have them rebuff him
at every turn with, 'There are no slave quarters!' or 'I don't know what you are talking
about.' Jared's experience exemplifies one of Greene's insights about race in response to
Ralph Ellison's (1952) *Invisible Man*: 'Invisibility represents a condition in the mind of
the one who encounters the black person' (p. 129). The disappearance of the slave
quarters from plantations, thus rendering them invisible, and the unwillingness of proprietors even to acknowledge that the quarters once existed constitute a conditioned forget-
fulness that results from such memories having no place in an acquiescent, old-fashioned
celebration of freedom.

On 3 July *The Advocate*, the daily newspaper out of Baton Rouge, contains nearly
40 references to Independence Day. Perhaps not surprisingly, the majority adorn advertisements, including those for restaurants, automobile dealerships, furniture stores, hard-
ware stores, banks and credit unions, clothing stores, super stores, and mattress warehouses.
A plethora of images consisting of stars, stripes, furling flags, exploding fireworks, Uncle
Sam caricatures, stern-faced bald eagles, and revolutionary-war-era cannons reminds readers
to honor the nation's origin as they support its economy. One advertisement, which
decrees, 'The Home Depot declares freedom from high prices!' (p. 17A), epitomizes
Greene's critique of the role of negative freedom (i.e., freedom as *freedom from* constraint or coercion) and its link to the promotion of consumerism in society. Greene
(1988) argues that the contemporary world embraces 'a social reality in which the existence and the uses of freedom in its negative sense are continually affirmed, while at the
same time Americans seem to be absorbed into a passive, consuming audience' (p. 22).

The merging of images of freedom and consumption, whether in linking Coca Cola
and Independence Day or in suggesting that Home Depot provides a safe haven to
oppressed shoppers, has its genesis, as Greene suggests, in

the late eighteenth and early nineteenth centuries, from . . . the early days of capitalism. . . . The themes derive from an early liberalism associated with *laissez-faire*
approaches to the economy. Deregulation, noninterference, privatization: All are
linked to the development of 'character,' to consumption, to merit, to (deserved)
material gain. (1988, p. 17)

My purpose in the introduction is not to single out St. Francisville or *The Advocate*
for criticism. Similar portrayals of passive consumption and negative freedom abound
throughout the United States. However, recent anecdotes from my own life and surroundings do illustrate Greene's contention that the concept of freedom as a given or an
endowment is pervasive and embedded in the social practices of daily living. In the
sections that follow, I will discuss *The Dialectic of Freedom* in the social context of the
1980s and address three primary and complex constructs: freedom, community, and
education. In particular, I will consider Greene's argument for a situated freedom in the

context of community and her plea for a transformation of the purposes and practices of education to foster freedom and democracy.

The Dialectic of Freedom and the 1980s

A decade ago Maxine Greene raised the following questions, questions that remain pertinent today:

> What is left for us then in this positivist, media-dominated, and self-centered time? How, with so much acquiescence and so much thoughtlessness around us, are we to open people to the power of possibility? How, given the emphasis on preparing the young for a society of high technology, are we to move them to perceive alternatives, to look at things as if they could be otherwise? And why? And to what ends? (1988, p. 55)

The publication of *The Dialectic of Freedom* in 1988 coincided with the completion of Ronald Reagan's eight years as President of the United States. While it is difficult, if not impossible, to generalize about the 1980s, the legacy of the Reagan Revolution underscored a climate of self-centered, self-righteous individualism that disdained the merits of an individual's responsibility to others in community or commitment to social action. On the contrary, the hallmark of freedom in such an atmosphere is the ability of individuals to pursue their own interests unfettered by social constraints or obligations. Some commentators even argued that this untempered freedom would benefit society as a whole. For example, economists justified the unbridled accumulation of conspicuous wealth through the trickle-down theory (Arndt, 1983), the rather dubious belief that as individual and corporate profits rise, the generated riches eventually would benefit members of all socio-economic classes. Unfortunately, however, for some members the benefits evaporated before they trickled down to them.

The emphasis on a self-righteous individualism guided the Reagan administration's response to social issues as well. For example, when the media publicized the problem of drug addiction, the first lady, Nancy Reagan, sent the following message to the American people: 'Just say no!' (Bennett, 1996). This slogan, which the First Lady's speech writers undoubtedly coined and she repeatedly uttered at every opportunity, suggests that individuals privately are liable for their own problems and, therefore, the government — the public — is absolved of responsibility and not obliged to offer support. This tersely phrased moral imperative accentuates the poignancy reflected in Greene's question regarding a compliant and senseless social climate that does not encourage people to take action together in their own best interests.

The attraction to ineffective, individualistic rhetoric and aversion to substantive, collaborative action conceivably stemmed from the Reagans' years living in California prior to their time in the White House, for California is replete with examples of self-centered individualism and inaction. Perhaps one of the most vulgar examples is Werner Erhard's EST Institute, an organization that acquired enormous wealth in part due to the establishment of The Hunger Project. The project, which Erhard founded in the late 1970s and continued to direct through the 1980s, encouraged people to simply pledge their word to end world hunger, along with sending the project a monetary donation. The rationale is that when enough people (a critical mass of people in the project's terminology) individually pledge their word to take responsibility to end world hunger, then hunger will end. No further action is necessary. As Gordon (1978) points out, 'The Hunger Project does not, you see, *do* anything about ending hunger' (p. 42, emphasis in original). As a result, the donations perpetuate the project, rather than benefit people who are hungry. Ironically in retrospect, Erhard claimed that he would be 'personally taking responsibility to end the starvation on this planet by 1997' (Gordon, 1978, p. 44).

Having lived in California for 17 years myself, I experienced numerous examples of such facile responses to the complex challenges of social life. In fact, in the 1980s as a high school teacher in the San Diego area, I observed first-hand the effects of the 'Just Say No!' campaign on the students in my school. Signs on the walls of the school building announced that the high school constituted a drug-free zone. Assembly speakers implored students to 'Just say no!' to drug use. Students and staff members wore red ribbons and buttons imprinted with the word drugs and the slash symbol through the word. However, in spite of, or perhaps as a result of, this kind of attention to the problem, drug use among the students increased.

Influenced by the ethos of self-centeredness and the shallow, ineffective rhetoric in response to the intricacies and difficulties in community, people in general increasingly withdrew from participation in a public life concerned with the well-being of others. In *Habits of the Heart*, Bellah, Madsen, Sullivan, Swidler, and Tipton (1985) describe this trend as a replacement of community in the public arena with lifestyle enclave in the private arena. According to Bellah et al., 'In a period when work is seldom a calling and few of us find a sense of who we are in public participation as citizens, the lifestyle enclave, fragile and shallow though it often is, fulfills that function for us all' (1985, p. 75). By living in lifestyle enclaves, people turn away from those who are different from themselves, opting instead for the superficial comfort derived from proximity to others with comparable interests. As the authors assert, 'Whereas a community attempts to be an inclusive whole, celebrating the interdependence of public and private life and of the different callings of all, lifestyle is fundamentally segmental and celebrates the narcissism of similarity' (Bellah et al., 1985, p. 72).

Freedom and Community

The idea of negative freedom is linked characteristically to the pervasive concept of freedom as a given or as an endowment in the United States. According to Greene (1988), negative freedom, which stems from the liberal philosophical tradition that predominates discussion of freedom in the United States, signifies an individual's *freedom from* constraint or obligation, 'the right not to be interfered with or coerced or compelled to do what one does not want to do' (p. 16). Noddings (1996) states that freedom from constraint or obligation, embedded in the fabric of the concept of freedom as a given, is particular to the United States, and as a result, individuals in the United States have lost the imperative to care for others in the community at large. Noddings points out that 'unlike some European nations, citizens in the United States have few, if any, positive duties. . . . The emphasis on negative duties has eroded not only a sense of responsibility for one another but even our understanding of human sociality' (1996, p. 252).

Through *The Dialectic of Freedom*, Greene critiques the social milieu of the 1980s, in which the effects of a self-righteous, self-centered social climate dispatched individuals into lifestyle enclaves and thus stripped away their sense of obligation to one another. Amid this ambience of intolerance toward social differences and immobility and indifference in reaction to social problems, Greene argues,

> There is almost no serious talk of reconstituting a civic order, a community. . . .
> [Instead,] there is a general withdrawal from what ought to be public concerns.
> Messages and announcements fill the air; but there is because of the withdrawal, a
> widespread speechlessness, a silence where there might be — where there ought to
> be — an impassioned and significant dialogue. (1988, p. 2)

Greene encourages individuals to re-enter public life through recovering their collective
voices and experiencing the agency that results from participation with others to produce
changes. Greene seeks 'to remind people of what it means to be alive among others, to
achieve freedom in dialogue with others for the sake of personal fulfillment and the
emergence of a democracy dedicated to life and decency' (1988, p. xii).

Unlike the prevailing concept of freedom as a passive, meaningless given, the concept of freedom as an active, meaningful dialogue does not represent a reified, context-
free social condition. For example, Greene suggests that 'freedom ought to be conceived
of as an achievement within the concreteness of lived social situations' (pp. 4–5). Moreover, she argues that individuals cannot afford to continue to take freedom for granted.
She observes that

> it [is] unthinking any longer for Americans to assert themselves to be 'free' because
> they belong to a 'free' country. Not only do we need to be continually empowered
> to choose ourselves, to create our identities within a plurality; we need continually
> to make new promises and to act in our freedom to fulfill them, something we can
> never do meaningfully alone. (1988, p. 51)

Dialogical freedom, then, arises out of particular situations in which individuals band
together to participate in a process that affirm their identities and fulfills their promises
through naming and overcoming obstacles.

Education

In turning to an analysis of education within the context of freedom and community,
Greene asks, 'How, in a society like ours, a society of contesting interests and submerged
voices, an individualistic society . . . can we educate for freedom?' (1988, p. 116). Moreover, how can we foster in students the ability to recognize, name, and overcome obstacles
that hinder the achievement of their goals? What role should the schools play in supporting the development of processes for the enactment of dialogical freedom?

Existing schooling practices and the rhetoric of current reform initiatives do not
offer much in the way of education for freedom. For example, Greene (1988) argues that
'a concern for the critical and the imaginative, for the opening of new ways of "looking
at things," is wholly at odds with the technicist and behaviorist emphasis we still find in
American schools' (p. 126). The technicist and behaviorist emphasis requires that students and teachers acquiesce to the given and ignore the possible. As Greene points out,
'The major focus is and will be on technical or "coping" skills. . . . The orientation has
been to accommodation, to fitting into existing social and economic structures, to what is
given, to what is inescapably *there*' (p. 12, emphasis in original). Obviously, in such an
environment, students are not encouraged to use their imaginations, recognize and name
obstacles, or learn to empower themselves and others. Instead, as Greene points out,
'schools [are] infused with a management orientation, acceding to market measures; and

[teachers] (seeing no alternatives) are wont to narrow and technicize the area of their concerns' (p. 13).

Even more disturbing, Greene asserts, is that the narrow, technical focus of a management orientation to schooling practices exhibits 'the apparent absence of concern for the ways in which young people feel conditioned, determined, even *fated* by prevailing circumstances' (1988, p. 124, emphasis in original). These deterministic, prevailing circumstances become reified into the larger phenomenon of cultural reproduction. As Greene points out,

> By that is meant not only the reproduction of ways of knowing, believing, and valuing, but the maintenance or social patternings and stratifications as well. The young people may not chafe under the inequities being kept alive through schools, as inequities often are; they are likely to treat them as wholly 'normal,' as predictable as natural laws. (p. 125)

In order to counteract the phenomenon of cultural reproduction, Greene argues that schools ought to become sites of intellectual and cultural transformation, places where students can learn to empower themselves and others to overcome the legacy of prevailing cultural practices. As Greene (1988) suggests,

> It is through and by means of education ... that individuals can be provoked to reach beyond themselves in their intersubjective space. It is through and by means of education that they may become empowered to think about what they are doing, to become mindful, to share meanings, to conceptualize, to make varied sense of their lived worlds. (p. 12)

However, for schools to create the conditions for students to reach beyond themselves and become empowered to think about what they are doing and make sense of their lived worlds, classroom expectations and practices must be transformed to foster the process of dialogical freedom. As Greene argues,

> In the classroom opened to possibility and at once concerned with inquiry, critiques must be developed that uncover what masquerade as neutral frameworks. ... Teachers, like their students, have to learn to love the questions, as they come to realize that there can be no final agreements or answers, no final commensurability. And we have been talking about stories that open perspectives on communities grounded in trust, flowering by means of dialogue, kept alive in open spaces where freedom can find a place. (1988, p. 134)

Conclusion

Ten years have passed since Maxine Greene published *The Dialectic of Freedom*. Her critique of the social conditions of the 1980s certainly hold true today. Little has changed in the way most individuals conceptualize freedom, and most demonstrate a lack of responsibility to community. Individuals passively accept social inequities as a given. Individuals characterize freedom in the negative sense as freedom from obligation or coercion. Little has changed in the way educators conceptualize and implement contemporary schooling practices.

In this climate of acquiescence to the given, Maxine Green continues, in her words, 'a lifetime's preoccupation with quest, with pursuit . . . [for] the possible: of what *ought* to be, from moral and ethical points of view, and what is in the making, what *might* be in an always open world' (1988, p. xi, emphasis in original). Unlike those who argue for the freedom of an unbridled individualism, Greene pursues a freedom grounded in the ethic of care and collective responsibility. Unfortunately, visionaries like Greene are few in number and do not have immediate access to mainstream media.

Writing in *The Village Voice* of his friend Allen Ginsburg, Robert Creeley (1997) pronounces,

> He wanted a freedom for us all, a recognition that could bring us home, the guilts and arguments and pained oppositions finally let go of. That burden is always in his writing, in his determined clarity of detail, in the care he has taken to understand. (p. 38)

Creeley's statement concerning Allen Ginsburg echoes what many of us experience in reaction to Maxine Greene's work in general and to *The Dialectic of Freedom* in particular. Greene wants a freedom for us all, grounded in the fabric of community, in the ethical and moral responsibility that individuals feel for one another when they come together to recognize, name, and overcome impediments to their becoming fully human. Greene's desire to reawaken in us a commitment to fight against an acquiescent acceptance of the given social environment is always in her writing, in her determined clarity of detail, and in the care she has taken to understand.

References

ARNDT, H.W. (1983) 'The "trickle-down" myth,' *Economic Development and Cultural Change*, **32**, pp. 1–10.

BELLAH, R.N., MADSEN, R., SULLIVAN, W.M., SWIDLER, A., and TIPTON, S.M. (1985) *Habits of the Heart: Individualism and Commitment in American Life*, New York: Harper & Row.

BENNETT, W.J. (1996) 'Just say sure: A lack of leadership,' *Rising Tide* [on-line], **4**, 1, http://rnc.org/news/tide/9611/art6.html

BROWN V. BOARD OF EDUCATION (1954) 347 U.S. 483.

CREELEY, R. (1997) 'Voice of the people,' *The Village Voice*, **52**, 15, pp. 36, 38.

ELLISON, R. (1952) *Invisible Man*, New York: Signet Books.

GREENE, M. (1988) *The Dialectic of Freedom*, New York: Teachers College Press.

GORDON, S. (1978) 'Let them eat est,' *Mother Jones*, **3**, 10, pp. 41–54.

NODDINGS, N. (1996) 'On community,' *Educational Theory*, **46**, pp. 245–67.

PLESSY V. FERGUSON (1896) 163 U.S. 537.

5   *Releasing the Imagination* and the 1990s

Patrick Slattery and David M. Dees

You can't depend on your judgment when your imagination is out of focus. (Mark Twain, 1935, p. 344)

When old and familiar things are made new in experience, there is imagination. When the new is created, the far and strange become the most natural inevitable things in the world. There is always some measure of adventure in the meeting of the mind and universe, and this adventure is, in its measure, imagination. (John Dewey, 1934, p. 267)

[Imagination] brings the severed parts together. (Virginia Woolf, 1976, p. 72)

What I am describing here is a mode of utopian thinking: thinking that refuses mere compliance, that looks down roads not yet taken to the shapes of more fulfilling social order, to more vibrant ways of being in the world. This kind of reshaping imagination may be released through many sorts of dialogue . . . When such dialogue is activated in classrooms, even the young are stirred to reach out on their own initiatives. Apathy and indifference are likely to give way as images of what might arise. (Maxine Greene, 1995a, p. 5)

Introduction

In *Releasing the Imagination*, Maxine Greene evokes a passion for education, the arts, and social change as she shares her journey 'to look through the others' eyes more than I would have and to imagine being something more than I have come to be' (1995a, p. 86). Maxine Greene is a prophetic voice challenging educators and students — indeed all persons — to connect the arts with lived experience for the purpose of opening 'spaces where persons speaking together and being together can discover what it signifies to incarnate and act upon values far too often taken for granted' (1995a, p. 68). Greene envisions classrooms and communities that value multiple perspectives, democratic pluralism, life narratives, and ongoing social change. This is best accomplished, she believes, through literary, artistic, and phenomenological experiences that release the imagination. She challenges the anxiety of a modern world that has reduced learning and living to fragmented and quantifiable components devoid of the aesthetic and narrative. Greene (1995a) summarizes:

> I have written *Releasing the Imagination* to remedy that anxiety. It grants a usefulness to the disinterest of seeing things small at the same time that it opens to and validates the passion for seeing things close up and large. For this passion is the doorway for imagination; here is the possibility of looking at things as if they could

be otherwise. This possibility, for me, is what restructuring might signify. Looking at things large is what might move us on to reform. (p. 16)

The possibility of creating a passion for looking at things anew and opening a doorway for imagination, education, and social reform is Maxine Greene's constant theme in the 1990s.

Maxine Greene's philosophical positions never stray far from her passion for narrative and lived experience which has been evident in her works from *Teacher as Stranger* to *The Dialectic of Freedom*. However, we believe that something unique has emerged in *Releasing the Imagination*. This text, as we read it, is Maxine Greene's artistic representation of her journey to create a new social and educational vision. In effect, *Releasing the Imagination* is an autobiographical narrative written in three parts: creating possibilities, illuminations and epiphanies, and community in the making. These chapters parallel the three movements in the symphony of Maxine Greene's life and career: transformations through literary encounters, the search for pedagogical possibilities, and creating a community with a passion for multiple voices and multiple realities. These movements coalesce in a harmonious process with the repetitive phrase of imagination through the arts. It is here that transformations, possibilities, and community emerge for Greene and others willing to engage in the process of releasing the imagination.

Transformations through Literary Encounters

The downbeat of the first movement in Maxine Greene's oeuvre is the aesthetic experience that can occur through encounters with the arts and literature. She writes: 'If we regard curriculum as an undertaking involving continuous interpretation and a conscious search for meanings, we come to see many connections between the grasping of a text or artwork and the gaining of multiple perspectives by means of the disciplines' (1995a, p. 96). Drawing upon Sartre, Dewey, and Iser, Greene posits that encounters with the arts are a transactional mode of being in which the individual's lived experience and the text become united in a process of understanding that leads to transformation. Literature and the arts are not merely decorative additions or supplemental ornaments; literature and the arts '... bring to curriculum inquiry visions of perspectives and untapped possibilities' (Greene, 1995a, p. 90). Literature and the arts elicit modes of being and are misunderstood when they are reified or objectified.

Positivist critics may ask why there are so many literary references in *Releasing the Imagination*, concerned that literature is a distraction from the rigorous logic of philosophical analysis or sociological surveys. For ourselves and for Maxine Greene this criticism is rooted in modernist notions of positivist science as 'instrumental rationality' (Greene, 1995a, p. 113) that seek certitude and tangible evidence and only uncover 'inert ideas' (Whitehead, 1929). However, it is in the ineffable, the experiential, indeed the imaginative, that philosophical understanding and social transformations occur. For Greene, literature has allowed her to lend her life to others. She writes (1995a), 'I was, through my reading, allowing them [literary figures] to emerge in my consciousness and, by so doing, to transform it, as social scientific accounts or even psychological ones would never do' (p. 94). By lending herself to others through literature, Greene has been able to pursue her quest of seeing 'from the other side of the looking glass' (p. 94), creating spaces for personal transformations. Greene's description of her pursuit of personal transformations is reminiscent of Dewey's insight into encounters with works of art. Dewey (1934) contends that knowledge is transformed and made more intelligible through the aesthetic experience. He writes, '[t]angible scenes of life are made more intelligible in esthetic experience: not, however as reflection and science render things more intelligible by reduction to conceptual form, but by presenting their meanings as the matter of a clarified, coherent, and intensified or "impassioned" experience' (p. 290).

We believe that one of the fundamental purposes of *Releasing the Imagination* is to inspire educators to begin the quest of encountering literature and the arts from the phenomenological perspective, that is, to engage the arts in ways that the lives of teachers and students will be transformed through the autobiographical narrative. For those who have already begun this journey, Greene provides a narrative of her life through literature as an example of the way that the arts have created spaces for transformation. Greene (1995a) explains:

> In this time of interest in narrative and storytelling as a way of knowing . . . my hope is that the story disclosed here will move readers to tap their own stories, their experiences in finding projects by which to create identities. It is important to me, for example, to summon up the ways in which I was demeaned in my early days of college teaching by being told I was too 'literary' to do philosophy. That seemed to mean that I was thought ill equipped to do the sort of detached and rigorous analysis of language games and arguments that for a long time dominated the academic world. I could not objectify nor separate my subjectivity from what I was perceiving. I could not separate my feeling, imagining, wondering consciousness from the cognitive work assigned for me to do. Nor could I bracket out my biography and my experiences of embeddedness in an untidy, intersubjective world. (p. 113)

Here Greene articulates her passion for supporting educators in the process of incorporating literature and the arts along with personal narrative into the process of transforming lives, and thus creating meaningful learning spaces for pedagogical possibilities.

Pedagogical Possibilities

If the downbeat that began the musical movement in Maxine Greene's work is the aesthetic experience, then the instrumentation that allows for the creation of the symphony is the pedagogical process. Greene (1995a) explains that 'we all believe that our efforts to understand the young and recover our own landscapes must be linked to notions of pedagogical praxis and that the pedagogies we devise ought to provoke a heightened sense of agency in those we teach, empower them to pursue their freedom and, perhaps, transform to some degree their lived worlds' (p. 48). Greene believes that this transformation can occur through pedagogical practices grounded in the arts because the arts serve to open vistas of possibility and experience that draw from and move beyond a student's lived world. Additionally, she reminds us that teaching is a transactional event that occurs between teachers and students, thus allowing for the opening of new vistas for both. Greene (1995a) writes:

> If we teachers are to develop a humane and liberating pedagogy, we must feel ourselves to be engaged in a dialectical relation. We are more likely to uncover or be able to interpret what we are experiencing if we can at times recapture some of our own lost spontaneity and some awareness of our own backgrounds, either through communication with children, psychotherapy, or engagement with works of art. (p. 52)

Thus, pedagogical encounters with works of art not only allow our students to give their 'lives' to others like Greene, but also to understand and appreciate multiple perspectives and creative interpretations. These pedagogical encounters serve as a means of allowing teachers to step into lived worlds of students, perhaps allowing educators to find and create new spaces for personal, pedagogical, and social transformations.

Through the arts, aesthetic consciousness is awakened, allowing our students to see multiple perspectives and educators to hear the multiple voices of their students. This aesthetic consciousness also increases our imaginative possibilities which can serve to engender school reform. However, current school reform efforts remain rooted in reductionism and modernist philosophy. For example, in many ways, school reform is entrenched in the 'old quantitative models' (Greene, 1995a, p. 18) and 'the quest for certainty' (Dewey, 1929). In response, many citizens yearn for the predictable and assurances that their children have mastered the basics. Greene (1995a) challenges these assumptions, and asserts that we must also use imagination in the ways we think about school reform and school restructuring:

> To tap into imagination is to become able to break with what is supposedly fixed and finished, objectively and independently real. It is to see beyond what the imaginer has called normal or 'common-sensible' and to carve out new orders in experience. Doing so, a person may become freed to glimpse what might be, to form notions of what should be and what is not yet. And the same person may, at the same time, remain in touch with what presumably *is*. (p. 19)

Exploring imaginative possibilities not only transforms classroom practice but also opens up vistas to new ways to envision the schooling process, evaluate the learning environment, and create educational experiences.

A Community with Passion for Multiple Voices and Multiple Realities

The third phrase in the symphonic movement of Maxine Greene's oeuvre as reflected in *Releasing the Imagination* is the creation of a community inspired by a passion for multiplicity and social change. This is the rhythm that underscores her life performance. This is the *raison d'etre* for turning to the arts and literature to release the imagination. Greene contends that in order to imagine a democratic community accessible to students we must 'summon up the vision of the "conjoint experience," shared meanings, common interests and endeavors described by John Dewey' (1995a, p. 33). Interconnectedness and communion are the characteristics of such a community for Greene: 'A continuing search for intellectual freedom and freedom of articulation . . . give vibrancy and energy to the *possible* community' (1995a, pp. 33–4). Perhaps it is the belief that such a community is not only *possible* but also essential for growth and survival that inspires Maxine Greene to write with such passion and commitment. There is an urgency in her commitment to a democratic community that integrates multiplicity into the fabric of its existence. Greene contends that in recent years invisibility has been refused by many people, '[o]ld silences have been shattered; long repressed voices are making themselves heard . . . We are challenged as never before to confront plurality and multiplicity' (1995a, p. 155).

As Greene so eloquently notes, this is an assiduous challenge for educators. Struggling to understand how our students are processing and 'living' the information we share with them, as educators we can become frustrated and disenchanted with our students' perspectives. Greene (1995a) writes:

> Listening to them [students], we frequently find ourselves dealing as never before
> with our own prejudgments and preferences, with the forms and images we have
> treasured through most of our lives. What we have learned to treat as valuable, what
> we take for granted may be challenged in unexpected ways. We find ourselves
> stopped in our tracks — to wonder, to protest sometimes, to lash out in anger or
> contempt, to retreat now and then to think about our own thinking. (p. 188)

However, by tapping into the imagination through aesthetic consciousness, educators can
find a space for allowing the multiple perspectives in our students' voices to emerge and
grow within a social dialogue.

As noted above, for Greene, awakening her awareness to the voices of 'others'
occurred in many respects through her engagements with literature. For her, literature
taps '. . . all sorts of circuits in reader consciousness . . .' (1995a, p. 186). From this
awakened state both teachers and students can see, hear, and connect with the lives of
others which in turn helps to re-position and re-create their own sense of self. As Greene
notes, this state of awakened awareness allows us to '. . . participate in some dimensions
that we could not know if imagination were not aroused' (1995a, p. 186). Thus, through
the aesthetic consciousness aroused through artistic encounters, teachers and students can
develop a space for the 'other' to enter into their own lived world. However, Greene
warns that releasing this imagination does not instantaneously provide the answer for
understanding silenced voices and multiple perspectives. Releasing the imagination creates an environment in which more interesting questions can emerge which in turn will
'. . . lead us on more and more far-reaching quests' (1995a, p. 187).

Maxine Greene calls for a community of teachers and students who are questioning
and searching for possibilities of social justice and equality:

> I say these things about the possibility of shared commitments not because I believe
> we can override pluralism or rediscover a 'general orientation' or some renewed
> faith in a 'universal reason'. I say them in the belief that a re-viewing ought to
> involve us in the continuing constitution and renewal of a common world, if we can
> keep in mind the idea that such a world may come into being in the course of a
> continuing dialogue, which we ourselves can provoke and nurture in the midst of
> change. (1995a, p. 196)

This challenge will not come easy; it requires visionaries and individuals that are not
afraid to break from their personal 'given,' everyday perspectives. This form of consciousness requires individuals to challenge one's own sense of being and awareness.
Greene (1995a) states '[t]he principles and the contexts have to be *chosen* by living
human beings against their own life-worlds and in the light of their lives with others, by
persons able to call, to say, to sing, and — using their imaginations, tapping their courage
— to transform' (p. 198). Releasing the imagination is not an easy quest — yet it is
vital to imagining a world in which social transformation and individual possibilities can
flourish. In musical terms this represents Maxine Greene's *de capo al fine* — her belief
that the imaginative quest for multiple voices and multiple realities never ends. We will
continue to be inspired by the music.

Maxine Greene in the 1990s

It is clear to us that the three movements in Maxine Greene's *Releasing the Imagination*
also can be heard in her other works published in the 1990s. This is particularly evident

in 'Notes on the search for coherence' (Greene, 1995b), published in the ASCD Year-book entitled *Toward a Coherent Curriculum* (Beane, 1995) where she challenges educators to ask the kinds of questions that have to do with meaning and with 'different ways of seeing and describing the landscapes people inhabit' (p. 139). Coherence in the curriculum emerges when questions about human experience are foregrounded. When devising curriculum, Greene insists, we must 'consciously create conditions that stir learners to reach out from their own vantage points to spaces where they can attain some reciprocity' (p. 139). Greene often refers to Walker Percy's (1979) character Binx Bolling in *The Moviegoer* as an example of what can happen when we are not consciously creating such learning conditions. Percy writes, 'Not to be on to something is to be in despair.' Likewise, not to be on the search for possibilities in education establishes a curriculum that is lifeless, meaningless, and incoherent. 'It is understandable that . . . boredom and a sense of futility are among the worst enemies of education. At a time of diminishing opportunity in so many lives, at a time when upward mobility cannot be guaranteed, feelings of futility are widespread' (Greene, 1995b, p. 141).

How do educators overcome pervasive malaise and futility to create a coherent curriculum? In the 1995 ASCD Yearbook, Maxine Greene argues that encounters with the arts and narrative can release the imagination and engender transformation — to see from another perspective — and transcendence — to go beyond an embedded existence — that will awaken possibilities for individuals as well as the socio-political, environmental, and global milieu. Greene (1995b) concludes:

> The coherence is to be found in the rhythm and vitality of the process itself, the willingness to turn outward, to enter into dialogues, to continue to create provisional relationships, to reach beyond. What is significant as well — deeply significant in what strikes so many as a chaotic world — is the weaving of wider and wider webs of relationship, what may become a common world . . . That may be where coherence is fulfilled — in the making of a common world. (p. 144)

Maxine Greene makes an impassioned plea for coherence, imagination, relationships, a common world, and landscapes of possibilities in the 1995 ASCD Yearbook, echoing the themes of her other works throughout the 1990s, especially *Releasing the Imagination*.

Addressing the issue of the angst in the 1990s and highlighting her theme of creating a community with a passion for multiple voices and multiple realities, Greene's (1991) article entitled 'The literacy debate and the public school: Going beyond the functional' posits that many of today's educators '. . . are responding to society's conceived survival needs, ordinarily defined first in economic terms' (p. 130). She continues noting that '[b]ecause of this, such discussions [regarding literacy] become purely functional' (p. 130). As a result of this perceived societal need for functional reading ability, Greene (1991) describes the dilemma of today's practicing educators in the following manner:

> Teachers tend to set aside their original visions of worlds that would be opened by various kinds of literacy — by imagination, for example, by the capacity to truly *see*, to attend to the particulars at hand. Somehow convinced that their professional self-definitions (as well as their own trade jargon) place decided social value upon functional literacy, they scarcely ever ask themselves about the difference literacy makes in various lives. (p. 130)

By learning and drawing from the post-modernists' questionings of reality, romantic movements in poetry, existentialism, phenomenology, and pragmatist perspectives, Greene

(1991) proposes that as a society we can move beyond the search for solutions based in '[m]easurements and prescriptions to accord with the deficit models on which we depend' (p. 133). This move away from modernist's reductionism can help us to include the 'other' in our conceptions of the public space as well as in our conceptions of 'self'. With Toni Morrison (1989) Greene moves us to see that 'the trauma of racism is, for the racist and the victim, the severe fragmentation of the self . . . We are not in fact "other"'' (pp. 16, 9). Greene (1991) writes:

> To include any of these 'other' views compels us (often against our will) to defamiliarize our accustomed worlds, to render strange what we have learned through our particular shared culture to read and see and say. Once we do allow for other consciousnesses with equal rights, including those of our students, we open ourselves to the *heteroglossia* or multiple voices of the social world . . . More than that, we may come to realize the language we speak does not belong to us alone but is social, as we ourselves are social, and that, whoever we are, we come in contact with the world through a great diversity of official and unofficial languages. (p. 164)

Greene contends that this awareness of the 'other' will allow for more honest and meaningful dialogue in our classrooms. Additionally, '[w]e might think of the many ways human beings have imposed narrative form on their experiences in an effort to create order and make sense' (1991, p. 164). Greene argues to reposition the dialogue regarding literacy away from reductionism's objectives of creating order, into an imaginative space in which new possibilities for social justice and equality can emerge.

Rather than creating, like E.D. Hirsch, Jr. (1987), a 'grand narrative' list to describe the culturally literate, Greene (1991) believes that the classroom dialogue can serve as a garden allowing imaginative possibilities and cultural awareness to bloom:

> What is important is for educators, in their own diversity, to think about creating the conditions under which the dialogue, the vital interplay being envisaged on so many sides, can occur. It is under conditions like these that a common language, a shared cultural literacy, may be achieved. (p. 167)

For Greene, these classroom interactions will serve to open aesthetic sensibilities and possibilities for our students. She continues:

> When I think of the literacy debate in relation to young people, I think of making opportunities possible for them to make the songs they sing; to tell, improve, and retell their stories; to gain a sense that they — talking together, writing together — are the authors of their world. (p. 167)

Thus, the literacy debate for Maxine Greene is more than just a reductionist 'list approach' to student knowledge. For her, the literacy debate should focus more on opening the imagination of teachers and students to help co-create a world that appreciates individual voice and is on a quest for social justice. For Greene, this is a space in which '. . . we cannot plan or chart in advance, but which is where we have not been' (1991, p. 168).

Another theme of Maxine Greene in the 1990s is that of a quest for pedagogical possibilities. This theme, highlighted in *Releasing the Imagination*, is placed in the foreground in 'Metaphors and multiples: Representation, the arts, and history' published in *Phi Delta Kappan* in 1997. In this piece, Maxine Greene charts her own pedagogical journey with her students by describing how she incorporates 'a range of literary works, paintings, and other art forms, as well as the more standard list of works in American history, educational and curriculum history . . .' into her classroom encounters (1997, p. 388). She details the results of these interactions when she states that '[i]n the process of our inquiries, we have found our perspectives opening, as imagination is released and one-dimensional explanations give way to a notion of multiple realities' (1997, p. 388).

Greene (1997) contends that 'this mode of teaching and curriculum-making does not lead to final answers' (p. 388), and she describes her intentions in this teaching style as having an aim for imaginative possibilities for future teachers and students:

> My aim is not to achieve certainty or to recapture some golden age of unassailable 'truth'. My aim is to awaken teachers-to-be to the ongoing quest for meaning in our history. If they can become the kinds of teachers who can enlist their students in that quest, then their involvement with the problem of representation will have been worthwhile. (p. 388)

Trying to move beyond rationalistic reductionism, Greene believes and models in her own classroom practice an educational philosophy that strives to release the imagination.

In this piece, Greene charts for the reader several personal reactions through using various pieces of literature in her classroom space. One in particular is Nathaniel Hawthorne's 'The May-Pole of Merry Mount' which is a 'tale of two colonies in old New England, the emblem of one being a maypole and of the other, a whipping post' (1997, p. 390). For her, this piece 'made me begin to understand the ways in which the *form* of representation feeds the life of meaning' (1997, p. 390). Greene contends that reading and experiencing Hawthorne's historical account translated into a metaphoric representation

> . . . requires the act of imagination, a deliberate bracketing out for a time of the ordinary and the taken-for-granted. Readers who lend their own lives to what happens, who shape the stuff of their experience in accord with the story's symbolic development, who recognize it as a 'denotative and expressive symbol' that reaches beyond itself may find perspectives opening and dimensions of experience disclosing themselves in wholly unpredictable ways. (1997, p. 391)

Greene believes that this metaphoric approach to history allows the students to find new and different perspectives toward their own place in the historical flow of our puritanical society. She continues:

> I discovered, as any teacher might, that a concentration on metaphor (in this case, with the maypole and the whipping post as examples) made far more difference to the students' search for meaning than an emphasis on divergent conceptions of reality, enlightening though they clearly are. A metaphor enables us to understand one thing better by likening it to what it is not. . . . A metaphor not only involves a reorientation of consciousness, it also enables us to cross divides, to make connections between ourselves and others, and to look through the other eyes. (p. 391)

Here Maxine Greene is modeling how she translates into the classroom her own passion for creating a space for seeing the world from the 'other's' eyes. This connecting of cultural divides that occurs through literary and artistic representations is a tangible means by which we can reposition society's conception of equality and justice.

Tapping into the imaginative possibilities of artistic representations is a main focus of Maxine Greene's search for pedagogical possibilities. She writes:

> In making central to our teaching the arts and the symbol system that present them, we may render conscious the process of making meaning, a process that has much to do with the shaping of identity, the development of a sense of agency, and a commitment to a certain mode of *praxis*. (1997, p. 394)

In this article Greene provides the reader with several tangible examples of how utilizing symbolic representations in the arts can open a conscious space for re-positioning identity and consequently for re-positioning the societal dialogue regarding issues of social equality and justice. For her, this can only happen through tapping into the imaginative possibilities that lie within ourselves. Additionally, for her, it is the educator's responsibility to help open the imaginative spaces of our students. As modeled in this article, her call to educators is achievable and quite exciting, relying very much upon the release of imagination. Clearly defined in her conclusion to this article is the insistence that imagination holds the key to this form of consciousness. She closes this article by saying that '. . . it is the imagination that empowers human beings to create and to engage consciously with works of art. As they do, the realms of meaning can only deepen and expand' (1997, p. 394). This is Maxine Greene's constructivist (Greene, 1996) and inclusive (Greene, 1993) vision that permeates her work in the 1990s.

Autobiographical Interpretations (*David M. Dees*)

Maxine Greene's work has always inspired in my own life as an educator. As I reflect on her life outlined in *Releasing the Imagination*, I am reminded of the ways in which aesthetic consciousness has influenced and re-positioned my perspective on the world as I gave my self over to certain artistic representations. For Greene, many of these moments of personal transformation occurred through literary encounters. For me, these moments have occurred especially through theatrical experiences.

I remember the first time I saw a performance of Martin Sherman's (1979) play *Bent*. This account of the holocaust describes the journey of a gay man from Berlin to Dachau. In an effort to hide his sexual identity and not be forced to wear the pink triangle (the lowest of the low), Max has intercourse with a dead women to prove to the Nazi soldiers that he is not 'bent.' As he describes both the pain and anger of this and other forced atrocities, he defends himself to the audience and his new found lover by noting that with his yellow star he is better off within the walls of the Nazi concentration camps. As Act II began, I watched these actors, trapped in a concentration camp, move large stone bricks from one side of the stage to the other. As the characters moved these bricks, they talked of their love, their pain, their anger, continually moving brick by brick back and forth across the stage. Not only did I feel first hand a small part of the agony of a concentration camp, but this performance made me begin to reflect deeply upon the question that many of us have had regarding the holocaust: How could Western culture come to such a horrific place? My reflection, however, did not end at this historical question.

During this performance I also began to reflect upon the society in which I find myself. Granted, we are not even near the atrocities of the concentration camps that were created to punish those who are 'a bit bent' from the 'norm.' However, this performance reminded me of the 'punishment' that many of my gay friends are forced to endure.

These human beings are forced to hide their identity for fear of verbal persecution, losing their job, and violence. I began to ask the question: How different are we in today's society? Do we force children and young adults into relationships to 'prove' their sexual identity? I started to think about school dances, proms, parties, etc. Do we welcome gay couples to these events? I thought about the high rate of suicide and drug abuse among gay teens. I realized that although we do not have official identity badges to persecute my gay friends, we have other more subtle forms of oppression in our society. This performance affected me much more than just remembering and learning about the atrocities of the holocaust. It made me realize that my friends are also living a nightmare of hidden love and hidden identity within my own 'new' society. Through this performance, I was able to give my life over to them, allowing me to 'see' the world through their eyes in ways I had never imagined.

From this point, I began to imagine a society in which people could love and accept each other for who they are. I imagined a society of people who would encourage others to live a life of realized potential. This, in turn, began to affect my perspectives towards my own class. I was beginning to imagine new pedagogical possibilities as I taught future teachers. For example, when dealing with issues of race in American society, what could my students learn from the lessons of Troy in August Wilson's (1986) *Fences*? Could they 'see' an image of the broken dreams of the African-Americans that moved from the south to the north in hopes of a better tomorrow? Could they begin to understand the pain of being 'fenced' in because of race and history? To me and my students, this type of aesthetic encounter affected us much deeper than any statistical measure of oppression and racism that I could cite for them.

The same type of transformation occurred for me and my students as we read Maria Irene Fornes' (1986) *The Conduct of Life*. Trying to create an understanding of the female voice in our world, this play dramatizes the oppression of women in a male dominated, destructive and aggressive society. We 'witnessed' in this play how the masculine values of control and domination are used to devalue and oppress the female activities of nurturing, educating, and caring for others. In the end we see Leticia, the wife of the oppressor, forced into killing her husband, thus representing how oppressive masculine societal values can overtake individuals, forcing them to contribute to the destruction of each other. Again, class members gave themselves over to this work, realizing how we devalue and persecute women in our society. As a class, we began to explore how our society values aggression and ruthless competition at the cost of our souls and the common good. We discussed how women are portrayed in popular culture as things of beauty to be lusted after rather than listened to. Granted, the students could have learned the same things by reading post-modernists' and critical theorists' discussions of this subject. However, inspired by John Dewey and Maxine Greene, I have come to appreciate the transformation of knowledge that occurs through encounters that engage the aesthetic consciousness, creating new levels of meaning and understanding, that allow us to give ourselves over to the 'other.'

Like Greene, these personal transformations have encouraged me to release my imagination with my students in an effort to imagine and create a better world. In this imaginative space, we can find new avenues for social justice and equality. We can find new spaces for appreciating individual identity in a complex and diverse society. Like a Monet painting or Samuel Beckett's (1976) *Footfalls*, we can imagine new perspectives towards the fundamental questions of reality itself. Maxine Greene has modeled for me in her life's work the power of autobiographical reflection and aesthetic consciousness. She has also inspired me to help co-create with my students a classroom space that encourages the releasing of the imagination in an effort to create pedagogical possibilities that allow the 'other' to speak to us all. Imagine the possibilities. Imagine the promise of a better world.

Autobiographical Interpretations (*Patrick Slattery*)

In the summer of 1995 I taught a graduate course in Columbus, Ohio, entitled 'Pupil Services Administration' to 30 educators seeking certification to become school administrators. I designed the course not only to address the technical skills related to student health services, special education, testing, counseling, athletics, and the like, but also to challenge administrators to broaden their vision of pupil services by investigating popular culture, aesthetics, and contemporary social issues as important dimensions for understanding students, especially marginalized youth in our communities. Several local and national events in the educational community in 1995 provided excellent opportunities to investigate the limitations of the traditional instrumental and functional approaches to pupil services administration in the schools: an alarming rise in the over-medication of active youngsters, particularly the use of the drug *Ritalin*, created a debate about the appropriateness of current trends in the diagnosis of ADD and ADHD. Legislation proposed by some politicians and religious leaders that would prohibit school counselors from discussing sexual orientation with students created a debate about the rights of students to have access, support, and information about important life issues as well as the freedom of counselors to address these issues. Reports of high school athletes who sustained permanent physical damage because coaches provided illegal performance-enhancing drugs and intimidated students to compete before serious injuries had healed sparked national debates about the role of competitive athletics in the schools. These and other media reports supported my belief that school administrators must examine pupil services from the perspective of the human person with sensitivity toward the impact that marginalization has on youth in the schools.

It was a difficult sell. Most of the educators in this class expected prescriptive information about the legal and technical requirements for administering tests, filing health forms, organizing extra-curricular schedules, and the like. While this information was provided, these educators revolted when asked to critically analyze the impact of current schooling practices and procedures on the lives of students. They were particularly indignant when asked to investigate the situation of marginalized youth and expand their vision of the role of the principal in supporting the needs of injured athletes, students struggling with sexual orientation, hyperactive youngsters, and others. In short, I asked these educators to imagine the lived world of students and find ways to free students to attend to their fears, anxieties, dreams, and aspirations. I struggled daily to find a way to help these future administrators to imagine an educational system where pupil services were more concerned about the lived world of students and less concerned about the technical aspects of administering programs. It was a frustrating experience.

At the end of the first week of class I received in the mail a copy of Maxine Greene's new book *Releasing the Imagination: Essays on Education, the Arts, and Social Change*. It was a glorious sunny afternoon; I decided to forget the frustrations of my graduate course and immerse myself in this new book. I went to the oval on the Ohio State campus and sat under a shady buckeye tree in front of the library. Maxine Greene's book was a gift at the most opportune time. *Releasing the Imagination* affirmed my vision that I was so desperately trying to convey to my graduate students. Throughout the book I was reminded that the focus of our work as educators must move beyond the technical dimensions of training and credentialing. We must counterbalance bureaucratic demands with an emphasis on the human person and the human spirit. It is the release of human imagination that will spark new visions for a just, caring, hopeful, and sustainable community. Maxine Greene's vision in the 1990s amounts to much more than an educational reform proposal; she is intent on developing a 'social imagination: the capacity to invent visions of what should be and what might be in our deficient society, on the streets we live, in our schools' (1995a, p. 5). Imagination is the key to unlocking doors that prevent the social imagination from emerging. 'It takes imagination to break with ordinary classification and come in touch with actual young people in their variously lived situations. It takes imagination on the part of young people to perceive openings through which they can move' (1995a, p. 14). In other words, it takes imagination to realize possibilities and make judgments and assessments about schools and society. After spending several hours on the OSU campus reading Maxine Greene's book and thinking about my graduate students' limited understanding of pupil services, I glanced skyward to ponder the connection between *Releasing the Imagination* and my own lived world experiences in the classroom. My eyes caught an anecdote by Mark Twain etched in stone above the entrance to the OSU library — 'Your judgment may be flawed if your imagination is not in focus.'

References

BEANE, J.A. (ed.) (1995) *Toward a Coherent Curriculum*, Alexandria, VA: ASCD Publications.
BECKETT, S. (1976) *Footfalls*, London: Faber and Faber.
DEWEY, J. (1929) *The Quest for Certainty*, London: Allen & Unwin.
DEWEY, J. (1934) *Art as Experience*, New York: Perigee Books.
FORNES, M.I. (1986) *Plays: Maria Irene Fornes*, New York: PAJ Publications.
GREENE, M. (1991) 'The literacy debate and the public school: Going beyond the functional,' *Educational Horizons*, **69**, 3, pp. 129–34, 164–8.
GREENE, M. (1993) 'Diversity and inclusion: Toward a curriculum for human beings,' *Teachers College Record*, **95**, 2, pp. 211–21.
GREENE, M. (1995a) *Releasing the Imagination: Essays on Education, the Arts, and Social Change*, New York: Jossey-Bass.
GREENE, M. (1995b) 'Notes on the search for coherence,' in BEANE, J.A. (ed.) *Toward a Coherent Curriculum* (pp. 139–45), Alexandria, VA: ASCD Publications.
GREENE, M. (1996) 'A constructivist perspective on teaching and learning in the arts,' in FOSNOT, C.T. (ed.) *Constructivism: Theory, Perspectives, and Practice*, New York: Teachers College Press.
GREENE, M. (1997) 'Metaphors and multiples: Representation, the arts and history,' *Phi Delta Kappan*, **78**, 5, pp. 387–94.
HIRSCH, E.D., JR. (1987) *Cultural Literacy: What Every American Needs to Know*, Boston: Houghton Mifflin.
MORRISON, T. (1989) 'Unspeakable things unspoken: The Afro-American presence in American literature,' *Michigan Quarterly*, Winter, pp. 1–34.
PERCY, W. (1979) *The Moviegoer*, New York: Knopf.
SHERMAN, M. (1979) *Bent*, New York: Avon Books.
TWAIN, M. (1935) *Mark Twain's Notebook*, New York: Harper Brothers.
WHITEHEAD, A.N. (1929) *Aims of Education*, New York: Free Press, Macmillan.
WILSON, A. (1986) *Fences: A Play*, New York: Plume.
WOOLF, V. (1976) 'Moments of being: Unpublished autobiographical writings' (J. Schulkind, ed.), Orlando, Fla: Harcourt.

Section Two

Themes

6 The Passion of the Possible: Maxine Greene, Democratic Community, and Education

Jesse Goodman and Julie Teel

Throughout her career, Maxine Greene has been concerned with the possible. She consistently encourages us to imagine our lives and culture as they could be. She frequently cites literature and the other arts in her effort to portray the way life is and the way that it could otherwise be. She (1995) cites Sartre's declaration that, 'It is on the day that we can conceive of a different state of affairs that a new light falls on our troubles and our suffering' (pp. 434–5). Greene's work represents a passion for the possible. This chapter will focus on her continual commitment to think of education as one of the many essential ways in which we can transform our culture into a more compelling democratic community. First, we explore Greene's images of democratic community. Next, her notions of 'wide-awakeness' and 'freedom' are discussed not only as illustrations of this community, but also as the means through which this community can evolve. Finally, we discuss her call to imagine a form of public schooling as perhaps the most important institution in bringing to life this renewed sense of a democratic community.

Democratic Community

Like Dewey, Greene suggests that visions of what is considered 'good education' are intimately rooted in the conscious and/or unconscious visions of what is considered a 'good society.' She rejoices in our ability, as human beings, to create culture. Greene's notion of the good society seems to be deeply rooted in a tradition of democratic community. There are several characteristics that form the basis of this community. First, and perhaps most importantly, she argues for us to assume a critical stance towards whatever community emerges from our efforts to create culture. Second, she suggests that we broaden our concept of democracy beyond the political realm of society. Third, the values of pluralism and cohesiveness are central to her vision of democratic culture. Fourth, her image of democratic community is rooted deeply in her existential notions of 'wide-awakeness.' Although there is not space to give full attention to these characteristics, we will briefly discuss each prior to exploring the educational implications that emerge from her cultural visions.

Critical

Perhaps no concept is more important to Greene than the idea that we need to view our efforts to create culture critically. That is, Greene warns us against ever taking the value of our culture for granted: 'Dewey found that democracy is an ideal in the sense that it is always reaching towards some end that can never finally be achieved. Like community itself, it has to be always in the making' (1995, p. 66). This healthy skepticism and questioning is especially important in our increasingly technological and information-based society. Like Wexler (1987), she notes that the concentration of power in our society has shifted from those who control the production of material goods and law enforcement agencies to those who control the means of knowledge production. Perhaps the greatest obstacle to creating a more democratic culture lies in the power of knowledge producers to mystify our lives.

> For us, the 'wall' [obstacles to democracy] may also be found in increasingly faceless bureaucracies, in a 'rule by Nobody' (Arendt, 1958), in the computeriza-tions by which so much of our life is administered and controlled. It becomes more and more evident, in fact, that we inhabit an administered world, and those who administer do so more often by mystifying messages than by containment or brute force. (Greene, 1988, p. 54)

Greene views much of her work as an effort to bring a critical awareness to the world in which we live.

It is noteworthy that Greene avoids taking even her own ideas for granted. Her ideas, like ours, are bounded by her life circumstances. However, recognizing the ultimate vulnerability of our ideas does not mean we should remain mute.

> My interpretations are provisional. I have partaken in the postmodern rejection of inclusive rational frameworks in which all problems, all uncertainties can be re-solved. All we can do, I believe, is cultivate multiple ways of seeing and multiple dialogues in a world where nothing stays the same. All I can do is to provoke my readers to come together in making pathways through that world with their students, leaving thumbprints as they pass . . . We cannot predict the common world that may be in the making; nor can we finally justify one kind of community more than another. We can bring in the dialogues and laughter that threaten monologues and rigidity. And surely we can affirm and reaffirm the principles that center around belief in justice and freedom and respect for human rights, since without these, we cannot even call for the decency of welcoming and inclusion for everyone, no matter how at risk. Only if more and more persons in their coming together learn to incarnate such principles and choose to live and speak in accord with them, are we likely to bring a community into being. (Greene, 1995, pp. 16 and 43)

Greene makes it clear that affirming the humility of our powers to create ideas should not keep us from acting upon those ideas. Even if in our hearts we know that our understanding of the world is not the ultimate understanding, it would be a mistake to let this insight paralyze our thinking and actions. On the contrary, Greene is deeply committed to offering her ideas about the nature of the 'good society,' and invites others to join her in this visionary quest.

Social Democracy

When most people in our country think of democracy, they consider various governmental structures such as the congress, courts, and the presidency. Many also think of cultural rituals such as campaigns and voting. Drawing many of her ideas from Dewey, Greene distinguishes between democracy as a living, social arrangement and democracy as a form of government. In our society, democracy is taken for granted as a purely political aspect of culture. Greene suggests by conceptualizing democracy within this limited framework, we have largely removed the public from creating a more comprehensive democratic culture. The same forces that established popular elections, jury by a trial of peers, and freedom of expression have also built conditions that make the above institutions and rituals work primarily for the benefit of those who have traditionally maintained economic and political power. Racism, poverty, sexism and other forms of oppression greatly undermine the democratic potential of our culture. Greene (1995) states, 'knowing this is part of the society we inhabit — we have to find ways of creating situations in which persons will choose to engage in cooperative or collective action in order to bring about societal repairs' (p. 66).

In response, Greene suggests that democracy is best conceptualized as a way of life, rather than merely a form of government. Democracy needs to be practiced in social as well as political locations. From this perspective, democracy is brought into our lives through work, personal relationships, recreation, and education. In particular, Greene calls upon us to create 'open spaces' within our culture as a means of bringing democracy into our everyday lives.

> There are open spaces to be created in living rooms on playgrounds, in workplaces, studios, waiting rooms, as well as classrooms and school yards. Dominion must be rejected, however, if dialogue is to occur — inquiry and critique. Moving in and out, from neighborhoods to classrooms, from classrooms to the surrounding world, from the world to localities again, persons must be provided opportunities for communication and concern. Taking social structures as well as knowledge structures as objects of study . . . they must be helped to move towards wide-awakeness as well as conceptual skills. They need to learn how to interrogate together and (acknowledging multiple perspectives) help each other to see. (Greene, 1976, p. 22)

Twenty years later, Greene continues her struggle to create these open spaces throughout our society.

> My concern is to find out what we can do to open such spaces where persons speaking together and being together can discover what it signifies to incarnate and act upon values far too often taken for granted. We well know that defining this society in terms of the American Dream or in light of life, liberty and the pursuit of happiness means nothing if the people in this society do not feel free to act upon such ideals and so realize them. We must intensify attentiveness to the concrete world around in all its ambiguity, with its dead ends and its open possibilities. And attending, as Dewey and Freire have helped us to see, is not merely contemplating. It is to come to know in ways that might bring about change. (1995, p. 68)

Human associations, whether public or private, are best organized around the values of giving its participants an authentic 'voice' in identifying and implementing their aspirations. As such, social democracy implies a commitment to broad-based distribution of knowledge and promotion of communicative experiences. It also implies a moral commitment to promote the 'common good' over any individual's right to accumulate privilege and power. It seems likely Greene would agree with Dewey's (1927) assessment that 'Democracy is the idea of community life itself' (p. 148).

Pluralism

There are many values that one can potentially associate with democracy. In our culture, we tend to think in terms such as freedom, liberty, and justice. In addition to these, Greene (1995) recently has stressed the value of pluralism, 'Because so many of us are newcomers and strangers to one another, I particularly emphasize pluralism and hetero- geneity, what is now called multiculturalism. I choose to do so in connection with the arts and community always in the making — the community that may someday be called a democracy' (p. 6).

In direct contrast to several scholars (e.g. Schlesinger, 1992; Hirsch, 1987; Bloom, 1987; D'Sousa, 1991; Brookhiser, 1991; Auster, 1990) who view attention to this plural- ism as a threat to our national unity, Greene suggests that our diversity should be cel- ebrated and recognized as the essence of our cultural cohesiveness.

> Proponents of what is called 'civism' (Pratte, 1988: 104–7) are concerned that pluralism threatens the existence of a democratic ethos intended to transcend all differences. The ethos encompasses the principles of freedom, equality, and justice, as well as regard for human rights, and there is fear that the new relativism and particularism will subvert the common faith. (Greene, 1993, p. 14)

Greene is particularly concerned that these scholars view the recognition and legitimacy of our diversity as a menace to the survival of our society:

> When such observers look around and hear the contesting voices, the clashing interpretations, they perceive what strikes them as a slippage, a shaking of the foundations. The language of community seems to be fundamentally in danger. They erect walls of cultural literacy and plan 'excellence networks.' They deliver jeremiads about the 'closing of the American Mind' and calls to turn the eyes of our minds to a supersensible realm again to find our anchorage in something objective and enduring, transcending cacophony and heteroglossia, as well as the stranger in our midst. (1995, p. 187)

In their effort to stem the legitimacy of our diversity and thus preserve the union, these scholars identify and advocate for a common culture 'as Americans' which would over- whelm all other identities based upon ethnic, gender, or class. Greene rejects this perspec- tive because it has historically marginalized those individuals who are not members of the dominant European heritage of our nation. Adrianne Rich (in Maher and Tetreault, 1994, p. 1) clearly articulates her concerns:

> When those who have the power to name and socially construct reality choose not to see you or hear you, whether you are dark-skinned, old, disabled, female, or speak with a different accent or dialect than theirs, when someone with the authority . . . describes the world and you are not in it, there is a moment of psychic disequilibrium, as if you looked into the mirror and saw nothing.

Although critical of this call for a 'common culture,' unlike many progressive scholars who merely dismiss this line of thinking, Greene (1993) recognizes the potential danger that an overemphasis on plurality can have in creating a democratic culture: 'It is important to hold this [conservative's concern for a common culture] in mind as we try to work through a conception of pluralism to an affirmation of the struggle to attain the life of a "free and enriching communion" John Dewey identified with democracy' (p. 14). Concern for pluralism, from Greene's perspective, must be balanced with a commitment to create unity and cohesion among all who live in our society.

> We realize we have moved far beyond simplistic notions of melting pots and social balance. We are challenged to come to terms with conceptions of difference and heterogeneity . . . We are asked to acknowledge contingency, meaning the dependence of perspective and point of view on lived situation, on location in the world. We are only beginning to realize the significance of perspectivism, of the rejection of objectivism, of fixed authorities, of standards residing in some higher realm — standards that apply to everyone and everything . . . (Greene, 1994, p. 12)

The creative challenge before us is not to preserve some artificial cultural norm in the face of our increasing diversity, but to establish some means of collective identity that does not undermine our commitment to pluralism.

Rather than identify a common cultural cannon to hold us together, Greene suggests we consider the value of pluralism itself. That is, a recognition by all of the unique strength we have as a nation due to our diversity.

> It [the ideal society] is a community attentive to difference, open to ideas of plurality. Something life affirming in diversity must be discovered and rediscovered, of what is held in common becomes always more multifaceted — open and inclusive, drawn to untapped possibility, nor can we absolutely justify one kind of community over another. Many of us, however, for all the tensions and disagreements around us, would reaffirm the value of principles like justice and equality and freedom and commitment to human rights since, without these, we cannot even argue for the decency of welcoming. (Greene, 1993, pp. 17–18)

She later argues that the values which should hold us together are those that help us overcome our historical divisions based upon such human traits as race, gender, class, or language.

> Knowing this [e.g. racism, sexism, ethnocentrism, homelessness] is part of the society we inhabit — we have to find ways of creating situations in which persons will choose to engage in cooperative or collective action in order to bring about societal repairs. (1995, p. 66)

Creating a community based upon a nation state identity (i.e. 'We're all Americans'), will not, according to Greene, provide us with the ideas needed to establish a truly enlightened society:

> Only if more and more persons, in their coming together, incarnate such principles [e.g. human and civil rights, economic and social justice] and choose to live by them and engage in dialogues in accord with them are we likely to bring about democratic pluralism and not fly apart in chaos and cacophony. All we can do is to speak with others as passionately and eloquently as we can about justice and caring and love and trust; all we can do is to look into each other's eyes and squeeze each other's hands. (1994, p. 25)

Rather than try to discount our diversity or drown it in an ocean of our traditional European heritage, Greene suggests that our society be based upon, not just the tolerance, but the celebration of our pluralism. It is through our embracing of 'the other' and his/her uniqueness that an authentically democratic culture can be established. A culture that helps its people rise to the challenge of experiencing our fundamental unity as we revere our diversity is, Greene suggests, the struggle before us.

Existential Freedom

A fourth characteristic of Greene's democracy finds its roots in European existentialism. In particular, the notion of existential freedom or 'wide-awakeness' has been central to her thought regarding both schools and society. Indeed, one of her primary criticisms of our society is that it has not generated institutions, rituals, myths, and other cultural structures which encourage us, as a people, to become more fully conscious: intellectually, emotionally, or spiritually. Given the degree in which we take our lives for granted, we are in many ways, Greene suggests, asleep.

> We are all familiar with the number of individuals who live their lives immersed, as it were, in daily life, in the mechanical round of habitual activities. We are all aware how few people ask themselves what they have done with their own lives, whether or not they have used their freedom or simply acceded to the imposition of patterned behavior and the assignment of roles. Most people, in fact, are likely to go on in that fashion, unless — or until — 'one day the "why" arises,' as Albert Camus put it, 'everything begins in that weariness tinged with amazement.' (1978, pp. 42–3)

It is far too easy for powerful individuals within our culture to dominate and keep democracy from becoming fully operational as long as we remain in this sleep-like state. Democracy in a society in which its people are not awake can be too easily manipulated by those who control the means of knowledge production and dissemination.

> I am suggesting that, for too many individuals in modern society, there is a feeling of being dominated and that feelings of powerlessness are almost inescapable. I am also suggesting that such feelings can to a large degree be overcome through conscious effort on the part of individuals to keep themselves awake, to think about their condition in the world, to inquire into the forces that appear to dominate, to interpret the experiences they are having day to day. (Greene, 1978, pp. 43–4)

A culture cannot be comprehensively democratic unless, according to Greene, its people are existentially free; are 'wide-awake.'

The concept of being 'wide-awake' is not easy to understand. Greene quotes Alfred Schutz to explain this state of mind.

> By the term 'wide-awakeness' we want to denote a plane of consciousness of the highest tension originating in an attitude of full attention to life and its requirements. Only the performing and especially the working self is fully interested in life and, hence, wide-awake. It lives within its act and its attention is exclusively directed to carrying its project into effect, to executing its plan. This attention is an active, not a passive one. Passive attention is the opposite to full awareness. (1977, p. 121)

Perhaps one way to comprehend this plane of consciousness and freedom is to juxtapose it against more functionalist notions of human consciousness and group life (e.g. Comte,

1853; Durkheim, 1938). Functionalist perspectives of socialization view the 'normal' life of individuals as being assimilated into the given social order. As Burrell and Morgan (1979) state, functionalism 'regards society as ontologically prior to the man and seeks to place man in his activities within that wider social context' (p. 106). From this perspective, human beings are relatively passive in face of the cultural status quo and social order. People are 'shaped' or 'molded' by the culture within which they exist. Society consists of unified arrangements and values, and tensions are viewed as the result of personal recalcitrance against societal standards. Conflict is seen merely as an inability of individuals to integrate themselves in the normative order. Western culture is viewed as a reflection of pre-existing laws of 'human nature.' One's 'place' in society is thus determined by these laws. Distinctions among people within society such as class and status are thus relatively easy to explain. 'Social inequality is thus an unconsciously evolved device by which societies insure that the most important positions are conscientiously filled by the most qualified persons' (Davis and Moore quoted in Homans, 1967, p. 66).

Most importantly for the purpose of this discussion, social functionalism is closely allied with behaviorism in its explanations of human action. People are controlled by external stimuli and thus react according to the previously mentioned laws of nature. Freedom, according to the noted social scientist, George Homans (1967), is merely an 'illusion . . . what each of us does is absolutely determined [by external stimuli]' (p. 103).

From an existential perspective the illusion of which Homans refers is merely a human construction. The view that one's life is externally determined is exactly the state of sleep to which existentialists refer. As Dewey (1896) noted long ago, functionalists ignore a crucial aspect of human psychology. Insightfully, he points out that as human beings, we do not merely react to external stimuli, but rather *interpret* this stimuli, and then we act upon our unique interpretations; not the stimuli, itself. Existential freedom exists because although we do not always control the external stimuli that come our way in life, we always have the potential power to decide our *experience* of and the way in which we choose to act in response to this stimuli. Foucault notes that being 'awake'

> allows one to step back from this way of acting or reacting, to present it [external stimuli] to oneself as an object of thought and question it as to its meanings, its conditions and its goals. Thought is freedom in relation to what one does, the motion by which one detaches oneself from it, establishes it as an object, and reflects on it as a problem. (1984, p. 195)

People who are 'asleep,' who respond without thought to life's situations, who take much of what is presented to them for granted, or who act merely by habit seem to be truly 'determined' by their surroundings. However, the potential power to control our own experience and thus make our lives meaningful is always with us, if only we awaken.

> If, in any event, we are to take seriously the notion of detaching ourselves now and then from what we do, we would be breaking with what we ourselves take for granted, perhaps opening ourselves to a pluralism of diverse visions. (Greene, 1995, p. 190)

One who is 'wide-awake' is never the captive of an external world, for s/he always has the power to determine his/her own experience of life and thus the way in which s/he chooses to act upon his/her world. People who are existentially free actively make meaning out of whatever situations and circumstances confront them (Frankl, 1985).

From Greene's perspective, a fully democratic culture is one that supports, encourages, and celebrates our struggle to be existentially free, that is, to be fully awake. As a culture becomes more existentially free, it evolves into a more morally just and caring society. As she (1978) states, 'Only as they [people in a given culture] learn to make sense of what is happening, can they feel themselves to be autonomous. Only then can they develop the sense of agency required for living a moral life' (p. 44). She goes on to suggest that,

> The moral life [culture] is not necessarily the self-denying life nor the virtuous life, doing what others expect of one, or doing what others insist one ought to do. It can best be characterized as a life of reflectiveness and care . . . In active attention, there is always an effort to carry out a plan in a place where there are others, where responsibility means something other than transcending . . . one's own everyday. (1978, p. 152)

It might seem to some that Greene's notions of wide-awakeness and existential freedom are overly individualistic. However, it must be remembered that building a strong democratic community would be exceedingly difficult without individuals who are 'wide awake.'

> In thinking of community, we need to emphasize the process words: making, creating, weaving, saying, and the like. Community cannot be produced simply through rational formulation nor through edict. Like freedom, it has to be achieved by persons offered the space in which to discover what they recognize together and appreciate in common; they have to find ways to make intersubjective sense. Again, it ought to be a space infused by the kind of imaginative awareness that enables those involved to imagine alternative possibilities for their own becoming and their group's becoming. Community is not a question of which social contracts are the most reasonable for individuals to enter. It is a question of what might contribute to the pursuit of shared goods: what ways of being together, of attaining mutuality, of reaching toward some common world. (Greene, 1995, p. 39)

In this sense, existential freedom is both a goal of democratic living and a means to creating this life. In particular, individuals who are not awake, who have not assumed responsibility over the way they experience their lives are easily distracted by external fears, hate, bigotry, and dogma. Existential freedom gives individuals the power to create a moral community with 'others.'

Educational Implications: Three Powerful Ideas

Given Greene's vision of open spaces and the importance of these in fostering existential freedom among people, it is not difficult to understand why she has given so much of her creative and intellectual energy to the field of education.

> If we are seriously interested in education for freedom as well as for the opening of cognitive perspectives, it is also important to find a way of developing a praxis of educational consequence that opens the spaces necessary for the remaking of a democratic community. For this to happen, there must of course be a new commitment to intelligence, a new fidelity in communication, a new regard for imagination. (Greene, 1988, p. 126)

It is primarily through education, rather than coercion or ideological dominance that a culture can become genuinely democratic and free. Fortunately, she has provided a coherent and provocative vision for the education of young people in our society. Due to the limitations of space, we cannot explore each of these in depth; however, we will provide some insight into three of her more powerful ideas.

Making Meaning through the Humanities

Perhaps due to her existential roots, the ultimate purpose of education, according to Greene, is to help students and their teachers create meaning in their lives. That is, education ideally awakens teachers and their students to the personal and cultural possibilities and challenges that life offers. As a teacher, Greene states, 'My goal is to challenge the taken-for-granted, the frozen and the bound and the restricted (quoted in Ayers, 1996, p. 124). Education, at its best, is a process of teaching people to explore ideas about themselves and the world in which we live, to ask questions about this experience called living, to embrace ambiguity, to notice the unusual without fear, and to look upon the ordinary with new eyes.

> In the classroom, open to possibility and at once concerned with inquiry, critiques must be developed that uncover what masquerade as neutral frameworks [ideologies] . . . Teachers, like their students, have to learn to love the questions, as they come to realize there can be no final agreements or answers, no final commensurability. (Greene, 1988, p. 134)

Given the purpose of education, Greene suggests that the humanities curriculum be emphasized throughout one's schooling.

> There are works of art; . . . works deliberately created to move people to critical awareness, to a sense of moral agency, and to a conscious engagement with the world. As I see it, they ought — under the rubric of the 'arts and humanities' — to be central to any curriculum that is constructed today. (1977, p. 120)

The humanities (e.g. art, literature, music, philosophy, history), according to Greene, serve as a catalyst through which teachers and their students can explore deeply and thus make meaning out of life and culture.

Contrary to many educators and politicians who howl about the importance of emphasizing utilitarian skills and subjects such as mathematics and science in schools, Greene calls upon us to avoid jumping on the 'bandwagon.' Certainly there is a need for some of our young people to be engaged in science, mathematics, and technological studies, and given our advanced industrial economy, anyone who doesn't understand basic information in these fields is at a serious disadvantage. However, an overemphasis on these subjects, Greene warns, can dull rather than sharpen our intellects.

> . . . as technology has expanded, fragmentation has increased, and more and more people have felt themselves impinged upon by forces they have been unable to understand . . . with the advance of scientific and positivistic thinking . . . an alternative tradition has taken shape, a tradition generated by perceptions of passivity, acquiescence, and what Thoreau called 'quiet desperation.' (1977, p. 120)

Our society is currently dependent on advanced scientific and technological work; however, Greene points out that not everyone has to focus on these areas of inquiry. While it is not really necessary for everyone to be deeply knowledgable in the fields of mathematics and science, it is crucial for everyone to seriously contemplate who we are as individuals and as members of a culture. As Greene (1977) stated many years ago, 'The arts are of focal significance . . . because perceptive encounters with works of art can bring human beings in touch with themselves' (pp. 123–4). It is vital for us to 'awaken' in order to continue our efforts to build a just, compassionate, and meaningful democracy. As previously mentioned, it is the arts and humanities rather than science and math that provide teachers in our schools with the curricular opportunities to explore these questions. For example, exploring the human condition of personal rigidity and inability to view life from multiple perspectives through *Moby Dick* typifies the type of opportunities the humanities offer.

> Only an artist [e.g. Melville], it has always seemed to me, could release meanings like this from stored-up meanings of industrializing society, order them as never before, shock readers into an awareness of, among other things, what it signifies to experience oneself so grooved and at once so manically in charge, so dreadfully free. (Greene, 1997, p. 392)

Of course, the power of exploring these ideas through the arts and humanities is that students have the potential to interpret the meaning of the text, share insights with others, and re-evaluate their thinking in light of other ideas. She argues that even subjects such as history can and should be taught in this manner.

> Histories . . . can involve their readers in dialogue. [When taught correctly] he or she [students] cannot but gain a sense of a living human being posing questions to the past from his own standpoint . . . Engaging with [this kind] of history, the individual human being can locate himself or herself in an intersubjective reality reaching backwards and forwards in time. These are the reasons I would include certain works of history in an arts and humanities program — works that provoke wide-awakeness and an awareness of the quest for meaning, which has so much to do with feeling alive in the world. (1977, pp. 122–3)

Best of all, this intellectual adventure holds the promise of passion. As Greene (1986) states, 'They [artists] remind us of absence, ambiguity, embodiments of existential possibility. More often than not they do so with passion; and passion has been called the power of possibility' (p. 427). Education imbued with the study of the humanities and arts has the power to awaken the imagination, the critical consciousness, and multiple perspectives that raise our consciousness and thus make it possible to create meaningful social worlds.

Authenticity

Much of what goes on in schools results in alienation. As Weis and Fine (1992) note, students often feel silenced by their schooling experience. There are few opportunities for them to express themselves in meaningful ways about meaningful topics. Even the arts and humanities often fail to engage students in authentic ways. Pinar's (1975) comments are unfortunately as true today in many classrooms as when he wrote them twenty years ago.

> Works of art come to have little or no impact upon the perceiver, unless it be a narrow cognitive one. . . . We see but do not see. We respond but do not feel. Inspection renders the object lifeless, analysis murders and the intellectual's gaze turns to stone. Ours is the age petrified by cognition, moribund by scholarship. (p. 381)

When issues that are potentially meaningful to students are discussed in schools they are often sanitized and thus left sterile.

> There have been many reports on classroom discussions of issues ostensibly of moment to the students: cheating, betraying confidences, nonviolent resistance, sexual relations, discrimination. Not only has there been little evidence that the participants take such issues personally; there has been little sign of any transfer to situations in the 'real' world, even when there were opportunities (say a peace demonstration) to act on what we affirmed as guiding principles. (Greene, 1988, p. 119)

Although it is not solely the fault of our educational establishment, it is nevertheless true that most young children in our culture come to school willing to learn and to share who they are, but in just a few years their spontaneity, honesty, and uniqueness begin to atrophy within the walls of our schools.

Unfortunately, the same can be said about many young teachers. During the last several decades, teachers in our schools have increasingly become 'deskilled' or 'disenfranchised' (e.g. Apple, 1986; Goodman, 1988). Instead of establishing relevant and meaningful curricular goals, developing original and stimulating content, and designing thoughtful learning experiences based on an intimate knowledge of their own and their students' interests and talents, many teachers have been relegated to a managerial rather than an educative role. Especially in elementary schools, most teachers are encouraged to become 'educational technicians' who merely coordinate the day's work rather than authentically engage students in the exploration of knowledge. As Zeichner (1986) notes,

> . . . numerous analyses, conducted from a variety of ideological and political perspectives, have concluded that the effect of many of the recent policies affecting teachers has been to promote greater external control over the content, processes, and outcomes of teachers' work and to encourage teachers to adopt conformist orientations to self and society as well as technical orientations to the role of teacher. (p. 88)

In short, teachers often feel that they cannot 'be themselves' that their voices are largely muted in areas of extreme educational importance (e.g. curriculum content, organizational structure, instructional experiences).

Greene wants to see teachers bring themselves into their schools and use their own lives, their knowledge, and their explorations as elements within the curriculum:

> The quest involves me as a woman, as teacher, as mother, as citizen, as New Yorker, as art-lover, as activist, as philosopher, as white middle-class American. Neither my self or my narrative can have, therefore, a single strand. I stand at the crossing point of too many social and cultural forces; and in any case, I am forever on the way. (1995, p. 1)

It is difficult to create a meaningful education for children if teachers are disconnected from themselves. Greene suggests that, in part, teaching is best viewed as a form of artistic expression in which the teacher manifests his/her creative energies through his/her pedagogical craft.

Perhaps most importantly, Greene wants teachers and students to come together for the purpose of honest, open, and genuine exploration of ideas through the collective study of written, visual, and verbal texts.

> I have been working to engage students with literary works and, as time has gone on, with paintings and music and film, in order to enable them to perceive more, to hear more, to grasp more in their lives and the surrounding world. Eager to counter-act what Dewey called the 'anesthetic' in life, I have wanted, as Dewey did, to release more and more people for reflective encounters with a range of works of art, works that have the potential to awaken, to move persons to see, to hear, and to feel in often unexpected ways. (1997, p. 392)

Greene knows that schooling that is not genuine; that what is not authentic leads to alienation and, for many, silent desperation. If schools are to become 'open spaces,' this education must be deeply rooted in the authentic experiences of teachers and their students.

Social Responsibility

As previously mentioned, some might consider Greene's deep involvement with existentialism as overly individualistic. However, this perception represents a misreading of her work. Greene's particular interests are closely connected to Sartre's efforts to find links between existentialism and more socially engaged ideologies such as those advocated by Marx. In particular, Sartre suggested that there is a covenant between freedom and responsibility. One can be existentially free only when s/he willingly accepts responsibility for his/her experience of the world. It is through consciously taking this responsibility that one becomes truly empowered.

Given this intellectual tradition, it is understandable that Greene's views on education would convey a strong concern for responsibility. However, Greene goes beyond personal responsibility for one's own experience and subsequent actions. Throughout her works, she draws our attention to the necessity of educating children to take responsibility for our collective well-being. Far from the promotion of education as merely a means to obtain employment, Greene insists that schools provide students with the understanding that it is their social responsibility to be thoughtful and well informed.

> Therefore, an important dimension of all education must be the intentional bringing into being of norm-governed situations, situations in which students discover what it is to experience a sense of obligation and responsibility, whether they derive that sense from their own experiences of being cared for or from their intuitions and conceptions of justice and equity. (1995, p. 66)

Children must come to understand the reason for learning is to nurture their intellectual talents for the construction of our society into a more democratic, just, and caring place to live. Students need to hear that democratic societies cannot grow and develop (let alone survive) unless their citizens are well informed and have the educational abilities and sensitivities needed to critically examine the world in which we live. As Greene writes,

> We should think of education as opening public spaces in which, speaking in their own voices and acting on their own initiatives, [students] can identify themselves and choose themselves in relation to such principles as freedom, equality, justice and concern for others. We can hope to communicate the recognition that persons become more fully themselves and open to the world if they can be aware of themselves appearing before others, speaking in their own voices, and trying as they do so to bring into being a common world. (1995, p. 68)

Students need to be repeatedly asked to consider the viewpoint that their learning is not just for their own benefit, but for the well-being of our culture (and other cultures) as a whole.

Greene calls upon teachers and their students to take responsibility for creating classrooms in which democratic living can flourish.

> We want classrooms to be just and caring, full of various conceptions of the good. We want them articulate, with dialogue involving as many persons as possible, opening to one another, opening to the world. And we want them to be concerned for one another, as we learn to be concerned for them. We want them to achieve friendships among one another, as each one moves to a heightened sense of craft and wide-awakeness, to a renewed consciousness of worth and possibility. (1993, p. 18)

Education, according to Greene, should help students realize their deep connection to and responsibility for, not just their own individual experience, but also for other human beings who share this world. The importance of this goal cannot be underestimated, given the increasingly mechanized and impersonal culture that characterizes our society. The pedagogical implications of this view are multiple, and it is hard to conceive of a set of educational purposes that does not include a concern for human freedom and a sense of agency in the face of a more and more controlled and administered world.

Greene makes it clear that freedom and democracy do not imply, as so many of our politicians would like us to believe, the absence of responsibility for those who share our world. Freedom and democracy do not mean that one can live his life without regard for the common good. Greene is clear that schools play a crucial role in helping our young people to understand this vital concept throughout the course of their studies.

Conclusion

This chapter began with the assertion that Greene's work was filled with passion for the possible. Her ideas about schooling and society express a politics of hope for what we can become as human beings and for the type of culture we can potentially create. Greene rarely lectures to her readers, rather she invites us to join her in the grand exploration of life's meaning. 'My field of study is lived situations. My goal is to challenge the taken for granted, the frozen and the bound and the restricted' (Greene quoted in Ayers, 1996, p. 124). She asks us to resist accepting our social world for what it is and to release our imaginations to what it can become. She envisions a society that is thoughtful, socially democratic, pluralistic, and existentially free. She promotes an education that is not based upon prescriptions of the 'truth,' but rather is a stimulant for our collective thinking.

In this light there are two points to be made that would perhaps enrich Greene's on-going efforts to understand and then reform our schools and society. First, we agree with the comments (although not the tone) of Bowers' (1991) insight regarding the anthropo-centric focus of Greene's work. In conceptualizing humanity and culture, it is crucial that we do not forget our connections to other living organisms that share this planet. We are only visitors here for an extremely short period of time, geologically speaking. As humans, we do not 'own' this planet. Our ability to create culture does not give us the right to do so without regard for the other living things here. It seems to us that we would do well to situate any conception of the 'good society' within an ecological context. Our 'field of study' is enriched when we expand it beyond the 'lived situations' of human beings. It is vitally important for us to remember that although we are unique, we are merely another species that occupies space for a brief moment as this planet rotates around its sun. This planet was here long before we arrived, and it will no doubt be here long after we, as a species, have departed. Although our ability to create culture sets us apart from other living species, we would do well to remember that we are also part of nature. Diamond's (1992) book, *The Third Chimpanzee* and Wrangham and Peterson's (1996) *Demonic Males* which examine humans as a variety of apes rather than a species completely detached from other life forms, provide important perspectives of ourselves and the cultures we have created, within a context of natural history and socio-biology. It would be wise to remember that our social worlds cannot be understood as if independent from the environment within which they exist.

Second, although Greene has been insightful in her analysis of our culture and the schooling of our children and in her visions of our potential, she has not devoted as much attention as we would like to issues of classroom pedagogy. In particular, it would be helpful to her readers if Greene would express herself visually as well as verbally. That is, it would be useful to have images of pedagogy that illuminate and portray the educational experiences of which she speaks so elegantly. For example, her call for using art and the other humanities to help students awake to the wonders and miseries of our culture touches our sensibilities, but we are left wanting an image of a teacher who does this with students. Certainly, having students read European and other cultural classics provide the potential to help them see beyond the ordinary but, as Pinar (1975) points out, in most classrooms this does not happen. Far too often, *King Lear* is a text in which students are asked to memorize character actions and plot sequence rather than explore the themes of power, questions of honesty, family dynamics, or matters of fate and human agency. In what ways might a teacher who is committed to 'disrupting' students' thinking approach the teaching of history, creative writing, or math?

We understand Greene's reluctance to provide these images. As she stated many years ago,

> We are unwilling to end this book by spelling out overarching purposes or slapping still another proclamation on the schoolroom wall. It makes no difference if the proclamation calls for the defense of the nation or personal liberation, citizenship or spontaneity. Once we spell out aims in general, we are in danger of embarrassing ourselves. Moreover, the teacher's feelings of responsibility may well be eroded by an implicit demand that he be the agent of an externally defined purpose, which he can only understand as slogan or still another expression of prevailing piety. We would emphasize once more the need for self-consciousness and clarity on the part of the individual, the need to frame conditional orders. His aims therefore can only be specific ones, identified in concrete situations with respect to concrete tasks and subject matters, where structures and relevancies are not always clear. They must be pursued as lacks are perceived and actions undertaken. Because persons differ, achievements vary, horizons shift, perspectives alter, his aims can never be twice the same. (1973, p. 272)

Although we agree with her sentiments, it is important to emphasize that in calling for more detailed illustrations of people working in classrooms and schools as a basis for Greene's conceptual insights, we are not suggesting she provide 'cookbook' descriptions of 'how it should be done.' Rather we ask for scholarship that, like Greene's vision of pedagogy, has a 'conscious concern for the particular, the everyday, the concrete' (Greene, 1995, p. 69). Our call to situate the conceptual within a context of actual or hypothesized practice is done not so readers can mimic what is presented, but rather to learn from the images as well as the ideas provided and then apply what is vicariously experienced to one's own particular situation and limitations.

We are not suggesting that a discourse of imagery should replace Greene's philosophical commentary as if the former is superior to the latter. It is important that our call for imagery not be viewed as 'the way' Greene (or others) should do scholarship. It is not being suggested that educational discourse reflect a narrow and particularistic style. Greene's insights into schooling and society clearly make a valuable contribution to our thinking in their present form. Calling for Greene or other scholars to integrate visual narratives into their work can be used to justify a form of essentialism that is counterproductive to the free exchange of ideas. At the same time, however, we do believe that Greene's scholarship would be more compelling and powerful if efforts were made by herself or others interested in her work to situate the conceptual within the visual.

Finally, Greene's work not only provides us with insights, it also inspires. The spirit within human beings from which concepts such as compassion, democracy, intellectual freedom, and social equity emerge is woven deep within her scholarship. It is the type of intellectual effort that powerfully expresses our dreams about how schooling and society can help young people develop their rational and creative talents, moral character, and civic courage that will be needed as we move into the next century.

References

APPLE, M. (1986) *Teachers and Texts: A Political Economy of Class and Gender Relations in Education*, London: Routledge & Kegan Paul.

ARENDT, H. (1958) *The Human Condition*, Chicago: University of Chicago Press.

AUSTER, L. (1990) *The Path to National Suicide: An Essay on Immigration and Multiculturalism*, Monterey, VA: American Immigration Control Foundation.

AYERS, W. (1996) 'Doing philosophy: Maxine Greene and the pedagogy of possibility,' in KRIDEL, C., BULLOUGH, R.V. Jr., and SHAKER, P. (eds) *Teachers and Mentors: Profiles of Distinguished Twentieth-century Professors of Education*, New York: Garland Publishing Company.

BLOOM, A. (1987) *The Closing of the American Mind*, New York: Simon and Schuster.

BOWERS, C.A. (1991) 'An open letter to Maxine Greene on the "The problem of freedom in an era of ecological interdependence,"' *Educational Theory*, **41**, 3, pp. 325–30.

BROOKHISER, R. (1991) *The Way of the W.A.S.P.: How It Made America and How It Can Save It, So To Speak*, New York: Free Press.

BURRELL, G. and MORGAN, G. (1979) *Sociological Paradigms and Organizational Analysis*, London: Heinemann.

COMTE, A. (1853) *The Positivist Philosophy*, London: Chapman.

DEWEY, J. (1896). 'The reflex arc concept in psychology,' *Psychological Review*, **3**, pp. 357–70.

DEWEY, J. (1927) *The Public and Its Problems*, Athens, Ohio: Swallow Press.

DIAMOND, J. (1992) *The Third Chimpanzee: The Evolution and Future of the Human Animal*, NY: Harper Collins.

D'SOUSA, D. (1991) *Illiberal Education: The Politics of Race and Sex on Campus*, New York: Free Press.

DURKHEIM, E. (1938) *The Rules of Sociological Method*, Glencoe, Il: The Free Press.

FOUCAULT, M. (1984) 'Polemics, politics, and problemizations: An interview,' in RABINOW, P. (ed.) *The Foucault Reader*, New York: Pantheon Books.

FRANKL, V. (1985) *Man's Search for Meaning*, New York: Washington Square Press.

GOODMAN, J. (1988) 'The disenfranchisement of elementary teachers and strategies for resistance,' *Journal of Curriculum and Supervision*, **3**, 3, pp. 201–20.

GREENE, M. (1973) *Teacher as Stranger: Educational Philosophy for a Modern Age*, Belmont, CA: Wadsworth Publishing Company.

GREENE, M. (1976) 'An approach to the constitution of democracy,' *Theory into Practice*, **15**, 1, pp. 15–22.

GREENE, M. (1977) 'Toward wide-awakeness: An argument for the arts and humanities,' *Teachers College Record*, **79**, 1, pp. 119–25.

GREENE, M. (1978) *Landscapes of Learning*, New York: Teachers College Press.

GREENE, M. (1986) 'In search of a critical pedagogy,' *Harvard Educational Review*, **56**, 4, pp. 427–41.

GREENE, M. (1988) *The Dialectic of Freedom*, New York: Teachers College Press.

GREENE, M. (1993) 'The passions of pluralism: Multiculturalism and the expanding community,' *Educational Researcher*, **22**, 1, pp. 13–18.

GREENE, M. (1994) 'Multiculturalism, community, and the arts,' in DYSON, A.H. and GENISHI, G. (eds) *The Need for Story: Cultural Diversity in Classroom and Community* (pp. 11–27), Urbana, IL: National Council of Teachers of English.

GREENE, M. (1995) *Releasing the Imagination: Essays on Education, the Arts, and Social Change*, San Francisco: Jossey-Bass.

GREENE, M. (1997) 'Metaphors and multiples: Representation, the arts and history,' *Phi Delta Kappan*, **78**, 5, pp. 387–94.

HIRSCH, E.D., JR. (1987) *Cultural Literacy*, Boston: Houghton Mifflin.

HOMANS, G. (1967) *The Nature of Social Science*, New York: Harcourt, Brace, & World.

MAHER, F.A., and TETREAULT, T.M.K. (1994) *The Feminist Classroom: An Inside Look at How Professors and Students Are Transforming Higher Education for a Diverse Society*, New York: Basic Books.

PINAR, W.F. (1975) 'Sanity, madness and the school,' in PINAR, W.F. (ed.) *Curriculum Theorizing: The Reconceptualists* (pp. 359–83), Berkeley, CA: McCutchan Publishing.

SCHLESINGER, A.M., JR. (1992) *The Disuniting of America: Reflections on a Multicultural Society*, New York: Norton.

WRANGHAM, R., and PETERSON, D. (1995) *Demonic Males: Apes and the Origins of Human Violence*, Boston: Houghton Mifflin.

WEXLER, P. (1987) *Social Analysis of Education: After the New Sociology*, London: Routledge & Kegan Paul.

ZEICHNER, K. (1986) 'Social and ethical dimensions of reform in teacher education,' in HOFFMAN, J. and EDWARDS, S. (eds) *Reality and Reform in Clinical Teacher Education* (pp. 87–107), New York: Random House.

7   From Both Sides of the Looking Glass: Visions of Imagination, the Arts, and Possibility

Carol S. Jeffers

To understand the dynamic and dialogical relationship among imagination, the arts, and possibility — the relationship that opens unexpected vistas and meanings in Maxine Greene's life, in others' lives, and in my own — is to look from both sides of the looking glass. It is to look at the releasing of imagination in context of the viewer's encounter with a work of art and in context of the artist's creation of one. It is to understand what a work of art does to, for, or with persons such as Maxine Greene and also, what she, in particular, does with works of art.

Setting for myself two emancipatory tasks for understanding, I will use these pages to look first from the side that opens visions of Maxine as active viewer and at what her imaginative encounters with the arts do (and have done) for her, as she describes them. Then I will look at my own encounters with two particular works of art. Created by the late Michael Whirledge, a living artist and master of fine arts student with whom I worked, these pieces engaged me, releasing imagination and revealing the shining possibility that Maxine Greene is an artist in her own right. Through Michael's side of the looking glass, I have come to see that what Maxine does with works of art and the imagination they release is to create with them. In a postmodern sense, Maxine appropriates, recontextualizes and reinterprets works, presenting imaginative new art — her art — in new forms. From both sides of the glass, these perspectives on imagination and the arts converge, bringing a laser focus to explorations of what Suzi Gablik (1995) has called a 'connective aesthetics' — the possibility that the arts connect imagination, questions, and meaning; that they connect us with the world and to each other.

Encountering Works of Art: Maxine's Ways of Seeing, Releasing Imagination, Questioning, Searching, Being

Maxine Greene speaks often and eloquently about her encounters with the arts, with 'imaginative literature' — and graciously, publicly — she shares what these personal encounters do (and have done) for her. Of her early encounter with Hawthorne's *The Scarlet Letter* and Hester Prynne's 'estranged point of view,' for example, Maxine writes that 'the imaginative vision launched me then — and continues to launch me — on quests I hope will never cease' (1991, p. 109). During a session at the annual meeting of the American Educational Research Association some years later, Maxine described openly her struggle to write a paper that she was to present. About her experience of writing what became 'Cherishing the earth: Toward a pedagogy of peace' (1989a), she said: 'I had to write the peace paper and I didn't know what to write — everything's been said and written. So I read a poem — I used it in the paper. It recaptured me, gave me new perspectives. . . . You can never use up Cezanne or Picasso or Melville' (1989b).

Hoping that others are similarly recaptured and launched on quests of their own, Maxine also writes:

> Questions about the arts and perceptive encounters with the arts at least have the potential, it seems to me, of arousing persons to what Alfred Schutz called 'wide-awakeness,' defined as 'a place of consciousness of highest tension originating in an attitude of full attention to life and its requirements.' The very asking of such questions, the very exploration of ways of fostering such encounters (and, indeed, the investigation of what such encounters *are*), may very well open new perspectives on what it is to learn and what it is to see. (1978, p. 169)

Seeing — the capacity to see both the particularities and the possibilities — becomes a powerful theme in understanding imagination, and a means of understanding Maxine's perceptive encounters with the arts. Conscious that 'seeing comes before words,' Maxine is drawn to Claude Monet's ways of seeing, to his multiple paintings of grain stacks and of Rouen's Cathedral. His studies of the particularities, of shapes and shadows — as they revealed themselves in the changing light over days and months — in turn, reveal multiple realities and meanings to Maxine. About her own way of seeing, Maxine explains: 'I wanted to see through as many eyes and from as many angles as possible . . . to feel what Alfred Schutz called the "multiple realities" or "provinces of meaning" that mark lived experience in the world' (1991, p. 112). To see in this way, Maxine writes that we must be 'willing to feel, to imagine, to open windows, and to go in search' (1991, p. 122). Like Monet and his views of what might have been ordinary-looking grain stacks, we 'need the ability to take a fresh look at the taken-for-granted' (1991, p. 117).

To take a 'fresh look' is to take the view of the stranger — the view that 'defamiliarizes' and arouses imagination. Maxine urges us to become aware of how particular pieces of art and literature defamiliarize experience. As she puts it, 'the taking of odd or unaccustomed perspectives can make a person "see" as never before' (1991, p. 110). Seeing through many eyes, from different angles, or as never before, empowers us to resist boredom, the habitual, the routine, and the familiar.

Meaningful encounters with the arts are not possible without the release of imagination — 'the capacity to look *through* the window of the actual, to bring "as ifs" into being in experience. Imagination creates new orders . . .' (1995, p. 115). Maxine goes on to describe imagination in terms of its importance to conscious, connective experiences of reality and to the arts:

> Imagination connects human consciousness and works of visual art, literature, music, dance. Imagination may be the primary means of forming an understanding of what goes on under the heading of 'reality.' Imagination may be responsible for the very texture of experience. . . . Once we do away with habitual separations of the subjective from the objective, the inside from the outside, appearance from reality, we might be able to give imagination its proper importance and grasp what it means to place imagination at the core of understanding. (1995, pp. 115–16)

To release imagination, to see into a work of art is to raise questions (many of which will remain forever unresolved), and it is to go in search of more questions. For Maxine, 'engagement with imaginative literature [and the arts] feeds into interrogation' (1991, p. 109). The idea of the question, the unceasing quest or search, vitalizes the relationship among imagination, the arts and possibility, just as it energizes and opens Maxine's own life. For her, 'the search involves a consciousness of what is not yet, of what might be' (1991, p. 110).

Such consciousness opens new spaces. Concerned with opening spaces and enabling young people to open them for themselves, Maxine writes that these are 'spaces for communicating across the boundaries, for choosing, for becoming different in the midst of intersubjective relationships. . . . To move into these spaces or clearings requires a willingness to resist the forces that press people into passivity and bland acquiescence' (1995, p. 112). Moreover, Maxine believes that:

> . . . shocks of awareness to which encounters with the arts give rise leave persons (*should* leave persons) less interested in the everyday, more impelled to wonder and to question. It is not uncommon for the arts to leave us somehow ill at ease or for them to prod us beyond acquiescence. They may, now and then, move us into spaces where we can create visions of other ways of being and ponder what it might signify to realize them. (1995, p. 112)

Creating spaces and moving into them, releasing imagination, opening to unexpected vistas, tensions, and particularities, encounters with the arts — these 'shocks of awareness' — disclose 'alternative ways of being in and thinking about the world' (1991, p. 108). Such encounters are (ought to be) themes in our being; they fold into modes of sense-making and thinking — what Maxine calls 'emancipatory thinking' (1991, p. 109). Elaborating on such themes, or 'moments of being,' Maxine writes:

> It seems to me that encounters with the arts make possible moments of being — the exceptional moments of which Virginia Woolf spoke. By that I mean that those who can attend to and absorb themselves in particular works of art are more likely to effect connections in their own experience than are those who cannot. (1978, pp. 185–6)

By sharing her personal encounters and wide visions to which they open, Maxine makes a compelling yet elegant case for the arts and their connective relationship to imagination and possibility. From this side of the looking glass, Maxine's views reveal how this relationship empowers persons to see, to question, to search, to open spaces, and to disclose moments of being.

Encountering Michael's Works and Moving into Opened Spaces

Turning now to my own encounters with Michael's work, I should like to share two of his installations which absorbed me and effected connections in my own experience — connections that disclosed the ground of Maxine Greene's being as an artist — which, for her and for Michael, is also the 'ground of learning and reaching beyond where one is' (1991, p. 111).

When engaging them, I found that Michael's pieces emerged in a particular context of meaning; that is, they emerged in context of the spaces they both occupied and created — and made meaningful. As Maxine points out, such meanings are not in the pieces themselves, nor in the person who comes to them. 'Meanings *happen* in and by means of an encounter with a painting, with a text, with a dance performance' (1995, p. 115). For me, these meanings happened in the students' gallery space known as the 'COMA' (an acronym for the 'Closet of Modern Art'), and on the patio off the main gallery, both of which are located in the Fine Arts Building on my campus.

In the COMA, Michael built a set of wooden bleachers which completely filled the 15′ × 15′ space. The bleachers beckoned to me and other passers-by (would-be viewers or spectators), ready to encounter the work. Indeed, the installation of bleachers invited us to come and sit, to imagine and question. What's more, we came to participate in the art — to *become* the art — and to give meaning to its metaphor. As participants, we took on the role of spectator, sitting on these inside bleachers, watching the game of life going on outside in the main corridor or in the world beyond. Reversing the inside and the outside, striving to do away with their 'habitual separation,' Michael enabled me literally, humorously, to take new perspectives of the game of life — the game of art — to release imagination and to place it at the core of understanding.

The COMA became a 'place of consciousness,' defamiliarizing my experience of a gallery space and enabling me to see as never before. I understood Michael's questioning of the separate roles of player and spectator, artist and viewer. He used the gallery space to open a space that gave rise to questions, not only about *where* meaning happens, but also about where art is created and by whom. The very asking of such questions opened new perspectives on what it is to see — to see myself and others as art, in a lived sense, and then, in the same sense, to see Maxine Greene as an artist. In this opened space, I began to look from both sides of Michael's looking glass at Maxine's release of imagination that empowers her both to encounter the arts and to create with them.

One Ton of Potential

In a different space (on the patio), Michael installed the piece he called, 'One Ton of Potential.' He constructed an overhead framework of large wooden beams from which was suspended by several steel chains a 5′ × 5′ wooden pallet. The pallet, hanging 18 inches above the patio, carried one ton of clay, arranged in a step pyramid consisting of 80 20-pound blocks. Sealed inside clear plastic bags, each block bore a hand-lettered tag that read, 'potential.'

The space between the suspended pallet and the patio captured me, causing me to wonder and go beyond bland acquiescence. Those 18 inches of space, which released imagination and left me slightly ill-at-ease, opened new perspectives on the meaning of potential. In a dim memory, the space — which illuminated a potential to fall or to *fail* — carried me back to an eighth grade physical science class — to lessons on gravitational force and the 'potential to do work.' This perspective on potential — on what is impending, on 'what else' is possible — seems somehow different from visions opening on to human potential, on to the possibility of 'what might be.' And yet, the former perspective literally illuminated Maxine's notions of resistance and her hope that we be willing to resist downward forces that press and oppress. Together, both perspectives revealed new dimensions in meanings about potential and in Michael's one ton of it.

At the opening of his exhibition, Michael invited interested persons to become participants, to take a bag of clay, to open to the 'not yet,' and 'what might be,' and to liberate their own human potential, to imagine and create. Removing the clay, lightening the load on the pallet, also seemed a symbolic gesture that lifted us beyond the downward forces pressing us into passivity and bland acquiescence. Had she been among those gathered on the patio in the soft evening air, I feel certain Maxine Greene would have seen the potential, the 'as if,' and taken a bag with which to create new visions. I also feel certain that Michael Whirledge lives on through this potential in Maxine and in others.

From the Other Side: Views of Two Artists

Though my encounters with Michael and his work released imagination, enabling me to understand him *and* Maxine as artists, it is Michael's 'Artist's Statements' that allowed me to see from the other side of the glass. Through Michael's writings, my vision of Maxine as an artist was clarified and intensified.

About his way of being in the world with art, Michael wrote the following, excerpted from his final 'Artist's Statement':

> I have chosen to live within direct experience and not the representative. . . . To create art, then, I identify with life and to exist takes on the meaning of re-inventing at every moment a new fantasy, pattern of behavior, aestheticism of one's own life. What is important is not to justify it or to reflect it in the work or the product, but to live it as work to be surprised in knowing the world, to be available to all facets of life. . . . To communicate with people and things means to be in aesthetic communion with the world. . . . Thus, art begins creating to place itself as a possibility in all things; its own dimension that identifies itself with knowledge and perception — living in art — that fantastic existence continually at variance with daily reality that opposes the building of art, resulting in the place of art. (Whirledge, 1996)

Though they never met, I feel that Michael and Maxine knew each other — as persons who chose themselves to be in the world as artists. Like Maxine, Michael appears to be aroused to 'wide-awakeness,' which has originated, indeed, in an 'attitude of full attention to life.' Like Michael, Maxine's 'concern is to enable diverse persons to break through the cotton wool of daily life and to live more consciously' (1978, p. 185). For my part, both Maxine and Michael, as artists, have invited me to look from both sides and to encounter and create with them. In so doing, I can begin to understand the fullness, the wholeness, and the connectedness of the relationship among imagination, the arts, and possibility.

References

GABLIK, S. (1995) *Conversations Before the End of Time*, New York: Thames and Hudson.

GREENE, M. (1978) *Landscapes of Learning*, New York: Teachers College Press.

GREENE, M. (1989a) 'Cherishing the earth: Toward a pedagogy of peace.' Paper presented at the annual meeting of the American Educational Research Association, San Francisco, March.

GREENE, M. (1989b) 'Provoking and invoking the public school — A conversation with Maxine Greene.' Invited address, annual meeting of the American Educational Research Association, San Francisco, March.

GREENE, M. (1991) 'Blue guitars and the search for curriculum,' in WILLIS, G. and SCHUBERT, W.H. (eds) *Reflections from the Heart of Educational Inquiry: Understanding Curriculum and Teaching through the Arts*, Albany: State University of New York Press, pp. 107–22.

GREENE, M. (1995) 'Texts and margins,' in NEPERUD, R.W. (ed.) *Context, Content, and Community in Art Education: Beyond Postmodernism*, New York: Teachers College Press, pp. 111–27.

WHIRLEDGE, M. (1996) 'Artist's statement,' Unpublished document, California State University, Los Angeles.

8 Confinement, Connection and Women Who Dare: Maxine Greene's Shifting Landscapes of Teaching

Mary-Ellen Jacobs

Prelude

Always my first-day-of-school anxieties are the same; and, on this sunless, bitterly cold January morning, the start of the spring semester, I once again wrestle with familiar demons. When I arrive at the door of GE 130 a few moments before my nine o'clock sophomore English class, the room — a windowless, neon-lit cavern — is already jammed: 30 students neatly aligned in 30 gun-metal gray desks. Many have crisp new notebooks already open, pens poised expectantly over immaculate white paper. I immediately sense my strangeness, the immense gulf between me and this sea of nameless young people 'required' in the interest of an associate degree to wend their way through the intricacies of American literature. I take a deep breath and push open the door. Dragging three heavy canvas sacks of books and syllabi, I gingerly weave my way through the rows to the front of the room.

Suddenly, unaccountably, I am homesick for last semester's students and the community we shared. How can I possibly create the same sense of warmth and purpose this term? I step toward the heavy mahogany podium positioned squarely in the center of the front of the room. How easy, I imagine, to glide behind it and build an unbreachable wall with my red, white, and blue canvas bags. How easy merely to dispense information — authors, works, standard interpretations. To offer Scantron tests. To not bother to learn students' names. Unnerved by the wilderness of unfamiliar faces, I hesitate on this first morning of a new semester. The choice, I realize with a blinding sense of epiphany, is entirely mine. I turn . . .

Daring the Wilderness

I begin and end this essay with glimpses of my own lived experience as a teacher as a way of illustrating the contradictory ways of being which form the backdrop of Maxine Greene's writings on women and teaching. My own uncertainties as a teacher, as I debate seeking the safety of the podium or daring the wilderness of students, mirror the recurring imagery of confinement and connection evident in both *Landscapes of Learning*, Greene's 1978 essay collection where she first explored the lifeworld of women, and *The Dialectic of Freedom* (1988a), published a decade later. Imagery of confinement, so stark in *Landscapes of Learning*, is gradually replaced in Greene's later essays by more connected ways of being. Although the transition from confinement to connection is neither smooth nor unequivocal, what seems crucial to the shift is Greene's gradual disavowal of one of the hallmarks of patriarchal culture, individual autonomy.

This essay, then, traces Greene's movement away from insularity and toward relatedness, an ideological awakening which coincided with her growing interest in examining the lifeworld of women and in analyzing the gendered nature of the constraints she faced in her own career. First, I examine the imagery of confinement and connection associated with women in *Landscapes of Learning* and *The Dialectic of Freedom*. I next discuss Greene's recent writings on women and teaching to consider how Greene herself has dared the wilderness. Finally, I conclude with a brief coda which brings my own story to a close.

The Prisonhouse of Patriarchy

Greene first publicly questions a patriarchal worldview in *Landscapes of Learning* by noting 'the constructs normally used for mapping and interpreting the common sense world are largely those defined by males' (1978, p. 214) yet internalized — dutifully — by members of both sexes. Consequently, all constructs, even 'those having to do with insubordination, natural inferiority, and unequally distributed rights are taken-for-granted' (p. 214). Because a male-centered universe dramatically constricts women's horizons, images of confinement predominate in Greene's descriptions of women negotiating 'the daily treadmill of life' (p. 214).

Rooted in the Latin *confinis*, 'confinement' translates as *boundaries* or *limits*. Repeatedly, it is the limits of women's lived world that Greene so poignantly evokes in the three essays she includes in 'Predicaments of Women,' the final section of *Landscapes of Learning*. In these essays, positioned at the outermost limits of the book itself, we come to understand confinement as a persistent narrowing of boundaries, an insidious, often taken-for-granted limiting of possibilities. Greene forces us to peer 'into the darkness, into the terrible blankness that creeps over so many women's lives, into the wells of victimization and powerlessness' (1978, p. 218). Citing the French feminist Helene Cixous, Greene grimly reminds her readers that, linguistically, women have always functioned within male discourse, within a discourse not entirely their own. Hence, women have had to play roles, create 'fictitious selves' (p. 215) so that they might survive in a masculine universe.

Roles themselves are social constructs which compel us, regardless of gender, to adapt ourselves to the reality of others. In so doing, 'we are likely to lose touch with our projects, to become *invisible* . . . to think of ourselves as others define us, not as we create ourselves' (1978, pp. 216–17). To prevent invisibility, Greene urges women to become truly present to themselves by reconsidering their own lived experiences: 'I am arguing for an intensified awareness of women's own realities, the shape of their own lived worlds' (p. 219).

What, though, do these worlds look like? Women often become so enmeshed in patriarchal culture that they fail to question what seems natural even though there are frequently startling discrepancies between the world as *constructed* through the eyes of a man and as *perceived* through the eyes of a woman (1978, p. 215). Schooled to submission in a society dominated by males, women, Greene laments, often find it difficult 'to grant to perceived realities the integrity they deserve' (p. 215). Perhaps it is women's terrible vulnerability which prompts many to retreat into the circumscribed, though seemingly secure, world of roles.

In real life and in literature, women's horizons are so relentlessly limited that an overwhelming powerlessness often pervades female existence. Greene draws on de Beauvoir in describing a woman 'who is shut up in the kitchen or boudoir . . . deprived of all possibility of concrete communication with others . . . she stays obstinately within the one realm that is familiar to her where she can control things and in the midst of which she enjoys a precarious sovereignty' (p. 217).

In fiction, a similar confinement is experienced by the female narrator of Grace Paley's short story *The Used-Boy Raisers* — 'a woman who stays obstinately in her own realm, who submits to what she thinks of as her destiny' (in Greene, 1978, p. 217). The same is true of Edna Pontellier in Chopin's *The Awakening* and Lily Bart in Wharton's *The House of Mirth*. Both are disturbing icons of nineteenth-century American literature — two women who, because of their obsessive need for male approval, are incapable of developing an identity of their own. For each, life eventually becomes a negation, and suicide the inevitable affirmation of the terrible strictures of their worlds.

Images of confinement also recur in Greene's account of the history of the education of American women, 'a history of unfairness and inequity' (1978, p. 225). Though traditionally perceived as a means of promoting equality, education was, in the nineteenth century, designed to perpetuate 'the existence of a separate (and subordinate) female sphere' (p. 225). In the deeply entrenched patriarchal culture of the Victorian era, 'women were considered predominantly spiritual creatures, emotional and delicate; if they were to be educated at all, the purpose was to educate them for dutiful and dependent lives — for subordination and powerlessness' (p. 227). Consequently, women endured both physical and psychological confinement.

Although considered a progressive institution, Oberlin College, from its inception in 1833, continually 'reinforced the idea that educated women were to be helpmates responsible for the mental health and moral balance of men doing evangelical work upon the frontier . . . Women were segregated from men at the college, and they were required to do domestic work, including the laundry of their male fellow students' (Greene, 1978, p. 234). Though this might seem an extreme example of female segregation, it was not atypical of the constraints placed on women so that they might be educated 'to live their lives as inferior and sustaining beings' (p. 235).

Throughout the nineteenth century, educated women experienced psychological confinement by being routinely infantilized. As students, women were benignly viewed as 'helpless, docile, and insistently happy' (1978, p. 230). As teachers, they were patronizingly perceived as eager to play the part of the ever-acquiescent 'good daughter' to their father-like superintendents (p. 228). Whether confinement was physical or psychological, most women remained trapped in the female sphere and, unlike their male contemporaries, were summarily cut off from discovering the depth and breadth of their own possibilities. It seems appropriate, then, that Greene defines sexism as 'emblematic of constraints and closures . . . an attitude, a posture that shuts persons off from occasions, stimuli, and opportunities for continuing growth in new directions' (p. 244).

Limitations, Greene believes, are transcended by freedom, 'the capacity to identify openings in situations, possible courses of action' (1978, p. 245). Such openings create an intense 'struggling against all labels, falsifications, and finally all enclosures' (p. 221). Though there are 'countless difficulties in the way of creating the open spaces for freedom we have in mind' (p. 253), how might it be possible for women to experience limitlessness? In all three essays, Greene advocates *praxis*, an intelligent interplay of action and reflection: 'Clearly, more critical reflection is required if what is limiting is to be properly exposed and what is humane is transformed. This is, in many respects, the same as working for openings' (p. 254). *Praxis* promises to unlock the prisonhouse of patriarchy so that 'lacks can be defined, openings identified, and possibilities revealed' (p. 223). It is through *praxis* that women might once again 'regain touch with their lived worlds' (p. 222).

Paradoxically, the key to authentic freedom is autonomy — we transcend limitations by moving deeper into the narrow confines of self. In the opening paragraph of 'The Lived World,' Greene announces: 'My concern is for the release of individual capacities now suppressed, for the development of free and autonomous personalities' (1978, p. 214). Similarly, in 'Sexism in the Schools,' Greene conceptualizes teaching as 'encouraging the autonomy of each of the students in the class. Autonomy signifies a sense of personal agency . . . It requires a profound self-understanding on the part of the teacher, who has to live in a kind of tension simply to function as a free agent, to make choices appropriate to the often unpredictable situations that arise' (p. 248).

By valuing autonomy, Greene places herself firmly within the context of a liberal philosophical and political tradition, a tradition which feminist scholars (Pateman, 1983) have convincingly linked to patriarchy. Liberalism is grounded in the assumption that humans are unique because of their capacity for rational thinking, a worldview contingent on equal, autonomous individuals making reasoned moral and civic choices. Though all persons are capable of autonomy, the term itself, because it is both abstract and universal, can be deeply deceptive. The taken-for-granted tendency to decontextualize autonomy leads Pateman to conclude that 'the ostensible individualism and egalitarianism of liberal theory obscure the patriarchal reality of a social reality of inequality and the domination of women by men' (1983, p. 283).

'Autonomy,' thus, is an abstract concept which, because of its lack of historical specificity, allows us to consider all persons — regardless of race, class, or gender — as equal. Carefully divorced from the social practices of everyday life, 'autonomy' is effectively de-politicized and, consequently, non-threatening to patriarchal society (Weedon, 1987, p. 135). In the best liberal tradition, Greene's call for 'autonomy,' though laudable, lacks the specificity which would turn an admirable thought into a potent political deed.

Ironically, it is often 'possible for liberal discourses of equality to work against women's interests, and it is only by looking at a discourse *in operation*, in a specific historical context, that it is possible to see whose interests it serves at a particular moment' (Weedon, 1987, p. 111). Within the context of the liberal tradition which Greene seems to espouse in *Landscapes of Learning*, 'autonomy' suggests that persons are fully capable of individually liberating themselves by throwing off historical conditions and unilaterally rejecting traditional sex roles (Tong, 1989, p. 38). Such sentiments, however admirable, fail to encompass the tangled web of social structures, which, despite countless 'individual efforts,' have proven to be enduring sources of inequality. Thus, Greene's urgent call 'for the release of individual capacities now suppressed, for the development of free and autonomous personalities' (1978, p. 213), in actuality, masks the gendered inequalities of day-to-day social realities. By confining her discourse to the realm of the personal and the resolutely non-political, Greene unintentionally locks women even more securely within the prisonhouse of patriarchy.

Reaching from Private to Public

In the decade following the publication of *Landscapes of Learning*, Greene's critique of social norms becomes more trenchant as she dedicates herself to helping women as well as other minorities escape the heavily guarded prisonhouse of patriarchy. Contemplating how women might move from a cramped to a more spacious existence, Greene began challenging patriarchal power structures and 'making questionable the categories that have contained feminine lives' (1988a, p. 58). In so doing, her own horizons open out.

Rejecting the 'chill structures of autonomy' (1988b, p. 478) — the same structures she had so vigorously advocated since the 1960s, Greene increasingly associates genuine becoming with the thoughtful interweaving of the many diverse strands which color our daily lives. Greene's new focus on relationship rather than solitariness is perhaps most evident in *The Dialectic of Freedom's* (1988a) central chapter 'Reaching from Private to Public: The Work of Women.' For Greene, women are most attuned to interconnection because their often precarious freedom may ultimately hinge on the graceful 'integration of the felt and the known, the subjective and the objective, the private and the public spheres' (1988a, p. 79).

In *The Dialectic of Freedom*, Greene deepens the themes she first introduced in *Landscapes of Learning*. Though many of the same threads run through the tapestry, the pattern becomes infinitely more intricate as Greene heralds her intent 'to *unconceal* . . . to create clearings, spaces in the midst of things where decisions can be made' (1988a, p. 58). Just as in *Landscapes of Learning*, space and confinement are pivotal images woven into the text so that we might visualize women's heroic day-to-day 'struggle against confinement and constriction, usually against what Virginia Woolf was to call "the cotton wool of daily life"' (1988a, p. 60).

Not unlike *Landscapes of Learning*, Greene meshes literature and history to recount how women attempt to make sense of their lives. She reacquaints us with Edna Pontellier, Catherine Beecher, and the Grimke sisters, all of whom appeared in Greene's earlier books. Greene also introduces us to heroines like Anna Dunlop in Sue Miller's *The Good Mother* or nineteenth-century 'literary domestics' like Elizabeth Stuart Phelps — all exemplify women whose "space of freedom has been narrowed hopelessly . . . It was, most often, the infinity of small tasks, the time-consuming obligations of housework and child that narrowed the spaces in which they could choose' (1988a, pp. 59–60).

Like columns of glittering coins, Greene stacks up example after example depicting the narrowed circumstances of American women, whether they be members of the dominant culture or women of color, whether they be historical figures or literary creations. Greene carefully notes that women, such as Jane Addams and Harriet Jacobs, who successfully eluded the strictures of race, class, and gender in order to achieve a more spacious existence could, without exception, 'name' those obstacles to their freedom and, in naming, were able to begin to transform what seemed unjust or unbearable (1988a, p. 65).

Naming the barriers to one's freedom, a recurring theme throughout *The Dialectic of Freedom*, enriches Greene's own thinking and seems to move her beyond the generalities of *Landscapes of Learning*. The act of 'naming' points Greene toward narrative, the stories individuals create to situate themselves within the whirl of daily life. Ideally, such 'situatedness' links us firmly to the lived world, making it possible for us to connect with others in 'a fabric of mutuality and concern, of ongoing dialogue and conversation, of cooperation rather than competition' (1988a, p. 84).

Situatedness — 'the will to be good, to remain in caring relation to the other' (1988a, p. 85) — seems profoundly antithetical to the autonomous coming-to-be that Greene had so ardently championed in her earlier essays. In the ten years since *Landscapes of Learning* was published, Greene has, it seems, grown increasingly critical of liberal ideology. 'Developed in the tradition of male autonomy' (1988a, p. 69), liberalism values abstraction and universality; yet, 'women's efforts to reach out for their own freedom have been most often contextualized and concrete. With rare exceptions, they did not initially identify themselves as autonomous citizens' (p. 60).

Liberalism's unambiguous distinction between 'universal' and 'particular' makes it appear natural to divide the world into the 'public sphere' of abstract male thought and the far less prestigious 'private sphere' of minutely contextualized female emotion. Greene reminds us that, during the nineteenth century, women's 'situated knowledge claims' (1988a, p. 71) were so thoroughly suspect that, desperate for equity, women would often 'suppress their own lived experiences in order to claim an equality in the domain of formal reason identified with the public sphere' (p. 71). Inevitably, such a strategy had disastrous consequences: 'Women's concrete historical realities . . . are such that the particularities of everyday life are inescapable. They cannot simply claim their freedom and their rights (at least not ordinarily) and escape the sphere of obligation and concern. When they do so, they very often alienate themselves from what might be called the ground of their being' (1988a, p. 71). Lacking a sense of connectedness with themselves or with others, it becomes nearly impossible for women 'to transform, to find openings, or to resist' (p. 82).

Situated rather than abstract freedom is so precious to women because it allows them to maintain their relational way of being for 'a person can achieve an authentic freedom only by finding her allotted place in the cosmic order of things' (1988a, p. 78). Similarly, 'freedom cannot be conceived apart from a matrix of social, economic, cultural, and psychological conditions. It is within the matrix that selves take shape or are created through choice of action in the changing situations of life' (p. 80). Ideally, for Greene, freedom is possible only by living dialectically within the endless tensions between self and others, subject and object, public and private.

Women, according to Greene, reach from private to public most meaningfully within the context of care, concern and connection, though she warns: 'Mutuality and concern (if, indeed, they characterize most women's lives) are not in themselves enough to change the world; nor is the affirmation of responsibility for others' (1988a, p. 85). Greene also cautions women that 'freedom cannot be treated as an endowment. It does little good for a single mother, for instance, to assert her natural rights and her God-given liberties, if she cannot engage dialectically with the determining forces around her' (p. 72).

Greene's critique of liberal thought prompts her to see the shadowy political underside of freedom which demands women move swiftly and purposefully from the language of 'female virtue to a language of social activism' (1988a, p. 73). Genuine freedom necessitates individuals working collectively to make: 'Structural and systemic changes. Employment opportunities must open; options must be expanded; support systems must be strengthened to keep families viable and secure' (p. 83). Care and mutuality, though essential, are, Greene gently reiterates, not quite enough.

Thus, in *The Dialectic of Freedom*, Greene weaves women's lives into far more complex patterns than in *Landscapes of Learning*. Only if we dare 'make questionable the categories that have contained feminine lives' (1988a, p. 58), dare live dialectically in an ongoing, never quite comfortable tension, dare move among others with care, concern and sensitivity to multiple ways of seeing might we as women begin the arduous work of reaching from private to public so that 'what is indecent can be transformed and what is unendurable may [at last] be overcome' (p. 86).

Coming Full Circle

Greene's gradual movement from confinement to space, from autonomy to relationality has particular resonance for us as women who teach. In 'Sex Equity as a Philosophical Problem' (1985), she points out: 'To work for sex equity in education and the social order as a whole is to move to alter the oppressiveness that makes individual autonomy antithetical to social concern. It is to rediscover what it signifies to be a person and a woman, while discovering what it signifies to transform' (p. 42).

Although Greene rallies us as women to explore the gendered limitations and possibilities of our own lifeworlds, she rarely reveals her own experiences as a teacher, a learner, or a philosopher. Instead, she speaks almost exclusively through literary and historical allusions. By habitually relegating her own story to the margins, she avoids any personal 'rediscovery' in her own texts and remains reticently along the sidelines. Since the publication of *The Dialectic of Freedom*, however, Greene's voice has grown increasingly candid. No longer is 'transformation' an arid abstraction but rather Greene invites us to witness her own richly contextualized struggles to break free of the constraints of patriarchal thinking and discourse. In a 1989 interview, she remarked: 'Up to ten or fifteen years ago, if someone introduced me as a woman who thinks like a man, I'd be flattered. It's terrible what we went through. . . . Now when I tell my story to classes like I did here last night, the problem of being a woman becomes very prominent even though I'm not sure I lived it with quite that feeling of centrality. But when I tell about it, it's absolutely crucial.'

Greene's sense of herself as a woman deliberately writing against the patriarchal grain reverberates provocatively through her most recent texts. For example, in her 1994 essay 'Teaching for openings: Pedagogy as dialectic,' Greene demonstrates how far beyond her earlier quest for an autonomous self she has moved as she invites us to listen to her own story: 'I wanted so much to be accepted in the great world of wood-paneled libraries, authoritative intellectuals, sophisticated urban cafés. My response to the criticisms I received early on was to turn away from the local and particular in my life, to strive for an incarnation of values that promised to transcend gender and class and race" (1994, pp. 4–5). Instantly, we understand why autonomy, with its deft erasure of particularities, had such a powerful appeal to Greene as she struggled to mask her own 'otherness' in a hostile patriarchal world.

In 'Teaching for Openings,' we once again encounter images of confinement but with a crucial difference. For the first time, Greene publicly details the constraints she herself felt: 'It has taken many shocks of awareness to realize how I existed within the tradition (or the "conversation") as within a container' (p. 4). As her story unfolds, she recalls her growing discomfort with 'ungrounded knowledge that is its own excuse for being' (p. 7) and acknowledges that this realization prompted the 'rupture of some of the containers in which I had lived and thought I wanted to live' (p. 7). As the walls of Greene's containers collapse, she sheds the chrysalis of autonomy and emerges as a woman who, through compelling personal examples, challenges us to dare to live dialectically in the tensions between self and other, between what is and what might be. No longer do we teach exclusively for 'autonomy,' the siren song of self that three decades ago was Greene's anthem in *Existential Encounters for Teachers* (1967), but rather we use our teaching to create relational ways of knowing and being. By choosing to enter into dialogue with students, Greene advocates a classroom grounded in diversity and compassion: 'I want us to work together to unconceal what is hidden, to contextualize what happens to us, to mediate the dialectic that keeps us on the edge, that may be keeping us alive' (pp. 5–6). Teaching for openings, Greene acknowledges, will always be fraught with risks, yet only by daring to seek such openings can we hope to survive — and perhaps even transform — an uncertain world.

Coda

I turn. Thirty pairs of eyes watch me drop my heavy canvas bags on the podium like unwanted lead weights. I grasp the edge of the lectern, pause to catch my breath, then decisively shove the podium to the far edge of the room where it remains unused except as a repository for my red, white and blue sacks. Noisily — metal furniture whining and squealing its way across the freshly polished floor, we drag our chairs into a large circle and begin.

References

GREENE, M. (ed.) (1967) *Existential Encounters for Teachers*, New York: Random House.

GREENE, M. (1978) *Landscapes of Learning*, New York: Teachers College Press.

GREENE, M. (1985) 'Sex equity as a philosophical problem,' in KLEIN, S. (ed.) *Handbook for Achieving Sex Equity Through Education* (pp. 29–43), Baltimore: The Johns Hopkins University Press.

GREENE, M. (1988a) *The Dialectic of Freedom*, New York: Teachers College Press.

GREENE, M. (1988b) 'What are the language arts *for?*' *Language Arts*, **65**, pp. 474–80.

GREENE, M. (1989) Personal interview, 15 September.

GREENE, M. (1994) 'Teaching for openings: Pedagogy as dialectic,' in SULLIVAN, P.A. and QUALLEY, D.J. (eds) *Pedagogy in the Age of Politics* (pp. 1–12), Urbana, IL: NCTE.

PATEMAN, C. (1983) 'Feminist critique of the public/private dichotomy, in BENN, S.I. and GAUS, G.F. (eds) *Public and Private in Social Life* (pp. 281–303), New York: St. Martin's Press.

TONG, R. (1989) *Feminist Thought*, San Francisco: Westview Press.

WEEDON, C. (1987) *Feminist Practice and Poststructuralist Theory*, New York: Basil Blackwell.

9 Signifying Self: Re-presentations of the Double-consciousness in the Work of Maxine Greene

Denise M. Taliaferro

From a Situated Being

The way things are for our life and body allows us only a partial view of things, not the kind of total view we might gain if we were godlike, looking down from the sky. But we can only know as situated beings. (Maxine Greene, 1995, p. 26)

I have come to know the work of Maxine Greene as a student of education. However, I have come to feel and live the meaningfulness of Maxine's thoughts as an African-American, a woman, and a teacher. In no certain order, but in no uncertain terms, these are my ever intermingling, interdependent, transforming selves. My ability to understand the complexity of these selves and their corresponding others lies in my struggle to confront the 'walls' that have grown in the way of my dreams. Maxine often writes of these 'walls' that stand between people and their dreams. They are the same walls that stand between people and their others. Interestingly, Maxine does not propose that we blow up or somehow destroy these walls. Instead, she encourages us to examine them and see who may be on the other side. Freedom, according to Maxine, is a quest, an existential project which means it is a lifetime of confronting walls. In the process of examining one of my biggest, baddest walls, I have come to think about Maxine's work as it brings new meaning to an old situation.

The Memory Is My Wall

Only in reflection, many years later, can I pinpoint the exact moment it began to happen. I think the first fissure appeared around age 7. The sun was warm and inviting and the sky a bright, cheery blue. When my aunt, sister, and I walked into the picture-perfect day, we were all fancied up for a special party at the high-rise apartment buildings across the big street that separated the city from the suburbs. My sister and I hopped into Auntie's gold-colored Plymouth, and excited and delighted, the three of us were on our way. By the time we arrived and parked the car, we opened the doors to a blast of heat from a sun that had quickly grown hotter since we had been driving. I remember the intensity of the sun that day, because we walked for several minutes trying to find the right building. Finally, coming back to where we began, Auntie insisted that we go into the building across from the car to ask for directions. So we started that way.

The nice cool air blew gently across my face as I stepped from the revolving doors, which I spun through twice, into the air-conditioned lobby. By the time I reached the counter where my aunt and sister were standing, I heard the tall lady say, 'You must be in the wrong place. We can't help you.' I looked up into her ice blue eyes disappointed at that point, because I thought we were never going to get to the party. It was not what she said, because I really believed she could not help us, but it was the unfriendly tone in her voice and the disgust in her ice blue eyes that caused the first fissure, the initial split in my consciousness.

This is perhaps one of my most vivid memories, one that, for the longest time, I could not understand. I thought the lady was angry because I was playing in her revolving doors. And, in memory at age 7, the lady was angry because I was playing in her doors. But, as I grew older, I came to remember her disgust differently. In an article entitled 'Memory, Writing and Creation,' Toni Morrison (1984) elaborates on the meaning of memory:

> Memory (the deliberate act of remembering) is a form of willed creation. It is not an effort to find out the way it really was — that is research. The point is to dwell on the way it appeared and why it appeared that particular way. (p. 385)

I have decided to dwell on how and why the memory of that experience has changed.

I renamed the memory/experience after reading *The Souls of Black Folk* by W.E.B. DuBois (1973). Although it lingered in works of black scholars like Paul L. Dunbar before DuBois actually named it, the double-consciousness has, since DuBois' naming, become a, perhaps *the*, most significant consideration in black ontological thought. The literature of black lived experiences can hardly escape the situation of the Negro characterized by DuBois as one who

> . . . is sort of a seventh son, born with a veil, and gifted with second-sight in this American world — a world which yields him no true self-consciousness, but only lets him see himself through the revelation of the other world. It is a peculiar sensation, this double-consciousness, this sense of always looking at one's self through the eyes of the others, of measuring one's soul by the tape of a world that looks on in amused contempt and pity. One ever feels his twoness — an American, a Negro; two souls, two thoughts, two unreconciled strivings; two warring ideals in one dark body. (1973, p. 13)

I read these words for the first time as I curled up in the corner where the edge of my dorm bunk met the wall. I felt so strongly, then, that these words were the long-anticipated diagnosis for the symptoms I had been suffering since leaving the security of my home-grown blackness to venture into the academic and social culture of the University of California in Los Angeles. Not only did the many white faces upset my Being, so did many of the black ones who seemed so very different than myself. Finally, I knew what my problem was. Problem? Yes, problem — that's the optimal word. I, along with everyone I know who has written about or discussed the phenomena of the double-consciousness, have considered it pivotal if not the ultimate, burden of being Black.

More recently, in my graduate studies, I have been trying to make sense of the current postmodern explosion of identity as static and necessarily constructed around binary oppositions. Somewhere in that rhetoric is a subtle suggestion that could support a reappropriation of the double-consciousness as a gift of 'second-sight in this American world' which is indeed a diverse world, one in which 'looking at one's self through the eyes of others' might be our only chance to journey in freedom. Thus, double-consciousness need not be only a burden, but might be a virtue as well. And, it need not be only a situation of blackness, it can also describe, albeit differently, the experiences of being a woman, a poor person, a disabled person, a homosexual person — any of America's oppressed. Not only that, but we should all seek to understand it and those who have escaped the pain of a splitting soul should surrender to the possibility. At this moment, it is from this situation of being that I turn anxiously to the work of Maxine Greene to explore understandings of freedom, art and imagination as they bring new meaning to that infamous double-consciousness.

Making Meaning with Maxine

One does not have to pluck apart the pages of Maxine's work, *The Dialectic of Freedom* (1988) and *Releasing the Imagination* (1995) in particular, to discover a woman who has, perhaps not intentionally, tapped into the powerful potential of the double-consciousness as a provocation of true freedom. As she frankly challenges our notions, as Americans, of freedom, imagination, and art, she bends the boundaries of difference. It is important that she only bends them without destroying them. For boundaries, as they are constructed by and construct identities, are important, yet they do not have to be exclusionary. Her words and thoughts dance on tiptoes across many boundaries in an attempt to signify self through the reimagination of the other, a manner of reconciling two souls, not just those being on either side of the boundaries, but the self and other that manifest in any humans Being. The coming together, not the merging, of self and other in Maxine's work repre-sents the 'dialectic of freedom.'

For Maxine, freedom is a continuous quest, the conscious exercising of imagination is the work to be done on the quest, and art, particularly literature, is the bridge from imagination to imagination. One of the ways in which Maxine weaves these threads into a rich tapestry for being Self and Other is through a metaphorical dialogic signifying with literary imaginations that capture both the tragedy and the potential positive power of the double-consciousness. These imaginations include those of Ralph Ellison, Zora Neale Hurston, Richard Wright, Martin Luther King, Jr., Paula Giddings, Notzache Shange and still others. However, many of the points Maxine makes most often are those that are represented in her repositioning (hooks, 1992) of self in the others that come to life in the writings of Alice Walker and Toni Morrison.

Faces of Freedom

There is always the Self and the Other constitutive, of course, of many selves and many others. The Self is the combination of identities we choose to claim, and the Other is the combination we choose not to claim. Although they are often theorized in binary opposi-tion, the Self and Other can, more productively, be understood in dialectical relation. Maxine describes this relation as one 'which exists between two different, apparently opposite poles; but it presupposes a mediation between them' (1988, p. 4). The mediation is the tension that occurs between the two.

Because the Self and Other are in dialectical relation, we are all, at one and the same time, both. Yet, we are all not both in the same way. People who are oppressed from positionalities of race, gender, class, sexual orientation, age, disability, or some other nexus see their Self through the eyes of the Other. In contrast, those who are in a position of privilege where certain identities are concerned, see their Other through the eyes of the Self. Thus, the thin line between Self and Other gets constructed and acted upon differently according to which positionality — oppressed or privileged — one is acting/being at any given moment.

From an oppressed positionality the double-consciousness emerges. It is founded on the ability of the person to see Self through the eyes of the Other. Historically this ability, typically associated with blackness in relation to whiteness in America, has been characterized as an unfortunate, tragic burden. Without a doubt, the double-consciousness possesses a tragic element. We need only look beyond our 'selves' to see those children of color, like Toni Morrison's Pecola Breedlove, who so desperately want to be white. We need only to look and see people so poor and destitute, like Alice Walker's Celie, that they sacrifice their dignity, their self-respect, their lives to live as the other. We need only to look and see the children who are so confused — in a society that rejects such ambiguity, about who they are or want to be — that they need to, want to, and do kill themselves. We need only look and see these situations of being, these lived experiences and others, to understand the pain and horror associated with warring souls.

Yet, it is from positions of oppression that one, in her/his twoness, has the predisposition to understand freedom as an ongoing quest, a continuous search that is realized in the intersubjectivity of community. It is from these positions that people have the capacity to realize that freedom is not just dependent upon effort, protest, and determination, but that acceptance is also imperative. Unfortunately though, even possessing a double-consciousness is not enough if one does not recognize its dialectical character. Then, the Self becomes submerged in images defined only by the Other and the face of freedom is not what it seems. Maxine exemplifies these dynamics by challenging taken-for-granted notions of freedom, by offering a new perspective on freedom, and most importantly by signifying her self through others.

In *The Dialectic of Freedom* (1988), Maxine deconstructs what has become, for many Americans, taken-for-granted assumptions about freedom. She challenges the idea of the American Dream that is dangled, so deceitfully, before us all:

> Talk of the free world today is intertwined with talk of economic competitiveness, technology, and power. Talk of personal freedom refers to self-dependence and self determination; it has little to do with connectedness or being together in community. Americans assume that they were born free. If they can function with any degree of effectiveness, they feel entitled to do as they please, to pursue their fulfillments on their own. To be autonomous and independent: this seems to many to be the American Dream. (Greene, 1988, p. 1)

She goes on to point out how black people, as an oppressed people, have been privy, although painfully, to experience, along with others, the underside of such a dream. However, it is from this underside view that we tend to define our 'selves' by others' standards alone. Consequently, when one sees the Self only through the eyes of the Other then they accept a dream that is self-defeating instead of self-freeing.

Maxine illustrates the consequences of collapsing Self and Other by making meaning of Celie in Alice Walker's *The Color Purple* (1982):

> Celie is victimized in the sense that she can scarcely use the first person singular or the active case when talking about herself. It becomes starkly clear that this kind of experience is linked to an almost total lack of understanding about the lived world; and, without such understanding freedom appears to be unthinkable. (Greene, 1988, p. 104)

Accordingly, Miss Celie's inability to say 'I am' is a reflection of her submerged consciousness. In essence, Celie's self is completely constituted in her others — her sister Nettie, her father, Mister and his children. Celie cannot imagine her self outside of her others. Here the double-consciousness is negative because Celie lacks an understanding of the dialectic between Self and Other. She only sees her self through the eyes of others believing of her self what they believe of her.

It is not until Shug encourages Celie to question her world and imagine her self outside of, but in relationship to, her others that Celie can be free from her oppression. Maxine's reading of Miss Celie emphasizes that only through connection with Shug is Celie able 'not only to put questions to her familiar world, but to begin to name it and act so that she can transform, through her own actions her own life' (1988, p. 104). In essence, the double-consciousness manifested in Celie as a war between the Other and the submerged Self aching to be in relation instead of submission. And her freedom from the war was only possible because of the presence of Shug's very different world.

Through her connection with Celie as an other, Maxine is able to question our understanding of freedom as some 'thing' gained for oneself by oneself. At the same time, she is also able to redefine freedom as something that occurs between the Self and the Other, in communal space. Maxine's ideas about freedom bring new significance to the phenomena of the split consciousness. If freedom lies in the intersubjectivity of community, then it necessitates the ability to see one's self through the eyes of others without constituting it completely within the imagination of the other.

It is intriguing, however, that the profundity of her message lies not in the words themselves, but how she uses them in her own quest for freedom, to get in touch with herself by repositioning self in relationship to others. Maxine reveals her own dialectic between self and other:

> [N]ow and then, when I am in the presence of work from the border, let us say, from a place outside the reach of my experience until I came in contact with the work, I am plunged into all kinds of reconceiving and revisualizing. I find myself moving from discovery to discovery; I find myself revising and now and then renewing the terms of my life. (1995, p. 3)

With a vision of freedom perceived through reconciliation between the Self and the Other, we can now turn to the arduous work to be done to realize that vision. Imagine.

Images of Imposition — Impositional Images

No matter how precisely we choose to define our existence, we do not 'become' in a vacuum. It is only through interactions with others that we are actually able to become. In 'The Politics of Recognition,' Charles Taylor (1994) focuses on the dialogical character of human interaction:

> People do not acquire the languages needed for self-definition on their own. Rather, we are introduced to them through interaction with others who matter to us — what George Herbert Mead called 'significant others.' The genesis of the human mind is in this sense not monological, not something each person accomplishes on his or her own, but dialogical. (p. 79)

The dialogical nature of the human mind is manifested in the relationship between the Self and the Other, and it is through the imagination that they dialogue. Maxine's philosophy of freedom is strongly rooted in and dependent upon using the languages of imagination:

> One of the reasons I have come to concentrate on imagination as a means through which we can assemble a coherent world is that imagination is what, above all, makes empathy possible. It is what enables us to cross the empty spaces between ourselves and those we teachers have called 'other' over the years. If those others are willing to give us clues, we can look in some manner through strangers' eyes and hear through their ears. That is because, of all our cognitive capacities, imagination is the one that permits us to give credence to alternative realities. It allows us to break with the taken for granted, to set aside familiar distinctions and definitions. (1995, p. 3)

What is fundamental about Maxine's characterization of imagination is not only what it allows us to see or to understand in other realities, but in essence, how those other realities shape our own, how the very act of imagining shapes our own realities. The task, then, of those of us who possess a double-consciousness is to imagine beyond those images fixed upon us by the inner-eye of the Other. Maxine urges us to engage in a 'continuing consciousness of new beginnings' so that we may avoid the 'sense of being fixed by someone else's categorization or inner-eye, of being caught up in trends and tendencies, of behaving not acting, since acting means taking initiatives' (1995, p. 40). On the other hand, for those of us who do not have or are not conscious of the phenomena of the split consciousness, Maxine challenges us to imagine beyond the images we hold of our 'self' and seek the perspective of the Other. What is it that we learn about our 'selves' as we exist in the imaginations of others?

Maxine, herself, does a great deal of exercising her imagination not only as a writer but also as a reader. And, these activities, as Toni (Morrison, 1992) suggests, are not all that distinct for a writer:

> Both exercises require being alert and ready for unaccountable beauty, for the intricateness or simple elegance of the writer's imagination, for the world that imagination evokes. Both require being mindful of the places where imagination sabotages itself, locks its own gates, pollutes its vision. (p. xi)

In her analysis of African-American literature, Maxine disrupts a point of sabotage, releases her imagination, and extends her vision beyond her 'self.' In order to reveal what Maxine accomplishes, it is important to consider the context.

A close analysis of African-American literature discloses, sometimes implicitly and sometimes explicitly but always, an acute awareness of the double-consciousness. In some works the focus is on a tragic desire for whiteness such as in James Weldon Johnson's *The Autobiography of an Ex-colored Man* (1990) or Toni Morrison's *The Bluest Eye* (1970). In other pieces, such as Toni's *Beloved* (Morrison, 1987) or Richard Wright's *Native Son* (1940), there is a commentary on the sheer fear of whiteness. And in still other writings including Ralph Ellison's *Invisible Man* (1952), Zora Neale Hurston's *Their Eyes are Watching God* (1937), or Nathan Macall's *Makes Me Wanna Holler: A Young Black Man in America* (1994) and Bebe Moore Campbell's *Brothers and Sisters*

(1994) there is reflected the mixed bevy of desire for and terror of whiteness in the black imagination.

In an essay entitled 'Representations of Whiteness in the Black Imagination,' bell hooks (1992) speaks poignantly of the terror often evoked by whiteness in the black imagination. She remembers her own terror as a child having to venture into a white neighborhood:

> It was a movement away from the segregated blackness of our community into a poor white neighborhood, I remember the fear, being scared to walk to Baba's, our grandmother's house, because we would have to pass that terrifying whiteness — those white faces on the porches staring us down with hate. Even when empty or vacant those porches seemed to say danger you do not belong here, you are not safe. (p. 175)

What bell highlights in her essay is not only the presence of the terror but white people's tendency not to see the terror for what it is.

Essentially, talking about the white students that she has taught, bell suggests that they do not often reflect on how they exist in the black imagination. They do not, in other words, see their 'selves' through the eyes of the Other (speaking of course specifically about racial difference). bell recognizes this inability or unwillingness to see white self in the imagination of black other as a manifestation of racism:

> Usually, white students respond with naive amazement that black people critically assess white people from a standpoint where 'whiteness' is the privileged signifier. Their amazement that black people watch white people with a critical 'ethnographic' gaze, is itself an expression of racism. Often their rage erupts because they believe that all ways of looking that highlight difference subvert the liberal belief in a universal subjectivity (we are all just people) that they think will make racism disappear. (1992, p. 176)

By turning to the work of Gayatri Spivak who suggests, 'what we are asking for is that the hegemonic discourses, and the holders of hegemonic discourse, should dehegemonize their position and themselves learn how to occupy the subject position of the other,' bell defines the act of repositioning. The process of putting Self in the subject position of the Other has, as bell suggests, 'the power to deconstruct racism and make possible the disassociation of whiteness with terror in the black imagination' (1992, p. 177).

Gayatri's dehegemonizing and bell's repositioning are reiterated by Toni's (Morrison, 1992) demand for 'a serious intellectual effort to see what racial ideology does to the mind, imagination, and behavior of master' (p. 12). Maxine's philosophizing is an attempt to hear and to respond actively to the call for dehegemonizing, repositioning, and a honing in, with a critical eye, on the imagination of the white racialized subject.

Maxine identifies her situatedness as white and woman, and it is from these positionalities that she uses her imagination to get in touch with alternative realities. Imagining for Maxine is what Toni (Morrison, 1992) refers to as becoming: '[I]magining is not merely looking or looking at; nor is it entailing oneself intact into the other. It is . . . becoming' (p. 4). Interestingly, in the places where her imagination could have sabotaged itself, Maxine, instead, exercises her imagination in such a way that does not victimize the Other, or assume to be the Other. Rather, she extracts from the other's experience that which leads to some broader understanding of self. This is her cultivation of a positive and powerful double-consciousness, one that gives credence to the dialectical rather than the oppositional nature of Self and Other.

It would be beyond the scope of this paper to identify the number of instances where Maxine looks to the Other for self-definition, whether the Other be people of color or men or some other reality outside her own. She relies heavily on the imaginative power of literature as art from a diverse plethora of imaginers — white and black, men and women. However, there is one example I find particularly powerful. Here, she turns to Toni's *Beloved* (1987) not with an inner-eye of pity but one that seeks understanding and relation. Her focus is Baby Suggs whom she understands not so much as a victim of slavery but more precisely as a deeply wounded mother due to slavery. Maxine could have conceived Baby Suggs as the Other outside the scope of her reality. Instead, she seeks dialectically to relate to Baby Suggs' reality as defining some aspect of her own. She reflects:

> There is no woman who has been a mother who will not discover a quite new aspect of mothering, of mother-loving, when she reads . . . how Baby Suggs felt having her children sold away from her. . . . We are likely to find what we have always considered cruelly subverted. How could any human being take responsibility for selling children, for depriving a mother of seven to whom she had given birth, and feel justified because of customs, codes, internalized images, and a taken-for-grantedness people are not willing to question? (1995, p. 71)

Although Baby Suggs' dilemma is painful, it is not her pain alone. Maxine reappropriates Baby Suggs' dilemma in such a way that it becomes every reader's pain and responsibility, albeit from differing positionalities.

In this one example Maxine accomplishes a number of complicated tasks. For one, she repositions her 'self' in the subject position of Baby Suggs as the 'other.' This enables her to see, to imagine, relationally instead of oppositionally. Second, she implicitly draws attention to the racist subject by questioning the humanity of his/her actions, while at the same time recognizing that these subjects, too, are pained by the possibilities of such a horrible reality. Finally, and perhaps most importantly, Maxine dehegemonizes the 'knowing of slavery' as the legacy of just black people. Heterogeneously, she alludes to, in her reading of *Beloved* (1987), that slavery is not only the history of black people but white people as well. The legacy bears down on all of us. In reflecting on her analysis of Baby Suggs' reality, Maxine admits that 'this is some of what can come from the presence of the subject standing in the public space — the space where visions should take shape, where at odd times and spontaneously people feel themselves part of the dance of life' (1995, p. 72).

In essence, Maxine not only calls for an arduous exercising of the imagination, but offers many re-presentations of the imagining she has done in her own quest for freedom. She questions and perceives anew images of imposition and impositional images as they contribute to the understanding, and lack thereof, of the relationship between Self and Other. Specifically, she views the imagination as a pathway between Self and Other. Thus, if we imagine not at all, or invisible-ize, the Other there is no double-consciousness. This is detrimental not only to the Other but to the Self as well. Although we are what we know, 'we are also,' as Pinar (1994) reiterates, 'what we do not know,' or choose not to see. Furthermore, even if we imagine oppositionally the relationship between Self and Other, there resides only the possibility of subversion of one into the other. That is the tragic element of the double-consciousness which can only perceive of a 'negative freedom' (Greene, 1988). If, however, we can imagine dialectically the relationship between Self and Other, then the double-consciousness can be represented as a provocation of true freedom, a freedom that is rooted in the intersubjectivity of community, a community of selves and others.

Perhaps, it is only through the conscious, positive cultivation of a double-consciousness that it is possible to escape the impositional images of freedom that contribute to what Maxine (1988) calls 'the opaqueness of a private life,' a life centered around nothing but itself. But . . . there is always a but.

But What?

The 'BUT' is that even if we are able to imagine dialectically Self and Other, the tension between the two is not and cannot necessarily be resolved, just better understood. Maxine emphasizes, emphatically, that the dialectic is always with a tension that cannot be overcome by a 'triumph of subjectivity over objectivity, of Self over Other.' Nor, she insists, 'is it the kind of dialectic that can finally be resolved in some perfect synthesis or harmony' (1988, p. 8). In other words, it will never be such that the Self and Other are in a tensionless state, because it is only at the border, the abyss, the wall where they meet that allows us to see them and be them. So freedom is no more about the quintessential American Dream than it is about the underside of that dream. What it is about is examining, together, the border, the abyss, the wall between the two.

With all said, thought, and reflected upon, the power of the double-consciousness does not presuppose a perfect, untroubled existence between Self and Other. Instead, it only calls for our awareness of how the two participate, dialectically, as Maxine demonstrates, in the 'dance of life.'

References

CAMPBELL, B.M. (1994) *Brothers and Sisters*, New York: Berkley Books.

DuBois, W.E.B. (1973) *The Souls of Black Folk*, Millwood, NY: Kraus-Thompson Organization Limited.

ELLISON, R. (1952) *Invisible Man*, New York: Signet Books.

GREENE, M. (1988) *The Dialectic of Freedom*, New York: Teachers College Press.

GREENE, M. (1995) *Releasing the Imagination: Essays on Education, the Arts, and Social Change*, San Francisco: Jossey-Bass Publishers.

hooks, b. (1992) *Black Looks: Race and Representation*, Boston, MA: South End Press.

HURSTON, Z.N. (1937) *Their Eyes Are Watching God*, New York: Harper & Row.

JOHNSON, J.W. (1990) *The Autobiography of an Ex-colored Man* (ed. and introduced by William L. Andrews), New York: Pilgrim. Originally published in 1912.

MACALL, N. (1994) *Makes Me Wanna Holler: A Young Black Man in America*, New York: Vintage books.

MORRISON, T. (1970) *The Bluest Eye*, New York: Bantam Books.

MORRISON, T. (1984) 'Memory, creation, and writing,' *Thought*, **59**, pp. 385–90.

MORRISON, T. (1987) *Beloved*, New York: Knopf.

MORRISON, T. (1992) *Playing in the Dark: Whiteness in the Literary Imagination*, Cambridge, MA: Harvard University Press.

PINAR, W.F. (1994) 'Notes on understanding curriculum as racial text,' in McCARTHY, C. and CRICHLOW, W. (eds) *Race, Identity and Representation in Education* (pp. 60–70), New York: Routledge.

TAYLOR, C. (1994) 'The politics of recognition,' in GOLDBERG, D. (ed.) *Multiculturalism: A Critical Reader* (pp. 75–106), Cambridge, MA: Blackwell Publishers Ltd.

WALKER, A. (1982) *The Color Purple*, New York: Washington Square Press.

WRIGHT, R. (1940) *Native Son*, New York: HarperCollins.

10   Maxine Greene and the Project of 'Making the Strange Liberty of Creation Possible'

Paula M. Salvio

The question, for all those who cannot live without art and what it signifies, is merely to find out how, among the police forces of so many ideologies . . . the strange liberty of creation is possible. (Albert Camus, 1960, p. 251)

Introduction

The novel *Taste of Salt*, tells the story of modern Haiti at the time Bertrand Aristide has just been elected president.[1] Francis Temple writes this story from the perspective of two teenagers, Djo, one of Aristide's bodyguards and Jeremie, who is educated in a convent, where she is secluded from the violence continually erupting on the streets of Port au Prince. As the story opens, Djo is lying in a hospital bed weakened from the Macoutes' bludgeons. His eyes are swollen shut and he is barely able to speak. Aristide has asked Jeremie to sit by Djo's bedside and offer him what comfort she can. He has also re-quested that Jeremie tape record Djo's life story. 'If I tell my story,' whispers Djo, 'I will not die entirely . . . Titid loves me. Also, Titid is a politician. He knows how to use stories to make things happen, to make the way of the world change' (Temple, 1992, p. 7). During one of their visits, Djo remembers the following story that inspires his work with Pe Pierre, a friend of Aristide's, with whom he teaches a group of young boys how to read.

> Pe Pierre has a box full of books that he uses to teach the letters and the words. These books are called Taste Salt.
>
> The name makes me remember a story my mama told us. You know this story, Jeremie? How if a person dies, and their body is stolen by a zombie master, the zombie master will make the body rise and work all day and all night as a slave. The zombie understands only his suffering. He has no power to break away. He can only work and work.
>
> But there is one little trick that can save the zombie. Do you remember what it is, Jeremie? Did your mama tell you this? If the zombie can get a taste of salt, he will understand. He will open his true eyes and see that he has been made a zombie. And he will turn against his master. He will obey him no longer. He will make himself free.
>
> I am not so quick, Jeremie. Among us boys, Lally is the smart one. I use these books with Pe Pierre and not think anything about the title. Then one day I see why the books be called Taste Salt. Is because that is what being able to read and write is like. You understand things you didn't before. (Temple, 1992, p. 27)

In voodoo cults in West Africa, Haiti and the southern United States, the zombie appears as a snake god, endowed with supernatural powers that can enter into and re-animate a dead body. According to the parable that Djo tells Jeremie, when the zombie tastes salt, he is shocked into awareness and will turn against all that is oppressive, mindless and unjust — he will 'make himself free.' Djo believes that reading and writing can play an important role in liberating and arousing his people to a state of wide-awakeness; reading and writing, like the taste of salt, can shock the senses and move us out of malaise, or from, as Freud points out, 'the desire to ignore.' Freud maintains that ignorance is not an inert or static state of consciousness; rather, it is a dynamic state of being, which is marked by determination and resistance.[2]

The parable of the zombie who is aroused from ignorance to liberation by the taste of salt, calls to mind some of the literary figures who take a prominent presence in the scholarship of Maxine Greene: Henrik Ibsen's Nora, Albert Camus' Rebel, Toni Morrison's Sula, Jean Paul Sartre's Roquentin, Alice Walker's Celie. Each of these figures deliberates over and defies prevailing, normative codes of behavior that threaten to steal their bodies and enslave them. Their acts of defiance are not sentimental; they are acts of courage which require they leave people they love, confront tyranny and face unspeakable horror. I think of Celie in particular as I write this essay, specifically the moment when Celie feels her 'eyes are opening,' and she begins to see herself through loving, rather than disdainful eyes.

> Now that my eyes are opening, I feels like a fool. Next to any little scrub of a bush in my yard, Mr. __'s evil sort of shrink. But not altogether. Still, it is like Shug say. You have to git man off your eyeball, before you can see anytin a'tall. (Walker, 1982, p. 179)

Like the zombie who has awakened to his master's ways, Celie begins to feel the power to exert her own agency in the world, and through the love and support she is given by her friend and lover, Shug, she begins, as Greene writes, 'to question her familiar world, . . . to name it and act so that she can transform, through her own actions, her own life' (Greene, 1988, p. 104). Throughout Greene's writing she uses an ensemble of literary figures to dramatize the complex consequences inherent in refusing to abide by the language of the law or institutional and cultural practices that demand debilitating forms of compliance. Characters such as Celie and Shug also teach us that wide-awakeness can be as painful and wrought with loss as it is liberating.

In this chapter I consider how performance can be used as a medium through which to establish points of contact among students that inspire moments of wide-awakeness and shocks in the classroom. I specifically focus on how the dramaturgy of Bertolt Brecht can mediate an engaged awareness with the identity positions we take up when we encounter difficult art.[3] I take up these questions in light of Greene's concept of wide-awakeness to highlight the ways the act of becoming wide-awake requires emotional and political labor that brings us into contact with people as we make and remake ourselves.[4] These points of contact, whether they be made through face-to-face conversation, the exchange of a glance or the act of composing responses to literature through writing and other aesthetic media, must call our attention to the places in the curriculum where, writes Toni Morrison, our 'imagination sabotages itself, locks its own gates, pollutes its vision. Writing and reading mean being aware of the writer's notions of risk and safety, the serene achievement of, or sweaty fight for, meaning and response-ability' (1992, p. xi).

A Definition

Maxine Greene's use of the term 'wide-awakeness' is inspired by the work of the phenomenologist Alfred Schutz. Schutz characterizes wide-awakeness as an attitude that fully attends 'to life and its requirements' (1967, p. 163). To be wide-awake is to be engaged in intelligent deliberation about the norms by which we choose to live and to consider the consequences of identifying with one set of norms rather than another. Schutz goes on to suggest that a person who is wide-awake is interested and engaged in the world; this attitude emerges as one develops a heightened awareness of oneself in relation to human projects, human undertakings and political life, 'not,' Greene writes in her gloss of his text, 'in a withdrawal into the intersubjective world.' This form of attention is characterized by an interest in things rather than a disposition of compliance or indifference.

For both Greene and Schutz, human beings define themselves through the projects with which they become involved: Amnesty International, Habitat For Humanity, theatrical projects such as *Rent* written by Jonathan Larson or the performance art of Cindy Sherman. These are a few examples of projects that are determined both by present political and social factors as well as a vision of purpose for the future. By means of engagement with a project, the attitude of wide-awakeness develops and contributes to the choice of actions that lead to self-formation. Greene, who identifies strongly with existentialist philosophy, uses one of the central existentialist terms, *project*, to refer to the intentionalized vision of purpose, of making or constructing the self and the world. Jean-Paul Sartre defines the project in the following passage:

> The most rudimentary behavior must be determined both in relation to the real and present factors which condition it and in relation to a certain object, still to come, which it is trying to bring into being. This is what we call the project. (1968, p. 91)

The project of self-creation, an activity on which Greene places high value throughout her writings, is contingent upon continual acts of intelligent deliberation within the classroom community. The act of intelligent deliberation is enormously complicated when we stop to consider the ways in which specific values, ideas and issues are represented, ordered or condoned on the social surface of the curriculum. The grip of power is not simply imposed on us. As Nikolas Rose and Peter Miller argue, it is increasingly evident that power is becoming more a matter of '*making up* citizens capable of bearing a certain kind of regulated freedom' (1992, p. 174). I feel the pressures of making citizens who can withstand the pressures of regulated freedom each day in my life as a teacher, particularly in the locale where I live. Consider, for a moment, the case of Merrimack, New Hampshire. In September of 1995, despite many community members' continuing opposition to a new ban on any mention of homosexuality by teachers in Merrimack classrooms, the majority of the School Board imposed a policy that prohibited teachers and staff from 'any activity that might be perceived as encouraging or supporting homosexuality as a positive lifestyle or from giving students referrals for counseling to organizations that support homosexuality' (*The Boston Globe*, 7 September, 1995, p. 35; 5).

These 'policies' function to promote the very kind of uncritical absorption about which Greene is concerned. The consequence of taking in, without public, explicit critique, such rules and regulations, is equivalent to the forms of acquiescence and withdrawal that undermine the potential for freedom and the potential for living a moral life (Greene, 1978, p. 49). 'If individuals act automatically or conventionally,' writes Greene, 'if they do only what is expected of them (or because they feel they have no right to speak for themselves), if they do only what they are told to do, they are not living moral lives' (1978, p. 49). The policy passed by the Merrimack School Board has left many teachers I work with feeling inert, surveyed, and anxious. Educators speak of feeling dominated and powerless. The policy I describe above, while recently over-ruled due to the enormous labor organized by deeply committed and varied constituencies, has left long-lasting effects on many of the educators who teach in the schools of New Hampshire. Moreover, it has functioned to undermine the moral position Greene believes educators who are wide-awake must occupy. This can only be done, writes Greene,

> . . . if teachers can identify themselves as moral beings, concerned with defining their own life purposes in a way that arouses others to do the same. I believe, you see, that the young are most likely to be stirred to learn when they are challenged by teachers who themselves are learning, who are breaking with what they have too easily taken for granted, who are creating their own moral lives. (1978, p. 51)

Over the last two years, many of the teachers in my classes report that they feel prohibited from talking about death or suicide, despite the fact that New Hampshire has a disturbingly high suicide rate among our teens. Teachers report that they self-censor the material they read with their students for fear they will lose their jobs. Despite their familiarity with Justice Jackson's opinion from the Supreme Court holding that 'parental offense cannot be the barometer for educational decisions' (DeMitchell, 1994, p. 474), the educators in my classes continue to feel timid about the reading selections they choose for their students for fear they might be wrongly accused of inciting values and beliefs that are perceived to transgress the values held by school boards and parents.

For many educators, there is a profound gap between legal policy and the lives they lead in classrooms. I often hear teachers talking in hushed tones. They point out that when reading a rich, layered work of literature with their students such as *Shabanu: Daughter of the Wind* by Suzanne Fisher Staples (1989) or *The Giver* by Lois Lowry (1993), they feel compelled to treat it in the most 'neutral' of ways for fear they will be wrongly accused of promoting ideas that are 'immoral,' or 'evil,' — language I take from extended conversations with them during class discussions. It is not remarkable, given the political climate, that many teachers feel as if they must compose counterfeit identities that will function as armor, protecting them from the surveillance they have witnessed other teachers endure.

The move toward censorship, is a mark of our identity as a post-national entity, which Arjun Appadurai (1993) characterizes as a space marked, not only by its whiteness but 'too by its uneasy engagement with diasporic peoples, mobile technologies, and queer nationalities' (p. 412). If, as Gilles Deleuze and Felix Guattari (1991) argue, concepts need conceptual personae to bring to form their rhythmic characters, then I would like to assign to the concept of wide-awakeness the *persona* of trickster. The trickster introduces a condition for the exercise of thought that is distinct from stranger or outsider. The trickster is more inclined to insistently call things into question, demand why, ask for translations and ask that cultural and social practices be made accessible to students, educators and parents. By invoking this *persona*, I aim to short-circuit the categorical, normative order of things in the curriculum and to offer another perspective from which to view, as Greene urges us to do, the complexities of identity, difference, subjectivity and desire. The *persona* of the trickster has the potential to function as an alchemical figure in ways akin to the taste of salt. Writings on alchemical symbolization hold that whence salt is taken, the contents of our unconscious will come to the surface of consciousness: 'And that is the secret that we seek: all our secrets are contained in it' (Jung, 1955, p. 146). Salt, that sharp, lively element which can revive us, as smelling salts do, from a state of sleep, or which can help us to keep our wits about us when we have reservations about a person's position — we take what they say 'with a grain of salt.'

The dramaturgy of the German director and playwright, Bertolt Brecht, is built on the assumption that the theatrical performance offers us a means through which to put the concept of wide-awakeness and shocks into motion. Embedded in the scholarship of Maxine Greene is a Brechtian sensibility that I hope to make evident in this chapter. While Schutz offers us insight into the contours of Greene's use of the attitude of wide-awakeness, Brecht offers us a repertoire of interpretive practices on which we can draw to perform these concepts in our own seminar rooms. The aesthetic attitude of Brecht is present in Greene's commitment to shaking conventional certainties, to dislodging taken-for-granted assumptions so that we can clear a path for renewed insights and understandings. The kind of looking that Greene calls for is akin to the kind of looking that Brecht demanded, not only of his ensemble, but of his audience as well. Brecht called for art that is accessible to public life. He argued that reality must be changed by art and that it is the theatre's obligation to show that unjust social relationships can be subject to change (Brecht, 1957).

In ways quite similar to John Dewey, Brecht's theatrical process is structured on a scientific model that includes a form of social inquiry which requires the participatory acts of critical and imaginative thinking, formulating hypotheses, the open exchange of ideas, and a commitment to social deliberation and intelligence. The form of art that Brecht was committed to provoked individuals to critically appraise their everyday actions in society and intended to move them to take initiatives that would have social and political implications. Brecht invested art with the capacity to provoke more inclusionary practices of social justice.

Brecht's theatre is perhaps best recognized for historicizing dramatic events and re-examining history from various perspectives while at the same time revealing the social and political forces at work in our lives. His narrative methods of 'epic theatre' are useful for moving away from realism towards a presentational style that is not only jarring and discontinuous, but functions to help the audience see the specific and changeable conditions shaping a character's situation as alterable. In his 'Short description of a new technique of acting which produces an alienation effect,' Brecht writes:

> The actor must play the incidents as historical ones. Historical incidents are unique, transitory incidents associated with particular periods. The conduct of the persons involved in them is not fixed and 'universally human'; it includes elements that have been or may be overtaken by the course of history, and is subject to criticism from the immediately following period's point of view. (1957, p. 140)

Greene's 1977 essay, 'Towards wide-awakeness: An argument for the arts and humanities in education,' incorporates a call for such historization in her exploration of critical awareness and moral agency. In ways akin to Brecht, Greene argues that an artist is always an artist-in-society:

> . . . what he or she is presenting is presented against the social meaning system of the group to which he or she belongs. Moreover, many of the meanings in the individual's existential reality (perhaps most of them) have had a social origin. . . . Art can work to stimulate questions about the social world, with its lacks, its deficiencies, its possibilities. As individuals experience the work through and by means of their

own lived worlds, the realities they discover may well provide new vantage points on the intersubjective world, the world they share with others; the enrichment of the 'I' may become an overcoming of silence and a quest for tomorrow for what is not yet. (1978, p. 181)

Works of art can stimulate questions about the taken-for-granted assumptions and principles that govern our lives, and in so doing, art can shift our perceptions of self and society, if we are prepared to have the order of our lives re-arranged. Throughout Greene's writings on wide-awakeness, she emphasizes the potential that viewing an art object has to stimulate questions about the social world, or the possibilities that reading and discussing a literary text has for offering new vantage points on the intersubjective world. To what extent, however, do Greene's writings on wide-awakeness emphasize the *making* of art?

Greene's scholarship on wide-awakeness reminds me of the distinction that Elaine Scarry makes between *making up* and *making real*. For Scarry, 'making' involves two distinctly different stages. In the first instance, *making up*, a person may create an object that is a projection of the human body and its desires, capacities and spirit. This creation, however, occurs in the realm of the imagination. What is imagined has not yet been given shape, form or substantiation in the physical world. When what has been imagined has been made real, it takes on a vibrant presence through the use of form, rhythm, craft and attention. While Greene emphasizes the realm of the imagination, that is making in the first instance, she does not turn to those acts of making which take up a full-bodied, substantiated presence in the curriculum.

Brecht's dramaturgy can function to extend Greene's pedagogical framework to include a studio component that requires each of us to make things that move from the realm of the imaginary to the realm of the physical world. Like Scarry, I use the term '*make*' to invoke action in a physical playing space, a public space, akin to a *piazza*, a polis, a court system, a classroom. Like the trial audience — the jury — I struggle to engage students not only in mental exercises or counterfactual wishes, but to make real what the audience of a play can ordinarily only make up (Scarry, 1985, p. 298). Brecht's dramaturgy contains a repertoire of conventions that require, for example, that a story be told and retold and retold from myriad vantage points, because 'only by entering it countless times and from countless directions,' writes Scarry, 'does the jury learn what it must learn: was someone hurt (but this is not all), was there a defective product (but this is not all), most important for the legal question that must be answered, given the first two, is it the case that the second is the proximate cause of the first; did the two meet on "the path of the accident," did the two meet at "the crossroads of the catastrophe?"' (1985, p. 298).

For Brecht, the making of and participating in art has the potential to alter our sense of identity, our sense of longing and belonging. Brecht's theatre resonates with the work of Albert Camus, who believed that there is, 'in the work of art, an emancipatory force . . . which unites, whereas tyranny separates' (1960, p. 269). Brecht's theory of performance is a response to tyranny and to the social forces that undermine a sense of wide-awakeness and shocks. Drawing on conventions that distanced the audience from the performance, rather than seducing them into a sentimental state of over-identification, Brecht used, for example, non-naturalistic acting, separation of sound from image, self-conscious staging of scenes, quotations from diverse sources and frequent interruptions by voice-overs or inserts, to awaken in his audience a curiosity, a thirst for knowledge, a sense of happiness, capriciousness, anger and enjoyment in response to contemporary social and political issues. Brecht intended to show that we do possess the capacity to make change, to alter our social circumstances, and to engender historical possibilities for he believed that we are the actors, and hence, the progenitors of social norms, practices, beliefs and principles.

The intention of the Brechtian actor is to engage the audience in watching the actors' characters come to a new or fuller understanding — to utter or signify through gesture, new or unspeakable truths. As the audience watches the actor experience the shock of recognition, they become united with the actors — they are simultaneously moved to take, what Brecht referred to as 'the new world action' (1957, p. 149). In Brecht's theatre, the actor's self-observation and self-critique disrupts the audience from completely losing themselves in the character, as we might do when watching Dustin Hoffman in *Rainman*, or Meryl Streep in *Sophie's Choice*. A Brechtian actor engages the audience in acts of observation and critique, attitudes that promote wide-awakeness and shocks of recognition.

To illustrate the signatures of wide-awakeness, I render a series of scenes which portray my students and me reading *Krik? Krak!*, a collection of short-stories written by the Haitian-American writer, Edwidge Danticat (1991). In this collection, Danticat uses lyric language to usher her readers into a history that is rarely discussed in the social studies or English curriculum: the massacre of Haitian women at the hands of Dios Trujillos' soldiers in 1937 along the Dominican border, the terrorism of the Tonton Macoutes, and the linkage of generations of women through a tradition of storytelling. Danticat uses geographic locations, historical inheritances and family lineage to join together many women who stand apart in time, but who share the consequences of unspeakable historical circumstances. Her written portraitures are testimony to the way the 'nine-hundred and ninety-nine women who boiled in her [my mother's] blood lived and died and lived again.' 'The spirit of these women,' writes Danticat, 'lives in my blood' (1991, p. 224).

Although writing is seen by many of the women in her family as a grave transgression, an act of insolence, something 'as forbidden as dark rouge on the cheeks or a first date before eighteen,' writing becomes both a way to engage in active self-transformation and a rite of passage through which the women Danticat writes about move from being objects of history to being subjects within moving historical fields. If identities concern the way we position ourselves in the narratives of the past, then Danticat uses writing to contest the narratives produced by colonialists who aligned themselves with Dios Trujillos, if not explicitly, then through their silence and their refusal to know. Danticat re-writes the history for the women she is tied to and in so doing, she refuses to be treated as an object; she refuses to be reduced to simple historical terms (Greene, 1978, p. 169). Read through the eyes of Maxine Greene, we might say that Danticat uses writing to take on the role of a rebel, for Danticat is not only concerned with refusals — the refusal to be silent about horrific historical events, the refusal to forsake her identity as a Haitian woman — but she is concerned with recreations, as evidenced in her literary works of art. Danticat performs as a rebel with the intent to re-compose a history that endows her ancestors with a vivid, historical presence.

A Portrait of the Social Landscape on Which We Read

I began to read Danticat's work with my students in October of 1995. The students in this class, all women, were teachers working towards a masters degree in reading or in education or are fifth-year interns in elementary and high school classrooms throughout southern New Hampshire. The ethnic and socio-economic mix in this course, *Foundations of Reading Instruction*, is composed of a population of women that is similar to the population described in the writing and research of Susan Florio-Ruane (1994) and Cazden and Mehan (1989), a population that demographics show largely constitute the teaching profession. In 1989, Cazden and Mehan wrote:

> The typical beginning teacher in the 1990s will be female, in the early to mid-twenties, Anglo, and from a lower middle income to a middle income family. It is important to realize that these will be the characteristics of beginning teachers because they will not match those of the pupils. Their students, especially if they are as is increasingly the case assigned to an urban inner city school will be from linguistic minority backgrounds and lower income families. This means that teachers and their students will not share cultural and social experiences. (1989, p. 47)

The women who participated in this course are from working-class and middle-class backgrounds. Seven of the women are the first in their families to attend college, one woman was Italian-American, and two were Franco-American.

The composition of the students in this course represents the demographics throughout this predominantly white campus at the University of New Hampshire. Out of a student population of 12,500 students at this university (including both undergraduate and graduate students), there are 183 persons identified as Asian-American; 117 persons identified as Hispanic; 90 persons identified as African-American; and 12 students identified as Native American. The presence of students from diverse ethnic backgrounds in the education department in which I teach is limited to four African-Americans, two Asian-Americans and one Indian student from South Africa, all out of a group of 405 masters students in education. Pearl Rosenberg has characterized the figurative presence of race and racism at predominantly white universities where there is a virtual absence of people from diverse ethnic backgrounds as the *presence of an absence* (Rosenberg, 1996).

I intentionally select readings for this course, *Foundations of Reading Instruction*, that will engage students in developing a strong philosophical foundation on which they can articulate the educative value of the material they choose to read with their own students. This is an especially important focus to take given the political climate in the state of New Hampshire, a climate that is becoming more and more inclined toward the covert and overt censorship of reading material, as I stated earlier.

Given these social conditions, I suspected early on that one danger I would face in reading *Krik? Krak!* with the women in my class was that it was far too jarring and hence would be far too easy to dismiss because it so profoundly challenged the narrow field of vision and emotion that marks the social landscapes on which we teach. When asked how she experienced reading *Krik? Krak!* in the solitude of her home, Wendy, one of the women in this class, wrote:

> I had a very difficult time reading this book in private. I could not even finish reading the first short story alone . . . When I did not have anyone to share the book with I found myself reading quickly. I wanted to get away from the pain as quickly as possible. I think one of the reasons I did not understand what I had actually read when I finished the book the first time is that I did not allow myself to get close to it. I kept my distance so that I would not have to feel the pain or admit that such terrible things actually happened.

Like Wendy, I learned that this work could not be read silently. When I began to read *Krik? Krak!* during the summer of 1995, I too found myself reading the stories aloud. I began to talk about this book with family and friends and found myself spending time in the periodical section of the library tracking down the portrayal of the 1937 massacres in the United States newspapers. I wanted to match the testimony of Danticat to the accounts of political officials as represented in North American newspapers. For example, on 6 November 1937, *The New York Times* reported, the 'wholesale killings of Haitian emigrants to the Dominican Republic.' The *Times* goes on to report that 'although fragmentary reports of these killings have been filtering into the State Department for some time, official cognizance of these killings was taken only today.' The current reports of these incidents were based on stories from what the *Times* refers to as '*alleged* survivors' (my emphasis) who have reached Santiago de Cuba and on letters received by relatives in the Western part of Haiti. One document I found particularly disturbing includes a letter printed in the *New York Times* that was written by Andres Pastoriza, the Dominican Minister. It reads as follows:

> **November 6, 1937:** I have been authorized by my government to make the following statement: The Dominican government has not mobilized troops nor has had any reason to do so because the incident at the border is considered as closed with the exception of the investigation which is customary in incidents of such a nature where guilt is presumed in order to establish responsibilities and to determine judicial sanction against guilty parties. This incident is not of a different nature from many which have occurred since the year 1844 between Dominican and Haitian farmers, and the number of victims which is claimed is absolutely ridiculous.

Pastoriza's letter casts the massacre as an unremarkable 'incident.' He holds the testimony of survivors under suspicion and goes on to refer to the 'alleged' victims as 'squatters who for many years have been in the habit of taking up unauthorized land in the border territory.' Cast as squatters, the victims of the massacre are officially stripped of any national, local or familial identity. The official questioning of Haitian testimony signifies a pervasive cultural practice of casting as deviant or questionable the testimony of persons who challenge official power regimes and practices. Edwidge Danticat undermines these official reports by rendering portraits of the women in her life as full-bodied, complex persons who not only fear, but resist authority and comfort one another in the face of the unspeakable destructiveness that Pastoriza deems 'ridiculous.' In the following passage, Danticat joins Greene's ensemble of rebellious figures by drawing on the words passed down through persons who survived the blood shed in the Massacre River, the very river that binds the women of *Krik? Krak!* together.

> 'Sister, I do not want to be the one to tell you,' she said, 'but your mother is dead. If she is not dead now, then she will be when we get to Port-au-Prince. Her blood calls to me from the ground. Will you go with me to see her? Let us go to see her.' . . . 'She will be ready for burning this afternoon.'
> My blood froze inside me. I lowered my head as the news sank in . . .
> 'Sister,' she said, 'life is never lost, another one always comes up to replace the last.'
> 'Why did you not ask your mother, Jacqueline, if she knew how to fly?'
> Then the story came back to me as my mother had often told it. On that day so long ago, in the year nineteen hundred and thirty-seven, in the Massacre River, my mother did fly. Weighted down by my body inside hers, she leaped from Dominican soil into the water, and out again on the Haitian side of the river. She glowed red when she came out, blood clinging to her skin, which at that moment looked as though it were in flames.

> . . . No matter how much distance death had tried to put between us, my mother would often come to visit me. Sometimes in the short sighs and whispers of some-body else's voice. Sometimes in somebody else's face. Other times in brief moments in my dreams.
>
> 'There is that old Marie,' my mother would say. 'She is now the last one of us left.' Mama had introduced me to them, because they had all died before I was born. There was my great grandmother Eveline who was killed by Dominican soldiers at the Massacre River . . . and . . . my grandmother Defile who died with a bald head in a prison, because God had given her wings. (Danticat, 1991, p. 49)

As I read and studied the historical landscape of this book by taking cues from the text and moving to documentation in old newspapers, I began to collect a series of questions: Who is Dios Trujillo? Were the Dominican census reports of 1936–37 falsified in order to deny the mass slaughter of Haitians? If so, how was this accomplished and under whose direction? What role did Roosevelt play in mediating plans to settle the unrest between the Dominican Republic and Haiti? And, as I turned back to Danticat's stories, I fell silent in the face of accounts of women and men raped by soldiers, and the weekly journeys to prison to visit mothers who had been arrested for being accused of 'having wings of flames' (Danticat, 1991, p. 35). Like Aristide, Danticat uses stories to, in the words of Djo, 'make things happen, to make the way of the world change' (Temple, 1992, p. 7). Danticat writes:

> My mother had grown even thinner since the last time I had seen her. Her face looked like the gray of a late evening sky. These days, her skin barely clung to her bones, falling in layers, flaps, on her face and neck. The prison guards watched her more closely because they thought that the wrinkles resulted from her taking off her skin at night and then putting it back on in a hurry before sunrise. This was why Manman's sentence had been extended to life. And when she died, her remains were to be burnt in the prison yard, to prevent her spirit from wandering into any young innocent bodies. (1991, p. 36)

The act of reading *Krik? Krak!* made me feel as if I was walking along the streets of a foreign city where my customs of reading held little significance. I was thrust into a state of ignorance for I knew virtually nothing of Haitian history or the United States' relationship to Haiti. Carol, one of the participants in this class, writes the following entry in her process notes:

> I began reading *Krik? Krak!* over lunch one day and literally could not stomach the suffering and despair. I am impressed by the emotion that simple objects signify in Danticat's stories and how we as women or interpreters of the text began to react. We placed great value in a baby's bib, a quilt or a passport . . . It frightens me to think that in Haiti women and writers are killed. Perhaps there was a compulsion for Danticat's tales to be told as she is the voice of 'a thousand women before.' She speaks for them via 'the blunt tip of her pencil.'

While in the midst of preparing to read this book with my students, I found myself thinking against the thought of the interpretive frameworks that I used to read literature. Danticat's work reminded me of what the writer, Jeanette Winterson, says about looking at paintings. 'Long looking at paintings,' writes Winterson, 'is equivalent to being dropped into a foreign city, where gradually, out of desire and despair, a few key words, then a little syntax make a clearing in the silence. Art, all art, not just painting, is a foreign city, and we deceive ourselves when we think it familiar. . . . We have to recognize that the language of art, all art, is not our mother tongue' (1996, p. 4). Danticat's writing, itself a work of art, challenges the realities that we claim, and in so doing, it challenges the 'I' that we believe ourselves to be. This shift of perspectives on our sense of self is delicate and can often fade away if not given form and critically engaged. While reading a literary work of art such as Danticat's can potentially provoke a reader to confront her ignorances, it can also provide an occasion for the reader to slip into positions of sentimentality or feelings of empathy which allow the reader to efface the historical, social and economic distinctions among the people of Haiti and the United States, positions which undermine possibilities for using the curriculum as a site of intervention that inspires wide-awakeness and shock.

The forms of literary engagement I sought out are discussed by Toni Morrison in *Playing in the Dark*, a small book which has become one of Greene's sources of inspiration. Morrison is interested in 'transforming conceptions of knowledge from invasion and conquest to revelation and choice' (1992, p. xii). Morrison encourages us to study the social and historical forces that function to establish the parameters of how we read and interpret literature. Through critical exploration of these forces, Morrison believes that we might more fully understand the ways in which the literary imagination sabotages itself. How can we transform the aspects of interpretation that efface not only the ideologies, but the way race, socioeconomic class and sexuality shapes our reading lives? How can we bring the embedded assumptions of racial language and image to the surface of consciousness so that we can explore how these assumptions work in the literary enterprise? To what extent can the making of art enable us to more fully posit our readerly self as raced, particularly when, as white readers, we too often envision ourselves as unraced? (Morrison, 1992).

Reading *Krik? Krak!*, required that we locate and develop interpretive practices that lead us to new notions of literary praxis. This praxis includes writing *in*, rather than writing *off* or *over* the literary traditions and narratives of people who represent cultural practices, beliefs and longings that de-naturalize our own, and that remind us of the vital importance of re-inflecting the meaning of familiar texts with the shock of new questions, new modes of assessment and new critical configurations (see Donnell and Welsh, 1996).

Danticat's work infuses an unorthodox and diverse repertoire of literary forms into our use of literary praxis. Her recursive, fluid narrative structure, filled with diary entries, fictionalized letter-writing, autobiographical and poetic fragments, montage and oraliterary characteristics, suggests a more flexible concept of 'literature' and hence, modifies our conscious definitions of the 'literary.' Greene argues that an attitude of wide-awakeness can begin to emerge if we develop the desire and the stamina to radically modify our consciousness, that is, to modify what we consciously pay attention to. This requires, writes Greene,

> a 'leap' as Kierkegaard calls it, which manifests itself in the subjective experience of a shock. The shock, he explained 'is nothing else than a radical modification in the tension of our consciousness, founded in a different attention *a la vie*. These shocks, these shifts in attention, make it possible to see from different standpoints; they stimulate the wide-awakeness so essential to critical awareness, most particularly when they involve a move to the imaginary — away from the mundane.' (quoted in 1978, p. 173)

The montage of images and characters rendered throughout Danticat's collection make it possible for the reader to see from different standpoints and to alter the readers' conceptions of literature. The proliferation of motifs of exile, return and longing are not literary abstractions, they are rooted in the lived realities of Danticat and the women she writes for/about. Her writing developed, in part, out of acts of negotiation and crossing between different cultures, movement from one urban center to another — Port-au-Prince to New York City — and hence it is an extension of an extraordinary intellectual and spatial flexibility (see Donnell and Welsh, 1996, p. 25). The shifting standpoints presented in this collection could be made evident to us if we could be faithful to the book, that is, if we read it rather than rushed through it, put it aside or slipped into empathy or states of sentimentality as I stated above. In preparing to read this book with my class, I also found myself focusing on locating ourselves within this text; I wanted us to use presentational rather than representational forms to posit the identity positions we take as we encounter 'difficult art.'

Presentational forms are more stylized than representational forms. While the representational art form invokes a feel for the 'real' — a real kitchen, park, classroom — presentational forms engage actors in multiple roles, use imaginary props, and continually call upon the audience to generate meaning from what is performed rather than simply sit back and take in the show.

Robert Donmoyer and June Yennie-Donmoyer (1995) liken presentational forms of theatre to the transactional theories of reading comprehension developed by Louise Rosenblatt (1978) and Frank Smith (1982). Drawing on the work of Coger and White (1982), they quote, 'The members of the audience supply a portion of the performance in that their imaginations must complete all the suggestions of characterizations, action, and setting,' (in Donmoyer and Yennie-Donmoyer, 1995, p. 406). Presentational forms of art not only require active, imaginative participation from the reader, but they ask the audience to mimetically alter the scenes in ways similar to a jury who sits before a judge and a team of lawyers. In some sense the audience as jury is empowered to reverse the findings, and this possibility makes room for a particular form of making and re-making of the plot structure of the text, intentions of characters and outcomes of the story.

With this in mind, I turned to the dramaturgy of Brecht, particularly his use of montage. Brecht's use of montage is useful for putting Maxine Greene's concept of wide-awakeness and shocks into motion. His method of composing montage is infused with an obligation to move beyond the sentimental feelings a work of art might generate. (A short-hand example might be a viewing of *Terms of Endearment,* or crying at an AT&T phone commercial. A less sentimental viewing, one moving toward Brecht's notion of montage, is the series of scenes in *Good Morning Viet Nam* in which Louie Armstrong sings 'It's A Wonderful World' against footage of invasions, marches and terrified children running in the streets of Saigon.) A Brechtian montage does not simply present us with images to critically appraise, rather, it functions to transform the ways in which we perceive the social world. A Brechtian montage does not resonate, it reverberates within the body of the spectator, and it is by virtue of its resonance that we have incorporated (literally taken into our bodies) the significance of the material images before us.

Gaston Bachelard's phenomenological doublet of resonance and reverberation is useful for talking about the educative value inherent in Brecht's dramaturgy. 'The resonances of a work of art,' writes Bachelard,

> are dispersed on the different planes of our life in the world, while the repercussions invite us to give greater depth to our own existence. In the resonance, we hear the poem, in the reverberations we speak it, it is our own. . . . It is as though the poem, through its exuberance, awakened new depths in us. (1958, p. 56)

The images that reverberate are those that we incorporate into our consciousness, into our bodies, and in so doing, these images transform our perspectives and our very sense of where we stand in relation to others. The reverberating image can open up in each one of us the imaginative capability of perceiving history — that is the events that have happened to others — in our own bodies. As a form of literary response to *Krik? Krak!*, montage offered us a means through which to make the 'literary whiteness' that accompanied our readings, so that we could begin to study the epistemic and political influence it had on our interpretations.

Montage offers a way into literature that potentially generates a sense of wide-awakeness by moving the reader beyond words, to images, metaphors, tropes, and icons that broaden their field of emotions. It is in the ever-widening field of emotion that I believe we can learn to exceed the limits of our thought and to move out of ignorance. By locating an image and then identifying the cultural conversations lodged within the image, students begin to make strange what was once familiar, or what they thought they once understood. What degrees of shock might we provoke and what degrees of insight might we gain, if we use montage as a poetic device to interpret the disorderly images in literature?

'New York Day Woman'

During the second week of our discussion of *Krik? Krak!* I asked students to choose from among three different theatrical conventions to interpret this work. The group I will discuss chose to focus on one of Danticat's stories entitled 'New York Day Woman.' 'New York Day Woman' is, like other selections in this collection, a play within a play, a smaller story nested within a larger story of the women of Haiti. The reader of 'New York Day Woman' observes an older Haitian woman walking the streets of New York City through the eyes of her Americanized daughter.

> Today, walking down the street, I see my mother. She is strolling with a happy gait, her body thrust toward the DON'T WALK sign and the yellow taxicabs that make forty-five degree turns on the corner of Madison and Fifty-Seventh street. . . . I follow my mother, mesmerized by the many possibilities of her journey . . . Even in a flowered dress, she is lost in a sea of pinstripes and gray suits, high heels and elegant short skirts, Reebok sneakers, dashing from building to building. My mother, who won't go out to dinner with anyone.
>
> **If they want to eat with me, let them come to my house, even if I boil water and give it to them.**
>
> She stops by another vendor selling sundresses for seven dollars each. I can tell that she is looking for an African print dress, contemplating my size. I think to myself, please ma, don't buy it. It would just be another thing that I would bury in the garage or give to Goodwill.
>
> **Why should we give to Goodwill when there are so many people back home who need clothes? We save our clothes for the relatives in Haiti.**

Time and space is marked by the mother's rounds of meetings and partings such as buying a hot dog from a local vendor, looking after a young child while his mother goes for a run, and much to the daughter's surprise, looking into the windows of Chanel and Tiffany's.

The following excerpt from Wendy's process notes documents the group's initial intentions to begin juxtaposing American images of New York City against images of Haiti. In a sense, we might say that the group's initial intention was to compare the two worlds by placing them side by side.

> We began our work by selecting a passage. After discussing the images from several of the short stories in *Krik? Krak!*, we settled upon 'New York Day Woman.' We felt this selection contained many striking visual images that could be used to challenge common stereotypes. Since the action in this story takes place on the streets of New York City we wondered how these 'American' images could be challenged by corresponding Haitian images. At the end of the first meeting, we decided to each pick out the images that we personally found the most compelling and bring them into class the following week.

The women in this group felt that by juxtaposing images of Haiti against images of New York City, they could 'instigate/initiate thoughts about how different life in Haiti and America is.' 'Our group's goal,' writes Wendy, 'is to get people thinking about the importance of point of view as well as the impact history has on the way each of us views the world we live in.'

Before Wendy and the four women in her group could even begin to identify and then represent the images in 'New York Day Woman,' they had to negotiate a communal reading of this book, a reading which relies on understanding the epistemic weight in one another's words as well as the epistemic weight carried by the text. Text, talk and image also functioned as signs to mediate an understanding of the political struggles through which this collection of stories was produced as well as the artistry that was used to create it. Throughout this group's initial discussions, properties of what M.M. Bakhtin (1981) refers to as the dialogic function emerge, a function that can promote the qualities of critical awareness and engagement that Greene believes to be contingent upon states of wide-awakeness. The dialogic imperative insures that our words are inflected with previous meanings, intentions, desires, all of which presumes the pre-existence of a language world, replete with competing norms and meanings (Bakhtin, 1981, p. 426). In the context of textual interpretation, our perspectives, insights and appraisals undergo 'dialogization,' when they become de-privileged, and, as readers, we become more aware of competing definitions, rather than fixing on an authoritative or absolute 'truth.' The dialogic function opens up systems of meaning and, in turn, it creates possibilities for readers to posit the racial language and perspectives that accompany them to their readings, but are too often cast as 'natural' or 'given.'

Krik? Krak! is itself a semiotic space in which multiple voices interact, contradict one another, talk over and through one another and vie for understanding. The utterances in text and social talk are not fixed or bound utterances; they do not demand unconditional allegiance, nor do they forbid playing at the borders of sign systems. The dynamic process of this semiotic space, as well as the dialogue that unfolds among the women in this group as they strive to move out of ignorance toward understanding, produces a continual stream of new interpretations of this material. Greene might describe this approach to interpretation as a perspectival reading, a form of literary praxis that she identifies with Bakhtin's concepts of dialogism and heteroglossia. To confront multiple voices and discourses in a novel, writes Greene, 'is to enlarge one's experience with a multiplicity of perspectives and, at once, with the spheres that can open in the midst of pluralities' (1988, p. 29).

The act of composing a montage for this text becomes a medium through which the readers' voices — expressed through the gesture, intonation and shifting movements of their bodies — can interact. I do not use the convention of montage to make an unalterable, univocal demand upon the participants in this group. The students in this class use social language to explore how they will compose their montage, and in so doing, they make of social language a medium through which to link the literary and actual worlds and awaken new insights. As teachers begin to incorporate images into their discussions, however, they move beyond the discursive borders of speech into the territory of the image, where meaning is composed in distinctly different ways.

Montage demands that participants play at double-dipping: an image against a word, jarring captions, mingling expose with poetry and literary prose. This mixing and mingling of genres and sign systems is used to engender a proliferation of questions and critiques, both of which potentially create the experience of 'shocks,' that state in which the reader breaks through the limits of one province of meaning to another. This shift brings about a breach of our emotional and intellectual horizons (Greene, 1978, p. 101). Greene identifies particular moments in modern history as moments of 'shock.' She cites, for example, the 1968 Democratic Convention, the Kent State and Jackson State killings, the disclosure of the murders at My Lai, or the so-called 'Saturday night massacre' during the Nixon days. Greene warns us, however, that the aftermath of these tragic events brought about cynicism and a desperate 'reaching out for positive images.' There was, writes Greene, a failure to problematize, little effort to intervene or comprehend linkages (1978, p. 102). Greene implies that shock is miseducative if it fails to be accompanied by an awareness of our historical existence, our biography, our local situations *and* a desire to intervene in these realities. In the context of our work together, curriculum became one site of intervention, one site where my students and myself could begin to intervene in the lost presence of Haiti in our curriculum.

I would like to go back for a moment and consider what happened after the students' first round of collecting images in preparation for their final montage. As it turns out, after planning to bring in a range of material, the women in Wendy's group came to class the following week with a collection of North American images. Not one of them brought in images that in any way represented Haitian life. Wendy writes:

> When we met the next week, we looked at the images that we had gathered and realized that most of them were American images. This was not surprising considering the story was being told from the point of view of a Haitian girl who had been raised in America. The reader of 'New York Day Woman' views the Haitian mother through the eyes of her Americanized daughter. As we began to examine these images we began to talk about how point-of-view profoundly affects the images in the reader's mind. For instance, we admitted that as North American women, we were unconsciously drawn to imagining the mother and daughter as Caucasians. All of the visual description seemed common-place to us because it is so American. We began to question whether the mother saw the city in the same way her daughter did and also whether our images differed from the images of the daughter. Eventually our group began to play with the idea of challenging the American images with the Haitian memories of the mother. Would busy New York streets remind the mother of crowded Haitian dirt roads? Would a woman jogging through Central Park remind the mother of the countless number of women she knew who ran away from life-threatening massacres? Our group decided that we would focus the viewers' attention on what an important role point-of-view plays in the reading/writing of a story by collecting American images and Haitian images to display to the class. The

American images will be accompanied by American music (Bruce Springsteen) as well as a re-written script of 'New York Day Woman' presented from the point-of-view of an American, Caucasian daughter. The Haitian images will be accompanied by Haitian music and also a re-written script presented from the point-of-view of the Haitian mother as she walks through the streets of NYC and remembers another life in Haiti. We still have a lot of fine tuning to do. This week we are focusing on collecting the images. Next week we will try to decide how we want to approach the re-writing of the script.

Here Wendy and her colleagues concretize the images that accompanied them during their 'private' readings of *Kirk? Krak!* Wendy writes, 'When we looked at the images, we realized they were mostly North American images.' They conclude that this was not surprising for two reasons. One, the story was told from the point of view of a Haitian girl who had been raised in North America and two, they were 'unconsciously drawn to imagining both the mother and daughter as Caucasians. 'All of the visual images,' writes Wendy, 'seemed commonplace to us because they were North American.'

During the composing process of their montage, the women in this group continually re-work and question the meanings lodged in their literary interpretations. By exploring representations and perspectives and keeping alternatives within the text alive, there is more potential that they will question the images that accompany them to their readings. The women place on the table, for critical appraisal, the prejudices, ignorances and beliefs that impinge on their readings and interpretations. The hermeneutic task involves a process of learning to interpret ourselves as readers as well as to interpret authors as writers. The poetic framework of montage offers readers opportunities to learn to understand themselves as culturally situated readers. This experiment does not privilege the text or the reader, rather it establishes active communication links among author, readers and the larger matrix of culture by engendering dialogue among these varied constituencies.

What provoked the women in this group to critically analyze the images they collected to represent their readings? Why might they shift their point of view as readers and decide to take on the *persona* of the Haitian mother rather than sustaining the identifications they had as North American Caucasian women or sustaining their identification with the Haitian-American daughter?

As the women in this group begin to re-read the story from the mother's point-of-view, a point-of-view that is distinctly different from their own, they enter into what the anthropologist and director, Richard Schechtner (1985), refers to as *performative consciousness*. Performative consciousness asks that students 'imagine if' they were to take on another person's identity. This transformation of consciousness, however, is only partial, for the students are both themselves and not-themselves all at once. In Brecht's theatre, 'there is no illusion that the player is identical with the character and the performance with actual event' (Brecht, 1957, p. 195). The actor sustains multiple identities; they coexist in an unresolved dialectical tension. 'The beauty of performative consciousness,' writes Schechtner, 'is that it activates alternatives — this and that are both operative simultaneously' (Schechtner, 1985, p. 6). Performative consciousness functions to interrupt the potential for sentimentalizing or over-identifying with Others, in part because it demands active, critical commentary on the power relationships which the actor has to the character s/he portrays. Moreover, this performance operates in the subjunctive tense, an indeterminate space that is infused with possibility.

Because montage, as a form of composition, is knotted together, it prohibits the kind of flow and ease of interpretation of which Maxine Greene is so wary. Like Brecht,

Greene calls for an attitude of continually turning back and checking points, in much the same way the women in Wendy's group critically read the collection of images they initially brought in. Greene argues, not only for attending, but a 'reflective turning back to the stream of consciousness — the stream that contains our perceptions, our reflections, yes, and our ideas' (1978, p. 182). The act of continually turning back and checking points must happen in moments of stasis and crystallized habits, and this form of reflection, argues Greene, may make 'possible a pluralism of visions, a multiplicity of realities' (1978, p. 182).

Montage is composed of contradictory images, consequently the group could not be content to represent just one point of view or one perspective. 'We cannot invite the audience to fling itself into the story as if it were a river,' writes Brecht, 'The individual episodes have to be knotted together in such a way that the knots are easily noticed. The episodes must not succeed one another indistinguishably but must challenge us to interpose our judgment (1957, p. 201). The act of interposing their judgment of the initial images they would work with cleared the way for them to create a montage that would reverberate rather than simply resonate for the other members of the class. Moreover, because montage demands a continual and critical appraisal of the work at hand, students are less likely to engage in what Susan David Bernstein refers to as a 'promiscuous identification,' (1992) that is an easy slip into thinking, for example, that because I am a woman, I 'share' an easy or natural affinity with the women in Danticat's novel.

The longer the students worked with images from 'New York Day Woman,' the more focused they became on linking the images in the text to the images in their lives; they knotted together the localized images of Haiti and New York into the disturbing images within Danticat's writing. The final montage consisted of juxtapositions of Miami condos overlooking the ocean with shanty towns in Port-au-Prince and artifacts from Voodoo and Catholic rituals. The montage of images were rendered as inseparable from one another, ever contingent upon one another, but at the same time retaining their distinctive characteristics and histories. As the women in this group engaged in intelligent deliberation on the relationship among the images in this book, they became more aware of the multiplicity of possible perspectives they could pursue. Perhaps most importantly, their positions as white readers and the impulses they had to project their whiteness onto the literary figures in this text became evident and opened up points of contact among their group, the characters in the text as well as the classroom audience. These points of contact contribute to creating a literary praxis that treats literature and interpretation as art forms which, writes Greene, can only be brought to significant life when human beings engage with them imaginatively and deliberately, for one cannot make art unless one deliberates and imagines.

In closing, I asked the students to discuss and write responses to the following questions:

1 Based on your readings, discussion and ensemble work, what role does theatre play in the reading classroom? What insight did you gain into *Krik? Krak!* via performance that you do not believe you would have gained strictly through class discussion?
2 As you listened to others in our class describe their responses to this book, what insights or ideas have you gained?
3 What is this text asking of you?
4 How has your world changed upon your reading of this novel?
5 How did you experience the reading of this text in private?
6 How has your public life been affected by this private reading?

In responding to how her public life has been changed by this private reading, Wendy writes:

> I don't think that my public life has been affected very much . . . from my private reading. I did not take a lot from my private reading because it was too difficult to do it alone. My public life has been affected from the discussions I've had with others about the book and by the presentations in class. If I had stopped my experience with *Krik? Krak!* after my private reading, . . . the book would have been left closed upon a shelf and very little of positive value would have resulted from my reading. I don't think that I would now walk by women on the street and think about their histories and the struggles they face living today.
>
> I'm so glad I had the experience with others.
>
> This novel demands that I think about the lives of so many women who I do not have any daily contact with . . . I cannot leave this book on my bookshelf. I have to share it with others. This book was not meant to sit anywhere with its pages untouched. My first reaction is to pass this book on — to give it as a gift, lend it to a friend, teach it in my classroom. I can do this alone. As others read it, however, I can join in with them to question how to improve the conditions in Haiti.

Laura writes:

> This novel asks me to be more involved with the events in Haiti and other struggling countries. It opened my mind again to another world.

These responses capture some of the first moments of an attitude of wide-awakeness felt the women in this class. A number of the women believed that if they were asked to read this book alone, they would have left it on the shelf. 'It was far too difficult, far too painful,' writes Wendy. Performance functioned to interrupt the repetitions of normalcy that too often infuse pedagogy — repetitious talk, reading for plot and critical analysis rooted in traditions of the New Criticism. In the context of reading *Krik? Krak!* an attitude of wide-awakeness was made possible through theatrical conventions which offers techniques to make sense of and remark upon what we may be inclined to dismiss or cannot bear to know.

Concluding Thoughts

The attitude of wide-awakeness is neither morally nor politically neutral. Rather, it is rooted in an understanding of democracy that grew out of the progressive movement and is associated not only with John Dewey (1916, 1927), but with figures such as Charles Taylor (1985), Hannah Arendt (1958), and Jurgen Habermas (1971). For each of these thinkers, both freedom of mind and freedom of action develop through membership and participation in a community one values. A person develops a strong sense of self through participatory acts, that is, through the *projects* they take up in the world. Like the taste of salt, an attitude of wide-awakeness, can renew a person's sensibilities, widen their horizons and desires and enable them to, in the words of Djo, '. . . ponder on the question of what makes freedom' (Temple, 1992, p. 45) and 'understand things you didn't before' (p. 27).

In my estimation, Greene believes that social action and intervention are crucial to attaining and sustaining an attitude of wide-awakeness. Although Greene does not explicitly call for the making of artistic performances, she does imply that without generative action and intervention, the attitude of wide-awakeness will dissipate (1978, p. 102). Pedagogy, like any performance event, is a collaboration in which participants are both part of the group and a part from it. As a collective, our class creates 'a piece' which, as rendered in this chapter, is a critical and imaginative commentary about each person's relation — political, psychic, emotional, geographical, economic, physical — to the animation of the novel, *Krik? Krak!*

As the women in this class literally took materials into their hands, conducted technical research, selected images, made slides, composed and sound-tracked the montage, they practiced art. By virtue of crafting a montage, the members of this ensemble became attentive to the voices of Others; they both considered and deliberated over the historical and social perspectives of persons who may contradict or defy their own social values. They also came face to face with the prejudices, limits in experience and beliefs that influenced their initial literary interpretations. And as they worked to refine their montage, the teachers featured in this chapter developed a desire and ability to explore Haitian history and literature. They did not do so in ways that treated this history and literature as a textual commodity billed as 'exotically different,' or that simply highlighted the marginality of Haitians in ways that positioned them as victims, thereby further marginalizing them. Rather, the students in this course used Brecht's dramaturgy as a form of social inquiry through which they could begin to 'ponder' as Greene writes, 'the images of courage, the images of survival,' all of which are rich in history, heritage, taste even prejudices and cannot be used to fix any one Haitian woman in a congealed or abstract identity category (Greene, 1993, pp. 191–3).

It is not a question of whether or not my students performed a great work of art, or whether or not they are artists (indeed, most of them are not and would never claim to be). The issue at hand is what they gained in composing this performance piece. And, what might they do next if they were to try and refine their montage? In what ways do the reflection and thinking required to craft the montage in light of the audiences' responses deepen not only the technical work of doing art but open up the opportunity to think again about the issues being represented? They might have gone on to explore the ways, for example, that their performance pieces captured and took seriously the lived experience of acting, thinking and writing in fragmented times. How does the insight we gained into how we read this novel fit into how we exercise our power as teachers? We might have further examined the anxieties that complicated our readings. Who are we as readers of this novel the second time around? Who are we to one another as we watch each other's performances? How do we account for our different responses to this novel? These are the types of questions that post-colonial scholars Alison Donnell and Sarah Lawson Welsh (1996) encourage us to ask if we hope to inflect our texts with the shock of new questions, new modes of assessment and new critical configurations.

Yes, the practicing of performance can accomplish a number of things, as I state above. One of the key accomplishments that I want to underscore here, however, is the way in which performance brings us face to face with limitations as well as possibilities. Like Susan Bordo (1993), I am cautious about the sometimes over-abundant use of the word 'possibility.' I worry that we may become intoxicated with the interpretive and creative possibilities inherent in cultural and literary analysis and forget about what is actually going on around us. What value is there in reading against the grain or challenging canonical texts when teachers feel surveyed by local, state or national policies and begin to survey themselves in their own classrooms? In what ways can we speak of possibility when so many educators work in the midst of severe budget cuts, sub-standard working conditions, destructive biases, and over-crowded classrooms?

When we use performance as a form of social practice, we confront both our own limits and our possibilities. We find limits in the form of economic resources, rhetorical or artistic skill, physical agility, failures of insight, intellectual and emotional depth, breadth and political experience. The making of a performance piece requires that we choose, for example, to work with this image and not that one, and in this act of choice, we exercise agency, intentionality and commitment. Throughout Greene's scholarship, she argues for an active intentional subject, however she does not lose sight of the mutual determination(s) of actors and structures. One can say about performance what Sartre said about the project: it is a 'moving unity of subjectivity and objectivity' (Sartre, 1968, p. 97).

As we choose this image over that one, we come to realize that what we know we see is not all that there really is. As we drive home after class, we think to ourselves, maybe the next time we'll do it better, include this piece of music, bring more insight to the readings, interweave this poem, or that newspaper clip. And in these musings and promises to ourselves, we hope for better, a hope bound to possibility. We are kept by hope, but not so seduced by it that we forsake the world around us.

Rather than seeing our limitations as inconsequential, pathological, or insignificant, or speaking of them in hushed tones, we might do well to direct our pedagogy to the limits of our thought and emotions, that is, to cast them as the place where inquiry begins to take hold and an attitude of wide-awakeness can flourish. Our limitations, our knowledge and our ignoraces mutually implicate each other. In this way, writes Deborah Britzman (1995), 'ignorance is analyzed as an effect of knowledge, indeed, as its limit, and not as an innocent state.' Britzman offers three pedagogical points of departure that I would like to reference here, as they offer a guide for using performance as a form of social inquiry: (1) the study of limits; (2) the study of ignorance; (3) the study of reading practices. Each of these points of departure require that we think against the thought of our conceptual foundations and develop the interest and capacity to study the anxieties that haunt our teaching and our learning and that we do so with compassion for one another (Britzman, 1995, p. 154). Perhaps then, through our limitations, knowledge and our ignorances we can also derive strength from our vulnerabilities.

Greene fully recognizes that while textual interpretations which go against the grain of canonical literary readings are powerful to the extent that they stimulate the intellect and imagination of the reader, social resistance and social transformation are, in themselves, performative. Greene herself states that *encounters* with the arts alone will not prepare people to take transformative initiatives. 'It is actually,' writes Greene,

> in the process of *effecting* transformations that the human self is created and re-created. Dewey, like the existentialist thinkers, did not believe that the self was ready-made or pre-existent; it was, he said, 'something in continuous formation through choice of action' (Dewey, 1916, p. 408). The richness, the complexity of the selves people create are functions of their commitment to projects of action they recognize as their own. As Sartre saw it, human beings create themselves by going beyond what exists, by trying to bring something into being. (1988, pp. 21–2, my emphasis)

As educators we must provide more than encounters with art; we must provide our students with opportunities to design projects of action that they identify with, projects that they will 'recognize as their own.' In this sense, the state of being wide-awake is made possible only in part by engaging art. To become wide-awake, one must *make* art in communal contexts recognizing the places in the curriculum where, to quote Morrison one last time, 'our imagination sabotages itself, locks its own gates, pollutes its vision.' Like the taste of salt, performance can create points of contact which cultivate attitudes of wide-awakeness in our classrooms. Through these points of contact, we hope, writes Greene, that we

> remain aware of the distinctive members of the plurality, appearing before one another with their own perspectives on the common, their own stories entering the culture's story, altering it as it moves through time . . . We want our students to achieve friendships among one another, as each one moves to a heightened sense of craft and wide awakeness, to a renewed consciousness of worth and possibility. (1993, pp. 194–5)

Acknowledgments

I would like to thank Donald Blumenfeld-Jones for his careful reading of earlier draft of this essay as well as the insights he gave me into the importance of *making* art. I am also deeply grateful to Barbara Houston for reading a preliminary version of this paper and offering me (as always) a series of substantive and generative responses. Additional thanks go to Bill Wansart and Bill Pinar for encouragement and generous critique.

Notes

1 This paper is dedicated to the memory of Frances Temple who, each day, made 'the strange liberty of creation possible' among her students and in her life as a writer and colleague.
2 For a provocative discussion about directing critical pedagogy toward ignorance, see Shoshana Felman (1982) 'Psychoanalysis and education: Teaching terminable and interminable,' in Barbara Johnson (ed.) *The Pedagogical Imperative: Teaching as a Literary Genre* (pp. 21–44), New Haven, CT: Yale University.
3 Before exploring the cultural concepts rendered in *Krik? Krak!*, concepts such as matrilineal heritage, intimacy and memory, the women in this class spent time reading and discussing 'The public curriculum of orderly images,' (1995) by Elizabeth Vallance. Vallance distinguishes between a curriculum of orderly and disorderly images, in part, by suggesting that the orderly image is often:

> designed to reach in some familiar, recognizable way. Also, very visible public structures such as public sculpture, billboards, and other elements of the built environment offer images that can remind us of what we think we know; that statue of a local hero, usually a soldier, in a city park is a common example. It doesn't challenge our assumptions at all. Its very purpose is to reinforce our shared image bank of what soldiering is like. The purpose of this kind of public image is usually distinctively narrative. It tells or reminds us of a story, or, in the case of billboards, makes a statement or suggests a story that we are able to be enticed to join. (Vallance, 1995, p. 6)

Vallance explores why the public resists what she refers to as 'difficult art.' Her work is especially useful for working with 'difficult literature' that possesses disorderly images which challenge our everyday perceptions and beliefs. She encourages educators to work with students to develop a capacity to interpret the disorderly images in art that challenge the social values and beliefs we take for granted and to 'propose new worlds, different from the one's we know' (Varnedfoe, 1992). These propositions often make us pay attention to the things we think we know intimately. There are, maintains Vallance, vital cultural conversations recorded in disorderly images (1995, p. 7).

4 In *The Body in Pain*, Scarry (1985) argues that the act of making cannot be conceived of without a consideration of ethics, justice and moral pressure (p. 281). 'As in an earlier century,' writes Elaine Scarry, 'the most searing questions of right and wrong were perceived to be bound up with questions of "truth," so in the coming time these same, still searing questions of right and wrong must be reperceived as centrally bound up with questions about "fictions"' (p. 280).

References

APPADURAI, A. (1993) 'Patriotism and its futures,' *Public Culture*, **5**, 3, pp. 411–30.

ARENDT, H. (1958) *The Human Condition*, Chicago: University of Chicago Press.

BACHELARD, G. (1958) *The Poetics of Space*, Boston: Beacon Press.

BAKHTIN, M.M. (1981) *The Dialogic Imagination* (ed. Michael Holquist), Austin: University of Texas Press.

BERNSTEIN, S.D. (1992) 'Confessing feminist theory: What's 'I' got to do with it?' *Hypatia*, **7**, 2, pp. 120–47.

BORDO, S. (1993) *Unbearable Weight: Feminism, Western Culture, and the Body*, Berkeley: University of California Press.

BRECHT, B. (1957) *Brecht on Theatre: The Development of an Aesthetic* (trans. John Willett), New York: Hill and Wang.

BRITZMAN, D. (1995) 'Is there a queer pedagogy: Or, stop reading straight,' *Educational Theory*, **45**, 2, pp. 151–65.

CAMUS, A. (1960) *Resistance, Rebellion, and Death*, New York: Vintage International.

CAZDEN, C.B. and MEHAN, H. (1989) 'Principles from sociology and anthropology: Context, code, and classroom,' in REYNOLDS, M. (ed.) *Knowledge Base for the Beginning Teacher* (pp. 47–57), Oxford: Pergamon.

COGER, L. and WHITE, M. (1982) *Reader's Theatre Handbook: A Dramatic Approach to Literature*, Glenview, IL: Scott Foresman.

DANTICAT, E. (1991) *Krik? Krak!* New York: SoHo.

DELEUZE, G. and GUATTARI, F. (1991) *What is Philosophy?* New York: Columbia University Press.

DeMITCHELL, T. (1994) 'Witches, cauldrons, and 'wicca' in the public school curriculum: Is government establishing a religion? The courts think not,' *International Journal of Educational Reform*, **3**, 4, October.

DEWEY, J. (1916) *Democracy and Education*, New York: Macmillan Col.

DEWEY, J. (1927) *The Public and Its Problems*, Athens, OH: Swallow Press.

DONNELL, A. and WELSH, S.L.W. (1996) (eds) *The Routledge Reader in Carribbean Literature*, New York: Routledge Press.

DONMOYER, R. and YENNIE-DONMOYER, J. (1995) 'Data as drama: Reflections on the use of readers theatre as a mode of qualitative data display,' *Qualitative Inquiry*, **1**, 4, December.

FELMAN, S. (1987) *Jacques Lacan and the Adventure of Insight: Psychoanalysis in Contemporary Culture*, Cambridge, MA: Harvard University Press.

FLORIO-RUANE, S. (1994) 'The future teachers' autobiography club: Preparing educators to support literacy learning in culturally diverse classrooms,' *English Education*, **4**.

GREENE, M. (1977) 'Toward Wide-awakeness,' *Teachers College Record*, **79**, 1, pp. 119–25.

GREENE, M. (1978) *Landscapes of Learning*, New York: Teachers College Press.

GREENE, M. (1988) *The Dialectic of Freedom*, New York: Teachers College Press.

GREENE, M. (1993) 'The passions of pluralism: Multiculturalism and the expanding community,' in PERRY, T. and FRASER, J.W. (eds) *Freedom's Plow*, New York: Routledge.

HABERMAS, J. (1971) *Knowledge and Human Interests*, Boston: Beacon Press.

JUNG, C. (1955) *Jung on Alchemy* (selected by Nathan Schwartz-Salant), Princeton: Princeton University Press.

LOWRY, L. (1993) *The Giver*, New York: Houghton Mifflin.

MORRISON, T. (1992) *Playing in the Dark: Whiteness and the Literary Imagination*, New York: Vintage Books.

ROSE, N. and MILLER, P. (1992) 'Political power beyond the state: Problematics of government,' *British Journal of Sociology*, **23**, 2, pp. 173–205.

ROSENBERG, P. (1996) 'The presence of an absence,' in FINE, M., WEIS, L., POWELL, L.C., and WONG, L.M. (eds) *Off White: Readings on Race, Power and Society*, New York: Routledge.

ROSENBLATT, L. (1978) *The Reader, The Text and The Poem: The Transactional Theory of Literary Work*, Carbondale, IL: Southern Illinois University Press.

SARTRE, J.-P. (1968) *Search for a Method* (trans. H.E. Barnes), New York: Vintage Books.

SCARRY, E. (1985) *The Body in Pain: The Making and Unmaking of the World*, New York: Oxford University Press.

SCHECHTNER, R. (1985) *Between Theatre and Anthropology*, Philadelphia: University of Pennsylvania Press.

SCHUTZ, A. (1967) *The Problem of Social Reality: Collected Papers I* (ed. Maurice Natanson), The Hague: Marinus Nijhoff, p. 213.

SMITH, F. (1982) *Understanding Reading*, New York: Holt, Rinehart and Winston.

STAPLES, F.S. (1989) *Shabanu: Daughter of the Wind*, New York: Random House.

TAYLOR, C. (1985) *Hegel and Modern Society*, Cambridge: Cambridge University Press.

TEMPLE, F. (1992) *Taste of Salt*, New York: Orchard Books.

VALLANCE, E. (1995) 'The public curriculum of orderly images,' *Educational Researcher*, **24**, 2, pp. 4–13.

VARNEDOE, K. (1992) Untitled commencement address given at Stanford University, Stanford, CA: Stanford University News Service, 14 June.

WALKER, A. (1982) *The Color Purple*, New York: Washington Square Press.

WINTERSON, J. (1996) *Art (Objects)*, New York: Alfred A. Knopf.

Section Three

Influences on Greene's Thought

11 Existential and Phenomenological Influences on Maxine Greene

Marla Morris

Maxine Greene draws upon a variety of existentialists and phenomenologists to inform her educational theory. Jean-Paul Sartre, Simone de Beauvoir, Albert Camus, Alfred Schutz, Soren Kierkegaard and Maurice Merleau-Ponty appear prominently throughout Greene's work. Of these, I am interested in examining how Jean-Paul Sartre, Alfred Schutz and Maurice Merleau-Ponty have influenced Greene's writings. Ultimately, I want to suggest that Greene moves beyond these philosophers by offering a phenomenology of the imagination. Greene's phenomenology of the imagination opens doorways to lived experience; it is through the imagination that educators may hope for better futures.

In an effort to understand Greene's appropriation of existential phenomenology it becomes important to deconstruct the term itself and provide a brief backdrop of the field. Existentialism and phenomenology grew up differently. But over time these two movements became bedfellows, for phenomenology offered existentialism a method. However, existentialism and phenomenology are strained bedfellows as there is little agreement as to who fits in which bed and what issues concern each. John Macquarrie suggests that 'most existentialists are phenomenologists, though there are many phenomenologists who are not existentialists' (1972, pp. 21–2). Conversely, Robert Olson (1962) claims that most existentialists are not phenomenologists. Robert Solomon (1980) says there are only three philosophers who can be considered existential phenomenologists: Martin Heidegger, Maurice Merleau-Ponty and Gabriel Marcel. To this list I would add Alfred Schutz, Jean-Paul Sartre and Maxine Greene. To make matters even more complex, some existentialists refused the label altogether. Albert Camus (1970) said, for instance, that he was not an existentialist; in fact, he talked of writing a public statement to declare that he and Sartre had nothing in common. When asked in an interview whether he was an existentialist or a phenomenologist, Sartre (1981) declared that he saw no difference between these labels. Certainly, this comment would have horrified Husserl (1970), who many consider the father of phenomenology, since he felt that existentialism was nothing more than irrationalism. Maxine Greene (1973) and others refute this charge and claim that existentialism is firmly grounded in reason.

As confused as these movements seem, I think they do point to different ways of doing philosophy. Therefore, before attempting to grapple with what existential phenomenology is, untangling phenomenology from existentialism might be a good first move.

Most agree that phenomenology is concerned with method (Macquarrie, 1972; Heidegger, 1962; Husserl, 1980a, 1980b, 1980c; Olson, 1962; Sartre, 1977; Merleau-Ponty, 1962). And since many phenomenologists draw on Edmund Husserl in some way, highlighting some major themes scattered throughout his writings may be useful. Husserl is best known for *Ideas*, *Cartesian Meditations* and *The Crisis of European Sciences and Transcendental Phenomenology*. A good starting place is understanding what Husserl means by the 'natural attitude.' According to David Carr (1970), the natural attitude refers to naive realism in *Ideas*. But it becomes clear in Husserl's later work, especially in *Crisis*, that the natural attitude is a particular way of encountering lived experience. It is 'that of straightforwardly living toward whatever objects are given, thus toward the world-horizon, in normal, unbroken constancy, in a synthetic coherence running through all acts' (Husserl, 1970, pp. 143–4). Husserl contends that one must get above the natural attitude, 'above the world' (1970, p. 152) in order to embrace a 'total transformation of attitude' (p. 148). The epoché or reduction can cause this shift. The phenomenological epoché, reduction, or abstention is a 'certain refraining from judgment' (Husserl, 1980c, p. 115). One can 'alter [the natural attitude] radically' (Husserl, 1980c, p. 112) through the phenomenological method of 'bracketing' or 'disconnecting' particular aspects of the life world. After bracketing aspects of the lifeworld, a 'transcendental experience' (Husserl, 1970, p. 153) enables one to see the essences of phenomena through intuition. The epoché allows one to see things, in other words, as they really are. Once I see things as they really are, no extraneous interpretations are necessary. In fact, Husserl stresses that 'phenomenological experience as reflection must avoid any interpretative constructions. Its descriptions must reflect accurately the concrete contents of experience, precisely as they are experienced' (1980b, p. 53).

Drawing on Brentano's notion of intentionality, Husserl suggests that when I experience phenomena I am thrusting toward something, I am always conscious of something. Consciousness is not an interior realm, for it pushes out toward the world. As against traditional empiricism, Husserl suggests that phenomena are not sense-data pressing in upon me from the outside. Solomon (1980) reminds us that for Husserl, phenomena are objects as they are experienced. That is, phenomena are not objects in themselves or experience in itself; phenomena are things as they are experienced. Husserl has dispensed with the traditional dualism between things and experience. Further, Husserl collapses the dualism between appearances and reality. For Husserl, reality is appearance, nothing stands behind appearances, what we see is what we get. Kant's noumenal realm has been demolished. Moreover, the reduction yields indubitable descriptions. But in order to arrive at these, John Macquarrie reminds us, for Husserl it becomes necessary to 'clear [my] mind of all presuppositions and prejudices' (1972, p. 22). Thus, Husserl feels that one can arrive at truth through intuition by completely lifting oneself out of the natural attitude and the natural world.

Clearly, Husserl's method is problematic for many reasons. Obviously, it is highly improbable that I can, realistically, lift myself out of the natural world and perform a mind-cleansing ritual in order that I may see what really is. I am produced by a particular culture and time; I am the product of that culture. Since many of my views about the life world have been shaped by my world, I may be unconscious of precisely how my ideas have been produced. Although Sartre does not believe in the idea of the unconscious, he rejects Husserl's epoché for similar reasons. Solomon claims that Merleau-Ponty 'reinterprets [the epoché] beyond recognition' (1980, pp. 20–1). From my reading of Merleau-Ponty, I believe that like Sartre, he too rejects the epoché as he says that 'we are involved in the world and we do not succeed in extricating ourselves from it in order to achieve consciousness of it' (1962, p. 5). Unlike Merleau-Ponty and Sartre, Alfred Schutz (1967) appropriates Husserl's method and argues that it is indispensable for an examination of the social world. Like Schutz, Maxine Greene agrees that bracketing the life world is necessary. But Greene does not contend that by bracketing the world one arrives at indubitable truths. Rather, Greene suggests, bracketing the life world allows one to transcend passivity and indifference.

In sum, for Husserl, at least in his early work, phenomenology was considered a method. This method of reducing things to their essences allowed one to transcend the natural attitude and to see what really is. Further, the method was a path leading toward consciousness. At the end of the day, the final reduction for Husserl consisted of consciousness and its objects. It was not until Husserl's later writings that the lifeworld seemed to become important to him. One might argue that it was the pressure of being a Jew exiled from Germany during the rise of the Third Reich that forced Husserl to reflect on the crisis of the lifeworld and to concede that the existentialists had something important to say.

David Carr points out that Husserl finally understood that existentialism 'had given needed expression to something real: a deeply felt lack of direction . . . a sense of emptiness of European cultural values, a feeling of crisis and breakdown, the demand that philosophy be relevant to life' (1970, pp. xxv–xxvi). Thus existentialists take up the life world in all its suffering, absurdity. Some common themes, then, running throughout existential literature concern freedom, action, rebellion and pain. At the center of existential concern stands the individual as s/he is thrust into the world. For Soren Kierkegaard (1973), who is considered by many to be the father of existentialism, a turn toward the subject marks the movement: in fact, Kierkegaard goes so far as to say that 'truth is subjectivity' (p. 210). Truth, in other words, is not found in an objective reality independent of human life, truth is found in the human heart. Perhaps Kierkegaard can be criticized for encapsulating the individual too tightly within herself. The individual seems to live in a vacuum, a solipsistic place detached from others. Against this, many existentialists like Maxine Greene, Sartre, Schutz and Merleau-Ponty suggest that truths are found not only in the individual but also in intersubjectivity, in community. As Greene points out, many existentialists, and especially Kierkegaard, were reacting against philosophical systematizing and the subsequent abstraction of the individual:

> Unlike traditional philosophers, from Aristotle to Hegel, the existential thinker refuses
> to conceive man [sic] as an abstraction, a category, an 'essence.' To describe man as
> a 'rational animal,' as Aristotle did, or to see man in Hegelian fashion as a component part of a system of 'thought objectified' is . . . to eliminate the crux: the
> existing individual. (Greene, 1967, p. 7)

Precisely how existentialists portray the existing individual as a conscious, suffering being, of course, differs greatly from thinker to thinker. But, in sum, most are concerned with fleshing out lived experience, finishing what Husserl had left undone.

Existentialists who call themselves phenomenologists, then, combine the concerns of both schools of thought. Generally speaking, existential phenomenologists: 1) tend to agree with Husserl that consciousness is intentional and focus on consciousness and its intended objects; 2) tend also to agree with Husserl concerning phenomena and focus on phenomena as they are experienced (nothing stands behind appearances); 3) flesh out Husserl's ideas concerning the lifeworld and focus on lived experience in its concrete, suffering, absurd manifestations.

Thus I would say that Maxine Greene, Alfred Schutz, Maurice Merleau-Ponty and Jean-Paul Sartre are all existential phenomenologists since they satisfy the above conditions. At this juncture I would like to examine major themes of Sartre, Merleau-Ponty and Schutz, in turn, as they have relevance for Greene's work. Finally, I will turn to Greene's unique synthesis of these thinkers and her phenomenology of the imagination.

Jean-Paul Sartre wrote plays (*No Exit, The Flies, The Respectful Prostitute*), novels (*Nausea, Troubled Sleep, The Age of Reason*, to name but a few), biographies (*St. Genet, Flaubert*) and philosophic works such as *Search for Method, Critique of Dialectical Reason* and *Being and Nothingness*. Arguably, *Being and Nothingness* is Sartre's most important work, for it is here that he grounds the rest of his thinking. Let us, for a moment, turn our attention to *Being and Nothingness*.

Sartre's primary concern is describing the structures of consciousness and how consciousness relates to the world. Sartre claims that the ontological structure of consciousness is freedom. Freedom, says Sartre, 'is not a quality added on or a property of my nature. It is the very stuff of my being' (1977, p. 415). Dagfinn Follesdal comments that Sartre's is 'a philosophy whose sole dogma is the affirmation of human freedom' (1981, p. 392). Hazel Barnes writes 'In *Being and Nothingness* . . . the answer was clear. Sartre was recognized as the proponent of the most radical view of human freedom to appear since the Epicureans' (1963, p. vii). By 1960, however, especially with *Critique*, Sartre's position on freedom became less radical. Sartre sought to find a middle ground between freedom and determinism, between existentialism and Marxism. Andrew Dobson suggests that the 'theme of his dialogue with Marxism is that of historical materialism: the notion that we make history as it makes us' (1993, p. 3). And it is here that Sartre's influence on Maxine Greene becomes evident. Greene always stresses the dialectical nature of freedom. I never get the sense from Greene that freedom is radical. As far as freedom is concerned, then, it is this middle Sartre, not the early Sartre, that becomes quite important for Greene.

In order to understand Sartre's position on freedom, and to understand how it is that freedom ontologically coincides with consciousness, an examination of consciousness is in order. Sartre says that non-reflexive consciousness is freedom: 'Non-reflexive consciousness is absolutely rid of ego' (Sartre, 1981, p. 11). The ego, as 'a quasi-object of consciousness' (Sartre, 1981, p. 10) attempts to shield me from my own freedom. The ego 'appears only in reflexive consciousness' (Sartre, 1981, p. 11). Sartre calls consciousness being-for-itself (*être-pour-soi*) and describes it as a lack: 'being-for-itself is . . . being what it is not and not being what it is' (1977, p. xv). Being-for-itself, in other words, is never what it is since it surpasses itself at each moment. To surpass itself, the for-itself attempts to transcend nothingness. 'Nothingness must be given at the heart of being' (1977, p. 22). However, this nothingness is not 'nothingness in general but a particular privation' (1977, pp. 535–6). Ultimately being-for-itself attempts to 'nihilate the in-itself' (1977, p. 415). Being-in-itself (*être-en-soi*) is being. Sartre writes 'If being is in-itself, this means that it does not refer to itself as self-consciousness does . . . In fact being is opaque to itself precisely because it is filled with itself . . . being is what it is' (1977, p. xv). The in-itself, Sartre declares, is 'all positivity' (p. 62).

Sartre's ontology is clearly dualistic. Being-for-itself is quite distinct from being-in-itself. If being-for-itself coincided with being-in-itself I would be self-caused or God. And in fact, this is our desire, says Sartre. Thus human beings are useless passions, Sartre declares, because the quest to be self-caused is futile:

> The being of human reality is suffering because it rises in being perpetually haunted by a totality which it is without being able to be it, precisely because it could not attain the in-itself without losing the for-itself. Human reality therefore is by nature an unhappy consciousness. (1977, p. 66)

The freedom that emerges from being-for-itself is in the form of lacks, nihilations, and negative responses to being-in-itself. Sartre claims that I am 'condemned [to be free] because [I] did not create [myself] . . . once thrown into the world [I] am responsible for everything [I do]' (1965, p. 41). Not only am I responsible for everything I do, but I am also a 'law-maker who is, at the same time, choosing all mankind' (1965, p. 38). The burden of freedom and the 'anguish' (1965, p. 38) of freedom lies in this sort of Kantian dilemma: What I choose I choose for all. My choice becomes a categorical imperative because it reflects all.

Hubert Dreyfus and Piotr Hoffman (1981) point out that one of the first critics of Sartre's position on freedom was Maurice Merleau-Ponty as he suggests that Sartre 'does not offer an account of the body that makes it more than a pure hole in the center of a field of instruments, and that lacking any account of the body Sartre's account of a spontaneity — beyond freedom — ends up making freedom impossible' (p. 230). Sartre countered Merleau-Ponty's critique by insisting that Merleau-Ponty had it all wrong. The for-itself and the in-itself made freedom possible. What seemed impossible was Merleau-Ponty's ontology. Sartre said of Merleau-Ponty that he simply could not get his 'bearings in the philosophy of perception' (1982, p. 44). Sartre felt that Merleau-Ponty's approach was too slippery.

Let us turn briefly now to Merleau-Ponty's ontology to better understand what his philosophy of perception asserts. Monika Langer (1981) contends that Merleau-Ponty's entire philosophy serves as a corrective to Sartre's dualistic scheme. Merleau-Ponty attempts to find a continuum between the body and the world, to close the gap between these two poles. Like Sartre, Merleau-Ponty's philosophy primarily turns on describing consciousness. Unlike Sartre, Merleau-Ponty centers consciousness in perception and this perception is incarnated, embodied. Thus it is through my body that I perceive the world and am connected to the world. Merleau-Ponty works out this general thesis in *The Phenomenology of Perception*, *The Primacy of Perception* and *The Visible and the Invisible*.

Whereas Sartre claims that consciousness coincides with freedom ontologically, Merleau-Ponty suggests that consciousness is, most fundamentally, perceptual. 'Perceptual experience . . . gives us the passage from one moment to the next and thus realizes the unity of time. In this sense, all consciousness is perceptual' (1964, p. 13). Perception, by its very nature, is ambiguous, 'shifting, and shaped by its context' (1962, p. 11). A perceptual field stands out against another because 'it possesses in our perception a special structure: the structure of figure-ground' (1981, pp. 13–14). Merleau-Ponty avoids getting trapped in idealism by suggesting that phenomenology is a 'philosophy for which the world is always "already there" before reflection begins' (1980, p. 317). Thus the world is not in my head, it was there first; I perceive the world after I arrive on the scene. And what I perceive are 'relations' (1981, p. 14), not isolated terms or objects.

Merleau-Ponty situates consciousness in the body. 'Consciousness is being toward the thing through the intermediary of the body' (1962, pp. 138–9). Further, Merleau-Ponty calls the body the 'third term' (1962, p. 101). I wonder if by third term he is attempting to occupy the space between Sartre's two poles of the for-itself and the in-itself. Perhaps by the third term, Merleau-Ponty means to show that I am mixed up in the world, that I am a third thing in continuum with the world:

> We say therefore that our body is a being of two leaves, from one side a thing among things and otherwise what sees them and touches them . . . it unites these two properties within itself. (1968, p. 137)

It is through the body that I become present, says Merleau-Ponty. 'The experience of perception is our presence at the moment when things, truths, values are constituted for us' (1964, p. 25). This notion of presence is particularly important for Maxine Greene as she often talks of becoming present to ourselves and others in order to achieve authenticity.

Toward the end of his career, Merleau-Ponty's writings become more and more obscure. But one thing does seem clear: throughout his life, the body and our mixed-up place in the world consumed Merleau-Ponty. No other philosopher has made an attempt to show just how ambiguous this lifeworld is. It seems the more rigor Merleau-Ponty attempted to demonstrate around this ambiguity the more slippery his work became. A reading of *The Visible and the Invisible* illustrates this.

Let us turn now to Alfred Schutz and it will become clear that although Sartre and Merleau-Ponty share similar concerns, Schutz's philosophy differs greatly from both. Like Sartre and Merleau-Ponty, Schutz is concerned with describing the structures of consciousness in his work called *The Phenomenology of the Social World*. But unlike Sartre and Merleau-Ponty, Schutz suggests that these structures of consciousness are inherently related to time. And thus all action 'takes place in time . . . in the internal time consciousness' (1967, p. 40). Schutz borrows the notion of time consciousness from Henri Bergson. It is temporality that ultimately shapes experience. In fact, for Schutz, temporality shapes Husserl's phenomenological reduction. Thus the phenomenological reduction becomes a crucial element in Schutz's philosophy also. Natanson points out that Schutz 'more than anyone else, carried out the authentic impulse of Husserl's thought to the realm of everyday life' (1986, p. 1).

Schutz claims that one must first look to the structures of consciousness since 'the meaning-structure of the social world can only be deduced from the most primitive and general characteristics of consciousness' (1967, p. 12). Internal time consciousness is an 'irreversible stream of duration' (1967, p. 43). And through memory one can arrest time and 'lift' experience out of this stream (p. 43). In fact, Schutz says 'recoverability to memory is . . . the first prerequisite to all rational construction' (p. 53). When I choose to remember some experience I 'attach meaning to it' (p. 42). Meaning inheres only in things of remembrance past. Present experience, as it flows in the irreversible stream of time, is 'pre-phenomenal' (p. 56) and therefore 'not meaningful' (p. 57). This position, I think, is problematic for the present, in all its complexity, can indeed be meaningful, even if one calls it pre-phenomenal. Further, the present is so mixed up in the past that it becomes difficult to clearly separate them as does Schutz. The past impresses upon the present and the present enfolds the past.

For Schutz, the problem of meaning is paramount. Meaning inheres in past events because I can reflect upon them. Meaning, more fundamentally, is a 'certain way of directing one's gaze at an item of one's own experience' (1967, p. 42). And ultimately the problem of meaning is a problem of time, says Schutz. Generally speaking, Schutz's aim is to understand how time shapes meaning and how individuals then 'give meaning to social phenomena' (p. 6). If I direct my gaze toward some event with a 'particular kind of attention' (pp. 73–4) and 'transform something that is taken-for-granted into something problematical' (p. 74), by utilizing the method of bracketing elements of the life world, I can achieve 'wide-awakeness' (p. 74). Maxine Greene is particularly interested in Schutz's notion of wide-awakeness as it permeates her writings.

The Phenomenology of the Social World is largely an attempt by Schutz to correct Max Weber's account of action in the world. Schutz complains that Weber had not done enough to account for nuances and distinctions that are imperative for any social philosophy. Schutz says that:

> Weber makes no distinction between the action, considered as something in progress, and the completed act, between the meaning of the producer of a cultural object and the meaning of the object produced, between the meaning of my own action and the meanings of anothers. (1967, p. 8)

Schutz thus attempts to draw distinctions where Weber had not. Completed acts, for Schutz, have meaning because I can reflect on them; actions are still caught up in the stream of time and hence reflection is impossible; therefore, actions cannot have meaning. Although I think that Schutz's distinctions are strained and even laborious, I appreciate, generally, what he is trying to say. Temporality, as shifting, creates problems especially when one is trying to talk about meaningful acts and about meaning in itself. Schutz makes these distinctions to undergird the fact that ultimately consciousness is temporal.

How are the themes in each of these philosophers important for Maxine Greene's work? First, let us turn to Greene's views on freedom and action as they are informed by Sartre. The 'source of learning' (1995, p. 132), says Greene, is freedom. And this freedom can be 'attained through the refusals . . . of which Sartre spoke' (Greene, 1988, p. 9). Sartre suggests that to transcend and surpass the given is a refusal to align oneself with the status quo. If I align myself with the status quo I live in bad faith because I reject my inherent freedom. Bad faith is essentially lying to oneself.

Greene (1988) suggests that in embracing my freedom I may create myself. But the self is a social self and freedom or personal liberty does not mean 'an abandonment of social involvment' (1988, p. 21). To be free means to set others free. Freedom, for Greene, is freedom-in-community. Freedom has to do with 'connectedness or being together in community' (1988, p. 1). Freedom means dialogue, 'reinterpreting situations' (1988, p. 90), and 'opening perspectives' (1988, p. 5). Greene emphasizes that freedom is a dialectical movement between my own freedom and the freedom of others, between what is possible and what is not. As I mentioned earlier, it seems that Greene is in agreement with Sartre in his middle period (after 1960), as he too discusses the dialectical nature of freedom. Accordingly, Greene says that freedom 'cannot be conceived apart from a matrix of social, economic, cultural, and psychological conditions' (1988, p. 80). Greene attempts to demonstrate that both sociopolitical and psychological factors complicate and may even limit the possibilities of freedom. Like Simone de Beauvoir (1948), Greene claims that free acts are complicated because we do not know how they will turn out. Sometimes free acts with good intentions turn out badly, thus free acts are necessarily aporetic. Ultimately free acts, says Greene, are 'unpredictable' (Greene, 1988, p. 46).

Even if free acts are unpredictable, I must act in such a way as to free not only myself but others as well. Greene insists that one must not take refuge in negative freedom. Negative freedom is the sort of freedom espoused by J.S. Mill (1989) as a freedom from interference. Greene contends that negative freedom, or libertarianism, is merely self-serving. For educators, freedom cannot be conceived of in this manner. Greene says that freedom cannot mean 'autonomous achievement' (1988, pp. 121–2) since, most fundamentally, we are situated in community.

In community we are called to act. Social action comes by opening perspectives and, in fact, Greene suggests that for educators the 'problem . . . is not simply to interpret the world. . . . The point, as Marx wrote . . . is to change it' (1978, p. 109). Borrowing Sartre's phrase, Greene claims that, therefore, educators are 'condemned to action' (1978, p. 109). Following Sartre, Greene says that it is only after a 'crisis of consciousness' (1973, p. 268) that people act; when situations become unbearable action occurs. Fueled by a spirit of discontent, action moves one beyond and 'involves the transcending or surpassing of what is' (1973, p. 163). Moreover, Greene declares that action (praxis) must be a form of knowing: 'Praxis is a particular type of cognitive/action' (1973, p. 163). If action is to become meaningful it 'must be informed by critical reflection' (1978, p. 18). The emphasis upon cognitive capacities and critical reflection is important, for Greene frequently points out that existentialism is not blind irrationalism as critics have contended:

> . . . in the bulk of existential literature, there is a fundamental respect for reasoning as well as reflection, for experience as well as subjectivity. The existentialists

may deny the primacy of knowledge, as Sartre does when he talks about self-consciousness and the discovery of being the knower; but he will also vehemently challenge . . . someone who becomes an anti-semite because he is impervious to reason and experience. (1973, p. 138)

Greene is right to point out that reason is crucial for existentialists. Husserl's attack on existentialism as irrational was unwarranted and ill-informed. Existentialists do not automatically slip into irrationalism merely because questions of epistemology are not forefronted.

In sum, Sartre's influence on Greene's writings has mainly turned on the ideas of freedom and action. For Greene, the important concern has to do with the dialectical nature of freedom and action as it is grounded in reason. It is interesting to me that Greene does not discuss Sartre's ontology. Recall that Sartre's is a dualistic scheme which admits of very little ambiguity. Greene (1995) states that she does not like dualisms and in fact she says that dualisms may undermine a phenomenology of the imagination. Therefore, ontologically, I think Greene is closer to Merleau-Ponty than she is to Sartre.

Greene is primarily interested in Merleau-Ponty's treatment of perception and his notion of visibility as these have relevance for educational theory. Like Merleau-Ponty, Greene agrees that perception is primary. Perception is the fundamental structure of consciousness upon which all other cognitive capacities are built. Accordingly, Greene contends that 'the perceptual consciousness through which a child first comes in contact with his [sic] environment under-lie all the higher level structures that develop in his later life' (1973, p. 160). Further, like Merleau-Ponty, Greene stresses that perception is embodied: 'We first come into the world as embodied beings' (1995, p. 73). Because perception is embodied and situated, it is also limited. What I perceive is partial, incomplete. I cannot, therefore, without contradiction, pretend to have a God's eye view of anything. Greene declares that I 'inhabit varied and always incomplete multiverses of forms, contours, structures, colors, and shadows' (1995, p. 73). In this Heraclitean flux, Greene suggests that students 'perceiving profiles and incompletenesses all around live in a world of constantly shifting perspectives' (1995, p. 55). However, living in the flux of lived experience is not completely chaotic, for perception is embodied and situated historically, socially, psychologically.

Still, perception is slippery. Recall, Sartre said that he could not get his bearings in a philosophy of perception. But as difficult as it may be to get a grip in the throes of perception, Greene says we must attempt to do so. And we can do so through memory. Greene suggests that memory may lead us into our perceptual frontiers, our 'perceptual landscapes' (1978, p. 103). It is easy to forget that we are fundamentally perceptual beings, therefore, memory must be cultivated. It becomes difficult to remember our shifting, changing horizons. But Greene insists that 'critical educators [must] remain in touch with their lived worlds, their pre-understandings' (1978, p. 103). It is not that I need to return to a primitive form of consciousness; what is crucial is I recall who and what I am: I am fundamentally perceptual.

Following Merleau-Ponty, Greene insists that I become present to my perceptual landscapes. Memory enables me to do so; memory allows me to become present to myself and others. Through memory I become present 'in the midst' (Greene, 1995, p. 73) of others and the world. Still, presence does not mean totality. I see only 'profiles' (1995, p. 73), even of myself. Once present to myself in the midst of the world I may achieve what Greene terms transcendence: 'Only if educators remain in touch with their own histories, can they emerge with others, who are making . . . efforts to transcend' (1978, p. 103).

Transcendence for Greene means overcoming passivity and indifference. Transcendence, then, is a horizontal move, not a vertical one. Transcendence allows one to step more firmly in the world; it allows one to move beyond static/everyday things, to deeper levels of the everyday. Transcendence, for Greene, is thus grounded or immanent. This grounded transcendence enables me to interrupt static structures to 'reach beyond what is immediate, make horizons explicit, and transcend what is first a field of presences toward other future fields' (Greene, 1978, p. 103). Transcendence does not yield indubitable truths; it opens passageways and multiple ways of seeing.

Greene attempts to close the gap between immanence and transcendence by, in a sense, collapsing the two onto immanence. Phenomenologically this move is necessary if she wants to maintain that perception is embodied, situated and changeable. If Greene were to say that transcendence is a vertical move upward, this would drive a wedge between transcendence and immanence, between my body and the world, between heaven and earth. Further it would create a chasm between the body and the things it perceives. Greene is able to maintain, then, a philosophy of perception without falling into dualisms.

The upshot of a philosophy of perception is that lived experience must admit of ambiguities. The history of Western philosophy certainly is a testament against this sort of philosophizing. One need only look at Plato, Descartes, Locke and even Husserl, to see that ambiguities have not been tolerated. Since Plato, reason and/or sense data (Locke) or intuition (Husserl) served to ground ideas in certainty. Perception got a bad name beginning with Plato as the cave dwellers lived in the realm of shadows, incompletenesses. Philosophies of perception have been marginalized ever since Plato stuck these people in his cave. Another reason philosophies of perception have been marginalized is because perception is tied inextricably to the body. Philosophers have had a history of ignoring the body, or devaluing it. It is heartening to see that Maxine Greene and Merleau-Ponty bring the body and perceptions back into place.

Greene's interest in Schutz also concerns perception. But here she emphasizes Schutz's notion of wide-awakeness as a way in which to perceive things. For Schutz there are two ways of seeing: seeing from the standpoint of the natural attitude and seeing from the standpoint of wide-awakeness. Greene is interested in how we move from one standpoint to the next. Greene talks of Schutz's image of the 'homecomer' (1973, p. 260). The homecomer is that person who has yet to make the familiar strange; she is steeped in the natural attitude, stuck in the natural standpoint. Greene contends that those stuck in the natural attitude are 'polluted by something invisible' (1995, p. 47) and this something invisible is the 'cloud of givenness' (p. 47). Thus, overhanging the homecomer's house is this invisible cloud, the cloud of givenness.

Like Schutz's image of the homecomer, Husserl uses the image of a house to illustrate what he means by dwelling in the natural attitude. 'Natural reflection,' according to Husserl, occurs when I see a house standing in front of me and I look at it 'straightforwardly' (1980a, p. 152). I am caught in natural reflection until I become aware that I am perceiving a house; that is, when I become aware of my awareness, 'transcendental reflection' (1980a, p. 152) occurs. Schutz's homecomer, therefore, lives in a non-reflective house, or in the house of natural reflection. Greene's invisible cloud of givenness hangs over this house.

For Greene, what is important is that this familiar house becomes strange. But becoming a stranger means more than simple awareness. The stranger must interrupt the cloud of givenness by bracketing 'presuppositions that fix . . . visions of the world' (1973, p. 11). By bracketing assumptions one may become 'critically attentive' (p. 11) or wide-awake. For Greene, wide-awakeness concerns the 'concrete, the relevant, and the questionable' (1978, p. 51). And what is relevant and questionable not only concerns me but concerns others as well. It is not a solipsistic act.

Following Schutz, Greene contends that prior to wide-awakeness, an 'experience of shock' (1978, p. 101) usually occurs. Once this shock throws me into a new 'province of meaning' (p. 101) new visions arise. Therefore, an event or feeling may precipitate a change of attitude. Greene says:

> I think again of Alfred Schutz pointing to the 'fundamental anxiety' that he associated with the feeling that our lives may be . . . meaningless. . . . Yet out of such anxiety comes ideas for projects and plans of action. (1995, p. 51)

Greene suggests, like both Schutz and Sartre, that crisis situations thrust open new horizons. When new horizons open, action and change follow. Greene stresses, though, that any action will not do. Action must not simply be blind; action must not result in 'impulses of expediency' (1978, p. 43). 'Cognitive clarity' (1978, p. 48) is key; praxis must be grounded in reason.

Recall that Schutz draws a distinction between acts and actions. Actions are in progress and are caught up in an endless stream of duration. Hence, actions are pre-phenomenal and meaning cannot inhere in them. Acts, on the other hand, are complete; they can be remembered and reflected upon and hence meaning can reside therein. I find it interesting to note that Greene makes no reference to this distinction. For Greene, the main point, then, is to act, and act reasonably. She does not seem to be concerned to draw the same distinctions as does Schutz.

Finally, I want to suggest that not only does Greene synthesize Schutz, Merleau-Ponty and Sartre in unique ways, but she also recontextualizes and transforms educational theory by offering a phenomenology of imagination. Ultimately this distinguishes her from these other thinkers. Although Sartre and Merleau-Ponty discuss imagination, it seems that their treatments of it are peripheral. For Greene, especially in her later work, the imagination takes center stage. Imagination releases the doors of perception.

In order to open the doors of perception, we must first turn to Greene's ideas on consciousness. For Greene, consciousness is intentional. Consciousness 'thrusts toward the world . . . thrusts toward the situations in which the individual lives her or his life' (1978, p. 14). Greene stresses this point throughout her writings because she claims that the idea of consciousness as an interior realm is ontologically invalid and ethically disastrous. If I say that consciousness is interior, then I am responsible only for my own life. Greene feels that this is morally repugnant. Consciousness, rather, means moving toward the world and others. Acts of consciousness, says Greene, 'bring individuals in touch with objects, events, and other human beings, they make it possible for individuals to . . . interpret, to constitute a world' (1978, p. 14). More specifically, acts of consciousness include perceiving, intuiting, remembering, judging and, of course, imagining.

Most fundamentally, consciousness is perceptual, embodied and situated. Because consciousness is primarily perceptual, Greene contends that the world may yield multiple interpretations. Perception grounds us in 'shifting horizons' that reveal 'profiles and incompletenesses' (1995, p. 51). And our task is to achieve cognizance of these shifting profiles as they allow us to overturn sunkenness in the commonplace. The immanent life world for Greene is changeable. Interestingly, Greene's position runs counter to Husserl, who, as Paul Ricoeur points out, asserts that 'immanence is not doubtful, because it is not given by profiles and hence involves nothing presumptive, allowing only the co-incidences of reflection with what "has just" been experienced' (Ricoeur, 1995, p. 103).

Conversely, for Greene, immanence is indeed given by profiles and hence shifting, revealing nothing indubitable.

And there is nothing indubitable about the imagination. Greene contends that the function of the imagination is not to 'resolve' (1995, p. 28) things or clarify things. Imagination sparks us on toward new horizons into the 'unseen, unheard, unexpected' (1995, p. 28). Those things ordinarily unseen and unheard now come to the fore and allow us to 'break with the taken-for-granted' (p. 3). Thus imagination is the force behind 'awakening' (p. 28). And in this awakening 'new connections' (p. 30) in experience become possible. It is interesting to me that Greene suggests that new connections in experience come by imagination and not, say, by deliberative thought, although Greene certainly would not want to drive a wedge between thought and imagination. I suppose here I am thinking of Aristotle and how he suggests in the *Ethics* (1975) that it is from prudence, or deliberative thought, that all virtues flow; it is from deliberative thought that new connections in experience are made. Greene is saying something entirely different. What moves us is the imagination. Further, Greene points out that imagination must be grounded. Imagination is not simply a flight into the netherworld. Imagination, says Greene, is what grounds us in 'particulars' (1995, p. 140). Moreover, imagination allows us to connect with others. In fact, Greene suggests that 'the extent to which we grasp another's world depends on our existing ability to make poetic use of our imagination' (1995, p. 4). Finally, imagination is prophetic, for it allows us to envision better futures, better horizons.

Maxine Greene says that she wrote *Releasing the Imagination* to 'remedy that anxiety' (1995, p. 16) of which Schutz spoke. Anxiety can foster a sense of meaninglessness. For Greene, it is the imagination that is the key to overcoming this meaninglessness. Imagination opens possibilities 'for seeing things otherwise' (1995, p. 46). For educators, imagination is the key for change. Maxine Greene opens our future horizons with this hope.

By tracing influences in Maxine Greene's writings it is clear that she draws upon an eclectic group of philosophers as they have significance for educational theory. From Sartre, Greene draws on the notions of freedom and action; from Merleau-Ponty, she draws upon the primacy of perception and the notion of visibility or presence; from Schutz, she draws upon the idea of wide-awakeness. Greene's unique recontextualization of these various thinkers sheds light upon crucial educational issues. Moreover, I want to stress that Greene is an existential phenomenologist in her own right as she offers to education a phenomenology of imagination. It is here that Greene distinguishes herself from these philosophers. Greene's phenomenology of imagination is a gift to the field of education as it serves as our inspiration and hope, our bedrock and prophecy for future horizons.

References

ARISTOTLE (1975) *The Nichomachean Ethics* (H.G. Apostle, trans.), Iowa: The Peripatetic Press.

BARNES, H. (1963) 'Introduction,' in SARTRE, J.-P. *The Problem of Method* (pp. vii–xxx), (H. Barnes, trans.), London: Methuen and Company.

CAMUS, A. (1970) *Lyrical and Critical Essays* (E.C. Kennedy, trans.), New York: Vintage.

CARR, D. (1970) 'Translator's Introduction,' in HUSSERL, E. *The Crisis of European Sciences and Transcendental Phenomenology* (pp. xv–xiiii), Evanston: Northwestern University Press.

DE BEAUVOIR, S. (1948) *The Ethics of Ambiguity* (B. Frechtman, trans.), New Jersey: The Citadel Press.

DOBSON, A. (1993) *Jean-Paul Sartre and the Politics of Reason: A Theory of History*, Paris: Cambridge University Press.

DREYFUS, H. and HOFFMAN, P. (1981) 'Sartre's changed conception of consciousness: From lucidity to opacity,' in SCHILPP, P.A. (ed.) *The Philosophy of Jean-Paul Sartre* (pp. 229–45), La Salle, Illinois: Open Court Press.

FOLLESDAL, D. (1981) 'Sartre on freedom,' in SCHILPP, P.A. (ed.) *The Philosophy of Jean-Paul Sartre* (pp. 392–407), La Salle, Illinois: Open Court Press.

GREENE, M. (1967) 'Introduction,' in GREENE, M. (ed.) *Existential Encounters for Teachers* (pp. 3–18), New York: Teachers College Press.

GREENE, M. (1973) *Teacher as Stranger: Educational Philosophy for the Modern Age*, Belmont, California: Wadsworth Publishing Company.

GREENE, M. (1978) *Landscapes of Learning*, New York: Teachers College Press.

GREENE, M. (1988) *The Dialectic of Freedom*, New York: Teachers College Press.

GREENE, M. (1995) *Releasing the Imagination: Essays on Education, the Arts, and Social Change*, San Francisco: Jossey-Bass Publishers.

HEIDEGGER, M. (1962) *Being and Time* (J. Macquarie, trans.), New York: Harper and Row.

HUSSERL, E. (1970) *The Crisis of European Sciences and Transcendental Phenomenology* (D. Carr, trans.), Evanston: Northwestern University Press.

HUSSERL, E. (1980a) 'Natural and transcendental reflection,' in SOLOMON, R.C. (ed.) *Phenomenology and Existentialism* (pp. 151–6) (D. Cairns, trans.), New York: University Press of America.

HUSSERL, E. (1980b) 'The Paris lectures,' in SOLOMON, R.C. (ed.) *Phenomenology and Existentialism* (pp. 43–57) (P. Koestenbaum, trans.), New York: University Press of America.

HUSSERL, E. (1980c) 'The thesis of the natural standpoint and its suspension,' in SOLOMON, R.C. (ed.) *Phenomenology and Existentialism* (pp. 112–17) (W.R. Boyce-Gibson, trans.), New York: University Press of America.

KIERKEGAARD, S. (1973) 'Concluding unscientific postscript to the philosophical fragments,' in BRETALL, R. (ed.) *A Kierkegaard Anthology* (pp. 190–258) (D.F. Swenson, L.M. Swenson & W. Lowrie, trans.), New Jersey: Princeton University Press.

LANGER, M. (1981) 'Sartre and Merleau-Ponty: A reappraisal,' in SCHILPP, P.A. (ed.) *The Philosophy of Jean-Paul Sartre* (pp. 300–25), La Salle, Illinois: Open Court Press.

MACQUARRIE, J. (1972) *An Introduction, Guide and Assessment: Existentialism*, New York: Penguin.

MERLEAU-PONTY, M. (1962) *Phenomenology of Perception* (C. Smith, trans.), New York: Routledge and Kegan Paul.

MERLEAU-PONTY, M. (1964) *The Primacy of Perception* (J. Edie, trans.), Evanston: Northwestern University Press.

MERLEAU-PONTY, M. (1968) *The Visible and the Invisible* (A. Lingis, trans.), Evanston: Northwestern University Press.

MERLEAU-PONTY, M. (1980) 'The preface to the phenomenology of perception,' in SOLOMON, R.C. (ed.) *Phenomenology and Existentialism* (pp. 317–34) (C. Smith, trans.), New York: University Press of America.

MERLEAU-PONTY, M. (1981) 'The nature of perception,' in SALLIS, J. (ed.) *Merleau-Ponty: Perception, Structure, Language: A Collection of Essays* (pp. 9–20) (Forrest W. Williams, trans.), New Jersey: Humanities Press.

MILL, J.S. (1989) 'On liberty,' in GOLDBERG, D.T. (ed.) *Ethical Theory and Social Issues: Historical Texts and Contemporary Readings* (pp. 156–9), New York: Holt, Rinehart and Winston.

NATANSON, M. (1986) *Anonymity: A Study in the Philosophy of Alfred Schutz*, Bloomington: Indiana University Press.

OLSON, R. (1962) *An Introduction to Existentialism*, New York: Dover.

RICOEUR, P. (1995) *Hermeneutics and the Human Sciences* (J.B. Thompson, trans.), Paris: Cambridge University Press.

SARTRE, J.-P. (1965) 'The humanism of existentialism,' in BASKIN, W. (ed.) *Essays in Existentialism* (pp. 31–62), New Jersey: The Citadel Press.

SARTRE, J.-P. (1977) *Being and Nothingness: An Essay in Phenomenological Ontology* (H. Barnes, trans.), New Jersey: The Citadel Press.

SARTRE, J.-P. (1981) 'An interview with Jean-Paul Sartre,' in SCHILPP, P.A. (ed.) *The Philosophy of Jean-Paul Sartre* (pp. 3–51), La Salle, Illinois: Open Court Press.

SCHUTZ, A. (1967) *The Phenomenology of the Social World* (G. Walsh and F. Lehnert, trans.), Evanston: Northwestern University Press.

SOLOMON, R.C. (1980) 'General introduction: What is phenomenology?' in SOLOMON, R.C. (ed.) *Phenomenology and Existentialism* (pp. 1–41), New York: University Press of America.

12 Maxine Greene: Literary Influences

Thomas Barone

What is the greatest achievement of the scholarship of Maxine Greene? The candidates are numerous, but I will argue for one in particular. Maxine Greene has (almost single-handedly) managed to secure a permanent place for imaginative writing at the table of educational discourse, insisting on its equal seating beside the more familiar genres of the social sciences, history, philosophy, and educational theory. More than any other educational author — certainly more than any other philosopher of education — she has brought the works of imaginative literature to bear on the central concerns of education, and indeed, of life in general. She has accomplished this, I suggest, through wide-ranging examples, telling demonstrations of the undeniable relevance of particular pieces of poetry and storytelling to the general matters at hand. But whatever the strategy, Greene's unprecedented achievement is the result of her grasping (when others could not) the significance of works of literature, inviting them into her scholarly world in order that they might shape and influence it. The point of this essay is to comment (in a necessarily abbreviated fashion) upon the character of that influence.

It is impossible to fathom Maxine Greene's regard for literature without first understanding her enduring mission. The nature of her 'lifetime pursuit' is summarized with characteristic clarity and eloquence in the 'Introduction' to *The Dialectic of Freedom* (1988, p. xi), and then reiterated in the 'Introduction' to her latest book, *Releasing the Imagination* (1995, p. 1). The quest, she reveals, has been, on the one hand, deeply personal, 'reaching, always reaching, beyond the limits imposed by a woman's life,' and on the other, deeply public, 'that of a person struggling to connect the undertaking of education . . . to the making and remaking of a public space . . .' (1988, p. xi). Whether in her own personal/professional sphere or in larger public arenas, Greene's quest has been, like a life lived in narrative form, always open, always in the making (1995, p. 1), consistently longing for 'something better,' than unacceptable present conditions, that which '*might* be in an always open world' (1988, p. xi).

This is a motif discernible throughout her writings, Greene's conscientious objection to conditions under which people (especially school people) are forced (or sometimes led) to live closed lives, and her refusal to participate in a 'bland acquiescence' (1991, p. 27), a pervasive silence concerning those conditions. With the poet Rainer Maria Rilke, she has realized that 'many of the songs we have sung in the past have been to no avail' (1977, p. 283), and so hankers for a space of possibility beyond what is, beyond the 'real,' into clearings 'where we can create visions of other ways of being and ponder what it might signify to realize them' (1991, p. 27).

Of immediate interest here is her consideration of the literary arts as means for creating that space, for fostering the kind of critical awareness which moves us into the margins of the cultural text, there to become less immersed in the everyday and more impelled to wonder about features of a supplied script. Put more succinctly, good literature prompts new imaginings of the ideal and the possible. It can even stir action against the conventional, the seemingly unquestionable, the tired and 'true.'

From early on in her career, Greene revealed a fascination with the special character of literature which enables it to move the reader beyond taken for granted 'truths,' some of which are proffered by science and technology. These are seemingly privileged 'realities' which, nevertheless, Greene suggests, fail to provide a meaningful context for their presence in our lives. Unlike science, imaginative literature offers a means for *enacting* meaningfulness, for 'creating values as we live, values susceptible to continuous remaking' (1965a, p. 424). But grasping the nature of the process wherein poetry and fiction provide this means requires a shifting of frames of reference through which we understand encounters with such texts. Indeed, it demands a refusal of the usual dichotomies between the cognitive and the emotional, between the real and the imaginary.

In her essay, 'Real Toads and Imaginary Gardens,' Greene (1965a) borrows a metaphor for revealing one approach to understanding literary encounters. The metaphor (from Marianne Moore's poem, 'Poetry') suggests that literature is highly empirical, the poet scrutinizing the world in order to capture in words the particulars of recognizable objects — 'real toads,' for example. These particulars which the author explores and probes are parts of her personal experience with life. And they reside within a different discursive dimension from that of the scientist or even the educator, 'where general tendencies are dealt with, logical relations effected, inferences drawn, conclusions derived' (1965b, p. 6).

But the artist does more than merely represent these 'real toads' on the written page. Rather, she relocates them, transports them into an imaginary garden, into, that is, 'the artist's context, the consciousness of the poet' (1965a, p. 420). In the process, the particulars are themselves transformed, 'remade deliberately.' They are given symbolic form, a gift only an author of literature can possess. Others may see 'substance' and utility: scientists, for example, see individual toads as actual representatives of a species, and gardeners value them for useful purposes such as ridding a real garden of pests. But 'it takes an imaginary garden to . . . make [those toads] significant as forms.'

Elements of Greene's analysis are reminiscent of the thoughts of Wolfgang Iser, with whose work Greene (1991, p. 114) has expressed a sense of connectedness. Iser (1974, 1993) has similarly dismissed simplistic distinctions between the real and the imaginary, explaining how real objects, upon transposition into a the virtual world of a literary text, are turned into 'signs for something else' (Iser, 1993, p. 3), made to point to a 'reality' beyond themselves, moved beyond whatever purposes they served in an actual world outside of the text. Moreover, noted Iser, the elements of the virtual world unlike the irrelevant, diffuse fantasies and reveries which occupy our everyday (extra-textual) experiences. This is because they have been secured within the Gestalt of the text, placed into a 'fictional' context, or following Greene's borrowed metaphor, into a literary 'garden.' This attaches to them a distinctly literary sort of relevance, power, significance, purpose.

Greene, Iser, and others recognized that, in fact, *two* boundaries are crossed in the act of fictionalizing. Not only is the determinacy of reality exceeded by the placement of 'real toads in imaginary gardens,' there to mean more than they had previously meant. But simultaneously the 'diffuseness of the imaginary is controlled and called into form' (Iser, 1993, p. 30), there to mean more than *it* had previously meant.

But these are not meanings which can comprehend themselves. Resonating with the reader reception theorists (as well as Dewey, 1958; and Sartre, 1964), Greene cautions that it is only within the experiencing of the work of art, only when that work is given existence in relation to a human consciousness, only when it is understood through feelings, that meaning can happen. Meaning begins to happen when the reader, toting the luggage of her personal history, enters into the imaginary world, and responds to 'an initial tension and entanglement' (Greene, 1965b, p. 421). As the experience progresses, the reader, establishing ever more connections between the piece of literature and her own life story, becomes increasingly engaged. Indeed, aesthetic meanings may continue to build, and new questions arise, as the reader reflects upon the encounter even after the reading is complete. Ultimately it is the *action*, exploratory and productive, of the reader which must be emphasized (Green, 1991, p. 114).

Untold numbers of examples of the synergy between meaning and action within her own personal encounters with literature are provided in the writings of Maxine Greene, and they give her work its distinctive characteristics of richness, ideational fluidity, and audacity. One gauge of her commitment to the discovery through literature of meanings that would 'otherwise have been inaccessible' (1977, p. 294) is the sheer number of references from literary works which are sprinkled so liberally throughout her essays and chapters. Indeed, in one book of 198 pages (*Releasing the Imagination*, 1995), Greene manages to weave into her text relevant thoughts and excerpts from no less than 78 literary works.

But it is through a single telling example that we are granted an extended look at the birth of one particularly profound realization. It occurred upon Greene's reading of *To the Lighthouse*, a novel by one of her favorite authors, Virginia Woolf (1962). In one passage of that book Woolf describes how the reflected light of candles on panes of glass in an elaborate ballroom serve to shut out the darkness of the night, enabling the members of a cultivated British family to become 'conscious of making a party together in a hollow, on an island; [aware that they] had their common cause against the fluidity out there.' Writes Greene:

> For me . . . the idea that social life and even civilization are human creations in the face of nothingness may have been buried in the ordinary experience of the world, never quite confronted. To confront them here [in this novel] . . . is to come upon something unexpected and at the same time, shattering. In the novel itself, the passage prepares in some way for the intermediate section called 'Time Passes,' the period of the First World War, of death in childbirth and death on the battlefield, of the 'chaos and tumult of night, with the trees standing there, and the flowers standing there, looking before them, looking up, yet beholding nothing, eyeless, and thus terrible' (156). It is not that I learned anything altogether new. I was made to *see* what I had not particularly wanted to see; and once seen, it had moved me to summon energies as never before to create meanings, to effect connections, to bring some vital order into existence — if only for a time. (1991, p. 116)

Greene notes that it was this sort of securing of insights which prompted her to include novels, stories, and poems as readings in her educational foundations classes, in hopes that her students might experience such active encounters for themselves. And some of the encounters she fosters are located more directly within the domain of education and schooling. Take an early work, her book, *The Public School and the Private Vision* (1965b). What other educational historian would have dreamed of (to paraphrase the subtitle) searching for America in both education *and* literature? What other educational scholar could have managed with such aplomb the transpositions of the historical 'realities' found within the establishment of the American public school against the visions of 'authentic' American literary giants who were able to imagine education otherwise? This is precisely what Greene achieves in this still relevant work of educational history which honors alternative perspectives, gleaned from within pieces of fiction, as counterpoints to those of the champions of the American common school movement.

And how is the viewpoint of the literary genius distinctive? 'Each is concerned with identifying the insufficiencies he feels, the discrepancies between existence and prevalent descriptions of it, the strains of contesting values and ideals.' Here, again, we confront the theme of conscientious objection: Greene hears and honors oppositional voices. Of course a rigid critic might complain of certain limits to Greene's spirit of inclusion: not all oppositional voices are granted a hearing.

Consider that the prominent writers highlighted in this early work (and in some later ones, as well) are identified with a familiar canon. They include Emerson, Hawthorne, Melville, Whitman, and Twain, five authors whose writings would intrigue Greene through-out her quest, beckoning her back, for example, for one more revisiting of the meanings within the 'whiteness of the whale,' for an additional opportunity to reflect on what Huck Finn might teach a new generation of Americans. Throughout her career Greene has, undoubtedly, evidenced a selective passion for prominent authors with extraordinary talent and vision, for literary works with deep insights into issues that matter. Not every writer is, after all, adept at fashioning an exquisitely aesthetic garden for real toads. Authors possessing extraordinary keenness of vision and a high degree of craftsmanship are, of course, rare, and they do not necessarily include those writers who have rather recently begun to occupy the attention of narrative scholars — commonfolk (especially women and members of other traditionally marginalized social categories) whose jour-nals and diaries offer additional, if raw and often less than artfully composed, testimony to the personal struggles of the disenfranchised.

But despite her reluctance to honor 'narrative for its own sake' (Ayers, 1995, p. 328), who would dare suggest that Greene has ignored the critical importance of the multiplicity of vantage points which good literature can provide? Throughout the decades she has indeed conveyed a sense of urgency for the sharing of various perspectives on the world, argued for the proliferation of available frames of reference, urged attention to all sorts of voices previously silenced.

Moreover, in moving through Greene's body of work in a roughly chronological order, one gains a sense of the growth in her literary repertoire, the progress made in her quest for an ever wider experiential space, for tearing down one wall after another in order to attend to 'other voices in other rooms.' In each succeeding book or essay Greene's experience seems to undergo additional reconstruction due to the insights gleaned from one or more newly encountered novel or poem, or from a revisiting of beguiling favorites.

Since one of her original vantage points is that of a United States citizen who concerns herself with the 'predicaments of American selfhood' (Greene, 1978, p. 7), one might expect Greene to rely predominantly on American authors for inspiration and insight. The essayist, after all, like the artist, is always *in* society, and what she presents is necessarily 'presented against the social meaning system of the group to which he or she belongs' (Greene, 1977, p. 294). And indeed, especially in her early works, the fascination with American literature is undeniable — if never to the exclusion of classics by the likes of Flaubert, Dostoevsky, Ibsen, Camus, and many other Europeans (although I confess to some puzzlement regarding her omission of Charles Dickens, an author who had much to say concerning the prominent Greenian theme of utilitarianism in school and society).

Of course, to ignore texts which beckon from non-American cultures would be to betray her own premises concerning the potential uses for imaginative literature. For, while necessarily living within the contexts of her own self-understanding, Greene never-theless strives to use the imaginative text, whatever its point of origin, to move beyond the boundaries of her own selfhood. Her explanation is as follows:

Mimetic theory, it seems to me, makes it possible to focus on the question of our world's — each person's world's — horizons; since our ability to enter the universe of *Hamlet*, say, is partially a function of our perception of those horizons, partially of our ability to break through them, to transcend. And having transcended, having penetrated what is not, we see from another standpoint. We see critically, through new eyes. Granted, Shakespeare does not reveal our reality to us from the perspective of our own [modern-day, American] future. But he does disclose, through his own 'double vision,' the corruption of a state in an imaginary world contiguous to our own. This in itself, coupled with the action of the play . . . enables us to experience what Sartre called 'a true image of our time.' (1965a, p. 422)

But Maxine Greene is, of course, much more than just an American. She is also, among other things, a 'teacher . . . mother . . . New Yorker . . . art lover . . . activist . . . philosopher . . . white . . . [and a member of the] middle class' (1995, p. 1). She is also both female and Jewish, dimensions of her being which locate her within social categories whose members have, in various ways, felt the weight of oppression. One may surmise that personal struggles against gender-based and ethnicity-based obstacles have served to animate her 'enduring quest' for meaning and justice, sensitized her to long-standing exclusionary conditions within the public square and the distorted policies shaped therein, and to the role that imaginative literature might play in drawing attention to and changing those deplorable conditions and policies.

Indeed, some of the stories which Greene finds deeply attractive are those which bell hooks (1991) might classify as *narratives of struggle*, stories in which the writer speaks autobiographically as a member of an oppressed group. In the process of writing such a story the author comes to consciousness 'in the context of a concrete experimental struggle for self-actualization and collective . . . self-determination' (hooks, 1991, p. 54). And the reader who, seeing herself as a fellow member of that particular collectivity, struggles along with the author-character, may undergo a similarly emancipatory self-redefinition. Greene reveals how literature by other women writers enabled her to redefine part of herself, to 'reach the ground of her being' as a woman:

It took some time for me to confront what it signified that as a woman I was excluded, on some level, from the steamboats and sailing ships I imagined myself aboard [in reading Melville and Conrad]. It took perceptions gained from Charlotte Perkins Gilman in 'The Yellow Wallpaper,' Kate Chopin in *The Awakening*, and Virginia Woolf in *The Three Guineas* and *A Room of One's Own* to move me into concrete confrontations with exclusion, indifference, and contempt. I needed that mad vision of the women creeping out of the wallpaper in Gilman's work as I needed my own indignation at Edna's shortsightedness in *The Awakening* and my ambivalent indignation at her suicide. I, after all, was lending these people my life; I was, through my reading, allowing them to emerge in my consciousness and, by doing so, transform it, as social scientific accounts or even psychological ones would never do. Tillie Olson came later and Maya Angelou and Marge Piercy and Margaret Atwood and Toni Morrison; and I began, for the first time, seeing through many women's diverse eyes. (Greene, 1995, pp. 93–4)

Greene's explorations of selfhood are not confined within the boundaries of her own gender. Indeed, she understands that finding the ground of one's own being is crucial but that ground is also the 'ground of learning, of reaching beyond where one is' (1995, p. 93). Indeed, Greene admits that for a long time she deliberately sought out stories which would enable her to 'see through as many eyes and from as many angles as possible,' from men and women of all classes, backgrounds, colors, and religious faiths (1995, p. 94). The results of this seeking are apparent in her essays, for the writers and characters upon whom Greene calls to support and populate her literature-inspired multiculturalism are a varied lot indeed. A small sampling might include Walt Whitman, speaking, for example, in 'Song of Myself,' of the voices of prisoners and slaves, the 'voices of the diseas'd and despairing and of thieves and dwarfs . . .' (1995, p. 158); Ralph Ellison's Tod Clifton, the youth leader who is murdered by police in *Invisible Man* (1952); the Cuban immigrants of *The Mambo Kings Sing Songs of Love* (Hijuelos, 1989); the lady in brown from Ntozake Shange's *For Colored Girls who Have Considered Suicide, When the Rainbow is Enuf* (1977); 'the good and suffering people' in the works of Bernard Malamud; Thomas in *Native Son* (Wright, 1940); the Hindus and Sikhs of Bharati Mukherjee's *Jasmine* (1989); and, of course, the unforgettable characters, such as Pecola Breedlove, in *The Bluest Eye* (1970), upon whom Greene's beloved Toni Morrison has bestowed virtual breath.

And, again, the list includes characters brought into being within the significant portion of the traditional Western canon of literature which Greene reveres. Indeed, Greene notes that whether writers like Conrad and Melville proffered 'male views or not,' they conveyed a vision that binds all human beings to one another. Their capacity to promote human solidarity represents an important reason for honoring enlightened works written within less than enlightened cultural conditions. These works should be studied and, without ever ignoring exclusions and deformations past and present, paid tribute to, as has, Greene notes, a host of non-white authors — including Ellison writing about Melville and Hemingway, Alice Walker engaging with Muriel Ruykeyser and Flannery O'Conner, Toni Morrison mentioning Homer, Dostoevsky, Faulkner, Flaubert, and others (1995, p. 162).

Indeed, reading Maxine Greene provides encounters with a splendidly variegated mural composed of fragments from her own transactions with hundreds of literary texts. Or a different metaphor: Greene's innumerable allusions to literary characters may serve to recall Bahktin's notion of the novel as a carnival, a place for all sorts of embodied voices to join together in the dance of life. Greene herself notes that good literature, like a carnival, enables one to 'release the kind of energy that will permit familiar contact with everybody and everything' (1995, p. 63).

It is clear, therefore, that diversity, the widening of the discursive space to include many vantage points, really matters to Greene. But it would be seriously misleading to suggest that empathy and diversity represent her ultimate hopes for what literary encounters can provide. Greene does not advocate diversity for its own sake. She is not interested in newly strengthened voices contributing to a pointless and futile cacophony of individual interests. Diversity, she has commented, is important but we need to 'think hard about where we go with the multiple voices' (Ayers, 1995, p. 327).

Where do we go? Into a reconstructed human community. As suggested by her reaction to the Woolf novel, Greene deems the quality of human social life to be critical. Indeed, because there may be no objectively existent world outside of that life, our social entanglements are all that we can be certain exists. So the degree of connectedness we experience with others partially determines the quality of our lives. It is for that reason that we must move beyond the 'swamp of separateness,' to the creation of genuine community, a community in which we — its members — confront the stories of others who live, as Richard Rorty put it, 'outside of the range of "us"' (Rorty, 1989, p. 293). This community will be one of mutual regard, in which each of its members 'contribute to the pursuit of shared goods: . . . ways of being together, of attaining mutuality, of reaching toward some common world' (Greene, 1995, p. 39). Such a community of human solidarity is an 'ideal possibility . . . of unexpected moments when people feel their identity with other suppressed groups they never knew, and . . . acting in the experience of that mutual recognition, they open a space where they . . . [can] be free' (Ayers, 1995, p. 324).

So it is clear that the diversity and human solidarity about which she has so avidly written is, in fact, merely a context for a larger critique. That critique is entered into with a spirit of utopian thinking aimed at the construction of a new social order, with a hope for a 'community that may someday be called a democracy' (1995, p. 6). It is a mode of thought which, not surprisingly, on certain levels resonates with the politically conscious texts of the radical and progressivist left. Common ground is, in fact, identifiable between Greene and the so-called 'critical theorists': Greene would, it seems, endorse fully their dismay at prevalent notions of the individual as an existential, political, and economic isolate, at the debilitating reproductions of beliefs and ways of knowing, at the maintenance of rigid social stratifications, at the strong pull toward various sorts of commodification within our capitalist economy and culture. While they are not among her most often cited texts, it is clear that Greene has found time to acquaint herself with, and occasionally comment directly upon, the writings of Marx, Bowles and Gintis, Adorno, Lukacs, Marcuse, and Habermas (although, with the exception of Paulo Friere, rarely upon the writings of her prominent progressivist colleagues within the field of education).

So Greene does not directly reject the radicals' desires for 'socialist teachers and the creation of a working class consciousness,' their hopes for 'revolutionary educators being in the forefront of a movement to create a unified class consciousness' (1978, p. 107). Ultimately, however, Greene feels a sense of incompleteness about critical academic discourse. She is, perhaps, too prodigious a reader, too expansive a thinker, too closely acquainted with alternative sources of enlightenment, to confine herself to the specialized idiom and narrowly drawn arguments of critical theory. Her inspirations and hopes are derived from additional philosophical traditions, especially those of existentialism, phenomenology, and literary criticism.

Of direct interest here, however, is the distance Greene places between herself and the language usually employed by those 'generous intellectuals,' a language which is 'at odds with and often alien to the "natural language"' of those whom they want to teach (1978, p. 104), or, stronger, a well-intentioned but specialized idiom which is, paradoxically, 'associated with distrust of ordinary people' (1978, p. 105). Greene argues instead for a kind of verbal agility among intellectuals and educators which enables them to move among various symbolic forms, and of course, she ultimately emphasizes the emancipatory power of literary (and other artistic) modes of discourse. In this matter Greene's thinking might be characterized as strongly Sartrean.

Greene's appreciation of the emancipatory potentials of imaginative literature is indeed reminiscent of the work of Jean-Paul Sartre. But Sartre is a thinker who has apparently influenced her profoundly on several levels. She resonates strongly with his existentialist philosophy, and his leftward-leaning political commitments, as well as with the particular role he envisioned for literature in the development of a better social order.

Like Greene, Sartre viewed writing as a way of opening up imaginative spaces in hopes of transforming the world. For him words are invariably tools, 'the instruments of possible action.' But he was also insistent that the text was not merely the 'means for any end whatsoever' (Sartre, 1988, pp. 54–5). Indeed, long before Greene, Sartre (in *What Is Literature?*) specified what he considered to be a desirable end for a work of literature: 'whether he speaks only of individual passions or whether he attacks the social order, the writer, a free man, addressing free men, has only one subject — freedom' (Sartre, 1988, p. 55). In Sartre one finds presaged the Greenian theme (and that of other latter-day commentators) of literature's capacity to call attention to unendurable social conditions which serve to shackle bodies, minds, and spirits. Sartre elaborated upon this goal of literature in a speculation about the effects of *Black Boy* (1945), the novel by Richard Wright, on African-Americans: 'they understand with their hearts . . . [Wright] mediates, names, and shows them the life they lead from day to day in its immediacy, the life they suffer without finding words to formulate their sufferings. He is their conscience . . .' (Sartre, 1988, p. 79).

Sartre and Greene would agree that freedom cannot exist prior to this kind of naming, to such deep and immediate understanding. Nor can freedom be born and survive within an inability to imagine better states of affairs, and some imaginative literature can indeed inspire collaboration and conspiracy between writers and readers, can result in a 'coming together of those who choose themselves affected and involved . . . in order to break through the structures of their world and create something new' (Sartre, 1988, p. 17). For Sartre then, as for Greene (and Foucault and others), the writer is someone who is (like the critical theorist) engaged in an act of politics. The writer, as a human being, 'reveals himself by undertakings. And all the undertakings we might speak of, reduce themselves to a single one, *making history*' (Sartre, 1998, p. 104).

But if both Sartre and Greene have viewed literary texts as rhetorical tools for coaxing a reader toward a more just and humane view of social phenomena, they also have understood the potentially dangerous, anesthetic consequences of using those tools in a heavy-handed manner. Even as he called for 'committed literature,' Sartre cautioned that 'commitment must in no way lead to a forgetting of *literature*' (Sartre, 1988). This means that writer must avoid all tendencies toward the production of propaganda, 'closed' texts which eschew ambiguity in an attempt to impose their own final, totalized truths.

Instead, Sartre and Greene (with John Dewey, and phenomenologist aestheticians such as Susanne Langer), see literary language as embodying (rather than simply conveying) that which is not conceptual, as able to evoke in readers an image that is directly sensed. Works of imaginative literature could thereby help educators who align themselves with critical causes to remain in touch with their own 'lived worlds, their pre-understandings, their perceptual landscapes' (Greene, 1978, p. 108). They may locate specific characters within the alienating and oppressing contingencies of their own lives, thus grounding lofty critiques of the culture in the consciousness of the reader. Readings of, and conversations about, such texts can lead to the kind of critical reflection that can be carried on by persons who are situated in the concreteness of the world, by persons equipped for interrogation, for problematization, and for hermeneutic interpretation of the culture — of the present and the past (Greene, 1978, p. 108).

Sartre noted that 'we can no longer formulate general truths about ourselves which shall cover us like a house' (quoted in Murdoch, 1960, p. 78). But the writings of the critical theorists, like most other well-intentioned treatises of social science, philosophy, and religion, tend to hover high above the grounds upon which real injustices are dealt out. As such their power to promote the kinds of imagination, empathy, solidarity, and social action which Greene and Sartre have in mind may be somewhat vitiated. The authors of these texts may advocate, even argue passionately in favor of, a world of reduced oppression and humiliation, but somehow lack the degree of persuasive power of a text given to subtle suggestions about broad issues through vivid depictions of particular lives, and illustrations of how debilitating social and institutional forces intrude upon and distort those lives.

But what can be said about the irony in attempts — including those by Greene and Sartre — to persuade readers of the virtues of imaginative discourse through texts composed of and within a non-literary language and format? In proffering their essentially theoretical frames of reference neither Greene or Sartre offer texts which represent 'real toads,' or give them formal significance by relocating them into 'imaginary gardens.' Are their texts, which, unlike those of imaginative literature, do not locate characters within the contingencies of their lives, any more likely than those of the critical theorists to promote the kind of critical reflection which leads to a remaking of the reader's values?

The young Jean-Paul Sartre was so keenly aware of this irony that he bravely ventured into the territory of the artist, attempting to 'transpose the ideas in our books' into the languages of novels, radio broadcasts, film, and theater (1988, pp. 216–17). But despite his production of plays (*The Dirty Hands*), screenplays (*The Chips Are Down*), and novels (*Iron in the Soul*), Sartre never quite mastered the ability 'to speak in images' as well as he had mastered more theoretical forms of discourse. His literary attempts paled alongside his great works of philosophy and literary theory, and he knew it.

Maxine Greene also has a personal history of literary writing. She has revealed in an interview (Ayers, 1995) how she began writing stories at the age of seven, the first — 'what I called a novel' — for her father. Later, after having a story about women in World War II published in the magazine *Mademoiselle*, she took on a literary agent. But her first book was rejected for publication, and she was herself dissatisfied with the second. And then her third book, about a possible suicide by someone who had testified at an un-American Activities Committee, coincided with her own father's suicide, and:

> I suppose I was voodooed; certainly I was terribly guilt-ridden. I never wrote any fiction after that . . . Sometimes I think that I should unearth [those novels] and rekindle the researched sections; but then I lose heart. People tell me I should try writing novels today; but I know too much about what fine novels are and do not think I could write one. If I started again, I would want to do a *Madame Bovary* or *To the Lighthouse* or *Jazz*, not an item by the Maxine Greene I feel myself to be. (Ayers, 1995, p. 326)

Ultimately, of course, we must accept Greene's judgment about her own talents and abilities. She is, after all, privy to more information about these matters than are we. Nevertheless, when I confront a passage with such descriptive power as in the following, I find myself doubting that Greene's literary attempts could ever have been total failures:

> There are the worn-down, crowded urban classrooms and the contrasting clean-lined spaces in the suburbs. There are the bulletin boards crammed with notices and instructions, here and there interlaced with children's drawings or an outspoken poem. There are graffiti, paper cutouts, uniformed figures in the city schools; official voices blaring in and around; sudden shimmers when artists visit; circles of young people writing in journals and attending to stories. There are family groups telling one another what happened the night before, describing losses and disappearances, reaching for one another's hands. Clattering corridors are like the backstreets of ancient cities, filled with folks speaking multiple languages, holding their bodies distinctively, watching out for allies and for friends. There are shouts, greetings, threats, the thump of rap music, gold chains, flowered leotards, multicolored hair. Now and again there are the absorbed stares of youngsters at computer screens or the clink of glass and metal in school laboratories in front of wondering, puzzled eyes . . . (1995, pp. 10–11)

The elderly Jean-Paul Sartre, unable to meet his own standards for crafting graceful and politically insightful works of art, ultimately suffered a disillusionment with his notion of 'engaged literature.' ('For a long time I took my pen for a sword; now I know our impotence', Sartre, 1964, p. 212.) But Greene's hopes for the efficacy of her work continue undiminished, even as she describes her accomplishments, in her characteristically humble fashion, as 'modest' (Ayers, 1995, p. 328).

Occasionally, however, her hopes seem lofty, indeed. Consider her urgings, 'against conventional wisdom,' that teacher educators pay attention to novels by the likes of Flaubert and Balzac (1978, pp. 22–41), part of, Greene quite rightly observes, a critical literature 'that seems on the face of it, irrelevant to teacher education.' For Greene, the emancipatory function of these texts lies in their ability to provoke the kind of self-reflection, awareness, and hope in teachers as 'people whose lives have become attenuated.' Greene's assumption must be that at least a few thoughtful teacher educators can indeed be persuaded by her own masterful revelations of the relevance and power of literary classics to place their students within the proximity of those works.

For some, these hopes are too high: there are surely many teachers and teacher educators whom the writings of Maxine Greene cannot reach. First, some may not be willing to place themselves within the proximity of her works. And second, philosophy and literary criticism might (unlike imaginative literature) be insufficiently powerful discursive forms to awaken those asleep at the chalkboard to the unexpected and shattering, to enable them to 'understand through their hearts' that which they do not particularly want to see or understand.

The story, however, may be otherwise for those with different perceptual landscapes, whose own pre-understandings about the relevance of literature have already been shaped within other sorts of life experiences. I know that she has persuaded at least one such teacher educator (and I suspect, many others) to 'see and understand.' For even if she refuses to be an artist herself, her beautifully crafted and politically insightful writings have indeed performed for me that which John Dewey (1958) identified as the primary function of an art critic: Greene has educated my perception of the significance of particular pieces of literature for my own personal and professional quest for meaning. My own horizons have been broadened to include the additional vantage points of the authors of, and characters in, the literature she references. Finally, she has reinforced my belief in the importance of enticing my own students to join in the 'carnival' of imaginative literature. I attempt to lure them there with her amazing essays, 'item[s] by the Maxine Greene [she feels herself] to be.'

References

AYERS, W. (1995) 'Social imagination: A conversation with Maxine Greene,' *International Journal of Qualitative Studies in Education*, **8**, 4, pp. 319–28.

DEWEY, J. (1958) *Art as Experience*, New York: Capricorn Books. Originally published in 1934.

ELLISON, R. (1952) *Invisible Man*, New York: Signet Books.

GREENE, M. (1965a) 'Real toads in imaginary gardens,' *Teachers College Record*, **69**, pp. 271–6.

GREENE, M. (1965b) *The Public School and the Private Vision: A Search for America in Education and Literature*, New York: Random House.

GREENE, M. (1977) 'The artistic–aesthetic and curriculum,' *Curriculum Inquiry*, **6**, 4, pp. 283–95.

GREENE, M. (1978) *Landscapes of Learning*, New York: Teachers College Press.

GREENE, M. (1988) *The Dialectic of Freedom*, New York: Teachers College Press.

GREENE, M. (1991) 'Blue guitars and the search for curriculum,' in WILLIS, G. and SCHUBERT, W.H. (eds) *Reflections from the Heart of Educational Inquiry: Understanding Curriculum and Teaching Through the Arts* (pp. 107–22), Albany: State University of New York Press.

GREENE, M. (1995) *Releasing the Imagination: Essays on Education, the Arts, and Social Change*, San Francisco: Jossey-Bass.

HIJUELOS, O. (1989) *The Mambo Kings Sing Songs of Love*, New York: Farrar, Straus & Giroux.

hooks, b. (1991) 'Narratives of struggle,' in MARIANI, P. (ed.) *Critical Fictions: The Politics of Imaginative Writing* (pp. 53–61), Seattle: Bay Press.

ISER, W. (1974) *The Implied Reader*, Baltimore: Johns Hopkins University Press.

ISER, W. (1993) *The Fictive and the Imaginary: Charting Literary Anthropology*, Baltimore: Johns Hopkins University Press.

MORRISON, T. (1970) *The Bluest Eye*, New York: Bantam Books.

MUKHERJEE, B. (1989) *Jasmine*, New York: Grove Weidenfeld.

MURDOCH, I. (1960). *Sartre*, Cambridge: Harvard University Press.

RORTY, R. (1989) *Contingency, Irony, and Solidarity*, New York: Cambridge University Press.

SARTRE, J.-P. (1964) *Words* (Irene Clephane, trans.), London: Hamish Hamilton.

SARTRE, J.-P. (1988) *What Is Literature? and Other Essays*, Cambridge: Harvard University Press.

SHANGE, N. (1977) *For Colored Girls Who Have Considered Suicide, When the Rainbow is Enuf*, New York: Macmillan.

WOOLF, V. (1962) *To the Lighthouse*, London: Everyman's Library. Originally published in 1927.

WRIGHT, R. (1940) *Native Son*,

WRIGHT, R. (1945) *Black Boy: A Record of Childhood and Youth*, New York: Harper and Row.

13   The Slow Fuse of Aesthetic Practice

Rebecca Luce-Kapler

If imagination is the spark that ignites the possible, then aesthetic experience is imagination's tinder box. When I read Virginia Woolf's *Three Guineas* or Kate Chopin's *The Awakening*, I compare the societal constraints on women with those of my own time and understand more clearly what possibilities exist in my life. When I listen to Ofra Harnoy play a Vivaldi cello concerto, my body responds to her music and clears the way for an imaginative response through poetry. When I encounter Emily Carr's painting, *Blue Sky,* I find myself in conversation with the artist, learning more about who I am through my engagement with her work. My work as a writer and a teacher depends on this kind of imaginative possibility.

This is the aesthetic potential that Maxine Greene describes in much of her work; a potential which offers creative and transformative power for learning and teaching:

> At the heart of what I am asking for in the domains of the teaching of art and aesthetics is a sense of agency, even of power. Painting, literature, theater, film — all can open doors and move persons to transform. We want to enable all sorts of young people to realize that they have the right to find works of art meaningful against their own lived lives. (Greene, 1995, p. 150)

This imaginative vision through aesthetic engagement is what Maxine Greene and others have called experiencing the *as if.* The rich, *as if* hypothetical worlds (our own or those of others' creations) reconfigure experience and make it less familiar and repetitive so that we can become conscious of 'what is not yet, of what might, unpredictably, still be experienced' (Greene, 1995, p. 62). But such imaginative possibilities are not accidental or meandering occurrences like daydreams; that is, unlike a daydream which builds on preexisting assumptions, the imaginative experience that Maxine Greene describes is more disciplined, more of an aesthetic practice. Such a practice, Robert Grudin (1990) suggests, includes control with exuberance, precision with ambiguity, and exacting professionalism with childish fun (p. 50). We learn to bring together the disparate parts, to reconstruct whole contexts of experience, and to reconfigure them, finding strangeness in the familiar and disrupting 'the walls' (Greene, 1988, p. 133) which confine our thinking. Aesthetic practice requires conscious participation and an ability to notice rather than a predetermination of what will be discovered.

> Knowing 'about,' even in the most formal academic manner, is entirely different from constituting an [sic] fictive world imaginatively and entering it perceptually, affectively, and cognitively. To introduce students to the manner of such engagement is to strike a delicate balance between helping learners to pay heed — to attend to shapes, patterns, sounds, rhythms, figures of speech, contours, and lines — and helping liberate them to achieve particular works as meaningful. (Greene, 1995, p. 125)

The importance that Maxine Greene ascribes to aesthetic practice is most evident in her use of literature, beginning with her earliest writings and threading through her work to the present. (An early example is Maxine Greene's (1965) book *The Public School and The Private Vision: A Search for America in Education and Literature*, New York: Random House, Inc. A recent one is *Releasing the Imagination*. There are, of course, many examples in her articles and books in between these two publications.) The literature, besides being an integral part of her life, becomes part of her research text that she uses to illuminate human life and pedagogy and, like any good teacher, she uses these illustrations to draw our attention to the world in ways that help us understand our part in it as teachers and learners. 'I have discovered that literature (for me) has the potential of making visible what has sunk out of sight, of restoring a lost vision and a lost spontaneity,' she writes.

> If I can make present the shapes and structures of a perceived world, even though they have been layered over with many rational meanings over time, I believe my own past will appear in altered ways and that my presently lived life — and, I would like to say, teaching — will become more grounded, more pungent, and less susceptible to logical rationalization, not to speak of rational instrumentality. (1995, pp. 77–8)

For Greene, her relationship with literature, her understanding of past and present experiences, and her teaching are deeply interconnected. Maxine Greene, as teacher, learns how she learns and then shares such experiences with students.

To better understand her aesthetic practice, I will focus on three writers who have influenced both Greene's work and my own: Virginia Woolf, Elizabeth Bishop, and Toni Morrison. Using some of their writings, I will explore how Greene both teaches and learns, and how, in turn, she encourages me to reconsider my own work as teacher and learner.

Virginia Woolf's writing is a consistent influence in Greene's work, not only through Woolf's fictional pieces such as *To the Lighthouse* (1994), but also through her autobiographical and non-fictional accounts. In particular, the metaphor from Woolf's autobiography of breaking through 'the cotton wool of daily life' to 'moments of being,' (Woolf, 1976, p. 72) echoes through much of Greene's later writing: only when we question the taken-for-granted, she suggests, 'only when we take various, sometimes unfamiliar perspectives on it, does it show itself as what it is — contingent on many interpretations, many vantage points, unified (if at all) by conformity or by unexamined common sense' (Greene, 1995, p. 23). This breaking through the habitual and unquestioned is critical for classrooms. Students and teachers can take for granted the noisy and crowded hallways of schools, the routines of math following language arts, and the requirements that demand only expected performances. But when the habitual is seen as a contingency rather than a given, Maxine Greene believes that we may then consider alternative ways of living and making choices. Sometimes, however, breaking through the 'cotton wool,' the habitual, can only come through a shock that makes one take notice. There is value in such experience, Virginia Woolf writes, because

> . . . shock is at once in my case followed by the desire to explain it. I feel that I have had a blow; but it is not, as I thought as a child, simply a blow from an enemy hidden behind the cotton wool of daily life; . . . it is a token of some real thing behind appearances, and I make it real by putting it into words. It is only by putting it into words that I make it whole, and this wholeness means that it has lost its

power to hurt me; it gives me . . . a great delight to put the severed parts together. (Woolf, 1976, p. 72)

Without the imagination to 'rewrite' her experience, Virginia Woolf would have found it difficult to withstand the blows to which she refers. To be able to reconfigure experience, to see it differently requires that one be able to consider possibilities, to wonder about might be or could be, *as if* something were feasible. Imagination creates new order as it connects human consciousness to works of art. Indeed, Maxine Greene thinks, 'imagination may be responsible for the very texture of our experience' (1995, p. 140). In relating such thinking to education, she writes:

> What seems crucial is the noticing, the active insertion of one's perception into the lived world. Only after that does a project come to be, putting an explanation into words, fighting a plague, seeking homes for the homeless, restructuring inhumane schools. To ponder this is to become convinced that much of education as we know it is an education in forgetfulness. (1995, p. 74)

Only when teachers move individuals into imaginative awareness, she suggests, will they free students to make their visions real.

Virginia Woolf's writing not only inspired Maxine Greene to imagine change for education, but also led Greene to consider choices in her own life. Reading about Woolf's refusal to merge with a male society in *Three Guineas*, Greene asked herself about the need to be an outsider, to be herself and on her own. 'I needed, as I got older,' she writes, 'to struggle toward some new integrations of my perception of being alive as an American woman with my desires to commit myself to make things change and to live out that commitment' (1995, p. 85). Comparing her experience to Woolf's description of shocks, Greene reflected on the importance of her dialectic relationship with political, social, and historical environments. When those forces inhibited, demeaned, or interfered with her freedom, her response was shock that her space of choosing and acting was being narrowed. This shock sent her to writing and to calling upon her imagination where she discovered alternatives and became open to possibilities. Like Woolf, she could put parts together, reconfigure experience, and discover something different.

It is in Virginia Woolf's imaginative literature, however, where Maxine Greene describes the potential inherent in the aesthetic experience of literature both for herself and education. Literary texts invite readers into the *as if*, that place of potential revision and possibility, and readers accept these invitations as expressions of reality that have some existence of their own in the world. As Wolfgang Iser writes,

> . . . fictional texts constitute their own objects and do not copy something already in existence. For this reason they cannot have the full determinancy of real objects, and indeed, it is the element of indeterminancy that evokes the text to 'communicate' with the reader, in the sense that they induce him [or her] to participate both in the production and the comprehension of this work's intention. (1978, p. 24)

Because the literary text is open, it is able to initiate 'performances of meaning' (Iser, 1978, p. 27) rather than actually formulating meaning itself. Readers, then, (and writers) read and write *as if* the story can describe the reality of an event or an imagining or a feeling, *as if* language did not remove them a step from the event. The reading and writing assume a wholeness in the work that has no residue on its margins. Readers and writers come to the text *as if* their needs and demands can be met and *as if* they will not be left desiring. What such contingency does is broaden the possibilities for experiencing, acting, understanding, and creating. When Maxine Greene writes about how the poetic imagination enables us to enter the *as if* world of Toni Morrison's *Jazz,* journeying from the rural South to the sights and sounds of Harlem, or enables us to join the complex family life of the Ramseys in *To the Lighthouse*, she is speaking about the possibilities of knowing from other perspectives. Understanding other points of view is an 'imaginative leap [that] can lead to the leap that is *praxis,* the effort to remake and transcend' (Greene, 1978, p. 223).

To the Lighthouse begins during a day at the Ramsay's vacation home in the Hebrides. Besides the Ramsay family, there are a number of guests including Lily Briscoe, an unmarried artist and Charles Tansley, a student of Mr Ramsay's. As the day progresses, the reader finds himself or herself shifting from one character's perspective to another about the surroundings and events of that place. One moment readers are with Mrs Ramsay measuring her husband's mood while she reads to her young son James and the next they see events from James's perspective as his father interrupts the intimate reading time. The day ends, leading into a poetic 'hinge' entitled 'Time Passes' where there are short fragments of events that open into the last piece of the novel: a return to the Hebrides 10 years hence of the remaining family members and friends. Again the reader shifts through perspectives in the story, comparing not only how the characters' perceptions differ, but how they have changed with the passage of time.

For Maxine Greene, this story clearly reveals how reading literature asks the reader to continually shift and change to interpret and make meaning of the text. She describes how this act of reading takes place between two poles: the artistic pole which is the text, and the aesthetic pole which is the reader who actualizes the work in relation to his or her own experience. While reading, one moves between one's own experiences and understanding and the possibilities inherent in the text; there is a continual revision between what one knows and what offerings are realized in the text. Iser, in Deweyan mode, describes transactions between readers' presence to the text and their habitual experiences as the aesthetic experience somehow transcends that past experience. Discrepancies readers find as they make the effort to create patterns become significant. Lily Briscoe, unmarried woman painter, sees the sea-surrounded Hebrides world quite differently than does the analytical Professor Ramsay. Both viewpoints are at odds with those of the various children, the aged poet, or the lighthouse keeper. When the characters are seen to view things differently, this phenomenon may make the readers conscious of the inadequacy of some of the patterns or interpretations they themselves have produced along the way (Greene, 1995, p. 97).

The text offers the openness for sense-making as the relation between the reader's experience and the experience of reading the text co-emerge. The act of reading becomes one of engaging in a liberating constraint where imaginative potential resides within the parameters of the text and the reader's experience. The reader brings meaning to the page and through actively communicating with the words and looking through the multiple and transient perspectives, gradually constitutes an *as if* world, achieved against the background of his or her lived reality.

> The actualities of that lived reality, like the other facets of the everyday and mundane world, cannot be totally abandoned. All the reader can do is bracket them out, put them into parentheses within her/his experience, so that they do not prevent her/him *qua* reader from moving into another space, an unreal world made out of memories, stored images, dream fragments, ideas, fantasies that have been reordered by imagination. (Greene, 1994, p. 211)

To the Lighthouse, like other literary works, is not a storehouse of predetermined meanings, but rather is a source of possibilities where meaning is discovered by the reader through his or her active participation in bringing experience to the text.

Maxine Greene describes an example of how this act of reading occurs for her in a passage from *To the Lighthouse.* She begins by describing the dinner scene from the first section of the book:

> Now all the candles were lit, and the faces on both sides of the table were brought nearer by the candle light, and composed, as they had not been in the twilight, into a party round a table, for the night was now shut out by panes of glass, which, far from giving any accurate view of the outside world, rippled it so strangely that here, inside the room, seemed to be order and dry land; there, outside, a reflection in which things wavered and vanished, waterily. Some change at once went through them all, as if this had really happened, and they were all conscious of making a party together in a hollow, on an island; had their common cause against that fluidity out there. (Woolf, 1994, p. 354)

This scene, Maxine Greene explains, was not where she learned something altogether new, but where she saw things she did not particularly want to see and that were buried in her ordinary experience of the world: that is, the idea that 'social life and even civilization are human creations in the face of nothingness' (1995, p. 98). However, realizing these ideas summoned her 'to create meanings, to effect connections, to bring some vital order into existence — if only for a time' (1995, p. 98). This kind of insight also confirmed for her the importance of including literature in her history and philosophy of education classes. Literature engaged the imagination which reached beyond to the *as if* and brought 'integral wholes into being in the midst of multiplicity' (1995, p. 99). She also suggests that this approach to reading reveals how we might envision curriculum: not as discrete bits of knowledge, but as making sense of one's relationship to the world; a verb rather than a noun. There is no existing world waiting to be uncovered or discovered, Greene explains, but as the reader becomes entangled in the characters' thoughts and perceives new possibilities, ideas are brought into the foreground which then alter the background consciousness. The world of the text and the world of the reader intertwine, becoming something new, something changed. She writes, 'choosing contingency over the false clarity the arts help us combat, we want to release persons for a transfigurative initiation through our curricula and to become more likely, also, to discover transformative dimensions in what we ourselves do' (1995, p. 100). My own reading of Virginia Woolf's work begins with the memory of finding a copy of *A Room of One's Own* in a dusty Kelowna bookstore that had books from everywhere and all times. The copy I found had been published in 1935 by Hogarth, which was Leonard and Virginia Woolf's press. When I held the book, I had a sensation of Woolf's hands in mine and experienced an immediate and intimate connection with the author which followed into my reading of the book. Within a few pages, I read:

> It was thus that I found myself walking with extreme rapidity across a grass plot. Instantly a man's figure rose to intercept me. Nor did I at first understand that the gesticulations of a curious-looking object in a cut-away coat and even shirt, were aimed at me. His face expressed horror and indignation. Instinct rather than reason came to my help; he was a Beadle; I was a woman. This was the turf; there was the path. Only the Fellows and Scholars are allowed here; the gravel is the place for me. (Woolf, 1935, p. 9)

Suddenly the reverie of the narrator, which had become my reverie, was startled by the image of this flapping, horrified man, and I experienced a sense of being placed rather firmly back into the 'real' world. As Virginia Woolf promised earlier in the text, she was going to use the techniques of fiction so listeners/readers could draw their own conclusions about so controversial a topic as the role of women. Her image made the point more strongly than any didactic treatise could have, for my imagination was fully in play: I was on that path and a participant of the event. Like Maxine Greene describes, I could see both the presence and absence of possibilities unfold.

In spite of knowing many of Woolf's works, I had not read *To the Lighthouse* until I saw how deeply the novel affected Maxine Greene. I approached the book thinking about not only what I would learn regarding my experiences, but also what insights I would then bring to my teaching. What struck me about the story, and what continues to reverberate with me, is both the simplicity and complexity of the novel. If one were to describe the plot, it would seem very straightforward: a day in the life of a family at their vacation home followed by another day 10 years later. Yet, the focus on the different perspectives which each character brings to the setting and events reveal the complexity of everyday life. Each moment is rich and varied. Lily Briscoe's thoughts describe it well:

> And, what was even more exciting, she felt, too, as she saw Mr Ramsay bearing down and retreating, and Mrs Ramsay sitting with James in the window and the cloud moving and the tree bending, how life, from being made up of little separate incidents which one lived one by one, became curled and whole like a wave which bore one up with it and threw one down with it, there, with a dash on the beach. (Woolf, 1994, p. 319)

Like Maxine Greene, this was not something I did not know, but experiencing its revelation through the novel, being part of a world where I could wander from perspective to perspective, I experienced a new understanding of how complexity could be created and engaged through the imagination. From a writer's viewpoint, I noticed the careful attention Woolf paid to the details of perspective, contrasting both characters and genders: each individual sees the landscape, the light of the day, the shadows of the night just a little differently. The lighthouse, as a beacon which draws every character's attention, also differentiates between them. As Maxine Greene points out, although the lighthouse seems to represent an object in the real world, one which we can visualize, it is not like those in the real world. Rather, it acts as a series of signifiers that shift according to time and the characters' perspectives. For Mrs Ramsay, it was 'the hoary Lighthouse, distant, austere' (Woolf, 1994, p. 295), and later, 'the steady light, the pitiless, the remorseless, which was so much her, yet so little her, which had her at its beck and call (she woke in the night and saw it bent across their bed, stroking the floor)' (pp. 331–2). Lily views the lighthouse by its distances; sometimes it seems close and other times, in haze, it seems an enormous distance away. James, as a young man, remembers the lighthouse of his childhood as a 'silvery, misty-looking tower with a yellow eye that opened suddenly and softly in the evening' (p. 419). Now it seems more definitively phallic: 'the tower, stark and straight . . . was barred with black and white' (p. 419). Yet, he realizes that both perspectives are the Lighthouse 'for nothing was simply one thing. The other was the Lighthouse too. It was sometimes hardly to be seen across the bay. In the evening one looked up and saw the eye opening and shutting and the light seemed to reach them in that airy sunny garden where they sat' (p. 419). Even the reader, as a silent visitor accompanying the narrator to the empty house, is offered a perspective: 'When darkness fell, the stroke of the Lighthouse, which had laid itself with such authority upon the carpet in the darkness, tracing its pattern came now in the softer light of spring mixed with moonlight gliding gently as if it laid its caress and lingered stealthily and looked and came lovingly again' (p. 381).

Every point of view makes the story more complex, deepening the sense that the reader has visited a place that existed, as if it were a real world. In my writing I am aware of the importance of point of view, but this novel reminded me how such a view could be carefully drawn to reveal the multiplicity of living. In my teaching, to develop students' awareness of viewpoint, I ask them to begin by writing about a place well known to them. Then, I ask them to shift away from their personal perspective by choosing from a small list of characters to whom I've assigned particular restraints. They are to 'bring' that character into the scene, describing the place from her or his point of view. While reading Virginia Woolf, I began to think about how I should not have stopped at just one point of view, but asked students to write others as well, having characters of differing histories, cultures or gender focused on one location or event. Reading Maxine Greene reading Virginia Woolf and then becoming part of that literary conversation by delving into the novel myself, I realized more clearly what Greene was saying. Following how she had learned, I discovered more about her as teacher as well as more about my own under-standings as a reader, teacher and learner.

This personal and transformative potential in imaginative literature occurs through a text's landmarks and through the gaps readers have to bridge, what Iser calls 'fundamen-tal asymmetry' (1978, p. 167). This asymmetry offers readers the opportunity to rewrite 'the text of the work within the texts of [their] lives' (Barthes, 1975, p. 62). While Virginia Woolf's writing is one example where Maxine Greene 'rewrote' the story within the text of her life, Elizabeth Bishop's work is another. Like her personal response to Woolf's work, Greene describes the insights she discovered in Bishop's (1992) poem 'In the Waiting Room,' and how that text was important for her creation of a narrative about the shape of childhood. She discovers that the poem recalls a memory that she views from a new perspective, thus altering her past and influencing her presently lived life.

'In the Waiting Room' is a poem about the sudden realization of one's separation from and connection to the human race all at the same time. The young girl, Elizabeth, sits in a dentist's waiting room while her aunt has her teeth worked on, paging through a *National Geographic,* studying the pictures of volcanoes and explorers in Africa. When she sees the photographs of black women whose necks are wound round with wire, she is horrified by their naked breasts. As Elizabeth checks the cover of the magazine, the yellow margins, the date, her aunt suddenly calls out in pain. Elizabeth realizes that she also has cried out, and this cry is accompanied by a sudden sensation of falling with eyes (hers, theirs) glued to the cover and the date February, 1918. To stop the sensation, Elizabeth tells herself that soon she will be seven years old; still, she is overwhelmed by the sudden awareness of her humanity. She tells herself that she is an *I*, an *Elizabeth*, a one of *them.*

In reading the poem, Maxine Greene remembers a mountain cottage and a sudden crash of lightning striking the roof. She and her friend scurry to find their mothers, leaving their paper dolls leaning against the wall. Her friend immediately crawls into her mother's lap along with her baby brother, but Maxine finds no room with her own mother who is holding her twin babies. Suddenly, there is no safe place, no place to hide. Maxine feels rejected and thrust into the world alone. Years later, in her encounter with the poem, she realizes that the reading has enlarged this experience for her. 'The shape of childhood of the child falling off the blue-black world begins to inform my memory of lightning crash, frail little paper dolls against a bedroom wall, my mother's arms full of babies, my clinging to the hem of her skirt, afraid and scornful at once, wanting to let go, be on my own' (Greene, 1995, p. 79). This sensation of being an 'I' who is also 'one of *them*' that Maxine Greene remembered through the poem is one that is reiterated through her writing. 'As time went on and I came closer to discovering my own "voice," meaning my woman's voice, through the writing I was doing, I learned much more about vantage point and more about history' (1995, p. 107). The falling into space of the poem, the painful particularity introduced 'a vantage point that subverts the systematic, the complete' (p. 117) and enhanced her consciousness of the ongoing dialectic.

Greene's recounting of this reading experience interested me because I, too, had had such an experience with the poem. I first encountered the piece in a book about poetry writing. The writing exercise suggested that the writer read the poem several times and then try to create a poem that would reflect the tone of Bishop's piece. The suggestion was offered that the writer might locate a memory in childhood and give it some specificity by supplying the focus of a date as Bishop does. As I searched for a memory, rereading the lines where Elizabeth notes the date on the magazine, I remembered that a copy of the *Saturday Evening Post* had created a similar event for me. It was the first time that I realized my father had been young just as I now was. My sister and I had been playing in the dusty attic of my grandparents' garage, exploring their old gramophone and some belongings that seemed ancient at the time, including a box of old *Saturday Evening Posts*. Some of our discoveries, combined with that fact that my grandfather and father were working nearby, must have precipitated this realization about my father.

Now that I had remembered this event, I was ready to write. Following the exercise, I gave the memory a specific date after guessing I must have been about 10 years old; then I began to imagine the experience, bringing to the event an adult understanding. I wrote the poem, including the lines:

> We discovered a cache
> of *Saturday Evening Posts*
> with their Norman Rockwell covers
>> boys with cowlicks
>> men who looked like photographs
>> of my grandfather
>> a dog at his heels.
>
>> One pictured a prim teacher
>> in a long green dress
>> greeting a mother
>> who held the hand of a boy
>> in knickers and polished boots.
>
>> The teacher's manner was genteel
>> a backdrop of the western hemisphere
>> hiding the hazelwood switch in her left hand
>
> 'September 14, 1935,' I read to my sister
>> touching the picture of boy
>>> who could be my father
>>> back to school in fall that year
>>> just turning ten

I had put this poem aside, unfinished, but returned to it after I read Maxine Greene's story. It was no longer a poem that I had abandoned, but a rewriting of a memory that became part of a childhood narrative. Rereading what I had written, I thought further about my relationship with my father, about how this event occurring just before adolescence had been almost like a marker of the change in our relationship. The two of us were moving into a time when we grew apart, where I would not feel close to him again for years. Looking at the memory now, my realization seems to herald this turning point. Maxine Greene had reminded me of how reading Elizabeth Bishop, like other imaginative texts, offered room for me to explore and rediscover the shape of my living: the curves and dips; the silences and gaps; the excitement and disappointment.

As Greene also considered her own silences and uncertainties through her experiences of the imagination, she realized that 'we all try to carve a space in which we can break the peculiar silences and choose' (1995, p. 117). In her reading and writing about gender roles, in particular the spaces for women, Maxine Greene wondered how the uncertainty she had felt in seeking her own voice might help her to begin to understand the difficulties of silence and uncertainty that people of minorities face. In the work of Toni Morrison, among other writers, she finds the 'amazing shocks' that offer other perspectives against the background of her own life. Multiple perspectives serve to enlarge our interpretive communities, Greene believes. These communities then become spaces for individuals to be subjects, unique and distinct persons within the public space, who are still part of a whole. With such an identity, comes responsibility, a valuing of what is, and a straining toward what ought to be. For example, Maxine Greene reminds us of Toni Morrison's remarkable novel *Beloved,* the story of slavery and a young mother's escape from such conditions. The novel is haunted with the memory of past cruelties and the deaths and loss of children. As Greene points out, the story recalls cherished memories of having and raising children as well as the subversion of such memory, the often repressed dread where children are sold or killed.

> And this may be when outrage may flood in, authentic outrage — retroactively with regard to children sold into slavery, presently with regard to children abused or lost. We may, after the outrage and passion, also feel a longing for resolution and repair. This is some of what can come from the presence of a subject standing in the public space — the space where visions should take shape, where at odd times and spontaneously, people feel themselves part of the dance of life. (Greene, 1995, pp. 71–2)

Toni Morrison (1992), in her collections of essays, *Playing in the Dark,* recognizes the importance of broadening perspectives. She describes how the critical gaze and the perspective of the reader have often not attended to the presence of African-Americans in literature. Not only have critics not read African-American texts, she explains, but in their reading of established works of white literature, they do not see the presence (or even the absence) of black characters in those texts. Referring to how Ernest Hemingway wrote so compellingly about being a white American male, she suggests that

> ... it would be a pity if the criticism of that literature continued to shellac those texts, immobilizing their complexities and power and luminations just below its tight, reflecting surface. All of us, reader and writers, are bereft when criticism remains too polite or too fearful to notice a disrupting darkness before its eyes. (Morrison, 1992, pp. 90–1)

Toni Morrison's story, *The Bluest Eye,* Greene suggests, reveals the danger of such a singular point of view. In the novel, Pecola Breedlove is convinced by two of culture's master narratives — the Dick and Jane basal readers and Shirley Temple — that as a black girl she is ugly. She wants nothing more than to look like Shirley Temple with bright blue eyes. When Pecola succumbs to madness, we realize that to have only one master story, only one standard (which for Pecola was set by blue eyes) can be fatal. Instead, Maxine Greene writes, '[w]hen we see more and hear more, it is not only that we lurch, if only for a moment, out of the familiar and the taken-for-granted but that new avenues for choosing and for action may open in our experience; we may gain a sudden sense of new beginnings . . .' (1995, p. 123). She also reads other possibilities in the book by focusing on the narrator of the story, Claudia. In the process of telling, Claudia reconfigures her own memories of longing and helplessness, in ways that reinterpret her own past and ethnicity. 'Whatever meaning she can draw,' Greene writes, 'from the connections she makes feeds into an ethic that may be meaningful in the future, an ethic that takes her beyond her own guilt at watching Pecola search the garbage' (1995, p. 125). Understanding our lives through narrative, helps us to make sense of those lives, to find direction. In classrooms, Maxine Greene reminds us, students can articulate their stories as a way to pursue other meanings in their lives.

> But that is not all. Stories like the one Claudia tells must be able to break through into what we think of as our tradition or our heritage. They will if we can do what Cornell West has in mind when he speaks about the importance of acknowledging 'the distinctive cultural and political practices of oppressed people' without high-lighting their marginality in such a way as to further marginalize them. (1995, p. 165)

While reading imaginative literature is a shared activity, Morrison writes from her own perspective, not to replace any other point of view, but to open a shared space where readers can come to imagine other possibilities, to put themselves in the *as if* of her fictional world. Morrison (1992) explains that her 'project is an effort to avert the critical gaze from the racial object to the racial subject; from the described and imagined to the describers and imaginers; from the serving to the served' (p. 90). Greene believes that this does not mean that schools adjust the curricula to suit one particular cultural group, but rather that teachers should foster openness, variety and inclusion without stereotyping, developing broad interpretive communities. Educators can encourage multiple conversations in classrooms through literature and other aesthetic practices that encourage the interaction and intersection of multiple voices and discourses, what Bakhtin called the heteroglossia. Engaged in such a dialogical relation, Maxine Greene points out, we will begin to develop a more humane and liberating pedagogy. This is not, however, necessarily an easy or comfortable process. Greene (1995) reminds us that some of the tensions people feel may be 'partially due to the suspicion we all often define ourselves against some unknown, some darkness (in many forms, not only of skin color), some "otherness" that we chose to thrust away, to master rather than to understand' (p. 162).

She also suggests that because aesthetic practice engages the imagination and opens possibilities, other ethical concerns come to the fore. With an awakened consciousness, students are opened to the potential for interpreting experiences in different and meaningful ways. Referring to Mary Warnock's writing, Greene explains that, 'it is the obligation of teachers to heighten the consciousness of whoever they teach by urging them to read and look and make their own interpretations of what they see' (1995, p. 35). As teachers, we too must break with our habitual and unquestioned ways of seeing: 'Trying to open students to the new and the multiple, we want ourselves to break through some of the crusts of convention, the distortions of fetishism, the sour tastes of narrow faiths' (1995,

p. 146). This also will bring us to questions of the limitations of the aesthetic practices we do and do not bring to our students. Rather than just accepting pronouncements of what is and is not acceptable in the world of art, we need to learn and our students need to learn how to make judgments in relation to our own experience and community norms.

Like Maxine Greene's, my reading of Toni Morrison led me to rethink my way of teaching. Looking back at some writing I did while I read *Beloved,* I discovered how I had become deeply entwined in the story, searching for connections to my teaching:

> And so the ghost of Beloved is consumed until she is no longer distinguishable from those she haunted. Am I absorbed too? Can I separate myself from the reading of this novel enough to discern an author's view, to speculate on her philosophy, to connect it to curriculum? I follow different threads of the story and trace my memory trying to unravel the experience. There is Sethe, the young woman who escapes from slavery only to become enslaved by the ghost of her dead daughter. There are the living children — two sons driven away by the ghost and a daughter isolated in the house with her mother. And there is Paul D, a man from Sethe's past, whose coming stirs up memories and brings them to life. In my search, I become inextricably tangled in the threads until I am part of the texture.
>
> My memories and experiences intertwine with the text and tug at strings from the story as I create the world of a slave woman in my imagination: the pink glitter and cool smoothness of the baby's granite headstone; the stickiness of the chamomile sap against my legs; the fur of mossy teeth tugging at my nipple; the bitter smell of the flooding creek; the voices of women singing. Bit by bit I am absorbed into that place.
>
> Then I become aware of the physical world which I inhabit and I step back for a moment from the reading, remembering that I want to think about curriculum. When I re-enter the story, I pay closer attention to the hints of an author ducking behind words and peeking between lines. There is a polyphonic presence whose voice has the timbre of flesh and blood; an imagined character who speaks of the shared understanding between my memory and reading and the author and her story.

Added to this re-creation, this remembering, are Toni Morrison's words in an essay that I read between the chapters of the novel:

> The imagination that produces work which bears and invites rereadings, which motions to future readings as well as contemporary ones, implies a shareable world and an endlessly flexible language. Readers and writers both struggle to interpret and perform within a common language shareable imaginative worlds. And although upon that struggle the position of the reader has justifiable claims, the author's presence — her or his intentions, blindness, and sight — is part of the imagination activity. (Morrison, 1992, p. xii)

She describes what is happening as I read her novel, and I am reassured that my entanglement is meant to be.

> What does this experience tell me about curriculum? I begin thinking of a class where one voice is not privileged over others, where the teacher listens to students as much as they listen to her, where I am reminded of the potential of literature to deepen our understandings of what we remember and how we interpret our lives. (Luce-Kapler, 1993)

Now, returning to this paper, I would add: 'and where the teaching begins with learning.' As Maxine Greene has shown us, learning can happen through aesthetic practice, where what one reads, talks about, hears, sees, and senses in the world influences imaginative experiences. In turn, those imaginative experiences influence the way we discover meaning in the world and follow possibilities for acting — the unfolding of curriculum.

Revisiting Maxine Greene, remembering familiar literature, and acquainting myself with new pieces has reminded me of this interconnected power of aesthetic practice. Memory, rewritten within the text of imaginative works, can change the past, present, and future. Through Maxine Greene's example of aesthetic practice, where she shares her personal relationship with literature and discovers insights into her learning that influence her writing and teaching, she illuminates how to discover the possible through imaginative routes. She writes:

> So literature, with other works of art, can become a harbinger of the possible. There are no promises, no guarantees. Emily Dickinson wrote that 'The possible's slow fuse is lit by the imagination.' It may at least be time to light the fuse. (Greene, 1994, p. 218)

References

BARTHES, R. (1975) *The Pleasure of the Text* (trans. R. Miller), New York: Hill & Wang.

BISHOP, E. (1992) 'In the Waiting Room,' in BEHN, R. and TWICHELL, C. (eds) *The Practice of Poetry*, New York: HarperPerennial.

GREENE, M. (1965) *The Public School and The Private Vision: A Search for America in Education and Literature*, New York: Random House, Inc.

GREENE, M. (1978) *Landscapes of Learning*, New York: Teachers College Press.

GREENE, M. (1988) *The Dialectic of Freedom*, New York: Teachers College Press.

GREENE, M. (1994) 'Postmodernism and the crisis of representation,' *English Education*, **26**, pp. 206–19.

GREENE, M. (1995) *Releasing the Imagination: Essays on Education, the Arts, and Social Change*, San Francisco, CA: Jossey-Bass Publishers.

GRUDIN, R. (1990) *The Grace of Great Things: Creativity and Innovation*, New York: Ticknor & Fields.

ISER, W. (1978) *The Act of Reading: A Theory of Aesthetic Response*, Baltimore, MD: Johns Hopkins University Press.

LUCE-KAPLER, R. (1993) 'Excavating memory: Exploring Toni Morrison's *Beloved* as curriculum,' Unpublished paper, Edmonton: University of Alberta.

MORRISON, T. (1992) *Playing in the Dark: Whiteness and the Literary Imagination*, Cambridge, MA: Harvard University Press.

WOOLF, V. (1935) *A Room of One's Own*, London: Hogarth Press.

WOOLF, V. (1976) *Moments of Being: Unpublished Autobiographical Writings* (ed. Jeanne Schulkind), Orlando, FL: Harcourt.

WOOLF, V. (1994) *To the Lighthouse*, London: Chancellor Press.

14   What Are the Arts For? Maxine Greene, the Studio and Performing Arts, and Education

Donald Blumenfeld-Jones

Dear Maxine Greene

You don't know me but I know you, at least I know something of you through your work which I have read and heard at conferences for many years. When I first 'met' you I was just beginning to move away from my first career as a concert modern dancer/university dance teacher into my present life as an education scholar. I didn't actually know that I was making that move because I was enrolled in an M.F.A. in Dance program, fully intending to use the degree to continue what I had already done for 13 years — dance and choreograph professionally and teach and choreograph dance in university settings. As it turned out the die was cast from the very first day of this new experience called graduate school and I had cast it. I had delineated a program for myself that included, almost exclusively, scholarly work in philosophy and anthropology as a way toward better understanding of what dance was, both for my own interest and in order to teach it better. I had thought in such areas for many years, reading and thinking on my own and now I was going to seize the opportunity to do so in a more systematic and supported way. In the course of events that ensued, I was brought to your book *Landscapes of Learning* (1978a), especially the section on aesthetics, by my good friend Sue Stinson. You even came to Greensboro, North Carolina to speak (although I couldn't attend that event because my newborn son commanded, beautifully, my attention and presence). Later on I did have the good fortune to hear you speak at Duke University. You were brought in to speak about the Lincoln Center Institute.

At the same time, and initially unseen by myself, I began to rethink my relationship to dance. I no longer enjoyed the ways in which people would respond to me when they came to know that I danced for a living. There was an awe that often entered people's demeanor and a notion of 'what fun' it all must be to play all day. If only they could have made such a choice. I had come to dislike this sense that I was to be set apart because I had chosen to do this rather than that. Even before this I had been uncomfortable with it. When on tour and at a reception for the company given by the local sponsor, I always made a point of spending time with the local people at the party rather than holding back in the corner with the rest of the company. These people had come out for us. We were nothing special, I thought to myself.

I also knew that the profession was rife with difficulties. For one it was replete with contradictions such as 'it matters how you dance' versus 'it matters how you look.' I knew that modern dance choreographers had, originally, valued individuality both in movement and look but had become increasingly focused on move-alike, look-alike dancers. Much later on in my graduate work Sue Stinson, Jan Van Dyke and I (Stinson, Blumenfeld-Jones and Van Dyke, 1990) did a study of seven female adolescent dancers making the transition to college whose thinking about dance expressed many of these contradictions, and more, were choosing to move out of dance even though they were fine dancers and articulate, intelligent young women. In doing that study we thought, 'What a sad loss to the dance community.' Additionally, I knew that most dancers lived close to poverty. I knew that dance was a business, with all that such a fact entailed. I knew that it wasn't the pure world which most people envisioned. As I studied further and began to think more deeply about my own involvement and experiences, I became increasingly uncomfortable with how the dance world was structured and lived in by those involved and viewed by those outside it.

I tell you all this because as I think about your relationship to the studio and performing arts (as best I can discern it), I find that we are both close and not close on many points. I am both sympathetic and disturbed by your ideas. I hope you are glad that I am disturbed because it seems to me that wide-awakeness, that wonderful idea which you develop so eloquently, must have, as part of its character, an edge and edginess. I know that whatever thoughts I have about dance and the studio and performing arts in general, I can only have because I have read you. That is, as with any area of inquiry, my present work is inevitably based on what you have already done, affording me the luxury, pleasure, excitement of springing out from your thinking. If my springing lands me somewhere else, this is as much a tribute to you as it is anything else. Where I land, of course, is a development of my own, particular relationship to the studio and performing arts. If we do not share such a relationship we will, in all likelihood, not be in the same subsequent relationship to them.

And I tell you all this because I do not wish to deliver any species of authoritative interpretation or understanding of your ideas. My hermeneutics rejects the notion that we can enact interpretations which understand the text better than the author her/himself. I believe, from the reader response theory and standpoint-theorizing perspectives, that I must locate myself as a particular interpreter with a particular situation which grounds the interpretation which I develop. This in no way invalidates my inferences from your ideas but it does locate them so that you may better understand why I might say what I say, thus creating grounds for a more full conversation. Further, as I have already written, I recognize that your texts are a context and pretext for me to be able to say anything at all in this new text. In the end, therefore, I offer my ideas to you in the way of conversation, care, and concern for your work.

This said, I want to tell you how I see the influence which the studio and performing arts have had upon your work, by proposing that there are three questions which I think animate your thinking about them. These are: Who is the artist? What are the studio and performing arts for? And, how can or should the studio and performing arts influence both our individual lives and how we live with each other? You argue consistently that the studio and performing arts afford experiences of imaginative transformation and affective insight (which bring about wide-awakeness) into all aspects of living in ways that alter how one lives one's own life and how one relates to the lives of others, creating thereby the possibility for a more moral life (1988a, 1995). The three central ideas of transformation, imagination, and wide-awakeness become thematized in how you address these questions.

You also draw a distinction between art education and aesthetic education which may help me understand your relationship to the studio and performing arts. You write that art education involves 'the spectrum that includes dance education, music education, the teaching of painting and other graphic arts, and (I would hope) the teaching of some kinds of writing' (1995, p. 138).

By 'aesthetic education,' I mean the deliberate efforts to foster increasingly informed and involved encounters with art. The point of enabling our students to both engage in art as a maker and experience existing artworks is to release them to be more fully present to, for example, an Edward Hopper city painting, a Cézanne landscape, a jazz composition, a Béla Bartók folk song, or a Joyce novel . . . I would like to see one pedagogy feeding into the other: the pedagogy that empowers students to create informing the pedagogy that empowers them to attend (and, perhaps, to appreciate) and vice versa. I would like to see both pedagogies carried on with a sense of both learner and teacher . . . reflective about his or her choosing process, turning toward the clearing that might (or might not) lie ahead. The ends in view are multiple, but they surely include the stimulation of imagination and perception, a sensitivity to various modes of seeing and sense making, and a grounding in the situations of lived life (1995, p. 138).

A more detailed examination of the three questions which I have suggested underlie your thinking about the studio and performing arts coupled with your thoughts on art education and aesthetic education help me to understand how you have positioned yourself vis à vis these arts.

'Who Is the Artist?'

This question seems the best starting place given your existentialist underpinnings. The status of the individual in the world must first be established before we can begin to understand how her/his projects and actions are related to that world. This is not an affirmation of individualism but, rather, of the freedom which the individual must enact as s/he interacts with others.

You often write about aesthetic experience in relation to specific works of art as you adumbrate how they might make our world less opaque and more vibrant in strange new ways. The following is an example taken from your work with teachers who attend the Lincoln Center Institute for the Arts Summer Workshop with which you have been associated from its inception.[1] You are telling them about the possibilities of aesthetic experience and you begin by describing your experience in the early morning in New York.

> There is always the possibility of opening perspectives and attaining new visions at Lincoln Center. Sometimes, in fact, I am overtaken by something very like an aesthetic experience even before I arrive in the morning. I become suddenly and sharply aware, as I get off the bus, of the jutting angles of the Juilliard Building, of the shadows it casts on the pavement, of the rooftops against the sky. I pay heed to the shape of the sky between the buildings. I find myself resonating to the rhythms of people walking by; I am drawn by the misty river a few blocks down, with its glimmers here and there, the boats in the haze, the vague shape of the bridge beyond. (Greene, 1989, p. 1)

You then go on to distinguish between 'release . . . from the habitual and the practical' and 'an encounter with an Edward Hopper painting of a city street' asking 'about the differences between experiences in the natural world and experiences with works of art' (p. 1). You aver that 'the crucial difference' lies in a work of art being 'deliberately composed' in order to 'express something . . . by means of color and form and imagery' (p. 1). This 'something' does not carry a definable message but is only designed to 'open new possibilities of vision' (p. 1). By encountering Hopper, unlike encountering the natural setting of the Juilliard Building, we encounter Hopper's 'lifelong quest for his own vision, his own 'truth,' in a changing context of meanings' (p. 1). You go on to write that Hopper 'intentionally . . . provides the kind of pleasurable experiences we can have by fortunate chance' (p. 8).

Here is what I learn from this text about the question 'Who is an artist?' I learn, in part that when I view the world with fresh eyes I am not enacting artistry, for my pleasurable experiences in such situations come only 'by fortunate chance' and are only a 'release from the habitual and practical.' (While it may be possible that you mean 'by fortunate chance' that we are fortunate enough to encounter a Hopper painting, I believe you are referring to your own experience of early morning in contrast to the deliberate activity of Hopper.) Mature works of art, such as Hopper's painting, are special sources for opening the imagination for, by a sort of negative contrast, this art opens 'new possibilities of vision' through a deliberate expressive act which my noticing is not. My noticing would seem to be only 'something very like an aesthetic experience' but, by implication, it is not aesthetic experience itself. It seems as if aesthetic experience can only happen in the presence of objects which I designate as 'art.'

These ways in which I interpret this passage position people against the studio and performing arts; fracture the world into artists and viewers of art — consumers who can become informed by the visions of artists but are not, necessarily, artists themselves. We become admiring consumers of art, but not makers of art objects. There is a double movement which both draws us in through admiration and sends us away through relegating the process of making to some people and not to others. This echoes the response I often receive when I ask my students to be makers of art objects: 'Oh, I'm not an artist. This will be no good.' 'Good' is thought of in terms of good art hung on a museum wall or in a gallery and the student's art could not hope to compete with that image. Therefore, what will be made is of no worth.

Such a response seems to me to miss how art objects are made. Artists begin by a close noticing of the world, similar if not identical to your experience in the early morning of New York. Their impulse is to notice. You often imply this act when you write of painters. For instance, you wrote that Constable 'enabled spectators to perceive green in the landscape, rather than rendering it in the traditional manner in gradations of brown. He defamiliarized the visible world, in effect, making accessible shadings and nuances never suspected before' (Greene, 1988a, p. 130). You pointed out that 'Claude Monet [made] visible the modeling effects of light on objects once seen as solidly and objectively *there*' and that Pablo Picasso expanded 'Western observers' conceptions of humanity and space with his "Demoiselles D'Avignon" and its African and Iberian visages, or his imaging of unendurable pain in the "Guernica"' (1988a, pp. 130–1). In each of these cases their insights came from their noticing the possibilities and, then, seeking form to express that noticing.

Your example of 'Demoiselles D'Avignon' is particularly felicitous for me. I attended many years ago a Picasso retrospective at the Museum of Modern Art in which this painting along with a series of studies that preceded the final work were displayed. These studies revealed something of Picasso's thinking as he manipulated the placement of the figures in the spatial landscape, highlighting in the final canvas the dramatic juxtaposition of differing faces and bodies of the women peering through the curtains by peculiarly flattening the space (in the early studies the faces, bodies and space had more conventional qualities and depth), thereby increasing our perception of the planar quality of their faces and bodies while maintaining the drama of their interrelationships (why are these women peering as they are?). These developments could only come about as he noticed more and more the particular aspects of human physiognomy.

Perhaps it is only that most people do not think of taking the next step, of making something themselves. In not taking this step we allow art making to belong to a special class of people and deny ourselves the opportunity to think in these careful and playful ways. This 'vocationalizing' of the studio and performing arts denies a general human capacity to use the making of art to inform (meaning: bring form to) ourselves and instruct (meaning: bring structure to) ourselves about ourselves and our relationships to the world (in all its manifestations: people, things, animals, earth, plants, air, space). This is a unique way of coming into contact with the world and different from the ways in which the studio and performing arts bring us into contact with the world when we are being consumers of the studio and performing arts.

As I noted earlier, you have called for both art education and aesthetic education. On the art education side, in your work with the Lincoln Center Institute, you wrote of the need for individuals to enact art of their own. For instance, you wrote,

> The more shapes [people] make with their bodies, with sound, with language, the more embodied and engaged will be that knowing [the full range of human poten-tiality: the cognitive, the affective, the sensual, the perceptual, the imaginative]. Experiences of this sort . . . not only enhance the sense of agency and responsibility when it comes to learning; they suggest what it signifies to overcome passivity and the inattentiveness that keep so many people from becoming different, trying to reach beyond where they are. (Greene, 1986, p. 1)

And in thinking about mature art works you wrote, 'To "do" aesthetics while engaging personally with artists and with works of art may empower us to make clear what it means to pen vistas, to widen perspectives' (Greene, 1978b, p. 2). And you wrote,

> How can there be a future if individuals are deprived of visions of open possibility — their own visions of what might be? How can there be vigorous students in our classrooms, productive students aware of craft, striving for quality, if they are never empowered to create through their own efforts and their own mastery, their own imaginative vistas, their own alternative realities? This is what informed aware-ness of the arts makes conceivable, this and the joy, the plain untrammeled joy, for which no one need apologize. (Greene, 1983, p. 2)

On the other hand, in *Releasing the Imagination* you wrote that we need to '[a]cknowledge the difficulty of moving the young to bestir themselves to create their own projects or find their own voices' (1995, p. 27). You went on to elaborate why 'we must make the arts central in school curricula' (p. 27) by emphasizing the 'remarkable pleasure for those willing to move toward them and engage with them' (p. 27) through encounters with works of art which 'demand as much cognitive rigor and analysis as they do affective response . . . [which] cannot be counted upon to have beneficent, consoling, or illuminat-ing effects. Soul-chilling instances are multiple' (pp. 27–8). If we are to value enactment but acknowledge its difficulty and emphasize encounters with works of art then I worry that art education is marginalized, even if we argue for it as equal to aesthetic education.

It is this marginalization with which I am concerned. I take it as crucial from two perspectives that people enact art as well as observe it. From one perspective, no matter how active their looking, without an experience of the doing it is more difficult for people to understand the mature art with which they are confronted. You do take note of this when you write,

When students can share in learning the language of dance by moving as dancers move, entering the symbol system of novel writing and story weaving by composing their own narratives out of words, working with glass sounds or drums to find out what it signifies to shape the medium of sound, all these immediate involvements lead to a participant kind of knowing and a participant sort of engagement with art forms themselves. Aesthetic education ought to include adventures like these, just as it ought to include intentional efforts to foster increasingly informed and ardent encounters with artworks. (Greene, 1995, p. 137)

From another perspective, the doing of art cannot result in a sense that 'I can never be an artist' but, hopefully, can result in a sense of what it means to play and be serious in thinking about and through materials toward the representation of ideas/feelings. Rather than art being made by special human beings I prefer to think of it as art by human beings who engage in a particular practice. My agenda dovetails with my desire not to be set apart and made special because I danced. I dance; others do their work; we all engage in meaningful and important activity that contributes to our community.

You and I, then, choose to place differing emphases in answering the question 'Who is an artist?' and, thus, have been influenced differentially by the studio and performing arts. I agree that an artist is someone who deliberately composes images out of materials for the purpose of 'opening up new possibilities of vision,' embarked on a 'lifelong quest for [personal] vision ... [personal] "truth".' This intentionality 'provides ... pleasurable experiences.' Such an attempt does not come easily. Rather, we must have a 'swelling recognition of the need for the most delicate caring, for a sense of craft, even as we find a growing willingness to embark on the adventures into meaning only the arts can provide' (Greene, 1989, p. 8). But I worry that this contributes to an uncritical distancing from the arts. I tend to deny a vocational emphasis toward being influenced by the arts, preferring to emphasize to a much greater degree that what can be said of the artist can be said of anyone who seeks to fashion a life or anything in life. An artist can be any of us and our materials might be anything and our 'delicate caring' and 'sense of craft' might be applied any place. Quality, serious endeavor, and attention to craft can be enacted by many people. Our seemingly different emphases are, more than likely, attributable to my choice to pursue a career in dance, thus positioning artistic practice as central to living and your choice of a scholarly career, thus tending to emphasize how encountering already made objects can influence you. In both cases I believe we would agree that people's lack of seeing their lives in artistic terms is a sad fact, one we would both like to remedy.

'What Are the Studio and Performing Arts For?'

Some of the answer to this question has already been referenced in the above discussion. The studio and performing arts open up our imagination and allow us to see the world other than it may appear to us. Thus, the studio and performing arts ought to be able to influence us to see anew. You apotheosize this seeing in your term 'wide-awakeness.' You have written,

> To 'do' aesthetics in the contexts of the Lincoln Center Institute is to become more wide-awake with respect to our encounters with practicing artists and works of art. As we grow more familiar with certain concepts in aesthetics ... we cannot but find our experiences with art illuminated. A new understanding ... may enable us to

> *notice* more, to attend with greater sensitivity and discrimination. (Greene, 1978b, p. 1)

You are concerned here with how wide-awakeness vis à vis the studio and performing arts is achieved. It is so achieved through becoming more 'familiar' with art and its concepts which will, in turn, bring about this greater sensitivity.

Your interest in wide-awakeness, however, is more general than that. In *Landscapes of Learning* you wrote that Kierkegaard intended to 'make things harder for people' in order to 'awaken them to their freedom' and that Thoreau, similarly 'also talked of arousing people from somnolence and ease' (Greene, 1978a, p. 162). By wide-awakeness you mean (from Alfred Schutz) 'a place of consciousness of highest tension originating in an attitude of full attention to life and its requirements' (quoted in Greene, 1978a, p. 163). Wide-awakeness involves 'people . . . posing questions with respect to their own projects, their own life situations' (1978a, p. 165). This wide-awakeness enables one to be open to the world in the quest for meaning which, for you, is fundamental to human existence. The studio and performing arts are a special and specific avenue through which to achieve wide-awakeness: 'The studio and performing arts are special because they foster imagination.' Through imagination 'persons . . . [may] break through the cotton wool of daily life and . . . live more consciously' (1978a, p. 185). Also:

> [I]maginative openness [can] make [people] more sensitive to untapped possibilities in their own lives. Imagination has been conceived as the capacity to look at things as if they could be otherwise. It is the capacity to summon up the 'as if,' the might be, that which is not yet. Imagination, as has been pointed out, sets the mind free as it opens up new realms of experience and surely as it allows experience to reveal itself in ever-changing modes of artistic presentation which deepen apprehension (wonderfully, mysteriously) of the 'real world.' (Greene, 1988b, p. 1)

Beyond this, imagination affords an almost transcendent experience (according to Mary Warnock):

> [T]here is more in our experience of the world than can possibly meet the unreflecting eye . . . this kind of belief may be referred to as the feeling of infinity . . . there is always *more* to experience and *more in* what we experience than we can predict. Without some such sense . . . human life becomes not actually futile or pointless, but experienced as if it were. It becomes, that is to say, boring.' (Greene, 1987, p. 9)

The worth of imagination is that, through our imaginative interactions with the world, we will not be 'bored,' we will not 'ever succumb to a feeling of futility, or to the belief that they have come to an end of what is worth having' (Greene, 1989, p. 10). You do not stipulate here what worth there is in living imaginatively nor what it is we might feel futile about. That is to say, you have not described the values which you believe art might stimulate us toward or help us think about. This is both surprising and understandable. It is surprising because you are so passionate about the inequities which mark our world. It is understandable because I agree with what I think you are avowing, that art must remain a mystery, must be open to interpretation; otherwise it becomes mere propaganda. However I worry that the very act of imaginative interaction with art and/or with the natural world seems sufficient reason for cultivating aesthetic experience and understanding. It is possible that opening the imagination does not inevitably lead to goodness. I will return to this thought a bit later.

'How Can or Should the Studio and Performing Arts Influence Both Our Individual Lives and How We Live With Each Other?'

This act of art appreciation does have at least one particular end, that of meaning making. Your special concern is with young people of whom you write,

> . . . they desperately want to learn how to make [meaning], how to find it, how to put it into words or images or musical sounds that might make the world less alien, less inscrutable, so that they may read some of what is happening around, *name* it, resist the anaesthetic, the controlling, the banal. (Greene, 1994, p. 1)

It is their need for meaning which must animate our use of the studio and performing arts as a prime source of their ability to make meaning. You indicate that 'young people we now realize are capable of making meaning, are caught up in multiple acts of finding meaning' (Greene, 1994, p. 1). This is a very important statement, for you are noting that whereas in previous educational theories it was the job of the educator to deliver the meaning of a text or painting or mathematical formula to the students as if the students were blank slates upon which to inscribe society's traditions, we now know that people are in a constant state of making meaning. It may not be the teacher's meaning but it is, nevertheless, meaning. Not only are young people engaged in constant meaning-making but it is the human condition to be constantly, even 'desperately' making meaning. These are existentialist sentiments and they are important for reorienting teachers toward what is occurring for their students.

How does one make meaning? Meaning-making and imagination must have a vehicle around which to act. Art works are excellent vehicles for facilitating this process for we can be brought to understand that 'meaning does not originate within the narrow chambers of its own subjectivity but emerges as a response to the other' (William Kearny in Greene, 1996, p. 4) The 'other' in this case is multiple. The art-work is 'other' as it enables us to become distanced from the object of interest so that we may see it anew, making the familiar strange. The artist is 'other' because s/he has a position which is portrayed and experienced by the viewer/experiencer. Finally, the viewer, her/himself, becomes othered as distance is gained from which to re-encounter that which we are coming to know. Clearly the theme of meaning is closely related to your concern for wide-awakeness and for the existential desire to live authentically in the moment as you often contrast the aesthetic with the anaesthetic.

It must be clear that this 'othering' experience can only come about when we eschew 'knowing about' for 'personal meaning' (Greene, 1994, p. 2).

> There is no predetermined meaning buried in the enacted play or in the script. We have to seek out its multiple meanings, make connections, find for ourselves the 'figure in the carpet' Calderon wove. Like all works of art, it is susceptible to many interpretations; all we can say is that the text and the performance must be honored. (Greene, 1991, p. 10)

Experiences with the studio and performing arts, then, contribute to our daily lives because there is a reciprocity between these experiences and living, a mutual illumination which, however, must favor the wide-awakeness in living. If art cannot eventuate in that, then it is not worthy of being part of our education. It can, of course, do this and do it better than other experiences and is, thus, central to education. This means that

> . . . [o]ur crucial preoccupation . . . is not with . . . 'cultural literacy' . . . [but] with
> the way [background knowledge, the historical past of dances] can contribute to the
> moments of presentness . . . those moments of freedom and presence unattainable in
> ordinary common-sense life. (1988b, p. 2)

The art experience must be immediate if it is to be effective.

The Problematics of the Studio and Performing Arts: 'What Are the Studio and Performing Arts *Good* For?'

Given that the studio and performing arts can help us accomplish wide-awakeness and transformation through acts of imagination, I remain concerned that opening the imagination does not inevitably provide goodness. According to at least one ethical theorist, William Frankena (1963), we must distinguish between various senses of 'good.' There are, according to him, six possibilities:

> Usefully good — 'This brush is especially *good* for thick painting.'
> Utility, leads to a good end — 'Music soothes me and, thereby, helps my health.'
> Inherently good — 'This music provides a good feeling.'
> Intrinsically good — 'Arts experiences are good in and of themselves.'
> Contributorily good — 'Experiencing the studio and performing arts is part of the
>   good life.'
> Finally valuably good — 'On balance the studio and performing arts do more good
>   than harm.' (p. 66)

I am asking about the utility and final value of the studio and performing arts, for a useful good is too trivial to consider and I am not sure that inherent, intrinsic and contributory goods are justifiable given the state of our community and world. I am, therefore, wary of an implicit faith in the studio and performing arts.

As a way into describing my wariness, I will refer to John Le Carré's novel *The Tailor of Panama* (1996). In this work he develops the idea of 'fluence,' the creation of a convincing version of one's life and the lives of others out of whole cloth without any necessary reference to the facts of one's or others' existences. Le Carré's protagonist, Harry Pendel, the tailor in question, lives constantly under the spell of 'fluence' which, like a liquid ether, courses through his mind in a seemingly inexorable rush, driving forward his tales, his life. When in the spell of 'fluence' he is able to spontaneously provide convincing descriptions and analyses without concern for what he actually knows about a situation although his tales have credibility, utilizing elements of possible truth which ground the story. His is a calculated reality designed to influence others for purposes of his own. As long as the story is never investigated it does its turn well, accomplishing what must be accomplished, eschewing what must be ignored. It is a thing of beauty and harmony when it succeeds. In Le Carré's hands fluence is the con man's tool, often causing problems (as such fluence is impossible to sustain if one is caught in the lie) but irresistible in its play.

Under the spell of someone else's fluence, one may become influenced. It is possible that artists can be under the sway of fluence. It is even possible that artists must have fluence in order to work at all. Fluence is certainly a form of imagination but is it the sort of imagination in which we want our children to become adept? And when we encounter the studio and performing arts we experience confluence, that is the coming together of things: events merge, new streams of thought and activity flow out. Perhaps fluence ensues. Perhaps not. Something either enriched or degraded may result. Confluence, however, tells us nothing about the direction of the 'fluence' of influence. Who influences who? What influences what? All we know is that things come together, for good or ill.

'Fluence,' influence, and confluence present particular qualities directly pertinent to art: artifice, imagining, spontaneity with no necessary pre-plan, surprise even to the one engaging in 'fluence.' Le Carré's made-up word connects to the acts of art as you have described them: uncovering, discovering, play and wondering otherwise. And 'fluence' is a sort of project in the existential sense, an authentication of oneself in the face of uncertainty and no rules by which to guide one. Art might be thought of as just the kind of process oriented and existential project in which you are interested.

However, 'fluence,' as Le Carré has developed it, is about lying for uneasy and contradictory ends. What are the contradictions to which art can be party? There are several. For one, we live in a world in which, on a daily basis, media artists attempt to manipulate us to buy commodities which we do not need in any fundamental sense. You take note of this when you write about a Bronx teenager whose 'word universe is infused with media language, commercial talk, soap opera dialogue, MTV lyrics' (Greene, 1995, p. 190). This, too, is art and, for the youth of our country, important art which influences the ways in which they think about themselves and what constitutes appropriate interactions between people. As you also note, it is not art which is for the pursuit of an individual's project nor does it, necessarily, aid us in living a more moral life. What are we to do with this art aside from being wary of it? It, too, stimulates imagination and projections of the good life or a better life. Must we not counteract these images, this art, in order to allow ourselves the space in which to think freshly? I believe that these young people refuse to make the kinds of distinctions you and I might make between the commercial and the fine arts, a distinction between so-called 'low art' and 'high art.'

Their refusal is not based on mere obstinacy and this leads to another contradiction which can bring into question the goodness of art. You relate the story of an African-American teenager's feelings about the Cloisters (Greene, 1995, p. 188), a story which struck me quite powerfully for during my adolescence I visited the Cloisters yearly with my parents. I would insist on going to this specific museum, of all the museums we visited, because of its wholeness, its complete differentness, its art on its walls which made sense to me, the whole building becoming art for me. I became transported into another world within its environs. In your story you relate your encounter with this boy while 'meeting with a group of high school adolescents who had just completed a research project on New York City museums':

> I was stopped in my tracks when an African American teenager from the Bronx abruptly asked, 'You ever been to the Cloisters, lady?' 'Of course,' I murmured properly (and, more than likely, smugly). 'I'll tell you about the Cloisters, lady,' he said. 'The Cloisters sucks.' (Greene, 1995, p. 188)

You understood his refusal as possibly based in a tacit recognition that the Cloisters are 'emblematic of the excluding power of the dominant society . . . mediated by the consciousness of the one who feels himself to be excluded, discriminated against, shamed'

(p. 189). This constituted, as you rightly point out, the potential for an educative moment. But another point arises for me. While I understand the point that art works well when it shocks us, since the intention of this museum is not to shock but, rather, to celebrate and preserve, I believe we are forced to ask, 'What makes this art "good"?'

For yet a third contradiction, we live in a world in which so-called fine artists pursue their work at the expense of others. Walter Benjamin stated it well when he wrote, 'There is no document of civilization which is not at the same time a document of barbarism' (1986, p. 682). We may ask ourselves, 'Why was Hopper able to paint this painting of a street? What allowed him the leisure and the time to choose to live in the way that he did?' Benjamin (1986) wrote, '. . . cultural treasures . . . owe their existence not only to the efforts of the great minds and talents who have created them, but also the anonymous toil of their contemporaries' (p. 681). Further, '. . . barbarism taints also the manner in which [these cultural treasures were] transmitted from one owner to another for such treasures have, historically, passed from one conqueror to another (to the victor go the spoils), from one privileged person to another, with the bulk of society neither privy to enjoy them nor able to benefit from their passage' (p. 682). Hopper's work must be understood in the context of the whole of his society, as an expression of that society's inequities. While this may not be the 'theme' of the painting and while our imagination may not be stimulated by the painting to think in this way, nevertheless such considerations are also part of the painting.

These dilemmas lead to me to think about your quality as one of our most eloquent thinkers on issues of freedom, equity, and justice. When you write about these issues and fold the arts into your discussions, you tend to do so through the literary arts rather than the studio and performing arts. Occasionally you will reference the connection between a people's lives and such art as when you write,

> The ways in which the blues have given rise to rock music and what are called 'raps' testify as well to a power, not merely to embody and express the suffering of oppressed and constricted lives, but to name them somehow, to identify the gaps between what is and what is longed for, what (if the sphere of freedom is ever developed) will someday come to be. (Greene, 1988a, p. 129)

For the most part, however, you seem to see in the studio and performing arts transformations of sight or kinesthesia:

> It has been clear in music, pushing back the horizons of silence for at least a century, opening new frequencies for ears to risk new sounds. It has been true of dance, as pioneers of movement and visual metaphor uncover new possibilities in the human body and therefore for embodied consciousness in the world. In painting, it has been dramatically the case. (1988a, p. 130)

You write that while 'the arts cannot be counted on to liberate, to ensure an education' they ought to be understood as 'breaking through the surfaces, about teaching others to "read" their own worlds.' However, when you come to discuss in substance what this might mean you turn to literature (poetry, novels, and plays) rather than the studio and performing arts. You may follow up such a discussion with a listing of examples from the studio and performing arts but you soon turn back to literature to continue your discussion. It is the absence of equally substantial discussions about art pieces which makes me feel there is more that needs to be said. I am still left with the question, 'How have you been influenced by the studio and performing arts?'

'How Have You Been Influenced by the Studio and Performing Arts?'

It is this last question, 'How have you been influenced by the studio and performing arts?,' in which I am most interested. I thought I might end this letter by describing some of my own experiences in this area.

For obvious reasons dance has been particularly important, both in encountering dances by artists, in dancing itself, and in making dances. Images from other artists spring to mind: a Paul Taylor dance in one section of which the men, dressed in tuxedos, dance a bear dance, a men's drumming dance, sitting on the floor in a circle and pounding that floor and heavily galloping and grappling; Phyllis Lamhut's dance 'Passing' in which the dancers dance as if in a slow trance, upright and dead (a terrifying dance, seemingly of nuclear holocaust death, so terrifying that some audience members had to leave the theater); Alwin Nikolais' 'Tent,' a portrayal of the evolution of human beings into transcendent spirits, joyous and at one with their environment; George Balanchine's 'Four Temperaments,' states of being that move through my own life. These images of civilization cloaking our animalness, civilization at the end, civilization in harmony with its context, and civilization as experienced affectively are images that enable me to think about my own relationship to civilization. They are not calls to action, but they are visions through which I can think about fashioning my own actions. Further, I am influenced by the ideas of certain postmodern choreographers, chiefly Yvonne Rainer, who wrote about the problematics of modern dancers who thought they were expressing an authentic self through their movements (Martha Graham's famous dictum 'The body never lies' is strongly implicated here) when Rainer had become unclear as to what constituted 'the authentic self.' I am influenced by Robert Rauschenberg's response to authenticity in which he, first, painted a painting and, then, meticulously copied it and, subsequently, challenged viewers to decide which was the original, authentic work and which the copy, thus attempting to debunk the notion that artists inevitably paint out of an authentic, personal expression.

My own dancing experience has been very important for me as I attend to my bodily motion on a daily basis, notice how I move and emphasize my words and encounters with others with and through my body. My bodily connection to my experiences is as important as my cognitive connections as I may catch myself speaking in ways that are all too familiar, especially as I teach and begin to feel the teaching to be a performance already too well known to me. In noticing such moments I may feel disconnected from these particular people with whom I am working. I notice this connection because I notice my body, feel my corporeal presence to be in a specific state. And my choreographic efforts always reveal to me something about my state of being at a particular moment: are my ideas dark, heavy, light? In making a dance entitled 'Sneakers' I explored the fetish quality of sneakers for young college students. When I began this dance I did not immediately know this is how I was thinking. I had certain images with which I desired to work which embodied certain ideas. I wanted to make a dance that would address their immediate lives and which they would enjoy dancing. As I worked with my group of dancers the ideas evolved, both the humor and the worry of sneakers as symbols of obsession and community. I became educated through the choreographic process.

In all these ways I have been influenced by dance. Your call for 'a pedagogy that integrates art education and aesthetic education' (Greene, 1995, p. 147) resonates with my own experience.

A Conclusion? A Conversational Opening

Two final thoughts occur to me. I see a subtle shift in your relationship to the studio and performing arts as you have thought through these areas over the years. Whereas, much of your work has taught us how participant encounters with the arts can transform us, you have more recently introduced, in *Releasing the Imagination* (1995), the possibility that the arts are dangerous. I believe that the dangers must take a clearer place in our work within the arts and within both aesthetic and art education. By opening up the discourse to these possibilities, we may be able to find a fuller understanding of the worth of the arts for our individual and collective lives.

It is possible that you conceive of all the arts (studio, performing and literary) sharing substantive features. This seems to be the case, for instance, when you utilize Wallace Steven's poem, 'The Man with the Blue Guitar,' to examine imagination although your discussion is set in the context of the Lincoln Center Institute where you are discussing the studio and performing arts. I, too, have drawn parallels between texts and other arts when I used Paul Ricoeur's notion of meaningful social action as hermeneutic in character to discuss interpreting dance (Blumenfeld-Jones, 1995). In this we share a problematic assumption for we do not acknowledge, thereby, the uniqueness of each of the arts, how, for instance, viewing Hopper's painting of a city street is a thoroughly different experience from a poem about the street or hearing a music composition. While it might even be possible that all three pieces were composed with substantively the same attitude, as I viewed, read, and heard I would possibly have substantively different experiences by virtue of the different senses animated by the different pieces. I neither have an answer as to what these differences are nor how important they are, but it is an area requiring greater attention.

What is most necessary is to carry on the critical conversation you have begun, to find entryways into aesthetic experiences that help us to be influenced by and be thoughtful about both other people's productions and our own productions. What is necessary is to continue the talk you have begun, helping us to understand what the arts are for.

Sincerely and with thanks,
Donald Blumenfeld-Jones

Note

1   I am greatly indebted to Alison Quam, the Lincoln Center Institute for the Arts librarian who kindly provided me with extensive archival materials of Maxine Greene's writing about the studio and performing arts and her unpublished addresses to the teachers who attend the Institute Summer Workshop.

References

BENJAMIN, W. (1986) 'Theses on the philosophy of history,' in ADAMS, H. and SEARLE, L. (eds) *Critical Theory Since 1965* (pp. 680–97), Tallahassee FL: Florida State University Press.

BLUMENFELD-JONES, D.S. (1995) 'Dance as a mode of research representation,' *Qualitative Inquiry*, **1**, 4, pp. 391–401.

FRANKENA, W. (1963) *Ethics*, Englewood Cliffs, NJ: Prentice-Hall, Inc.

GREENE, M. (1978a) *Landscapes of Learning*, New York: Teachers College Press.

GREENE, M. (1978b) 'Words of welcome,' *Lincoln Center Institute Report*, November, pp. 1–2.

GREENE, M. (1983) 'Now more than ever', *Lincoln Center Institute Report*, September, pp. 1–2.

GREENE, M. (1986) 'On the need for aesthetic education,' *Lincoln Center Institute Report*, October, p. 1.

GREENE, M. (1987) 'New Openings,' *Lincoln Center Institute Report*, October, p. 9.

GREENE, M. (1988a) 'Education, art, mastery: Toward the spheres of freedom,' *The Dialectic of Freedom* (pp. 117–35), New York: Teachers College Press.

GREENE, M. (1988b) 'Moments of presentness,' *Lincoln Center Institute Report*, October/November, pp. 1, 11.

GREENE, M. (1989) 'The rationalists and the sombreros,' *Lincoln Center Institute Report*, October, pp. 1, 8, 10.

GREENE, M. (1991) 'The Dissonances Remain,' *Lincoln Center Institute Report*, September/October, pp. 10–11.

GREENE, M. (1994) Lincoln Center Institute Lecture to Teachers, First Lecture, Summer (Archival materials).

GREENE, M. (1995) *Releasing the Imagination: Essays on Education, the Arts, and Social Change*, San Francisco: Jossey-Bass Publishers.

GREENE, M. (1996) Lincoln Center Institute Lecture to Teachers, Third Lecture, Summer (Archival materials.)

LE CARRÉ, J. (1996) *The Tailor of Panama*, New York: Alfred A. Knopf.

STINSON, S., BLUMENFELD-JONES, D.S., and VAN DYKE, J. (1990) 'Voices of young women dance students: An interpretive study of the meaning of dance,' *Dance Research Journal*, **22**, 2, pp. 13–22.

15 Maxine Greene: The Literary Imagination and the Sources of a Public Education

James M. Giarelli

The distinguishing feature of twentieth-century educational study is the problem of the school. For it is only in the last, at most, 150 years that the problem of educating, what Dewey called the social necessity of life (Dewey, 1944), has been located in the formal institutions of schooling. This is a well-known story. In response to the multiple factors which mark the transition from a pre-industrial to what Lawrence Cremin (1988) called a 'metropolitan civilization,' the need arose for an intentional institution which could perform the social, political, and economic tasks previously associated with a wide range of non-formal educational agencies. Importantly, one of the main, though not only, characteristics of metropolitan civilizations is the manner in which knowledge is stored in symbols. Thus, the school arises with the special purpose of transmitting symbolic knowledge, the working capital of modernity. This mission, the transmission of knowledge stored in symbols, has dominated what Thomas Green (1988) calls the public school movement since its inception. Against this standard, the effectiveness of schooling has been assessed around goals of attainment; what and how much symbolic knowledge is appropriate to each level of the system and how many get it?

In many ways, the public school system has been an enormous success when measured against attainment goals. However, while the school arose with a distinctive task of transmitting symbolic knowledge, the rhetoric of the public school movement, past and present, has also linked public schooling to the wider social, moral, and political purposes of a democratic community. Put much too briefly, the public schools were not only to foster symbolic literacy, but equally, and perhaps more fundamentally, foster common sense, literally the sense it takes to live in a commons. While there are many variations on what this might mean, a central thread of the public school story has focused on the connection between public schooling and the formation and re-formation of publics. Addressing the tension between these two purposes, the attainment of symbolic literacy and the acquisition of those skills, dispositions, and sensibilities which would encourage the formation and re-formation of a community of distinct members, Dewey cast the problem 'Can schools educate?' as the fundamental problem of modern educational theory.

The evidence in this regard is much more disheartening. By the 1920s, Dewey and others were writing of the eclipse of the public, the phantom public, and more generally about the ways in which precisely those forces that had called forth the school in a metropolitan civilization were vitiating any sense of a meaningful public life. While the school was certainly not the main culprit, succeeding generations of critics, conservatives, liberals, and radicals of different stripes, have analyzed how the ever-increasing formalisms of modern life, the interlocking sets of bureaucratic institutions, the universalization of abstract and instrumental relations, and the disembodiment of reason and knowledge, have eroded what Arendt called a 'public space' in which people can appear before each other as 'the best they know how to be' (in Greene, 1988, p. xi). Accompanying this assault on public forms has been a concomitant diminishment of the private, with the 'individual,' stripped of all associations save those having market potential, confined to the resources of 'interiority' and self-interested 'choice.'

As the public school movement winds down and mainstream educational researchers and policy analysts debate the cost–benefit ratios of another round of pursuing attainment objectives, a different, reflective literature has emerged around the problems and possibilities of schooling for public life. David Mathews (1996) in *Is There a Public for Public Schools?* takes up the Deweyan question and argues for a reconnection of publics and schools through citizen movements. E.D. Hirsch (1987) in *Cultural Literacy* argues that a common culture does in fact exist in symbolic terms and it is the purpose of schooling to transmit this canon directly so that it can be assessed as an attainment objective. Henry Giroux, Paulo Freire, Michael Apple and others argue for an educational strategy that offers both a language of critique to resist the racist, sexist, and classist forms of dominant knowledge which divide and disempower students and citizens and a language of possibility and power to re-name the world, cross the borders of official knowledge, identity, and interest and create occasions of emergent solidarity. Despite the deep differences that exist, this latter literature returns our attention to the fundamental problem of twentieth-century education — the problematic relationship of the school and the conscious quest for a public education.

The work of Maxine Greene stands out as the most original and compelling response to this problem in the latter half of twentieth century educational theory. As she writes in *The Dialectic of Freedom*,

> This book arises out a lifetime's preoccupation with quest, with pursuit . . . the quest has been deeply personal . . . it has been in some sense deeply public as well: that of a person struggling to connect the understanding of education, . . . to the making and remaking of a public space, a space of dialogue and possibility. . . . The aim is to find (or create) an authentic public space. . . . Such a space requires the provision of opportunities for the articulation of multiple perspectives in multiple idioms, of which something common can be brought into being. It requires, as well, a consciousness of the normative as well as the possible: of what ought to be, from a moral and ethical point of view, and what is in the making, what might be in an always open world. . . . My hope is to remind people of what it means to be alone among others; to achieve freedom in dialogue with others for the sake of personal fulfillment and the emergence of a democracy dedicated to life and decency. (1988, pp. xi–xii)

In this brief essay, I would like to offer a beginning account of the sources of Greene's project. While nothing like a systematic analysis of her work is possible here, I would like to sketch an outline of an alternative understanding of her work. In the standard interpretation, an account of Greene's intellectual project would involve an analysis of the sources for her educational thought in social theory and philosophy. To be sure, such an account could be produced, with particular attention to the central texts and characters in her writing, including most prominently, Dewey, Arendt, Merleau-Ponty, Sartre, Schutz and more recently, Charles Taylor, Habermas, and Freire, among others. However, as much as this account would be instructive, I believe it would miss the fundamental point and original moment in Greene's work.

Instead, I want to suggest that Greene has located the question, 'Can schools educate?' in the tension between the formal and the imaginative, the treatise and the novel, the center and the margins, systematic philosophy and imaginative literature. In *The Public*

School and the Private Vision (1965), for example, the social history of the public school movement is thrown up against the literature of moral protest. As she writes, 'At the very moment the school reformers were speaking their rhetoric of assurance and hope, the artists were writing of ambiguities, of human impotence and fallibility, of wildernesses, wasters, dualities. Yet they lived in the same world and breathed the same air' (1965, p. 4). In *Landscapes of Learning* (1978), she argues that 'our comprehension of the ways in which persons bring meaning into being and constitute their shared realities' requires the study of imaginative literature, 'the powers of darkness,' the 'deep currents of culture,' not yet visible on the surfaces of life (1978, p. 22). In *The Dialectic of Freedom*, she writes of her movement back and forth between imaginative literature and philosophy, 'resisting the notion of a finished, predetermined reality, I became fascinated not merely with multiple modes of interpretation, but with all that feeds into interpretation from lived lives and sedimented meanings' (1988, p. xiii). For Greene, while symbolic knowledge is the working capital of modernity, the limited range of symbol systems deemed official and worth knowing constrains the possibilities of self and social renewal. The arts immediately expand the continuum of symbol systems through which we can experience and make meaning in the world through their insistence on interpretation. It is precisely because of their inexactness, uncertainty, and requirement that they be engaged perspectivally, that the arts are the basics of any authentic educational theory. The arts, always on the verge, always making things more difficult, are the primary sources of our efforts to 'break the crust of convention' in Dewey's terms, to reclaim an authentic public space in a culture which offers us the 'choice' between a social life marked by, as Arendt writes, 'rule by Nobody,' or a private life of mundane interiority and mindless consumption.

I am suggesting here that, for Greene, the arts, specifically imaginative literature, rather than systematic philosophy and theory, are the sources of social and educational thought. This might be understood as the tension between the treatise and the novel. As Richard Rorty (1985, p. 3) argues, historically there have been two ways to talk of solidarity: first, by telling stories of our contribution to community, and second, by describing ourselves as standing in immediate relation to a nonhuman reality. The second approach is the strategy of the treatise. Treatises attempt to teach by working inexorably toward the view that they can distinguish between reality and 'mere appearances.' Treatises claim to identify a foundational Truth or Reality lurking behind events which can ground thought in a place beyond logic and culture. Treatises seek to work within or toward the universal, abstract, the timeless, and to set the categories and boundaries of what counts as real, good, true, and meaningful. The treatise is the text of the school.

However, the sources of our education are multiple. This is to say more than that families, churches, workplaces, and so on teach us. It suggests that the most pernicious consequence of educational abstractions and formalisms is the construction of borders, taboos, categories of what and who counts. This is profoundly oppressive and miseducative. For Greene, all educational and social thought must be focused on the borders, the extremes, the margins where life is lived fully. Along with border crossing goes genre blurring, what counts as a discipline, a source of knowledge, a source of identity. In other terms, Greene offers an alternative source of thought in the novel, both in its meaning as a literary genre, but more fundamentally in its core meaning as the new, different, original, unordinary. The novel resists the didacticism of the treatise, the direct lesson, and substitutes adventure, narrative and choice into the order of events. The theorist of the novel thinks it a comical conceit to assume that any one life project is better than any others because of its participation or correspondence in some non-human foundation. Rather than draw borders between reality and appearances, the novel takes 'mere' appearances as the common curriculum of real events in which we learn of lived suffering and experienced joy. The novel has no interest in reducing option to objective truth; instead it relies on the diversity of viewpoints, the plurality of descriptions of the same events, the dialectic of naming, as the source of a public education.

Richard Rorty quotes Milan Kundera (1986) further on this difference: 'The novel's wisdom is different from that of philosophy. The novel is born not of the theoretical spirit but of the spirit of humor . . . the art inspired by God's laughter does not serve ideological certitudes, it contradicts them. Like Penelope, it undoes each night the tapestry that the theologian, philosopher, and learned men have woven the day before . . .' (p. 160). The novel and the arts more broadly focus us on stories of concrete liberation and the precursors of emancipatory activity, rather than the grand sweep of faceless events. So too, they tell stories, especially educational stories, that are just as much about loss as about growth, alienation as well as integration, submergence as transcendence. They entangle us in the dialectic of freedom and the common quest for individuality and community.

Rorty on Kundera again: 'Flaubert discovered stupidity. I daresay that is the greatest discovery of a century so proud of its scientific thought. Of course, even before Flaubert, people knew stupidity existed, but they understood it somewhat differently: it was considered a simple absence of knowledge, a defect correctable by education . . . Flaubert's vision of stupidity is this: stupidity does not give way to science, technology, modernity, progress; on the contrary, it progresses right along with progress!' (Kundera, 1986, p. 160). As Rorty comments, 'I take Kundera to be saying that the Enlightenment was wrong in hoping for an age without stupidity. The thing to hope for is, instead, an age in which the prevalent varieties of stupidity will cause less unnecessary pain than is caused in our age by our varieties of stupidity. To every age its own glory and its own stupidity. The job of the novelist is to keep us up to date on both' (Rorty, 1991, pp. 76–7). The point here is not to exalt stupidity. Instead, the novelist reminds us that our certainty is temporal, that our categories are contingent, that our realities are tenuous conventions.

For Greene, this doubt, uncertainty, contingency, is a prerequisite for any authentic educational venture. Indeed, this insistence on a world in the making has particular relevance for the education of a democratic public. Democracy, in any meaningful sense of the word, insists that we treat each other with respect and decency because we *want* to, not because we *have* to. Not because we will be punished if we don't, not because we've been told to, not out of obedience, but because we want to, that is, out of *freedom*. It is in this profound sense that the novel of moral protest, and imaginative literature more generally, rather than the philosophical treatise, is the most important cultural and educational resource in the struggle against authoritarianism of the right and the left and, as such, is the characteristic genre of democratic education, the curriculum most deeply associated with the struggle for freedom and equality.

If the problem of freedom cannot be solved by the treatises of the good citizen and if the notion of freedom as being 'free from' others flies in the face of the brute facts of existence and the quality of our experience, what can freedom be? For Greene, there is no ahistorical, universal, neutral standard to which we can appeal. However, just as clearly, we make judgments and seek to ground our judgments in common agreement. How can we judge, or more, judge with intersubjective understanding or common agreement, if we do not know what we are looking for?

Yet we do. And that we do suggests that there is something more in our stories that allows us to get at least a peek through the veils of mass culture and categories of the treatise at a world where multiplicity and relation, compassion, and intellectual understanding connect and inform each other. This does not solve our problem. We still do not know what freedom is or how to live as distinct members of a community. We are at a real disadvantage in the natural world. We have no claws, big teeth, we're not very strong or fast. We thought for a long time our brains would save us. So we built temples to the mind, to reason, the hope for transcending the facticity of lived experience. But where reason, at least in the modern sense, has helped us deal with what is, the problem of freedom is rooted in what is not, the possible, the could be. For Greene, imagination is the art of the possible and education is its object.

And so, educating for freedom becomes educating for solidarity and educating for solidarity will focus on the unknown, the novel perspective, the unfamiliar. The teacher as stranger. In a world of unfreedom and anomie, a public education must be grounded in an imagining of what freedom and community *might* be like. For Greene, a curriculum of social imagination with its concern for a range of human intelligences, multiple vocabularies, expansive and open symbol systems, is our best hope for becoming human in a resistant world.

Novels, imaginative literature, the aesthetic, are not enough. But by moving us out of the familiar and given, by making these categories problematic, they make choice a question of freedom and living a more difficult and beautiful problem. The problem of 'finding' the meaning of life, as if it were somewhere, is changed to creating the meanings of living. The problem of living well is transformed from the attempt to conquest some extra-experiential grounding to the emergent quest for forms of conduct that sustain human flourishing. For Greene, this creative struggle for individual freedom is at the same time the quest for a public space through which to imagine and pursue our common humanity.

In 1930 Dewey wrote that he believed the 'next synthetic movement in philosophy will emerge when the significance of the social sciences and arts has become an object of reflective attention in the same way that mathematical and physical sciences have been made the objects of thought in the past, and when their full import is grasped' (quoted in McDermott, 1973, p. 13). As is well known, this has not been the case in philosophy, social theory or the philosophy of education in the twentieth century. Maxine Greene stands as the shining exemption, and in that sense, her work stands itself as the source for those of us who think that the question 'Can schools educate?' presents the most lovely problem of social imagination for the next millennium.

References

CREMIN, L. (1988) *American Education: The Metropolitan Experience 1879–1980*, New York: Harper & Row.

DEWEY, J. (1973) 'From absolutism to experimentalism,' in McDERMOTT, J.J. (ed.) *The Philosophy of John Dewey*, New York: G.P. Punt's Sons.

GREEN, T.F. (1980) *Predicting the Behavior of the Educational System*, Syracuse, NY: Syracuse University Press.

GREENE, M. (1965) *The Public School and the Private Vision*, New York: Random House.

GREENE, M. (1978) *Landscapes of Learning*, New York: Teachers College Press.

GREENE, M. (1988) *The Dialectic of Freedom*, New York: Teachers College Press.

HIRSCH, E.D. (1987) *Cultural Literacy*, Boston: Houghton-Mifflin.

KUNDERA, M. (1986) *The Art of the Novel* (L. Asher, trans.), New York: Grolier.

MATHEWS, D. (1996) *Is There a Public for Public Schools?* Dayton, Ohio: Kettering Foundation Press.

RORTY, R. (1985) 'Solidarity or objectivity?' in RAJCHMAN, J. and WEST, C. (eds) *Post-Analytic Philosophy*, New York: Columbia University Press.

RORTY, R. (1991) *Essays on Heidegger and Others*, Cambridge: Cambridge University Press.

Section Four

Greene's Influence on Educational Theory

16   A Situated Philosopher

Wendy Kohli

City Life

It was the summer of 1973 and I lived on West 12th Street in Greenwich Village. I was a relative newcomer to New York City, having moved there from a small upstate college town with my 'counter-cultural squeeze,' Michael, an Abbie Hoffman look-a-like. We had been at the center of the political and cultural 'revolution' on our campus and were ready to expand our horizons. Part of our political involvement at Cortland was with alternative education, including a community 'free school' for elementary-age children where I was the headteacher. Having been influenced by such diverse thinkers as Jonathan Kozol, Paul Goodman, Sylvia Ashton-Warner, Herbert Marcuse, Wilhelm Reich, Theodor Adorno, A.S. Neill, Paulo Freire, Murray Bookchin, and yes — Maxine Greene — we saw the intimate connections between education and social–political change.

Michael was convinced by Murray Bookchin to pursue a PhD in critical social theory at the Graduate Faculty of the New School, the inheritor of the Frankfurt School of thought in the US. Vacillating between studying social theory or philosophy of education, I decided to take a year to decide on my PhD prospects. In the meantime, as a result of my connections in the alternative school movement, I got a job as a junior high school teacher at The Baldwin School, a private, progressive, secondary school on the upper west side. Although I liked the school's philosophy, my colleagues, and the culturally diverse student body, it was still a job, not a career move, since I had already decided that K-12 classroom teaching was not going to be my life's work. I was interested in social and educational change, but from the vantage point of a professor. Nevertheless, the teaching job allowed me time and money to support my urban cultural journey and to search for a graduate school I could call home.

In retrospect, it is impossible not to notice the gendered nature of my experiences and choices in those days. As 'counter-cultural' as Michael and I were, we still reproduced many of the gender dynamics of our parents, even with my 'raised feminist consciousness.' My social circle in New York consisted mostly of men I met through Michael. Even so, it was a heady time for us aspiring intellectuals and social critics: translations of Habermas were hitting the 8th Street Bookstore and visiting speakers from Germany, including Habermas himself, were a regular occasion. Hannah Arendt sightings made our day. And late-night conversations about Hegel or Heidegger over pizza and beer were the rule not the exception. Yet, as exciting as this was for me, it also left something to be desired. I felt a certain disconnection from the scene: a lack of groundedness coupled with no small aversion to the 'peacocking' that was going on around me.[1] And, I had this gnawing feeling that no matter what I read or said, I would/could never 'be one of the guys.'

There were, of course, multiple reasons for my dis-ease, including my own insecurities and 'lack'[2] of philosophical training. With both BS and MS degrees in social science and education, I read mostly in sociology and history, as well as that 'derivative field,' educational foundations. And as a young woman with a small town, working-class background,[3] I was intimidated by what felt to me to be more articulate, urbane male thinkers. I suffered what many women suffer — the invalidation of my own thinking and intuition. Yet, I knew in my gut that in order for me to engage wholeheartedly in doctoral studies, something more would have to happen to/for me than what occurred in our never-ending theorizing in the Village. The theorizing in and of itself wasn't the problem. But I wanted a more direct link between critical social theory and educational change, what Paulo Freire (1970) called *praxis*. I also wanted more resonance between me — *all of me* — and what I was learning. The intellectualism of our group at the New School felt like an 'out of body' experience to me. Although I couldn't name it yet, I wanted Maxine Greene.

The Seventh Avenue Subway to Freedom[4]

Luckily, my former social foundations professor, John Marciano, knew Maxine and had written a letter of introduction for me. With it and her recent book in hand, *Teacher as Stranger* — which I had just devoured — I headed uptown on the 7th Avenue IRT subway to meet with Maxine at Teachers College. I still have that same copy of *Teacher as Stranger*, now tattooed with the layered marginalia from multiple readings over the years. Even with the masculine pronouns, I felt that book spoke directly to me. Greene (1973) opens the preface by saying:

> This book is specifically addressed to the teacher or teacher-to-be who is in the process of choosing his [sic] 'fundamental project' the activity of teaching in a classroom. The vantage point of the reader is conceived to be that of a person who is involved and responsible, someone who looks out on the educational landscape from inside a specifiable 'form of life'. (Preface)

I felt as if I *was* 'choosing my fundamental project.' Still wrapped in the idealism and commitment of the 1960s, I wanted my choices to matter. I believed they would. And although I did not want to be a classroom teacher, I thought I might want to be a teacher of *future teachers* and change those 'educational landscapes' that limited our possibilities.

Greene (1973) spoke to me in other ways as well. She *situated* herself as 'a writer who cannot escape her own biographical situation, her own location in the modern world.' And this location, this 'standpoint of the author is that of a person who was reared and educated in an urban environment' (Preface). Although not an urbanite, I felt the general point Greene made was a powerful signal to me that one's place in the world, although not a strictly *determining* factor, was absolutely crucial in understanding how we come to know the world. She reminds us of this in a later book, *Landscapes of Learning*, when she says: 'it is important to hold in mind, therefore, that each of us achieved contact with the world from a particular vantage point, in terms of a particular biography. All of this underlies our present perspectives and affects the way we look at things and talk about things and structure our realities' (Greene, 1978, p. 2). So not only does Greene locate the *reader* in a specific life-context, she also situates herself as *author/philosopher*.

Details of our first conversation are vague. What remains is a visceral memory: I was smitten. Professor Greene invited me to take her Social Philosophy course that semester, which I did. Little did I know that this would be the beginning of a lifelong relationship, one that would profoundly shape my view of education and philosophy for years to come.

The 'IRT' became a connecting link between my various west-side worlds: Greenwich Village wannabe intellectual, junior-high school teacher, and uptown graduate student. But it was more than that. It was my train to freedom. As I shifted between the formal, heavy, male, 'Old World style' of lecturing at the New School, to the airy, literary, broadly Continental, multidisciplinary teaching performances of Maxine Greene, I felt my spirit lift and my mind open. There was something so refreshing and inviting about her oratory. It was engaged. It was connected. Just as in *Teacher as Stranger*, Greene contextualized her lectures in the lived-world; she made philosophy come to life (even John Rawls!) with her own and others' lived experiences. I could actually imagine myself doing what she was doing — 'doing philosophy.'

The influence of existentialism and phenomenology was evident in her pedagogical stance — a stance underscoring our embodiment as knowers, learners, teachers — and one with direct epistemological and political implications. Inhabiting this philosophical frame, Greene felt obligated to 'go beyond the situations one confronts and refuse reality as given in the name of a reality to be produced' (1973, p. 7). For her, 'it is simply not enough for us to reproduce the way things are' (Greene, 1995a, p. 1). Unlike many of her academic peers, Greene has never shied away from connecting philosophy to political commitment. Quite the contrary. She has continually implored us to apply our critical intelligence to any situation in which we find ourselves — to not take anything for granted. In 1973 she offered the following invitation to what she has often called 'wide-awakeness.'

> The reader is challenged to do philosophy, to take the risk of thinking about what he [sic] is doing when he teaches, what he means when he talks about enabling others to learn. He is asked to become progressively more self-conscious about the choices he makes and the commitments he defines in the several dimensions of his professional life. He is asked to look, if he can, at his presuppositions, to examine critically the principles underlying what he thinks and what he says. (Preface)

This call to critical consciousness resonated with my own intentions as a radical educator.

Making a Way in the Wilderness

Could it be that I had found a 'role model?' I think here not of an unproblematized 'heroine,' but of the way Alice Walker used the term. For Walker, in an account offered by Bernice Fisher (1988), role models are important to artists in their struggle 'to make their way in the world' (p. 237). They can 'enrich and enlarge one's view of existence' and support a 'fearlessness of growth, of search, of looking that enlarges the private and public world,' (p. 237). Fisher recalls that when Walker first encountered the work of Zora Neale Hurston, she felt that she 'had discovered a model . . . as if she (Hurston) knew someday I (Walker) would come along wandering in the wilderness' (p. 238).

I see a parallel between the artist and the female philosopher of education. Both are finding their way in their respective wildernesses as they 'risk ridicule' and overcome their fears of failure (Fisher, 1988, p. 238). They are also both on searches, trying to break down the loneliness and isolation as they create something new (p. 238). Maxine Greene speaks often of *her* search, *her* quest. We see this described eloquently in *The Dialectic of Freedom*:

This book arises out of a lifetime's preoccupation with quest, with pursuit. On the one hand, the quest has been deeply personal: that of a woman striving to affirm the feminine as wife, mother, and friend, while reaching, always reaching, beyond the limits imposed by the obligations of a woman's life. On the other hand, it has been in some sense deeply public as well: that of a person struggling to connect the undertaking of education, with which she has been so long involved, to the making and remaking of a public space, a space of dialogue and possibility. (Greene, 1988, p. xi)

This connection of the personal with the political was one more quality that drew me to Maxine. At the same time, my attraction to her and her way of doing philosophy was not without its contradictions and confusions. You see, I had internalized the masculinist bias that what was going on at the New School Graduate Faculty was the *real* work, the *real* arena in which to toss my hat. What made this the legitimate arena? To some extent it had to do with the fact that what they were teaching *wasn't education*. But perhaps most importantly, The New School was *where the boys were*.

Elizabeth Young-Bruhle (1988) reminds us women that 'there is a great deal in our personal and cultural histories suggesting that thinking is not our province, not our privilege, not even our possibility' (p. 9). Few women held teaching positions in the philosophy 'wilderness' of the early 1970s. In my mind's eye, philosopher equals man with beard, tweed jacket, and pipe. This was intimidating but also part of its allure, its legitimation, its power. I wanted to be like that. As JoAnne Pagano (1990), a feminist philosopher of education who writes about the (patriarchal) wilderness suggests, 'the male teacher, like the father, serves directly and unproblematically as the representative of the abstract world of order, method, beauty, justice, etc. He is the "reader," the "scientist," the "philosopher," the "lover," the "artist," the "he," whose voice we mimic' (p. 118).

So, even though I was drawn to what was happening on 120th Street in Main Hall at Teachers College, I was a bit suspicious of its 'seriousness,' of its 'rigor.' Having straddled the fence between the liberal arts and education in undergraduate school, I knew of the reputation education had in the academy. Social Theory and Philosophy were *true disciplines*. Education was not, even if it was *philosophy* of education. And those doing it were constructed as second rate in/by the knowledge hierarchy.

It was only years later, in fact in preparing to write this and another essay on Greene's place in philosophy of education,[5] that I learned through an interview that Maxine had internalized the same things about education and philosophy as I had. It was extremely difficult for her to name herself, to take up the identity of philosopher of education. For years, she had doubted her competence and legitimacy. At one point soon after getting her doctorate from NYU in Foundations of Education, she thought about going back to graduate school to 'get a *real* PhD,' to study a '*real* discipline' — philosophy. In a patriarchal institution like the academy, the double jeopardy of being in education and being a woman caused Maxine to second guess her intelligence and importance far too often, and for far too long.

Complicating my decision about graduate school and my future in the university was the way I saw Maxine Greene teach. Comparatively, those New School professors represented the received view of 'philosophical purity,' in both their process and content. She, on the other hand, created a space 'for the articulation of multiple perspectives in multiple idioms' (Greene, 1988, p. xi) by inserting references to contemporary politics, literature and the arts in her lectures. Maxine's approach to philosophy was not bound to the making of 'logical' arguments or to the exegesis of texts. Philosophy as noun was transformed into a verb in the Greene lexicon. For her, philosophy is not a dead body of knowledge, a static *thing*; it is an ever-evolving search for meaning and freedom; it is an opportunity to confront the world critically in order to change it; it is acting, choosing, deciding to live in-the-world, to experience the lived reality of one's existence.

With this perspective, Maxine opened a space in the wilderness for me, and others like me, as she embodied the passion that helped 'carry [me] into the future' as a female philosopher of education (Fisher, 1988, p. 243). Seeing her in action, I emerged out of my confusion, remembering that I was someone committed to transforming education and society. Consequently, I chose to study philosophy of education — to combine critical social theory and critical educational theory. I decided to study with Maxine at Teachers College. Unfortunately, it was not to be. Gender dynamics intervened once again to shape a woman's life-choices (and chances). Michael and I broke up. I thought Manhattan wasn't big enough for both of us, so I went back upstate to pursue a PhD.[6]

A Stranger in a Not-So-Strange Land

Writing as an existential-phenomenologist, Greene frequently evokes the image of the 'stranger.' She herself was a stranger — marginal — in her chosen field of philosophy of education.[7] In many ways, she was *in* it, but not *of* it. Early on in her career, she was thought of as 'too literary' to be in a philosophy of education program.[8] Greene thinks, in retrospect, that her critics were actually saying she was 'too female' or 'too soft' (1997, p. 25). I think it could also mean something more literal. Greene in fact did use literature to explicate her philosophical ideas. In *Landscapes of Learning*, for example, she tells us: 'I have referred to or used examples from works of imaginative literature. The reason is that, as many have pointed out, encounters with literary works of art make it possible for us to come in contact with ourselves, to recover a lost spontaneity' (1978, p. 2). She reiterates this years later in her book *The Dialectic of Freedom* when she says: 'I have found it increasingly difficult to limit myself to a single province or a single symbol system. From the beginnings of my career, trying with some difficulty to be accepted as a philosopher of education, I found myself moving back and forth between imaginative literature and philosophy' (1988, p. xii). Not only does she draw on literature to make her philosophical points, she constructs a particular literary style in her writings, a style that she later characterized as 'my poetico-feminine vein' (1991, p. 321).

Criticism of her work as being 'too literary' (i.e. not *real* philosophy) surfaced in other contexts as well, including the Philosophy of Education Society (PES), the discipline-defining bastion of the field. When Greene was establishing herself as a philosopher of education, she was often a lone voice speaking. Actually it was more like *multiple* lone voices speaking: as a woman, as a political activist, as a continental philosopher, and as a person committed to literature and the arts. As she tells it, 'I am a woman who has been drawn to social activism, obsessive about the importance of the arts, and much attracted by existential phenomenology; I am, therefore, quadruply marginal' (Greene, 1991, p. 321).

Positioned on the margins, Greene has struggled, as have so many women in academia with whether or not to become 'one of the boys.' This was not easy in an organization like PES. Even as she worked to claim space alongside her male peers through her particular enactment of philosophical thought, she repudiated that same space. In that early, influential philosophy of education text, whose complete title is *Teacher as Stranger: Educational Philosophy for the Modern Age*, Greene is obviously anchored in the philosophical traditions of her male predecessors. At the same time, her narrative strategies subvert and transform traditional epistemology through the infusion of literary and artistic allusions.[9] This resistant style was also evident in the presentations she gave at PES.

As I have written in another context,[10] when Maxine Greene entered the academic world as a philosopher of education in the late 1950s, early 1960s, the Anglo-analytic school of philosophy was the dominant discourse in the field. Maxine 'was terrified' of this way of doing philosophy: 'it was so scary, the analytic time.'[11] In fact, according to her, she was '*so* scared at PES' that when she had to give a paper, she would 'get all dizzy and almost faint.' Yet, she would decline the friendly offers of colleagues to read her papers for her; she would take deep breaths and speak through her terror. Her audience, virtually all-male, were into, as she puts it, 'doing a conceptual "mopping up," clarifying language, working on arguments, battling vagueness and ambiguity' (Greene, 1991, p. 321). In one of those skirmishes on the conference floor, Maxine's presentation was met by a respondent who opened his remarks with 'Fuck Rilke!' Years later, in a generous gesture of forgiveness, she says, 'what he actually meant [was] "Forget Rilke; get on with the argument"' (1991, p. 321). With encounters like this, it's no wonder that she would nearly faint at the thought of facing all of those men.

And it *was* mostly men. One need only do a cursory review of the PES Programs during those years to grasp the context in which she placed herself; to see how her marginality was constructed, by her and by the situation. Mary Leach (1991) doing a feminist reading of the Society, found that 'in 1961 . . . there was a lone female listed on the program, though a formidable one — Maxine Greene' (p. 287). By 1967, when Maxine gave her Presidential Address, the number of women on the program, counting her, had jumped to 4, out of a total of 35 presenters! By 1972 there were 8 out of 8, including Maxine. It was well into the 1980s before the number of women on the PES program approached anywhere near a representative sample of the membership, and even then it was a struggle to get women to submit papers for presentation.

Numbers of women on the program are not the only criteria to consider, however, when assessing the intellectual/political milieu in which Maxine found herself. It is also the *kind* of ideas and the frameworks drawn on that shapes the discursive practices of the field. Avoiding an essentialist trap, I want to suggest that just because one was a woman, one did not *necessarily* add a feminist or alternative philosophical perspective to the mix. After all, if we think of Pagano's warning about women's desire to 'mimic' the father, then it comes as no surprise that woman *qua* woman would not necessarily add anything *qualitatively* different to the discourse at these meetings.

There were others besides Greene who did work in existentialism and phenomenology, and even those who argued for political action. They were marginalized as well. But they did not suffer the double/triple/quadruple marginality to which she referred, primarily because they were men; at least as men, they 'fit in.'

What remains a mystery to her is why she was elected to serve as President of PES in 1967. Whatever the complex of reasons for this, she used the position as a platform to speak out against the Vietnam War and to challenge intellectuals to think about their commitments to the larger public. In her Presidential Address, she took a risk and questioned the 'analytic turn' philosophers of education had made toward language (Greene, 1967). It was her view that by attending in a narrow way to the teacher's speech and action in the classroom, philosophers of education were abandoning the public realm to the behavioral scientists. Here is a portion of that speech:

> As citizens, we may have served as consultants or participants; we may have raised our voices in debate; we may even have demonstrated and carried picket signs. *As*

philosophers, however, [emphasis added] we concentrated on the verbal moves characterizing learning situations, the implications of epistemological theories for curriculum-making, the structure of educational arguments, the contextual meanings of education concepts, the typical uses of educational terms. (1967, p. 145)

For Greene, however, this wasn't enough. Indebted to John Dewey for many of her views on philosophy and education, Maxine decried what she saw as the separation of public from private action on the part of professional philosophers. For her, we philosophers of education should be asking moral and political questions related to the purposes of schooling and education and the relevance of philosophy to a 'torn and conflicted world' (Greene, 1991, p. 324). These moral and political questions that have been the mainstay of Greene's work in the past three decades have become more complicated, however, in a postmodern context where there is, quoting Lyotard (1984), an 'incredulity toward metanarratives.'

A Postmodern Modern

Acknowledging the enlightenment metanarratives that have shaped her philosophical stance, such as freedom, democracy, community and justice, Maxine has not shied away from interrogating her own thought. She practices what she preaches: she examines her assumptions, resists 'sedimentation,' and wrestles with alternative explanations. A voracious and responsible reader[12], she keeps up with intellectual developments in many fields, particularly in philosophy, cultural studies, literary theory and educational thought. From her existentialist perspective, she is *obligated* to do so; not to would be to act in bad faith as a teacher, writer and public intellectual.

One of her most recent statements about the field of philosophy of education represents her willingness to challenge her position; to take nothing for granted. By describing Helene Cixous, Greene reveals her own struggles with the transformations in political thought and action that are infusing our postmodern world:

Like many philosophers in the West, she [Cixous] was aware of the loss of legitimation of what used to be taken for granted about human subjects: freedom, social justice, and equality; and she found herself in tension with regard to a desire for the old standards and an acknowledgement of postmodern skepticism and questioning. She accepted the invitation and then recalled the questions being posed today about traditional norms and principles. (1995b, p. 3)

Greene, too, has accepted the invitation to look anew at what it means to be a philosopher of education today. She tells us that:

Philosophy of education today must begin in queer questions, those not susceptible to logical or empirical resolutions. Whatever shape they take, they must be defined with the contexts of multiple transactions, those in which diverse human beings are ultimately involved. (1995b, p. 17)

It is this commitment to plurality, to multiplicity, to open-endedness, to situatedness, that ties together Greene's work over the decades, even as she attends to new ideas and paradigm shifts. Her current understanding of philosophy of education reflects this commitment as well when she says:

There is no final summing up the themes of what counts as Philosophy of Education. Passion should infuse all these: the passion of sensed possibility and, yes, the passion of poetry and the several arts. Thinking of ourselves as subjects reaching out to others and attending to the shapes and sounds of things, we may resist the anaesthetic in our lives and the drawing back to anchorage. We have to know about our lives, clarify our situations if we are to understand the world from our shared standpoints, our standpoints as philosophers of education ready to commit ourselves to small transformations as we heed the stories, the multiplex stories, as cautiously we work to transform. (1995a, pp. 20–1)

Maxine Greene's Gift to Us

Certainly there is evidence of Maxine's resistance to the 'anaesthetic' in the multiple ways she has transformed the educational world, as she has jarred us to 'wide-awakeness.' From young children in arts programs in New York City, down to policy makers in Washington, across the country to countless teachers, school administrators and curriculum workers, we all have been moved by Maxine's generosity, her imagination and her eloquence. Greene's unique gift of the word, both oral and written, brings philosophy to life for her diverse audiences. Her effort to make meaning out of the world in which she has been 'thrown' resonates with so many educators. By speaking from *her own place* in the world, she is able to speak convincingly to them about *their* lived realities, *their* search for meaning, *their* need to make sense of *their* worlds and to change them. She offers openings, not orders, possibilities not prescriptions.

This is especially true for those of us in the field of philosophy of education. Maxine has, through her own volition, through her own marginality, through her own *situatedness*, forced us to expand the parameters of what counts as a philosopher of education. She has forced the category to include her own renderings of what it means to be one, of what it means to 'decide' who we are, of what it means to *name ourselves*.

It is through this rendering that Maxine has made the field more hospitable for many of us who draw on continental philosophy, the arts, literature, feminism and discourses of the 'other,' to do our work. Perhaps this is one of her finest, most powerful contributions: the *openings* she has created for others, particularly for other women. Her own ambivalence toward philosophy of education, manifested in her multi-disciplinary writings, may be, paradoxically, the most *certain* of her creations. This ambivalence does not paralyze; if anything, it allows her to see multiple realities, to choose to act with passion, to know that there are always other voices to be heard.

For this, I will be forever in her debt.

Notes

1 My colleague Emily Toth at Louisiana State University has offered this term to describe a particular form of male academic behavior. See her recently published volume, *Ms. Mentor's Impeccable Advice for Women in Academia* (1997), Philadelphia: University of Pennsylvania Press (pp. 66–7).
2 Interesting how the notion of 'lack' seems to surface in the context of women's experiences in academia.
3 See my memoir, Kohli (in press) 'Crossing the borders: Remembrances of a class act,' in Susan Franzosa (ed.) *Ordinary Lessons: Reconstructing the Girlhoods of the 1950s*, forthcoming with Peter Lang Publishers, for an account of the effects of growing up working class.

4 Maxine Greene is known for her philosophical attention to the concept and practice of freedom, including her 1988 book *The Dialectic of Freedom*, New York, NY: Teachers College Press. She was also named in 1975 the William F. Russell Chair in Foundations of Education, endowed explicitly to promote the value of freedom (Greene, 1988, p. xii).

5 Portions of this essay first appeared in another one I did for a volume edited by William Ayers and Janet Miller (eds) *A Light In Dark Times: Conversations in Relation to Maxine Greene*, forthcoming from Teachers College Press, New York, NY.

6 There is a bittersweet irony to this decision in that I ended up studying with one of the influential (male) Anglo-analytic philosophers of education, Thomas Green, who was shaping the field in the 1970s — but that's another story for another time.

7 One could argue, however, that it wasn't her 'chosen' field. As I indicate in my essay in the Ayers and Miller volume (forthcoming), Maxine called it 'total chance.' I called it 'gendered serendipity.'

8 In an interview with me on August 16, 1993 in her New York City apartment, Greene recounted that her Dean at NYU had once told her she was 'too literary.' She immediately ran for cover to the English Department.

9 See the unpublished dissertation of Mary-Ellen Jacobs (1991), *Diary of an Ambivalent Daughter: A Feminist Re-Visioning of Maxine Greene's Discursive Landscapes*, University of Maryland, College Park. In this brilliant work, Jacobs explores the patriarchal constraints on female text production. She reveals a persistent tension in Greene between the 'good daughter' of the patriarchs and the more resistant, 'ambivalent daughter' who refuses to accept the taken-for-granted.

10 See my essay in the Ayers and Miller volume: Kohli (in press).

11 From an interview with Maxine on 16 August 1993.

12 By responsible in this context I mean to highlight Maxine's grounding in existentialism where she acts in good faith, on principle. Compared to many of her colleagues who are 'professional philosophers,' Greene reads widely, drawing on academic as well as popular sources to enhance her understandings.

References

AYERS, W. and MILLER, J. (1998) *A Light in Dark Times: Conversations in Relation to Maxine Greene*, New York: Teachers College Press.

FISHER, B. (1988) 'Wandering in the wilderness: The search for women role models,' in MINNICH, E., O'BARR, J. and ROSENFELD, R. (eds) *Reconstructing the Academy: Women's Education and Women's Studies* (pp. 234–56), Chicago: University of Chicago Press.

FREIRE, P. (1970) *Pedagogy of the Oppressed*, New York: Herder and Herder.

GREENE, M. (1967) 'Morals, ideology and the schools: A foray into the politics of education,' *Proceedings of the Twenty-third Annual Meeting of the Philosophy of Education Society* (pp. 141–61), Edwardsville, IL: Southern Illinois University.

GREENE, M. (1973) *Teacher as Stranger: Educational Philosophy for the Modern Age*, Belmont, CA: Wadsworth Publishing Co.

GREENE, M. (1978) *Landscapes of Learning*, New York: Teachers College Press.

GREENE, M. (1988) *The Dialectic of Freedom*, New York: Teachers College Press.

GREENE, M. (1991) 'A response to Beck, Giarelli/Chambliss, Leach, Tozer and Macmillan,' *Educational Theory*, **41**, 3, pp. 321–4.

GREENE, M. (1995a) *Releasing the Imagination: Essays on Education, the Arts, and Social Change*, San Francisco: Jossey-Bass Publishers.

GREENE, M. (1995b) 'What counts as philosophy of education?,' in KOHLI, W. (ed.) *Critical Conversations in Philosophy of Education* (pp. 3–23), New York: Routledge.

GREENE, M. (1997) 'Exclusions and awakenings,' in NEUMANN, A. and PETERSON, P. (eds) *Learning from Our Lives: Women, Research and Autobiography in Education* (pp. 18– 35), New York: Teachers College Press.

JACOBS, M.-E. (1991) 'Diary of an ambivalent daughter: A feminist re-visioning of Maxine Greene's discursive landscapes,' Unpublished doctoral dissertation, University of Maryland, College Park.

KOHLI, W. (ed.) (1995) *Critical Conversations in Philosophy of Education*, New York: Routledge.

KOHLI, W. (1998) 'Philosopher of/for freedom,' in AYERS, W. and MILLER, J. (eds) *A Light in Dark Times: Conversations in Relation to Maxine Greene*, New York: Teachers College Press.

KOHLI, W. (in press) 'Crossing the borders: Remembrances of a class act,' in FRANZOSA, S. (ed.) *Ordinary Lessons: Reconstructing the Girlhoods of the 1950s*, New York: Peter Lang.

LEACH, M. (1991) 'Mothers of in(ter)vention: Women's writing in philosophy of education,' *Educational Theory*, **41**, 3, pp. 287–300.

PAGANO, J. (1990) *Exiles and Communities: Teaching in the Patriarchal Wilderness*, New York: State University of New York Press.

TOTH, E. (1997) *Ms. Mentor's Impeccable Advice for Women in Academia*, Philadelphia: University of Pennsylvania Press.

YOUNG-BRUHLE, E. (1988) 'The education of women as philosophers,' in MINNICH, E., O'BARR, J. and ROSENFELD, R. (eds) *Reconstructing the Academy: Women's Education and Women's Studies*, Chicago: University of Chicago Press.

17　Maxine Greene and the Current/Future Democratization of Curriculum Studies

James G. Henderson, Janice Hutchison,
and Charlene Newman

This is what we shall look for as we move: freedom developed by human beings who have acted to make a space for themselves in the presence of others. . . . And we shall seek, as we go, implications for emancipatory education conducted by and for those willing to take responsibility for themselves and for each other. We want to discover how to open spaces for persons in their plurality, spaces where they can become different, where they can grow. (Maxine Greene, 1988, p. 56)

Introduction

We will explore two questions in this chapter: *what has been Maxine Greene's impact on the **field** of American curriculum studies, and how can her sophisticated philosophical inquiries into human freedom serve to critique this **field**?* The first question will be addressed through a carefully documented account of the direct and indirect ways her philosophical themes have guided curriculum study projects. The second question is more complex and requires a response that touches on the identity — the very *heart and soul* — of American curriculum studies. We begin by describing the general features of American curriculum studies before turning to the two questions that serve as the organizational frame for this chapter.

The Field of Curriculum Studies

As noted by Schubert (1986), curriculum studies is a 'subdivision' of education. Historically, scholarly projects in this subdivision have focused on 'the relationships among the school subjects as well as issues within the individual school subjects themselves and with the relationships between the curriculum and the world' (Pinar, Reynolds, Slattery, and Taubman, 1995, p. 6). Because this study focus is so general in nature, curriculum scholars often rely on broad, integrating disciplines such as philosophy and history to pursue their work. It is not surprising that an astute and productive philosopher such as Maxine Greene would have an important impact on the field.

Though the current field of American curriculum studies is fairly diversified and amorphous, with no overarching 'master narratives' (also called 'metanarratives') to structure its inquiries (Pinar et al., 1995, p. 5), it maintains its identity as a cohesive scholarly 'field' for at least three reasons. First of all, curriculum study projects are, in general, focused on questions of how to educate for the 'good life.' 'Curriculum' is a Latin term, first used in university educational discourses in the European Middle Ages

(Jackson, 1992, p. 5), which can be literally translated as an educational 'race course' (Marsh and Willis, 1995, p. 6). By definition, therefore, curriculum study projects directly or indirectly address the question of what educational **path** should be followed. These projects, either explicitly or implicitly, posit a conception of the 'good life' that justifies a particular educational course of action. Macdonald (1975) makes this point about curriculum studies by drawing an analogy between curriculum theorizing and Dewey's philosophizing: '[In light of] Dewey's comment that educational philosophy was the essence of all philosophy because it was "the study of how to have a world," curriculum theory . . . might be said to be the essence of educational theory because it is the study of how to have a learning environment' (p. 12).

Curriculum studies also remains an identifiable scholarly field because it serves as a cultural site where interested parties can come to contest their diverse ideas about educating for the 'good life.' American curriculum studies can be understood as a formal location for ideological and political struggle (Kliebard, 1986). Pluralistic societies with democratic ideals, such as the United States, require such cultural locations (Hatab, 1995). If the 'arena' of American curriculum studies didn't exist, it would have to be invented so as to allow for a democratic contest of educational ideas and ideals.

Finally, American curriculum studies remains an identifiable field because it has a material presence — a very specific history. Although the purpose of this chapter is not to present a detailed interpretative account of this history, several key historical points must be made as a prelude to a response to the question of how Maxine Greene's inquiry into human freedom can be used to critique the curriculum study field.

Though there are earlier influential curriculum study documents that can be traced back to, at least, Plato's *The Republic* (1956), the publication of Franklin Bobbitt's *The Curriculum* in 1918 can arguably be considered the beginning of formal curriculum studies in the United States (Jackson, 1992; Pinar et al., 1995). This book established the precedent that the focus of curriculum studies should be on creating and sustaining institutional curriculum development processes. Pinar et al. (1995) describe this focus as the institutional 'text' of curriculum studies, which they characterize as follows: 'Understanding curriculum as institutionalized text suggests understanding curriculum as it functions bureaucratically . . . ; [it is] an ameliorative approach linked explicitly to the everyday functioning of the institution' (p. 661). Between 1918 and 1969, curriculum development was the dominant, though certainly not the only, focus of curriculum studies. The Tyler Rationale (Tyler, 1949), which is a refinement of Bobbitt's curriculum development prescriptions (Jackson, 1992), emerged as the major curriculum study document of this period.

Beginning in 1969, curriculum development prescriptions began to lose their discursive dominance in the curriculum study field. Schwab's 1969 publication of 'The Practical: A Language for Curriculum,' based on a 1968 AERA presentation at which he received a standing ovation, is arguably the single most important stimulus for the broadening of the field. Schwab (1969) argued that the focus of curriculum studies should be on the construction of sophisticated, 'eclectic' solutions to educational problems. Within a few short years, curriculum scholars were studying all sorts of solutions to a diverse set of *'critical'* educational problems. The fact that this period is characterized by an ideological contest over the correct interpretation of 'critical' problems and solutions (Pinar, 1988) is not surprising given the fact that American curriculum studies serves a site for 'democratic' educational contests.

In 1975 Pinar characterized the diversification of curriculum studies as the 'reconceptualization' of the field, signaling the fact that the field was no longer dominated by any one particular inquiry focus (Pinar, 1975). As diverse critical inquiry projects increasingly came to constitute the field, arguments for 'curriculum reconceptualization' became moot and were replaced by various 'poststructural' interpretations of curriculum study. For example, Cherryholmes (1988) writes:

> The history of curriculum theory and practice can be read as a series of repeated invasions of organizing ideas that command attention for a while before they are turned out by the next invasion. Each new invader was beyond the control of any individual educator, reflected political events external as well as internal to education, represented prominent contemporary ideologies, and could be deconstructed. [p. 141] ... The norm for curriculum, then, is not consensus, stability, and agreement but conflict, instability, and disagreement, because the process is one of construction followed by deconstruction, by [further] construction ... of what students have an opportunity to learn. (p. 149)

In 1995, Pinar et al. appropriated this poststructural view of curriculum to argue for a sophisticated 'conversational' understanding of curriculum: '[Curriculum] is what the older generation chooses to tell the younger generation. So understood, curriculum is intensely historical, political, racial, gendered, phenomenological, autobiographical, aesthetic, theological, and international. Curriculum becomes the site on which the generations struggle to define themselves and the world' (Pinar et al., 1995, pp. 847–8).

This 80-year movement toward a more *intertextual* interpretation of curriculum studies can be viewed as important 'progress' in the *democratization* of the field. However, before exploring this topic, we will first examine Maxine Greene's already considerable impact on the field of American curriculum studies. In this way, we will be able to provide important background information on the normative context that we will use to critique the 'progress' of American curriculum studies.

Maxine Greene's Impact: A Thematic Analysis

> From the beginnings of my career, trying with some difficulty to be accepted as a philosopher of education, I found myself moving back and forth between imaginative literature and philosophy. Troubled by the kind of positivism that identified existential questions ... with 'pseudo-questions,' with a domain of meaninglessness, I kept on stubbornly seeking out those questions in fictive and poetic worlds, in personal narratives. Troubled by impersonality, by abstract vantage points, I wanted people to name themselves and tell their stories when they made their statements. (Maxine Greene, 1988, p. xii)

In the introduction to *The Dialectic of Freedom* quoted above, Maxine Greene provides a concise account of the critical-existential questions and concerns that have guided her work for over three decades. Posited against a backdrop of 'education' as a site for positivistic discourse-practices, her voice invites educators to examine curriculum, and the related fields of teaching and teacher education, through diverse frames of reference. Inspired by the arts and humanities, she challenges educators to think of their work in imaginative, poetic, and narrative idioms rather than in constraining management and technical terminologies.

Several recurring themes run through Maxine Greene's educational and philosophical discourses. We will draw on these themes to document her impact on curriculum studies. In taking this approach, we recognize that we are not doing justice to the organic richness of her writing. Her work is multi-dimensional and densely layered, and she uses themes synergistically to create an overall humanistic effect. She writes to celebrate the possibilities of the human spirit, and she selects themes with that *end in view* in mind.

One recurring theme in her work is that of conscious living or *wide-awakeness*. This theme provides a background context for her use of four other themes: *self-knowledge, aesthetic literacy, feminism,* and *public spaces*. These five themes provide a rich normative postmodern gestalt or 'constellation' (Bernstein, 1991) for her discussion of *human freedom*.[1] This sixth and final theme, which will be used to critique the field of curriculum studies, will be the focus of this chapter's concluding sections.

Although Maxine Greene's impact on curriculum studies has been far reaching and long lasting, some of her influences have been direct and obvious while others have been indirect and subtle. In cases where it is possible to document a direct influence, specific individuals will be indicated. The documentation of her more indirect and subtle influences is more inferential and has been handled in two main ways: by noting the scholars that have cited her work and by observing similarities between her work and specific curriculum studies projects. With this background understanding of this section of the chapter, we now turn our attention to the first of her recurring themes: *wide-awakeness*.

Wide-awakeness

One of Maxine Greene's major concerns is to implore individuals to engage in a more 'wide-awake' existence in life. In *Landscapes of Learning*, she contrasts this state of being to the general malaise of society: 'This attentiveness, this *interest* in things, is the direct opposite of the attitude of bland conventionality and indifference so characteristic of our time' (Greene, 1978, p. 42). Grounded in active involvement and reflective action, she explains, 'consciousness . . . involves the capacity to pose questions to the world, to reflect on what is presented in experience' (Greene, 1988, p. 21).

Maxine Greene identifies two characteristics of 'wide-awakeness.' First, drawing upon the work of Merleau-Ponty (1964), Polanyi (1969), and Gadamer (1976), she recognizes the contextual and positioned nature of consciousness: 'Human consciousness . . . is always situated; and the situated person, inevitably engaged with others, reaches out and grasps the phenomena surrounding him/her from a particular vantage point and against a particular background consciousness' (Greene, 1988, p. 21). Second, consciousness is a way of purposefully connecting with others and with the world. She writes: 'consciousness throws itself outward, *toward* the world. It is intentional; it is always *of* something: a phenomenon, another person, an object or event in the world' (Greene, 1973, p. 162).

While describing 'wide-awakeness,' Maxine Greene often shifts the focus of her advocacy to educators. Specifically, with regard to the professional preparation of teachers, she implores them to engage in and model this level of awareness as a prerequisite for their teaching: 'If teachers today are to initiate young people into an ethical existence, they themselves must attend more fully than they normally have to their own lives and its requirements; they have to break with the mechanical life, to overcome their own submergence in the habitual' (Greene, 1973, p. 46). Corroborating Dewey's (1933) ideas on pragmatic intelligence, she notes the difference between *reflective action,* which results from persistent, active, and careful consideration of beliefs, and *routine action,* which is based on impulse, authority, and tradition.

By integrating Dewey's pragmatic intelligence into her discussions of 'wide-awakeness,' Maxine Greene has helped foster the current interest in reflective curriculum and teaching practices. Her influence on 'reflective practice' discourse is cited by Clark and Yinger (1987) and Richert (1991). LaBoskey (1994) implies that, with the exception of Hullfish and Smith (1961), Greene's voice was one of the few which called attention to 'reflective practice' since Dewey's discussion in the 1930s. Her work on this topic (1973, 1978) predates that of Schön (1983), one of the major contributors to discourse on reflective teaching. Moreover, Zeichner (1993) argues that her understanding of 'professional educational reflection' is more comprehensive than Donald Schön's:

> Maxine Greene [1986c] and Nel Noddings [1987] are among those who have challenged the detached rationality that has dominated the literature . . . for a long time.[2] Their critiques go well beyond Schön's [1983] criticisms of technical rationality, because the problems they identify, the lack of care, compassion, and passion in actions, can also be a problem in the epistemology of practice that Schön proposes as the new paradigm for conceptualizing reflective practice. (Zeichner, 1993, p. 12)

Examples of her influence on reflective practice can be seen in specific curricular projects. In her work with graduate students in English education over two successive semesters, Britzman (1992) practices curriculum in ways that encourage her students to become more 'conscious' of the ideas and assumptions which they have previously taken for granted. In her work with preservice teachers, LaBoskey (1994) invites her students to become more 'reflective' in their teaching practices. In a collaborative group comprised of teachers, school principals, and university-based researchers, Berkey, Curtis, Minnick, Zietlow, Campbell, and Kirschner (1990) have worked together to assist teachers with their professional development. All of these scholars duly note that Maxine Greene's 'wide-awakeness' serves as a normative referent for their work.

Self-knowledge

Based on the work of Merleau-Ponty (1964), Maxine Greene notes the synergy between attentive, reflective living and an awareness of oneself:

> Each of us achieved contact with the world from a particular vantage point, in terms of a particular biography. All of this underlies our present perspectives and affects the way we look at things and talk about things and structure our realities. To be in touch with our landscapes is to be conscious of our evolving experiences, to be aware of the ways in which we encounter our world. (Greene, 1978, p. 2)

She notes that attention to one's personal history can help one become critically aware of that which is habitual or routine: 'It does appear . . . that attentiveness to one's own history, one's own self-formation, may open one up to critical awareness of much that is taken for granted' (Greene, 1978, p. 103). Furthermore, by reflecting on their life stories, teachers are better able to 'regain an awareness of what it actually means to be enabled to learn, to reach beyond where one is' (Greene, 1986a, p. 16). She also recognizes that self-knowledge cannot be cultivated in isolation from others: 'The self can never be actualized through solely private experiences, no matter how extraordinary those experiences might be, and surely not the ideal of the teacher's self. Connectedness is required' (Greene, 1986c, p. 74).

To put this connectedness into practice, Greene advocates encouragement of a dialogical 'self-reflection' in teacher education curricula: 'I am proposing . . . that teacher educators and their students be stimulated to think about their own thinking and to reflect upon their own reflecting' (Greene, 1978, p. 61). Important benefits result from this type of curriculum design. Teacher educators and students can both begin to envision possibilities that neither had seen previously; and teacher educators can begin to break from the dominance of 'positivist notions, notions of the given' (Greene, 1978, p. 61).

In addition to exploring one's life in general, Greene encourages teachers to pay specific attention to the meaning of their lives and articulate the purposes of their lives. In telling their stories, Greene believes that they will become 'connected . . . with their origins' (Greene, 1991b, p. 303). To construct these self-narratives, Greene suggests that teachers can begin with 'the sources of their own quests . . . , perhaps to childhood, to times when the voices of parents and grandparents could be heard' (Greene, 1991b, p. 303). Maxine Greene notes that fiction, in particular, can be useful inspirational sources for the creation of self-narratives; and she cites the works of Ellison (1952), Wiesel (1992), Levi (1988), and Morrison (1987) as potentially useful literary wellsprings.

Her impact in the area of self-knowledge can be noted throughout the genre of *auto-biographical* and *biographical* curriculum study, which gained momentum during the 1980s (Pinar et al., 1995). In fact, Butt, Raymond, and Yamagishi (1988) make a point of noting that her work has provided curriculum researchers with a rationale for *auto-biographical/biographical* study. Miller's (1990) work illustrates Maxine Greene's influence on this line of inquiry. Operating from the belief that curriculum is 'centered within students' and teachers' biographical, historical, and social relationships' (p. 2), Miller (1990) collaborates with five teachers on the examination of their teaching practices.

Aesthetic Literacy

Despite the emphasis placed on teaching toward particular competencies, Maxine Greene argues that teachers need to focus on the artistry of their work. She clearly articulates the dangers of technocratic interpretations of teaching: 'When the reward system of a school is geared toward guaranteeing certain predefined performances or the mastery of certain skills, teachers too often become trainers — drilling, imposing, inserting, testing, and controlling' (Greene, 1982, p. 327).

To break away from this remnant of the factory model and attempts to forcibly insert knowledge into students' memories (Ryle, 1967), Greene provides a more humanistic view of student learning. She wants teachers to view their students, not as empty vessels devoid of information, but rather 'as novices, as newcomers to a learning community extending back through time and ahead into a future' (Greene, 1982, p. 327). Both teachers and their students benefit from this view of learning, by becoming more open 'to all sorts of untapped experiential possibilities' (Greene, 1982, p. 327).

To begin to learn how to learn in this particular way, Greene notes that aesthetic literacy, which is 'an informed awareness of works of art or works in the humanities' (Greene, 1982, p. 179), must be cultivated through active learning: 'The more a person can come to know, the more he or she will come to see and hear, certainly where works of art are concerned' (p. 327). She would like to see teachers engage in diverse art activities because 'every encounter with a work of art represents a new beginning, even if the work is moderately familiar and has been encountered before' (Greene, 1982, p. 327). For her, the arts are an infinite source of educational inspiration.

Maxine Greene's passion for aesthetic literacy leads her to promote the arts in the curriculum:

> By that I mean that those who can attend to and absorb themselves in particular works of art are more likely to effect connections in their own experiences than

those who cannot. They are more likely to perceive the shapes of things as they are conscious of them, to pay heed to qualities and appearances ordinarily obscured by the conventional and routine. I believe that we can release people for this kind of seeing if we ourselves are able to recover — and help our students to discover — the imaginative mode of awareness that makes paintings available, and poetry, and sculpture, and theatre, and film. (Greene, 1977, p. 15)

Arts-based classrooms provide students with multi-intelligent possibilities: 'This is the point . . . of the creative encounters we try to nurture with works of art. If we do not do our work intentionally, if we do not have a clear sense of what aesthetic perceptions and aesthetic objects signify, we are likely to deprive our students of possibility (Greene, 1977, p. 15). Furthermore, by providing students with opportunities to explore the arts, students can transcend their own existence and begin to articulate their views of the world as they understand it. Greene (1977) explains: 'Provided with opportunities to speak about it [the fragmented, objective world], young people often express a desire to overcome their own *ennui*. They make groping efforts to bridge between the subjectivities and that which exists apart from them, to find ways of identifying with a reality that afflicts them like an alien presence' (p. 15).

Teachers are central figures in providing students with artistic experiences, and they must be willing to model an attitude of openness and receptivity to the arts:

Teachers must take risks if they are to enable students to open themselves to art forms, to overcome false notions, to take a 'humanistic view.' Moreover, teachers must themselves be sensitive to the qualities of things, as they must know personally what it means to be receptive to the arts. Only teachers like these can move the young to notice more, to attend more carefully, to express their visions, to choose themselves. (Greene, 1977, p. 20)

Maxine Greene not only wants to infuse the arts into curriculum, she advocates the integration of artistic forms of inquiry into curriculum study. Greene (1991a) writes: 'To speak of the arts in relation to curriculum inquiry is, for me, to summon up visions of new perspectives and untapped possibilities. Curriculum has to do with the life of meaning, with ambiguities, and with relationships. And, yes, it has to do with transformations and with fluidity, with change' (p. 107). Citing the works of Iser (1980), Sartre (1956), and Dewey (1934a), she goes on to explain: 'If curriculum is regarded as an undertaking involving continuous interpretation and a conscious search for meanings, there are many connections between the "grasping" of a text and the gaining of perspectives by means of the disciplines' (Greene, 1991a, p. 114).

With reference to the search for meaning, which is a central motif of both the arts and curriculum inquiry, Greene believes that educators have a particular role. They must 'feel the importance of releasing students to be personally present to what they see and hear and read . . . [and] to develop a sense of agency and participation and to do so in collaboration with one another' (Greene, 1991a, p. 122). This sense of collaborative 'presentness' resonates with the theme of *wide-awakeness,* which has been previously explored. Greene (1991a) summarizes her understanding of the relationship between the arts and curriculum inquiry as follows:

To conceive of the arts in relation to curriculum is, for me, to think of a deepening and expanding mode of 'tuning-in,' of communication. There have to be disciplines, yes, and a growing acquaintance with the structures of knowledge; but, at once, there have to be the kinds of grounded interpretations possible only for those willing to abandon 'already constructed reason,' willing to feel and to imagine, to open the windows and go in and search. (p. 122)

Her words are a poignant challenge for teachers and teacher educators to move beyond that which is known into *public spaces* that are saturated with feelings, imagination, and wonder — another theme that will be examined shortly.

Her passion for aesthetic literacy has broadened curriculum studies. Walker (1992) credits her with providing the field with 'kindred forms . . . of qualitative research' (Walker, 1992, p. 108). Vallance (1991) notes that, along with Huebner (1966), Maxine Greene has challenged educators to use language and metaphors to shape an understanding of education and 'balance the traditional emphases on technical, scientific, and political understandings of schooling' (Vallance, 1991, p. 157). Barone's work on 'critical story-telling,' which he acknowledges has been strongly influenced by Maxine Greene, represents a specific example of the integration of artistic methods with curriculum studies (Barone, 1992a, 1992b; Rothman, 1992).

Maxine Greene's interest in *aesthetic literacy* has also encouraged a more humanistic understanding of student learning. For example, Goodlad and Su (1992) credit Greene and Maslow (1968) with having a major role in the establishment of a curriculum that is self-actualizing. This type of curriculum 'is child-centered, viewing education as an enabling process that provides the means to personal development and liberation' (Goodlad and Su, 1992, p. 335). Furthermore, her arguments for more arts-based curricula encourages more imaginative approaches to curriculum development. Padgham (1988) reflects this perspective when he writes: 'When the imagination is sparked, the "will" to learn is engaged and the curriculum begins to become imbued with soul: the curriculum speaks to the student and the student begins to develop his own dialogue much the same way the artist develops his own imagery and dialogues with his canvas' (p. 130).

Maxine Greene's work on *aesthetic literacy* has also influenced perspectives on educational assessment. For example, Beyer (1988) and Wolf (1992) both note that she has played a major role in helping educators move from technical to more artistic forms of assessment. Based on Greene's work, Wolf (1992) makes the following remarks about the value of artistic practices such as studio classrooms, museum visits, rehearsals, critiques, performances, and artist residencies: 'In these practices are embedded complex tasks, sustained work, and instances of assessment that function as episodes of learning. Rather than regarding these practices as marginalia or oddities, educators in any number of subject areas might learn from them' (Wolf, 1992, p. 959).

A final contribution of her work on *aesthetic literacy* has been to challenge the literary and artistic canons that have served as the normative referent for Eurocentric curriculum studies. Since this topic strongly overlaps with the theme *feminism*, it will be examined in the next section.

Feminism

Using the heroine in Chopin's *The Awakening*, (1964) to express the complexity of the situation of women in the United States, Greene (1976) explains her interest in feminism: 'My concern is not simply to point to the many modes of constraint and manipulation suffered by women; it is also to suggest the multiple, often mysterious devices invented for achieving their own education — in spite of the exclusion, humiliation, and discrimination that dogged them over the years' (pp. 25–6). She cites many examples of the types of constraint and manipulation that women have endured throughout history and argues for transformative curricula in which '[sexist] beliefs, attitudes, values, and knowledge as those associated with traditional Protestantism' are challenged and supplanted with new ways of being (Greene, 1976, p. 26).

This feminist interpretation of curriculum provides a context that enables women to define themselves. Rather than focusing on the inequities and prejudices that women endured in educational settings, Greene takes a pro-active stance, concentrating on each woman's individual story:

> It is of greater import to determine how women defined themselves within the spheres of action allotted to them, why some complied and others flowered and still others rebelled. The crucial research question, as I see it, has to do with the ways in which women conceptualized their own condition and acted upon their conceptualizations, in ways in which they intervened in the sequences of causes and effects and constructed their own realities. (Greene, 1976, p. 26)

Although Greene acknowledges the limited opportunities that were afforded to women, she also cites examples of women who were not stifled by these limitations. For example, she notes that, in the middle of the nineteenth century, Emma Willard 'encouraged women to study the sciences and mathematics' (Greene, 1976, p. 27), while Catherine Beecher 'believed . . . that young women of all classes should be properly educated for productive work' (Greene, 1976, p. 27).

In addition to the struggle to acquire an education, women have also been limited in the roles that they play. Greene (1978) writes: 'I am so sharply aware of the degree to which they [women's lived worlds and perceptual realities] are obscured by sex and gender roles. I am convinced that the imposition of these roles makes women falsify their sense of themselves' (Greene, 1978, p. 213).

According to some scholars (Jacobs, 1991; Purpel and Shapiro, 1995), Maxine Greene has been a prominent voice in the establishment of feminist curriculum theorists. One example is Janet Miller who clearly acknowledges the influence of Maxine Greene in her work (Pinar et al., 1995). In keeping with the spirit of Greene's concern for the roles that women play, Miller (1983) has written about the political and psychological dilemma of women working in academia as evidenced in her own autobiographical inquiries. In commenting on this piece, Pinar et al. (1995) note that 'the male-identified character of academic work functions to move women to self-alienation' (p. 550). Grumet (1988), who acknowledges Maxine Greene's influence, also studies curriculum through a feminist lens. She notes the tensions that women feel in balancing the multiple responsibilities in their lives: 'They [women] go back and forth between the experience of domesticity and the experience of teaching, between being with one's own children and being with the children of others, between being the child of one's own mother and the teacher of another mother's child, between feeling and form, family and colleagues' (Grumet, 1988, p. xv).

Public Spaces

To achieve the level of conscious living and knowledge of self, Greene proposes the use of a *public space — a place* 'of dialogue and possibility' (Greene, 1988, p. xi). Calling to mind the words of one of her intellectual mentors, Hannah Arendt, Greene adds that in these spaces, diverse individuals can be 'the best they know how to be . . .' (p. xi). Greene (1988) amplifies the concept:

Such a space requires the provision of opportunities for the articulation of multiple perspectives in multiple idioms, out of which something common can be brought into being. It requires, as well, a consciousness of the normative as well as the possible: of what *ought* to be, from a moral and ethical point of view, and what is in the making, what *might* be in an always open world. (p. xi)

She argues that the creation of *public spaces* is a central challenge for education. In her view, the role of education is 'to discover how to open spaces for persons in their plurality, spaces where they can become different, where they can grow' (Greene, 1988, p. 56).

Embedded in her sense of public spaces in the exchange of information or what she refers to as dialogue, Greene critically notes that the scarcity of dialogue in public spaces today distorts our ability to understand and appreciate human diversity. She explains: 'The lack of dialogue in public spaces today makes people forget that there are other American traditions, other visions of what constitute the good life and the humane society' (Greene, 1986c, p. 71). Returning to the arts, Greene (1986c) cites the poetry of Moore (1966), Rukeyser (1973), and Rich (1981) to note that *public spaces* are infused with desire, hope, and expectation (p. 236).

Greene's sense of public spaces is also linked to a higher purpose and more global vision through her robust discussion of human freedom and social order. She implores educators 'to find out how to open such spheres, such spaces, where a better state of things can be imagined; because it is only through the projection of a better social order that we can perceive the gaps in what exists and try to transform and repair' (Greene, 1986b, pp. 247–8).

In speaking about the ability to create spaces, Greene remains resolute in the face of the sometimes grim realities that exist in the world today and the enormous challenges that face educators. Her vision is one of hope and inspiration: 'I would like to think that this [creating spaces] can happen in classrooms, in corridors, in schoolyards, and in the streets around' (Greene, 1986b, p. 248).

The normative concept of a *public space* has been used by several curriculum theorists — Miller (1992) being a prime example. In the collaborative work that she has done with teachers who examine the ways in which they perceived their roles as teachers, she notes: 'I began looking for ways to create spaces in which we might examine the myriad assumptions, generated by cultural contexts and biographical situations, that girded and framed our practice' (Miller, 1992, p. 20).

Maxine Greene's vision of *public spaces* is embedded in her robust discussion of *human freedom* which, as the culminating and overarching theme in her philosophical inquiries, will be used to critique the field of curriculum studies. We turn now to that critique.

Maxine Greene's Emancipatory Faith

We now turn our attention to the question of how Maxine Greene's sophisticated philosophical inquiries into the question of *human freedom* could serve to critique the field of curriculum studies. We have just documented how her dense, multi-thematic work has served as a source of foundational ideas and ideals for a diverse group of curriculum scholars. However, there is a central feature of her studies that we have not as yet addressed: *her faith in democracy as a moral way of life.* This faith is carefully and succinctly articulated in *The Dialectic of Freedom* (1988). There are several distinctive characteristics associated with her passionate evocation of democratic 'emancipation' in this book. After illustrating these characteristics, we will use them to critically examine the field of curriculum studies with reference to two questions: *how has the field of curriculum studies progressed*, and *how might the field continue its progress in the future?*

Greene (1988) introduces her book as an extension of a John Dewey lecture. She notes that she holds the William F. Russell Chair at Teachers College, Columbia University, which 'was endowed for the sake of advancing inquiry into the connections between education and freedom' (Greene, 1988, p. xii). She then describes the study of these connections as 'perhaps, the main theme of my life' (p. xii).

As a normative term, 'democracy' is interpreted in many diverse ways (Barber, 1984; Beyer, 1996). John Dewey approaches this topic as a 'public intellectual' concerned about Americans' moral way of life (Westbrook, 1991). In 1939, on the eve of World War II, Dewey contemplates the challenges that democratic societies faced from Communist Soviet Union and Fascist Germany:

> The democratic road is the hard one to take. It is the road which places the greatest burden of responsibility upon the greatest number of human beings. Backsets and deviations occur and will continue to occur. But that which is its own weakness at particular times is its strength in the long course of human history. Just because the cause of democratic freedom is the cause of the fullest possible realization of human potentialities, the latter when they are suppressed and opposed will in time rebel and demand an opportunity for manifestation. We have advanced far enough to say that democracy is a way of life. We have yet to realize that is a way of personal life and one which provides a moral standard for personal conduct. (Dewey, 1989, pp. 100–1)

This particular *moral* approach to 'democracy' emphasizes the connection between democracy and education (Dewey, 1916), a point that Maxine Greene continually stresses throughout *The Dialectic of Freedom*. For example, early on in her argument she writes that a 'teacher in search of his/her own freedom may be the only kind of teacher who can arouse young persons to go in search of their own' (Greene, 1988, p. 14).

Greene addresses the connections of democracy and education in the spirit of an *inquiry faith* not a *true belief*. This is a subtle but important distinction that cannot be overemphasized when attempting to understand her philosophical work. Dewey (1938) describes faith in the significance of any inquiry topic as an 'end in view.' An end in view is different from a precise belief. It is an organizing ideal that forever remains open to diverse perspectives. It is an 'inside' view of the good life that is radically (always already) open to the interplay of other, 'outside' discourse-practices (Derrida, 1988). Carlson (1997) characterizes Dewey's democratic end in view as a 'fuzzy' utopianism. It is a moral understanding of life that is constantly open to reinterpretation, or in Dewey's language, to 'reconstruction.' This approach to 'progressive' democratic living is suffused with poststructural irony: a Deweyan democrat does not bring ideological closure to his/her 'faith,' knowing full well that only through continuing radical inquiry can this democratic way of life be practiced. Greene (1988) articulates this point of view when she writes:

> I hope to develop a view of education for freedom that will take into account our political and social realities as well as the human condition itself. I hope to communicate a sense of things that is neither contemplative or self-regarding, a mood in which new initiatives can be imagined and dimensions of experience transformed. It

is, actually, in the process of effecting transformations that the human self is created and re-created. Dewey, like the existential thinkers, did not believe that the self was ready-made or pre-existent; it was, he said, 'something in continuous formation through choice of action' (Dewey, 1916, p. 408). (in Greene, pp. 21–2)

In the spirit of poststructural irony, Greene (1988) notes that perspectives on human freedom can never 'be finished or complete. There is always more. There is always possibility. And this is where the space opens for the pursuit of freedom' (p. 128).

As she goes about her hopeful inquiries into the connections between democracy and education, Greene (1988) presents a complex, layered understanding of *human freedom*: 'Freedom cannot be conceived apart from a matrix of social, economic, cultural, and psychological conditions. It is within the matrix that selves take shape or are created through choice of action' (p. 80). She wants the reader to understand that her inquiries are based on an understanding of reality as 'interpreted experience' grounded in 'sedimented meanings' (Greene, 1988, p. xii).

Maxine Greene further understands that this layered understanding of *human freedom* demands a sophisticated deliberative praxis — an 'experimental' practice informed by a multidimensional critical awareness. Locating her inquiry project in the context of the best of American progressivist and pragmatic thought, she notes that such individuals as Oliver Wendell Holmes, Thorstein Veblen, Vernon Louis Parrington, William James, John Dewey, Lincoln Steffens, Charles Beard, and Jane Adams all 'shared a profound faith in hypothetical and empirical inquiries; and they shared an understanding of the transactional relationships between living human beings and their environments' (Greene, 1988, p. 42).

Drawing on Hannah Arendt's understanding of praxis, she argues that the 'consequences of free action . . . are to a large degree unpredictable' (Greene, 1988, p. 46). Engaging in our best practical intelligence is 'the price we must pay' for democratic pluralism (p. 46). Millgram (1997) describes Aristotle's ideal of practical intelligence as decision making 'informed by the full range of considerations' (p. 53). This is the understanding of intelligence that accompanies Maxine Greene's inquiry into *human freedom*. She has faith that humans can help one another cultivate a sophisticated 'critical' deliberation (Greene, 1988, p. 4). She cites Dewey on this point: 'Social conditions interact with the preferences of an individual — in a way favorable to actualizing freedom only when they develop intelligence, not abstract knowledge and abstract thought, but power of vision and reflection. For these take effect in making preference, desire, and purpose more flexible, alert, and resolute' (Dewey, 1960, p. 287; quoted in Greene, 1988, p. 4).

Finally, Maxine Greene argues for a subtle 'dialectical' understanding of human freedom, in which critical concerns for freedom's constraints are balanced by considerations of human development. In her overview of American discourses-practices on 'human freedom,' she notes that this dialectical sensibility was particularly well-articulated by John Dewey:

Dewey . . . grew up in the Hegelian stream; and the Hegelian view of dialectical change and development remained alive in his thinking. What he rejected in time, however, was the idea of the World Spirit, the Absolute, the cosmic order. . . . The Hegelian view that autonomy and freedom are attained when human beings grasp, through the exercise of reason, the overarching order of things was revised. For Dewey, there was no cosmic purpose fulfilling itself in history. Nonetheless, there was a clear connection between identity and what he called the 'freed intelligence' necessary for direction of freedom of action. (Greene, 1988, pp. 42–3)

Maxine Greene's *The Dialectic of Freedom* is essentially a careful analysis and poetic evocation of this 'freed intelligence.' Through numerous illustrations, descriptions, and metaphors, she presents her understanding of democratically liberated consciousness. To acknowledge the dialectical implications of her philosophical inquiry, she continuously acknowledges both the 'negative' and 'positive' poles of her presentation. She uses these terms descriptively, as a physicist would. Negative freedom is not 'negative' in a moral sense, nor is positive freedom 'positive' in a moral sense. Negative and positive struggles are, simply, two sides of the same 'emancipatory' coin. Negative freedom refers to the deliberate rejection of 'oppression or exploitation or segregation or neglect' (Greene, 1988, p. 9). Without a critical sense of negative freedom, people remain anchored, submerged, or even, rootless. They lack an awareness of their psychological and/or social constraints and limitations.[3] Negative freedom connotes 'the right not to be interfered with or coerced or compelled to do what [one] did not choose to do' (Greene, 1988, p. 16). In contrast, positive freedom refers to expressions of 'self-direction.' The critical norm of positive freedom 'suggests that freedom shows itself or comes into being when individuals come together in a particular way, when they are authentically present to one another (without masks, pretenses, badges of office), when they have a project they can mutually pursue' (Greene, 1988, p. 16).

Greene's (1988) discussion of negative and positive freedom is quite comprehensive and cosmopolitan. She describes a variety of forms of oppression, exploitation, segregation, and neglect in American society. Not only those associated with racial, gender, and class relations, but more subtle forms such as 'constraining family rituals,' 'bureaucratic supervisory systems,' and, ironically, even freedom as a media 'icon' that benefits the wealthy (Greene, 1988, p. 17). She recognizes that struggles against freedom's constraints must be broad-based and multi-leveled.

Maxine Greene's analysis of positive liberatory endeavors is equally sophisticated. She draws on expressions of positive freedom from the writings of Thomas Jefferson, Mark Twain, Horace Mann, Ralph Waldo Emerson, Henry David Thoreau, Nathaniel Hawthorne, Herman Melville, Walt Whitman, Jane Addams, Emily Dickinson, W.E.B. DuBois, Martin Luther King, Virginia Woolf, Joan Didion, Alice Walker, Walker Percy, among many others. She summarizes these expressions of 'positive' human freedom as follows:

> Looking back, we can discern individuals in their we-relations with others, inserting themselves in the world by means of projects, embarking on new beginnings in spaces they open themselves. We can recall them — Thomas Jefferson, the Grimke sisters, Susan B. Anthony, Jane Addams, Frederick Douglass, W.E.B. DuBois, Martin Luther King, John Dewey, Carol Gilligan, Nel Noddings, Mary Daly — opening spaces where freedom is the mainspring, where people create themselves by acting in concert. (Greene, 1988, p. 134)

From the beginning sentences in her book, Maxine Greene is careful to stay critically positioned within the negative/positive dialectic of freedom. She continuously wants to acknowledge both constraints and possibilities and, in doing so, she wants to affirm the intimate relationship between personal and social liberation. In the opening sentences of her introduction, she writes:

> This book arises out of a lifetime's preoccupation with quest, with pursuit. On the one hand, the quest has been deeply personal: that of a woman striving to affirm the feminine as wife, mother, and friend, while reaching, always reaching, beyond

the limits imposed by the obligations of a woman's life. On the other hand, it has been in some sense deeply public as well: that of a person struggling to connect the undertaking of education, with which she has been so long involved, to the making and remaking of a public space, a space of dialogue and possibility. (Greene, 1988, p. xi)

A Critical Appraisal of Curriculum Studies

Our critical appraisal of the field of curriculum studies will draw upon the key characteristics of Maxine Greene's inquiry into *human freedom*. Though counter to her sophisticated, multi-layered writing style, that is, the careful way she weaves her themes into a coherent line of inquiry, these characteristics will be analytically identified and enumerated so as to establish a clear normative frame of reference for our critical examination. Five characteristics of her discourse on human freedom were documented in the last section: (1) her Deweyan interpretation of democracy, which stresses the relationship between education and a 'public moral' way of life; (2) her inquiry-based faith; (3) her celebration of the constructed and multi-layered nature of democratic 'social reality'; (4) her acknowledgment that democratic educational praxis requires a sophisticated deliberation; and (5) her 'dialectical' understanding of democratic liberation.

We will critique the field of curriculum studies with reference to the above five characteristics. The focus of our critical discussion will be the key historical points of the field as presented at the beginning of this chapter, and two caveats must accompany our evaluative comments. We are critiquing general trends in the curriculum studies field, and our comments may not necessarily be applicable to the work of individual curriculum scholars. This is an important point to keep in mind because the curriculum field is constituted by individuals who bring their own unique perspectives to their studies. In fact, in their comprehensive overview of the curriculum study field, Pinar et al. (1995) decided that the best approach would be to 'preserve the voices of individual scholars' instead of writing 'a history of the field in which the individuals comprising the field . . . disappear into *our* characterizations of their work' (p. 4).

The second caveat is equally important. Our critical evaluations are based on selected historical highlights of curriculum studies. Our selections are certainly guided by our own interpretive biases. Those with other biases would, undoubtedly, feature other aspects of the field; and given the nature of American 'curriculum inquiry,' a certain contentiousness is to be expected. Ideological diversity and contest is, after all, one of the identifying characteristics of the field.

The 'reconceptualized' focus of the curriculum study field away from curriculum development models, particularly the Tyler Rationale, to a diverse set of critical problems and solutions was an important step in establishing the *democracy-education* connection in curriculum inquiry. Since curriculum development models inevitably address the 'institutional text,' which in our current historical period is generally dominated by top–down management structures and strategies — the implementation of state-wide proficiency tests being one such current manifestation, they tend to stress a *management-education* connection.[4] Leadership studies in education, which tend to foster applications from military and business organizations, reflect this orientation (Maxcy, 1991).[5]

Establishing critical distance from curriculum development models possessing overt or tacit *management-education* orientations should only be viewed as a first step in embracing the *democracy-education* connection so elegantly articulated by Maxine Greene. Curriculum scholars can be against top–down management structures and strategies for a variety of reasons without necessarily becoming advocates of Deweyan 'public morality.' Pinar et al. (1995) conclude their book, in part, with such an advocacy: 'The point of school curriculum is to goad us into caring for ourselves and our fellow human beings, to help us think and act with intelligence, sensitivity, and courage in both the public sphere — as citizens aspiring to establish a democratic society — and in the private sphere as individuals committed to other individuals' (p. 848).

How many curriculum scholars embrace this *democracy and education* perspective? The answer to this question is unknown because, currently, the field of curriculum studies is 'balkanized' (Pinar et al., 1995, p. 5). There is no common ground, or in this case *common faith*, in curriculum scholarship. When Pinar et al. (1995) apply the 'conversation' metaphor to the field today, their use of this term is more an advocacy than a historical reality. In a field that is currently constituted by diverse critical projects, how can curriculum scholars dialogue with one another? What would be their common agenda? How can they agree on common 'problems' that could be collaboratively explored?

The current critical openness of curriculum studies, based on its movement away from implicit or explicit *management-education* endorsements, is a step forward in the democratization of the field. However, an additional step must be taken. Curriculum scholars must begin to collaboratively examine their professional beliefs in light of the Deweyan *democracy-education* connection. Until this dialogue across critical differences is established, they will never know if they share a *common faith*. They will never know if they are collectively inspired by Maxine Greene's poetic evocation of a robust democratic public morality. Without this collaborative step, the 'democratization' of the curriculum study field will only be partially realized.

Though faith in democracy and education is not widely articulated in the current curriculum field, Maxine Greene's multi-leveled inquiry is mirrored in poststructural approaches to curriculum study. As noted at the beginning of the chapter, these approaches reject 'all appeals to foundational, transcendental, or universal truths or metanarratives' (Pinar et al., 1995, p. 452). Curriculum inquiry projects informed by poststructural sensitivities are currently widespread in the field, often positioned under the general term of 'postmodernism.' As carefully documented by Slattery (1995), *postmodernism* 'can be defined in multiple ways to suit the needs of any author,' the term is generally linked to 'a burgeoning belief in scientific, philosophical, political, artistic, literary, and educational circles that a radically new global conception of life on the planet and existence in the cosmos is underway' (p. 16). This *paradigm shift* mood, which is quite prevalent in contemporary curriculum discourses (Brown, 1988), possesses a strong skeptical and ironical flavor. Slattery (1995) writes that 'Postmodernism celebrates the eclectic, innovative, revisionist, ironic, and subjective dimensions of historical interpretation' (p. 35).

Perhaps it is due to the prevalence of poststructural/postmodern skepticism and irony in the curriculum study field that explorations of 'common faith' are subtly suppressed or even more overtly rejected. From a poststructural point of view, collaborative social constructions could be viewed as oppressive metanarratives — as exercises in 'big brother' thinking — and, therefore, as artifacts of modernist thinking.

Curriculum scholars, however, could learn a lesson from Maxine Greene on how to proceed with an inquiry faith while rejecting dominating metanarratives. As documented above, her inquiry faith, which is inspired by a certain feel for democratic public morality, is radically open to diverse perspectives. Maxine Greene is not a 'true believer'; she is a scholar working in the Deweyan tradition who is dedicated to a life of inquiry.

With reference to Maxine Greene's inquiry faith, the curriculum study field exhibits a mixed record. On the one hand, the field's broad-based embrace of poststructuralism/ postmodernism reflects a critical openness consistent with Deweyan democratization. On the other hand, the general mood of skepticism and irony that underlies much of this critical openness is not conducive to this understanding of democracy. Connections between democracy and education must be nurtured in a climate of inspired hope, with a sense of cautious optimism. How else could educators proceed with the difficult, and often thankless, task of fostering a democratic public morality? Pinar et al. (1995) acknowledge the fine line between inquiry faith and true belief when they write:

> We aspire to point to a 'common ground,' maybe 'a common faith' [Dewey, 1934b], in which different traditions and understandings can contribute to a comprehensive and inclusive understanding of the present stage of the American curriculum field. Such a project cannot, we believe, be likened to the authoritarian tendencies of so-called 'master-narratives' which pretend to establish final truth. (p. 14)

Maxine Greene's ontological position that human 'reality' is a personally and socially constructed, multi-layered phenomenon is a widely embraced tenet of current curriculum scholarship. In a remarkable argument that plays out over the concluding pages of their book, Pinar et al. (1995) point out that this ontological commitment, which gathered momentum during the reconceptualization phase of the curriculum studies field, will result, over time, in a sophisticated, *intertextual* maturation of curriculum inquiry. Their argument begins with the following tenet: 'To understand educational experience requires being in the political, racial, aesthetic, spiritual, gendered, global, and phenomenological world' (Pinar et al., 1995, p. 852). They note that this subtle feel for educational experience is 'much more complicated than most politicians and many colleagues in arts and sciences realize' (p. 858) and points to 'a political phenomenological understanding of curriculum, influenced by gender analysis, autobiographical theory, situated internationally in a multiracial global village' (p. 864). They then conclude that this understanding of 'curriculum' can lead to the maturation of an independent and autonomous field characterized by a Deweyan approach to the study of self and society. They write:

> The intertextual understanding of curriculum that the reconceptualized field offers can lead us to ask with greater complexity and sophistication, the traditional curriculum questions: what knowledge is of most worth? what do we make of the world we have been given, and how shall we remake ourselves to give birth to a new social order? What John Dewey said in reference to philosophy might be said in reference to the contemporary curriculum field:
>
> > A [curriculum theory] which was conscious of its own business and province would then perceive that it is an intellectualized wish, an aspiration subject to rational discriminations and tests, a social hope reduced to a working program of action, a prophecy of the future, but one disciplined by serious thought and knowledge. (Dewey, quoted in Westbrook, 1991, p. 147)
>
> Here Dewey unites self-realization and society (Westbrook, 1991), two of the major currents in contemporary curriculum scholarship. An intellectualized wish expressed as a social practice, thoroughly theorized and subject to rigorous critique which functions to reformulate the wish, re-expressed as practice: a moving form, that is understanding curriculum today. (Pinar et al., 1995, p. 866)

Given her own understanding of human reality and her faith in personal and social possibilities, Maxine Greene would applaud Pinar et al.'s (1995) visionary account of curriculum studies. If their argument is historically accurate (which time will only tell), as curriculum scholars cultivate an intertextual understanding of curriculum, they will *democratize* their field, in the tradition of John Dewey and Maxine Greene. In this sense, Pinar et al.'s (1995) critical assessment of the curriculum study field is hopeful.

However, we would continue to argue that their sunny picture of the future of the field is only warranted **IF** curriculum scholars begin to talk to one another about the relationship between democracy and education and **IF** they are willing to engage in this critical dialogue in a spirit of cautious optimism. As we have noted, these are two big 'IFs.' The widespread emergence of an intertextual understanding of curriculum studies is certainly a healthy sign that these two **IFs** can be actualized — that there can be a further 'democratization' of the field.

Maxine Greene's acknowledgment of the sophisticated *deliberative praxis* that daily grounds the connections between democracy and education has its analog in the curriculum studies field. This is Joseph Schwab's argument that curriculum study is a practical, eclectic, deliberative art. This argument, noted earlier, begins with his 1969 publication of 'The practical: A language for curriculum' and is subsequently refined over three additional essays on the practical art of curriculum inquiry (Schwab, 1978).[6] The Schwabian argument has generated a vast amount of curriculum study literature on the topic of deliberation.[7] Drawing on this literature, McCutcheon (1995) describes curriculum deliberation as collaboration over means and ends in a context of conflicting ideological interests and in light of diverse possible outcomes and moral consequences.

McCutcheon's detailed analysis of curriculum and teaching deliberations is a sophisticated example of the Schwabian line of inquiry in curriculum studies. In general, this literature is *not* grounded in a careful articulation of the connections between democracy and education, which, as noted above, is an important characteristic of Maxine Greene's work. This lack of critical articulation can be noted in McCutcheon's (1995) discussion of the 'moral dimension' of educational deliberation: 'Deliberation is not an objective, value neutral, totally rational enterprise, nor should it be. While deliberators make purposeful, rational decisions, their decisions are inescapably informed by values and ethical commitments, a sense of social responsibility, and a vision of a better society . . .' (p. 5). This analysis of the moral dimensions of deliberation tacitly suggests, rather than directly advocates, a democratic outlook.[8] With reference to Maxine Greene's vision of *democratic liberation*, curriculum scholars who inquire into the topic of deliberation must become more explicit about their moral commitment to democracy and education; and they must begin to dialogue with one another over the relationship between practical educational intelligence and democratic public morality.

Maxine Greene's comprehensive inquiry into the *dialectic of freedom* provides additional insight into how the curriculum study field can be further 'democratized.' As we noted above, from the beginning sentences in her *The Dialectic of Freedom*, Maxine Greene is careful to stay critically positioned within the negative/positive dynamics of human freedom. She continuously acknowledges both the constraints to, and possibilities of, democratic liberation and, in doing so, she constantly refers to the intimate relationship between personal and social freedom. When she examines questions of human 'emancipation,' we not only know what she is *against* but what she is *for*.

This balanced negative–positive critique, though characteristic of the work of James Macdonald — one of the early leaders of curriculum reconceptualization — is often missing in the work of 'critical' curriculum scholars.[9] The negative/positive and personal/social binaries are not deconstructed. In the early days of curriculum reconceptualization, the tensions between Michael Apple, with his neo-Marxian critique of American education (Apple, 1982) and William Pinar, with his interest in the autobiographical subtext of curriculum (Pinar, 1994), is an historical example of this lack of deconstructive sensibility (Pinar, 1988). Since the early 1970s, both Apple and Pinar have moved toward a more balanced critical approach. This is illustrated in Apple's (1993) critical examination of democratic education and Pinar et al.'s (1995) argument for intertextual curriculum study.[10]

For the further democratization of curriculum studies, this deconstruction of negative and positive critiques of democratic liberation must become the norm of the field. Curriculum scholars who focus on the overt, covert, and tacit dimensions of human oppression/suppression must be willing to converse with those who think about the creative, aesthetic possibilities of life. This ongoing dialogue would not only further actualize a more balanced approach to critical curriculum work — in the spirit of Maxine Greene's inquiry into the dialectic of freedom, it would also help curriculum scholars to establish a common 'democratic' framework for their studies.

Conclusion

We conclude this chapter with a series of open-ended questions that grow out of our critical evaluation of the field. What if curriculum scholars would construct a common democratic framework for their work? We can envision at least three important consequences of such a personal–social act. First of all, it could lead to an increased professional presence in the educational profession. At the present time, curriculum studies is a relatively uninfluential subdivision of education (Pinar et al., 1995). This is, in part, due to the current cacophony of the field. A doctoral student in health education recently responded to this cacophony in the following way:

> Yesterday I started reading the Pinar et al. (1995) book, *Understanding Curriculum*. I must admit that it is like no other book that I have ever read before. I felt as if I was in a room where everybody was talking at the same time, and my task was to make sense of what they were saying. How could it possibly make sense to me? They were people I have never heard of, talking about things I know nothing about, all voicing their own opinions, and none reaching common ground. My first reaction was, 'What is going on here? Who am I supposed to listen to? Isn't there somebody who is an authority on whatever it is that you are talking about?' My frustration level was so high that I decided to put the book down and get back to it later.

How many educators share this student's frustration with curriculum study publications? What if curriculum scholars could establish a common framework for their work? Would they be more influential? Would their critical inquiries become more widely read and discussed? Do curriculum scholars even care about their impact on the educational profession?

Secondly, if curriculum scholars were to establish a common democratic framework for their field, they could help function as the moral conscience of American education. The United States is a complex, pluralistic society whose experiment in democracy is only partially realized (Barber, 1992; Elshtain, 1995). Without the help of dedicated educators, how will the further democratization of American culture occur (Eisner, 1994; Carlson, 1997; Goodlad, 1997)? Why couldn't curriculum scholars help provide this professional leadership? Collectively, they possess the requisite critical knowledge, abilities, and interests, but do they possess the moral will so elegantly articulated by Maxine Greene?

Finally, the profession of education has struggled with its semi-professional status throughout the twentieth century (Noddings, 1996). This is due, in part, to educators' identification of their work as an applied social science (Schön, 1983). The reconceptual-ization of curriculum studies in the 1970s was, at its core, a critical break from this positivist heritage. The field is now well positioned to contribute to an understanding of educational practice as a critical, and perhaps *the* critical, **professional art** for a society with democratic ideals. Will curriculum scholars make such a contribution? Will they become public advocates for educators' **professional holonomy**, defined as *inquiry inde-pendence in a context of collaborative interdependence* (Wheatley, 1992; Costa and Liebman, 1997)?

The answers to our concluding critical questions lie in the future of curriculum studies. The fact that the field has partially democratized itself is a hopeful sign that the answers to these questions will be in the affirmative. But the jury is still out. What, in fact, is the *heart and soul* of American curriculum studies? Is it limited to sophisticated but disparate critical work, or does it possess a deeper moral purpose?

Notes

1 Bernstein (1991) writes: '"Constellation" is deliberately intended to displace Hegel's master metaphor of *Aufhebung*. For . . . although we cannot (and should not) give up the *promise* and demand for reconciliation . . . , I do not think we can any longer responsibly claim that there is or can be a final reconciliation — an *Aufhebung* in which all difference, otherness, opposition and contradiction are reconciled' (p. 8).

2 Zeichner's remarks were made with reference to the literature in teacher education. It is believed that his comments are equally valid in the field of curriculum studies.

3 In classical Marxian terms, they possess 'false consciousness.'

4 For two discussions of curriculum development that establish critical distance from the management-education connection, see J.G. Henderson and R.D. Hawthorne (1995) *Transformative Curriculum Leadership*, Englewood Cliffs, NJ: Merill/Prentice Hall and P. Slattery (1995) *Curriculum Development in the Postmodern Era*, New York: Garland Publishing.

5 Thomas Sergiovanni's leadership studies is one exception to this generalization. For example, see his (1992) *Moral Leadership: Getting to the Heart of School Improvement*, San Francisco: Jossey-Bass.

6 It is interesting to note that the combined length of his four essays is equivalent to the length of Tyler's (1949) curriculum development 'rationale.'

7 For a concise overview of this literature, see G. McCutcheon's (1995) *Developing the Curriculum: Solo and Group Deliberation*, White Plains, NY: Longman.

8 Gail McCutcheon's discussion of curriculum and teaching deliberation is more consciously linked to democracy and education in her chapter, 'Deliberation to develop school cur-ricula,' which is to be published in James G. Henderson and Kathleen R. Kesson (in press) (eds) *Understanding Democratic Curriculum Leadership*, New York: Teachers College Press.

9 For a concise overview of James Macdonald's curriculum studies, see Bradley J. Macdonald (1995) (ed.) *Theory as a Prayerful Act: The Collected Essays of James B. Macdonald*, New York: Peter Lang.

10 This movement toward a more balanced critique is also evident in the voluminous critical work of Henry Giroux. A comparison of Giroux's (1981) *Ideology, Culture and the Process of Schooling*, Philadelphia: Temple University Press and his more recent (1992) *Bordercrossings*, New York: Routledge, 1992, clearly documents this change.

References

APPLE, M.W. (1982) *Education and Power*, Boston: Routledge & Kegan Paul.

APPLE, M.W. (1993) *Official Knowledge: Democratic Education in a Conservative Age*, New York: Routledge.

BARBER, B.R. (1984) *Strong Democracy: Participatory Politics for a New Age*, Berkeley: University of California Press.

BARBER, B.R. (1992) *An Aristocracy of Everyone: The Politics of Education and the Future of America*, New York: Oxford University Press.

BARONE, T.E. (1992a) 'A narrative of enhanced professionalism: Educational researchers and popular storybooks about schoolpeople,' *Educational Researcher*, **21**, 8, pp. 15–24.

BARONE, T.E. (1992b) 'On the demise of subjectivity in educational inquiry,' *Curriculum Inquiry*, **22**, pp. 25–38.

BERKEY, R., CURTIS, T., MINNICK, F., ZIETLOW, K., CAMPBELL, D., and KIRSCHNER, B.W. (1990) 'Collaborating for reflective practice: Voices of teachers, administrators, and researchers,' *Education and Urban Society*, **22**, pp. 204–32.

BERNSTEIN, R.J. (1991) *The New Constellation: The Ethical-Political Horizons of Modernity/Postmodernity*, Cambridge, MA: The MIT Press.

BEYER, L. (1988) 'Art and society,' in PINAR, W.F. (ed.) *Contemporary Curriculum Discourses* (pp. 380–99), Scottsdale, AZ: Gorsuch Scarisbrick.

BEYER, L. (1996) 'Teachers' reflections on the struggle for democratic classrooms,' *Teaching Education*, **8**, 1, pp. 91–102.

BOBBITT, F. (1918) *The Curriculum*, Boston: Houghton Mifflin.

BRITZMAN, D.P. (1992) 'Structures of feeling and curriculum and feeling,' *Theory Into Practice*, **31**, pp. 252–8.

BROWN, T.M. (1988) 'How fields change: A critique of the "Kuhnian" view,' in PINAR, W.F. (ed.) *Contemporary Curriculum Discourses* (pp. 16–30), Scottsdale, AZ: Gorsuch Scarisbrick.

BUTT, R.L., RAYMOND, D., and YAMAGISHI, L. (1988) 'Autobiographical praxis: Studying the formation of teachers' knowledge,' *Journal of Curriculum Theorizing*, **7**, 4, pp. 87–164.

CARLSON, D. (1997) *Making Progress: Education and Culture in New Times*, New York: Teachers College Press.

CHERRYHOLMES, C.H. (1988) *Power and Criticism: Poststructural Investigations in Education*, New York: Teachers College Press.

CHOPIN, K. (1964) *The Awakening*, New York: Capricorn Books.

CLARK, C.M., and YINGER, R.J. (1987) 'Teacher planning,' in CALDERHEAD, J. (ed.) *Exploring Teacher Thinking* (pp. 84–103), London: Cassell.

COSTA, A.L., and LIEBMANN, R.M. (eds) (1997) *Envisioning Process as Content: Toward a Renaissance Curriculum*, Thousands Oaks, CA: Corwin Press.

DERRIDA, J. (1988) *Derrida and Difference* (D. Wood and R. Bernasconi, eds), Evanston, IL: Northwestern University Press.

DEWEY, J. (1916) *Democracy and Education*, New York: Macmillan.

DEWEY, J. (1933) *How We Think: A Restatement of the Relation of Reflective Teaching to the Educative Process*, Chicago: Henry Regnery.

DEWEY, J. (1934a) *Art as Experience*, New York: Minton, Balch & Co.

DEWEY, J. (1934b) *A Common Faith*, New Haven, CT: Yale University Press.

DEWEY, J. (1938) *Experience and Education*, New York: Macmillan.

DEWEY, J. (1960) 'Philosophies of freedom,' in BERNSTEIN, R.J. (ed.) *On Experience, Nature, and Freedom* (pp. 261–87), New York: Liberal Arts Press. (Original work published 1928.)

DEWEY, J. (1989) *Freedom and Culture*, Buffalo, NY: Prometheus. Original work published 1939.

EISNER, E.W. (1994) *Cognition and Curriculum Reconsidered* (2nd edn), New York: Teachers College Press.

ELLISON, R. (1952) *Invisible Man*, New York: New American Library.

ELSHTAIN, J.B. (1995) *Democracy on Trial*, New York: Basic Books.

GADAMER, H. (1976) *Philosophical Hermeneutics* (D.E. Linge, ed. and trans.), Berkeley: University of California Press.

GOODLAD, J.I. (1997) *In Praise of Education*, New York: Teachers College Press.

GOODLAD, J.I. and SU, Z. (1992) 'Organization of the curriculum,' in JACKSON, P.W. (ed.) *Handbook of Curriculum Research* (pp. 327–44), New York: Macmillan.

GREENE, M. (1973) *Teacher as Stranger*, Belmont, CA: Wadsworth.

GREENE, M. (1976) 'Honorable work and delayed awakenings: Education and American women,' *Phi Delta Kappan*, **58**, pp. 25–30.

GREENE, M. (1977) 'Imagination and aesthetic literacy,' *Art Education*, **30**, 6, pp. 14–20.

GREENE, M. (1978) *Landscapes of Learning*, New York: Teachers College Press.

GREENE, M. (1979) 'Liberal education and the newcomer,' *Phi Delta Kappan*, **60**, pp. 633–6.

GREENE, M. (1982) 'Literacy for what?' *Phi Delta Kappan*, **63**, pp. 326–9.

GREENE, M. (1986a) 'How do we think about our craft?' in LIEBERMAN, A. (ed.) *Rethinking School Improvement: Research, Craft, and Concept* (pp. 13–25), New York: Teachers College Press.

GREENE, M. (1986b) 'In search of a critical pedagogy,' *Harvard Educational Review*, **56**, pp. 427–41.

GREENE, M. (1986c) 'Reflection and passion in teaching,' *Journal of Curriculum and Supervision*, **2**, 1, pp. 68–81.

GREENE, M. (1988) *The Dialectic of Freedom*, New York: Teachers College Press.

GREENE, M. (1991a) 'Values education in the contemporary moment,' *The Clearing House*, **64**, pp. 301–4.

GREENE, M. (1991b) 'Blue guitars and the search for curriculum,' in WILLIS, G. and SCHUBERT, W. (eds) *Reflections from the Heart of Educational Inquiry: Understanding Curriculum and Teaching Through the Arts* (pp. 107–22), Albany, NY: State University of New York Press.

GRUMET, M.R. (1988) *Bitter Milk: Women and Teaching*, Amherst, MA: University of Massachusetts Press.

HATAB, L.J. (1995) *A Nietzschean Defense of Democracy: An Experiment in Postmodern Politics*, Chicago: Open Court.

HUEBNER, D. (1966) 'Curricular language and classroom meanings,' in MACDONALD, J.B. and LEEPER, R.R. (eds) *Language and Meaning* (pp. 8–26), Washington, D.C.: Association for Supervision and Curriculum Development.

HULLFISH, H.G. and SMITH, P.G. (1961) *Reflective Thinking: The Method of Education*, New York: Dodd, Mead.

ISER, W. (1980) *The Act of Reading: A Theory of Aesthetic Response*, Baltimore: Johns Hopkins University Press.

JACKSON, P.W. (1992) 'Conceptions of curriculum and curriculum specialists,' in JACKSON, P.W. (ed.) *Handbook of Research on Curriculum* (pp. 3–40), New York: Macmillan.

JACOBS, M. (1991) 'Diary of an Ambivalent Daughter: A Feminist Re-visioning of Maxine Greene's Discursive landscapes,' Unpublished doctoral dissertation, University of Maryland, College Park, MD.

KLIEBARD, H.M. (1986) *The Struggle for the American Curriculum: 1890–1958*. Boston: Routledge & Kegan Paul.

LABOSKEY, V.K. (1994) *Development of Reflective Practice: A Study of Preservice Teachers*, New York: Teachers College Press.

LEVI, P. (1988) *The Drowned and the Saved* (R. Rosenthal, trans.), New York: Summit Books.

MACDONALD, J.B. (1975) 'Curriculum theory,' in PINAR, W. (ed.) *Curriculum Theorizing: The Reconceptualists* (pp. 5–13), Berkeley, CA: McCutchan.

MARSH, C., and WILLIS, G. (1995) *Curriculum: Alternative Approaches, Ongoing Issues*, Englewood Cliffs, NJ: Merrill/Prentice Hall.

MASLOW, A.H. (1968) 'Some implications of the humanistic psychology,' *Harvard Educational Review*, **38**, pp. 685–96.

MAXCY, S.J. (1991) *Educational Leadership: A Critical Pragmatic Perspective*, New York: Bergin & Garvey.

McCUTCHEON, G. (1995) *Developing the Curriculum: Solo and Group Deliberation*, White Plains, NY: Longman.

MERLEAU-PONTY, M. (1964) *The Primacy of Perception and Other Essays on Phenomenological Psychology, the Philosophy of Art, History and Politics* (J.M. Edie, trans.), Evanston, IL: Northwestern University.

MILLER, J.L. (1983) 'The resistance of women academics: An autobiographical account,' *Journal of Educational Equity and Leadership*, **3**, 2, pp. 101–9.

MILLER, J.L. (1990) *Creating Spaces and Finding Voices: Teachers Collaborating for Empowerment*, Albany, NY: State University of New York Press.

MILLER, J.L. (1992) 'Teacher spaces: A personal evolution of teacher lore,' in SCHUBERT, W.F. and AYERS, W.C. (eds) *Teacher Lore: Learning From Our Own Experience* (pp. 11–22), White Plains, NY: Longman.

MILLGRAM, E. (1997) *Practical Induction*, Cambridge, MA: Harvard University Press.

MOORE, M. (1966) *Tell Me, Tell Me*, New York: Viking Press.

MORRISON, T. (1987) *Beloved: A Novel*, New York: Knopf.

PADGHAM, R. (1988) 'Thoughts about the implications of archetypal psychology for curriculum theory,' *Journal of Curriculum Theorizing*, **8**, 3, pp. 123–46.

PINAR, W. (1975) 'Preface,' in PINAR, W. (ed.) *Curriculum Theorizing: The Reconceptualists* (pp. ix–xii), Berkeley, CA: McCutchan.

Pinar, W.F. (1988) 'Introduction,' in PINAR, W.F. (ed.) *Contemporary Curriculum Discourses* (pp. 1–13), Scottsdale, AZ: Gorsuch Scarisbrick.

PINAR, W.F. (1994) *Autobiography, Politics and Sexuality: Essays in Curriculum Theory 1972–1992*, New York: Peter Lang.

PINAR, W.F., REYNOLDS, W.M., SLATTERY, P., and TAUBMAN, P.M. (1995) *Understanding Curriculum: An Introduction to the Study of Historical and Contemporary Curriculum Discourses*, New York: Peter Lang.

PLATO (1956) *The Republic* (B. Jowett, trans.), New York: The Modern Library.

POLANYI, M. (1969) 'The logic of tacit inference,' in GREENE, M. (ed.) *Knowing and Being* (pp. 138–58), Chicago: University of Chicago Press.

PURPEL, D.E. and SHAPIRO, S. (1995) *Beyond Liberation and Excellence: Reconstructing the Public Discourse on Education*, Westport, CT: Bergin & Harvey.

RICH, A. (1981) *A Wild Patience Has Taken Me This Far*, New York: W.W. Norton.

RICHERT, A.E. (1991) 'Case methods and teacher education: Using cases to teach teacher reflection,' in TABACHNICK, B.R. and ZEICHNER, K.M. (eds) *Issues and Practices in Inquiry-oriented Teacher Education* (pp. 130–50), London: Falmer Press.

ROTHMAN, R. (1992) 'Researcher urges colleagues to use "storytelling" techniques: A conversation with Thomas E. Barone,' *Education Week*, **12**, pp. 6–7, 25 November.

RUKEYSER, M. (1973) 'Käthe Kollwitz,' in GOULIANOS, J. (ed.) *By a Woman Writ: Literature from Six Centuries By and About Women* (pp. 363–79). New York: Bobbs-Merrill.

RYLE, G. (1967) 'Teaching and training,' in PETERS, R.S. (ed.) *The Concept of Education* (pp. 105–19), New York: Humanities Press.

SARTRE, J.P. (1956) *Being and Nothingness* (H.E. Barnes, trans.), New York: Philosophical Library.

SCHÖN, D.A. (1983) *The Reflective Practitioner*, New York: Basic Books.

SCHUBERT, W.F. (1986) *Curriculum: Perspective, Paradigm, and Possibility*, New York: Macmillan.

SCHWAB, J.J. (1969) 'The practical: A language for curriculum,' *School Review*, **78**, pp. 1–23.

SCHWAB, J.J. (1978) *Science, Curriculum, and Liberal Education: Selected Essays* (I. Westbury and N.J. Wilkof, eds), Chicago: University of Chicago Press.

SLATTERY, P. (1995) *Curriculum Development in the Postmodern Era*, New York: Garland.

TYLER, R.W. (1949) *Basic Principles of Curriculum and Instruction*, Chicago: University of Chicago Press.

VALLANCE, E. (1991) 'Aesthetic inquiry: Art criticism,' in SHORT, E.C. (ed.) *Forms of Curriculum Inquiry* (pp. 155–72), Albany: State University of New York Press.

WALKER, D.F. (1992) 'Methodological issues in curriculum research,' in JACKSON, P.W. (ed.) *Handbook of Curriculum Research* (pp. 98–118), New York: Macmillan.

WESTBROOK, R.B. (1991) *John Dewey and American Democracy*, Ithaca, NY: Cornell University Press.

WHEATLEY, M.J. (1992) *Leadership and the New Science*, San Francisco: Berrett-Koehler.

WIESEL, E. (1992) *The Forgotten* (S. Becker, trans.), New York: Summit Books.

WOLF, D.P. (1992) 'Becoming knowledge: The evolution of art education curriculum,' in JACKSON, P.W. (ed.) *Handbook of Curriculum Research* (pp. 945–63), New York: Macmillan.

ZEICHNER, K.M. (1993) 'Research on teacher thinking and different views of reflective practice in teaching and teacher education,' Keynote address presented at the Sixth International Conference of the International Study Association on Teacher Thinking, Göteborg, Sweden, August 10–15.

18   Of Friends and Journeys:
Maxine Greene and English Education

Robert J. Graham

On the wall above my friend Ruth's mantelshelf is an artifact that never fails to occupy a great deal of our interpretive attention each time my wife and I visit Ruth's house. Contained within a rectangular wooden frame are three ceramic tiles, on each of which is depicted a number of characters from Chaucer's *Canterbury Tales*. Taken as a whole, the tiles show the entire company of pilgrims at the start of their journey. The gap-toothed Wife of Bath is there as is the impressive Knight, the attentive Squire, the scatological Miller and the vilified Pardoner, represented here as a figure already set at some remove from the main body of the group. From the expressions on each pilgrim's face it is clear that in this company of strangers certain 'natural' affiliations are already making themselves manifest. The group looks tightly knit as everyone gathers expectantly at the beginning of their travels together, but closer inspection shows that small groups have already begun to form and that there are individuals who look as though they would be happier if left to their own devices. For me, the more I have stared at this artifact over time, the more it seems to me emblematic, not only of crucial aspects of my own journey as an English teacher and as a teacher of aspiring English teachers, but in particular emblematic of the larger journey of 'subject English' (Morgan, 1995) itself over the last 30 years.

As a way of exploring some of the central conversations that have occupied English education on that journey, and as a way of helping us appreciate more fully the compelling nature of Maxine Greene's contribution to those conversations, I look to anecdote and autobiographical recollection as my preferred rhetorical method. I have opted for this approach because I want to show that the kind of legacy English teachers have inherited from Maxine Greene's writing is the kind whose influence is less immediately apparent than, say, that of Louise Rosenblatt (1978) whose prescriptions are derived from a particular theory of literary response. Rather, I will hold instead that Maxine Greene has exercised a benign influence on how English teachers *think* about the work they do, and that this influence will persist long after the latest fad, fashion, or strategy-of-the-month has come and gone. My hope is that in what follows, some aspects of my own journey as an English teacher will resonate with the experience of other teachers, for in van Manen's (1990) words, 'In drawing up personal descriptions of lived experience [we] know that one's own experiences are also the possible experiences of others' (p. 54). Consequently, by making it clear the extent to which I believe Maxine Greene (or 'Maxine Greene' the implied author I have encountered in her writings) has become one of the few true friends on my own journey in English education, I want to celebrate the staying power of her vision for a literary curriculum theorized as an aesthetic, political, and liberatory project of personal and social transformation.

Robert J. Graham

Entering the Conversation

In the fall of 1967, I enrolled at Jordanhill College of Education in Glasgow, Scotland with the (not very firm) intention of 'becoming' a secondary school English teacher. Like most of my classmates, I had chosen English teaching because I had been 'good at it' in high school and had majored in English at university. But early on, as we watched and listened to Sydney Smith, our charismatic methods instructor, we were plunged immediately into a great debate over a number of competing conceptions of English teaching, and in particular, several different visions for its future development (c.f. Applebee, 1974). The now famous Anglo-American conference on the teaching of English held at Dartmouth in 1966 had not yet percolated into our consciousness in the way it would later with the publication of John Dixon's *Growth Through English* (1967). Our 'guru' at that time was Frank Whitehead, and we dissected in detail the views in his groundbreaking book *The Disappearing Dias* (1966). This book challenged our preconceptions of English teaching as primarily an academic undertaking and enjoined us never to underestimate the power of literature to transform minds, hearts, and lives. In the opening paragraph of that book, Whitehead offered a vision of English teaching that had a galvanizing effect on most of us in the room, since it seemed to capture a crucial element, an unarticulated aspect of our collective experience of schooling as Scottish kids from predominantly working-class backgrounds. We lived our everyday lives speaking the glottal-stopped dialect of industrial Lanarkshire, while inside school we were ruthlessly graded on our ability to master the vagaries of Standard English. Imagine, then, how we felt as would-be teachers when Whitehead (1966) said this to us:

> . . . we need to have brought to clear focus in our minds the way in which a child's acquisition of his [*sic*] native language is inseparably intertwined with his developing consciousness of the world in which he is growing up, with his control of his inner phantasies and the feelings they give rise to, and with his possession of the values by which he will live his life in the civilisation he forms a part of. (p. 11)

For us, we wouldn't have said that our 'native language' was Standard English, but rather the Scots dialect we spoke at home, in the streets, in the playgrounds, and in the pubs. And although we were acutely aware that our accents didn't carry the same social cachet as the accents of Oxford or Cambridge, I certainly can't claim that we felt excluded from any of society's conversations in the way that non-native speakers of English or people of color are still excluded today. I believe what we did discover was the first clear, unambiguous intimation that literacy teaching and learning was a profoundly political project, and that this realization assisted in the process of waking us up from some deep sleep or from a collective sense of denial. Whitehead's book, like Dixon's *Growth Through English* and its US counterpart, Herbert Muller's *The Uses of English* (1967), offered us a language-centered, and hence, *political* view of the English curriculum, a curriculum that looked to literature as a way of bringing any number of different voices (neither better nor worse, just different) into the classroom. It was thought that these literary voices would add to the multiple perspectives that students already brought with them from their own lives. Therefore, in classrooms that would increasingly be given over to talk and writing as the active uses of language, these would be the mediums through which students would build their own representational worlds and give shape to their own experiences. It was with this Anglo-American vision for a 'new' English education and a 'new' role for the English teacher that I began my teaching career as a Canadian immigrant in 1968.

The Primacy of Imagination: A Social Role for Literature

Paint me a picture, then, of the 10 years between 1968 and 1978 as I struggled to find my feet as a beginning English teacher. For us in Ontario, this was the time of the Hall-Dennis Report, a document that enshrined as public policy a progressive view of education, a view that began crumbling under public pressure even as we were trying to find ways to make its view of experiential learning and open classrooms a reality. I still possess reams of poems written during that time, poems in which I tried to capture the wonder, the banality, the contradictions and tensions of English teaching. As might have been predicted, I was experiencing such an all-consuming sense of growth as a person and involvement as a teacher that it was hard to tell where my personal life ended and my professional life began. Professionally (which was also personally) I railed against what I called 'The Confused Conspiracies,' the title of a (deservedly) unpublished manuscript I wrote in a fury of disillusionment in 1971–72. This philippic was my way of trying to reconcile the contradictions between the official, espoused positions of Ministry Guidelines and Eduspeak with the daily realities of teaching 120 Grade 9 and 10 students. And so, as with my earlier reaction to Frank Whitehead, imagine my feelings when at this crucial juncture in my career I stumbled over these words:

> We do not ask that the teacher perceive his existence as absurd; nor do we demand that he estrange himself from his community. We simply suggest that he struggle against unthinking submergence in the social reality that prevails. . . . How does a teacher carry out the educational policies he is assigned to carry out within his school? If the teacher does not pose such questions to himself, he cannot expect his students to pose the kinds of questions about experience which will involve them in self-aware inquiry. (Greene, 1973, p. 269)

Maxine Greene's *Teacher as Stranger*, as other writers in this volume have also testified, made an immediate and lasting impression. Here was someone whose finger was clearly on the pulse of her times, a pulse which was also my pulse and times which were also my times. This was someone whose existential frames of reference I could relate to and whose vision of teaching I had only begun to grope towards as I tried to make English language and literature come alive in the classroom and in the lives of my students. For Greene (1973) the teacher as stranger (and this was certainly true for me as an immigrant) must 'interpret and reorder what he sees in the light of his changed experience. He must consciously engage in inquiry' (p. 268).

This kind of hermeneutic, problem-posing inquiry was at once congenial and difficult for myself and for other English teachers in Canada and elsewhere at the time. Many of us shared the impression from reading the professional literature, from staffroom conversations and from attending national and regional conferences, that we were struggling with the personal and political ramifications of trying to extricate ourselves and our students from what Greene (1973) had rightly identified as our 'unthinking submergence in the social reality' (p. 269). So how could we invest our literary labors at the chalk face with a reinvigorated sense of their social importance, of their counting for something? For many of us in Canada, Northrop Frye's dictum that 'we have only the choice between a badly trained imagination and a well trained one' (1963, p. 57) represented one answer to that question, an answer that I would find echoed at greater and more meaningful length in Greene's *Landscapes of Learning* (1978).

In the important second chapter of that book, 'The rational and emancipatory: Towards a role for imaginative literature,' I experienced the 'phenomenological nod' of recognition, the 'Aha!' moment when Greene said in 10 pages what I had struggled to say in 300. By offering provocative readings of Blake, Wordsworth, Baudelaire and Flaubert, she documented the ' "romantic" revolt against utilitarian culture' (1978, p. 25), a culture that had 'placed primary emphasis on the *consequences* of human actions, even if that meant excluding the question of values altogether' (p. 25, original italics). For Greene, literature and more importantly, literature from the 'Western adversary tradition' (p. 24), contained 'a special capacity to arouse wide-awakeness in our own time and that this kind of arousal is necessary if there is to be transcendence' (p. 37). Greene counselled the need for teachers to combat those forces that turned people and particularly teachers, into objects so that their roles could be 'defined by others' (p. 39). Only a 'committed rationality' grounded in 'self-reflection' could effectively keep teachers in touch with 'their own landscapes' (p. 39).

Likewise, Northrop Frye's challenge for us as English teachers was to concern ourselves with the 'total verbal experience' of our students, with everything that was made out of words, from poems to advertisements, for it was through words that our society produced its 'adjustment mythologies,' those stories whose purpose was 'to persuade us to accept our society's standards and values' (1963, p. 60). For Frye, only good literature well taught contained the capacity to hone our imaginations to the extent that they 'would protect us from falling into the illusions that society threatens us with' (p. 60). In this instance, both Greene and Frye were saying similar things at the same time with only minor differences in emphasis. Together, they (re)alerted and (re)focused English teachers in Canada and elsewhere to the social, political, and transformative effects entailed by the study of literature, and in particular to the way this study could not be separated from the larger question of free speech in a democracy. For Frye no less was at stake than a Manichean battle between two forms of social speech, 'the speech of a mob and the speech of a free society' (p. 64). The overriding educational issue was that, for Frye, there could be no free speech without a corresponding sense in our citizens of how language operates and how to use it, and this knowledge 'is not a gift; it has to be learned and worked at' (p. 64). Consequently, the training and development of a social imagination was a necessary condition for communicating our *vision* of society, for beginning to see more clearly how things are and for imagining how they might be different.

Greene and Frye both wrote against the background of the radical student politics of their time. And as Pine (1992) writes, Greene 'saw these young people devoting too much time to self-contemplation and deciding too easily that they could have no impact on the world "out there" ' (p. 65). Greene's idea of wide-awakeness — the dialectical movement from examining personal landscapes to inquiring into how talk and language creates the mystification of false consciousness — was essentially a form of social praxis, 'a type of radical and participant knowing oriented to transforming the world' (1978, p. 13). I felt heartened.

But later, for teachers in the 1980s who hoped for an outward-looking, socially-oriented English curriculum fueled by imaginative literature and the effort to make students' writing have real effects on real audiences, the succession of social panics occasioned by reports of declining literacy levels and the ireful pronouncements of the 'back-to-basics' movement threw many English teachers into a tailspin of self-doubt. On the level of responding to the supposed deficiencies in our teaching of 'the basics,' many of us were asking what these 'basics' were that we were supposed to get 'back' to? Weren't we already grappling with the practical implications of viewing literacy as a set of *social practices* rather than mythologizing literacy as the unidimensional 'skills' of decoding and encoding (Olson, 1990)? Weren't we already helping our students to make a difference as Freire had asked by ensuring that they could read both the Word and the World?

Answers to these questions blew in from a chillier quarter on the prevailing political winds, and our previous successes in creating (at least some of the time) the kind of wide-awake, critically literate citizens that a robust democracy requires were considered less appropriate to the new realities of our increasingly inward-looking society.

Similarly, the impassioned striving to establish whole language as a kind of New Orthodoxy drew attention (rightly enough) to the *how* of language learning, to the "conditions under which language develops most easily and best, and about how teaching can support this development" (Goodman, 1996, p. 85).

But this fixation on how language was learned siphoned off important professional energy from the *what for* of language learning. As the internecine battles raged over phonics, invented spellings and authentic assessment, and as a 'you're-either-for-us-or-against-us' mentality permeated the professional ranks, we perhaps lost sight of the need to ask the harder questions, questions that went straight to the heart of our purpose as public school English teachers in the first place.

> So how do public schools, presumably dedicated to equality in the midst of plural-
> ism, even out the playing field? . . . How do we as teachers . . . provoke all our
> students to learn how to learn in a world we and they know is neither equitable nor
> fair? (Greene, 1995, p. 171)

Greene's questions were especially difficult for English teachers to confront, because they placed all the messy issues of language, interpretation, representation, race, gender, and identity squarely in the center of our classroom practice. These issues had always been with us, of course, but they were taken up in educational circles with a new sense of urgency, exacerbated perhaps by 'Postmodernism and the Crisis of Identity' (Greene, 1994), and by the need to respond to those proliferating social panics, some of which gave more of an *effet de reel* than others to an anxious public.

Who were our students now, these Generation Xers, these 'aliens in the classroom' (Green and Bigum, 1993)? As schools increasingly began to look like omnibus social agencies; as the Siren-song of standards and accountability filled our ears; as Hirsch (1987) snapped at our heels about our students' lack of cultural literacy; and as an aging, predominantly white, middle-class cadre of English teachers struggled with the curricular and instructional ramifications of this insurgent multiculturalism, Maxine Greene had already surveyed the layout of our postmodern habitat and was offering us a redrawn set of floor plans.

Travelling Hopefully: Back to the Future

The 1990s find me still travelling in search of subject English, but my companions are now mostly preservice teachers of English in their final, certification year. Matthew Arnold's poem 'Dover Beach' is, for them and for me, a generative text, a text that causes us to interrogate issues that remain central to their own emerging identities as English teachers, as well as highlights the contradictory, recalcitrant, and all-too-fixed aspects of my own identity as a teacher educator. I have discovered over the last few years that Arnold's poem also acts as a touchstone (would Arnold have appreciated the irony?) or, better, as a Rorschach test that elicits statements about the kinds of collective anxieties that appear to have my current crop of students in their grip.

This year, as my students' attention turns to how the existence of a mandated Provincial Literacy Standards Test will alter the expectations they have for their careers as English teachers, some are expressing serious misgivings about finding time to teach any serious literature at all, let alone any pre-twentieth-century literature. Arnold and his ilk are difficult, they say; you would need to give kids all kinds of historical background before it could make any sense; and just who are these 'ignorant armies' anyway? If they are other competing belief systems, why would you want to bring a poem to class that might offend people with different religions and belief systems? If the Standards Exam doesn't test the kids' knowledge *of* literature but only their reading comprehension and ability to write a persuasive essay, why waste time on a poem written by a dead white male when there are other important tasks to be done?

Others in the class claim that these would be the very reasons why they would want to work with 'Dover Beach' in the first place, not with the aim of valorizing Arnold's perspective, but because the issues he deals with in the poem are still alive and well, still with us wreaking personal grief and social discord. Real teaching and learning, they say, will always offend someone. By its very nature literature is always open to interpretation, and we teachers dare not sit on the moral sidelines like spectators at someone else's game. Unlike Arnold, whose 'solution' to the crises of his day was to withdraw and turn away from the madness outside the window, as teachers, we need to commit ourselves to understanding how our students cope with the daily struggle to make meaning out of the constant whirl of events. Again, under these circumstances, Greene (1995) comes to our rescue:

> Most of us are finding out how necessary it is to discover how the things we want to teach appear to young people who are often so unlike our remembered selves. Listening to them, we frequently find ourselves dealing as never before with our own prejudgements and preferences, with the forms and images we have treasured through most of our lives. (p. 188)

Looking into the mirror is never an easy thing to do, especially when the mirror happens to be an adolescent's eyes. The 'forms and images' that we have learned to treasure, culled perhaps from our lifelong encounters with literature and the expressive arts, are dear to us, they have been our fellow travelers, our own best teachers. Yet, says Greene, in spite of our increased awareness to the fact of difference, to the multiple and often contradictory realities that both we and our students inhabit under the taxing conditions of postmodernity, 'the central questions' we learned in the early days of our careers, 'will continue to haunt us' (Greene, 1995, p. 197). For Greene, one of those central questions centers around how we hold on to our beliefs about teaching and learning as 'an opening of ourselves to a pluralism of diverse visions' (1995, p. 190). And if this is what we must do for ourselves as persons and as teachers:

> Can we do the same for the teenager from the Bronx? Can we enable him to name his own recalcitrance, to see it in a dialectical relation to the structures that oppose . . . his becoming? Can we attune ourselves sufficiently to his word universe or create classroom conditions that make that universe audible? Can we enable him, at least, to chart a field of possibilities for himself and for those with whom he shares a world? (p. 190)

Throughout her career, one of the answers Maxine Greene has offered English teachers to questions like these is that we should align ourselves with our students' existential quests to understand and construct a meaningful life, a life full of meaning. We can assist in this undertaking in a number of ways, not the least of which is through the study of imaginative literature and through the creation of expressive objects, 'prefer-ably among others who are also in quest, who recognize us for what we are striving to be and who win our recognition for what they are not yet' (Greene, 1994, p. 218). As a talented interpreter of a vast and varied corpus of canonical and oppositional literary texts, texts that she has returned to again and again in her writing for inspiration and fresh sources of insight, I believe Maxine Greene has shown a way for us in the lessons she has derived from the practice of her own inimitable brand of ethical criticism.

As ethical critic, Greene views encounters with imaginative literature in an emergent way. She selects a 'particular work because it is, in so many senses, a drama having to do with the tension between the natural and the cultural and because that tension seems to me of profound educational importance' (Greene, 1988, p. 177). In addition, this tension is always already an ethical tension, for when 'we see the texture of our experience, we discover the text-like character of our lives. And it is then that meaning has an opportu-nity to emerge' (Greene, 1994, p. 217). It may be fair to say that Maxine Greene, like Frye (1976) views literature as a culture's 'secular scripture,' an inexhaustible source of multiple perspectives on the human condition and on ways to live more fully in the world. Thus, if others are attracted (as I am) by Postman's (1988) view of social research as an interpretive, ethical practice, a form of moral theology, then most assuredly Maxine Greene has proved herself one of education's pre-eminent moral theologians. For whether she is offering the study of literature as a form of qualitative research, or interpreting Julian Barnes's novel *Flaubert's Parrot* to remind us 'that description, like language, is contingent on vantage point, or on location, on gender, class or on ethnicity' (Greene, 1994, p. 207), Greene has rediscovered, reinterpreted, and re-enacted for us 'what people once were told and need to be told again' (Postman, 1988, p. 18).

Encomium as Conclusion

In *The Company We Keep* (1988), a book-length meditation on the ethics of fiction, Wayne Booth comes to regret the 'striking . . . decline in talk about books as friends' (p. 171). Although Booth realizes that not all books, like people, are equally friendly, nor equally benign in their intentions, he wants to go in search of 'a vocabulary of discriminations among *kinds* of friendship, [where] true friendship is a primary goal of life, and the study of how to achieve it a center of all ethical activity' (p. 172). By theorizing stories as 'friendship offerings' (p. 174), Booth draws attention to what he sees as the different kinds of friendship and the different kinds of gifts that a would-be friend might offer. The highest gift, and hence the highest kind of friendship, is given and received neither for pleasure nor for profit, but *'for the sake of the friendly company itself, the living in friendship'* (p. 173, original italics).

Throughout my own career as an English teacher, I have felt at times that I was simultaneously occupying two different and contradictory positions. On the one hand, like one of Chaucer's pilgrims, I felt like a participant in what had all the surface appearances of a common undertaking. I sometimes huddled near what I took to be the center of the group, for the sense of belonging and for the feeling that I was travelling in the right (or socially approved) direction. On the other hand, I felt as I imagined Chaucer himself might feel as the author of the work, a spectator, creating unflattering portraits and dispensing ironic judgments on the motivations of nearly all the story's principal actors. And equally ironically, as a minor actor and from the safety of the margins, I could disagree with that sense of direction but could never quite muster up the courage to turn my back on the entire enterprise.

On this journey, in these contradictory moods and at the most uncanny moments, it has been this living in friendship with the words and work of Maxine Greene that has proved for me and for countless other English teachers a source of fresh ideas, supportive conversation and boundless humanity. Her belief in the primacy of the imagination and in the teaching of literature as an emergent, ethical undertaking, an undertaking by means of which we and our students can learn to live more fully, is a lesson that is never learned once and for all time. It is a lesson whose relevance we have to rediscover, reinterpret and reapply for ourselves in the contexts of our own teaching and learning. No, Maxine Greene hasn't told us how to construct an integrated unit plan, and she most certainly hasn't made grading student papers any easier. But throughout her career, as a sign of her unswerving and lasting commitment to teachers everywhere and to English teachers in particular, Maxine Greene has accomplished something much more lasting and important. She has challenged us to focus our energies and allegiances precisely where they belong: with our students as a collection of individuals-in-process. For, as she states:

> The point is to live our lives because they are ours. Or to shape our narratives in ways that do not duplicate other narratives. At least we can work to render them the kinds of stories that open out to possibility. (Greene, 1994, p. 218)

All texts and practices that close off or limit that developing sense of who we are or might be diminish us by seeking to control us. Maxine Greene never seeks to control, never condescends; instead, she demonstrates true respect and true friendship by never minimizing for us the strength of the social forces arrayed against our bringing this vision of a multivocal, multicultural education in subject English to fruition. It is this vision that should inform both the method and manner of our work with a literary curriculum that is at one and the same time a literacy curriculum and a *curriculum vitae*, a way of living and being in the world (Graham, 1990).

In ancient Greece, an encomium was the practice of praising or eulogizing an individual's accomplishments. Interestingly, the encomium was sung or chanted in the procession which escorted the victorious individual back home. If this volume as a whole is that procession, then on behalf of this English teacher and English teachers everywhere, this chapter is one verse of our collective song, our collective singing.

References

APPLEBEE, A.N. (1974) *Tradition and Reform in the Teaching of English: A History*, Urbana, IL: National Council of Teachers of English.

BOOTH, W.C. (1988) *The Company We Keep: An Ethics of Fiction*, Berkeley: University of California Press.

DIXON, J. (1967) *Growth Through English*, Oxford: Oxford University Press.

FRYE, N. (1963) *The Educated Imagination*, Toronto: CBC Publications.

FRYE, N. (1976) *The Secular Scripture: A Study of the Structure of Romance*, Cambridge: Harvard University Press.

GOODMAN, K.S. (1996) 'Language development: Issues, insights, and implementation,' in POWER, B.M. and HUBBARD, R.S. (eds) *Language Development: A Reader for Teachers* (pp. 81–6), Englewood Cliffs, NJ: Prentice-Hall.

GRAHAM, R.J. (1990) 'The aesthetics of literacy in *The Courtier*,' *Journal of Aesthetic Education*, **23**, 4, pp. 91–103.

GREEN, B. and BIGUM, C. (1993) 'Aliens in the classroom,' *Australian Journal of Education*, **37**, pp. 119–41.

GREENE, M. (1973) *Teacher as Stranger: Educational Philosophy for the Modern Age*, Belmont, CA: Wadsworth Publishing Co.

GREENE, M. (1978) *Landscapes of Learning*, New York: Teachers College Press.

GREENE, M. (1988) 'Qualitative research and the uses of literature,' in SHERMAN, R.R. and WEBB, R.B. (eds) *Qualitative Research in Education: Focus and Methods* (pp. 175–89), London: Falmer Press.

GREENE, M. (1994) 'Postmodernism and the crisis of representation,' *English Education*, **26**, 4, pp. 206–19.

GREENE, M. (1995) *Releasing the Imagination: Essays on Education, the Arts, and Social Change*, San Francisco: Jossey-Bass.

HIRSCH, E.D. (1987) *Cultural Literacy*, Boston: Houghton Mifflin.

MORGAN, R. (1995) 'Television, space, education: Rethinking relations between schools and media,' *Discourse: Studies in the Cultural Politics of Education*, **16**, 1, pp. 39–57.

MULLER, H.J. (1967) *The Uses of English*, New York: Holt, Rinehart and Winston.

OLSON, D.R. (1990) 'Mythologizing literacy,' in NORRIS, S.P. and PHILLIPS, L.M. (eds) *Foundations of literacy policy in Canada* (pp. 15–22), Calgary: Detselig Enterprises.

PINE, N. (1992) 'Three personal theories that suggest models for teacher research,' *Teachers College Record*, **93**, 4, pp. 656–72.

POSTMAN, N. (1988) *Conscientious Objections: Stirring Up Trouble About Language, Technology, and Education*, New York: Vintage.

ROSENBLATT, L. (1978) *The Reader, the Text, the Poem*, Carbondale IL: Southern Illinois University Press.

VAN MANEN, M. (1990) *Researching Lived Experience: Human Science for an Action Sensitive Pedagogy*, London, ONT: Althouse Press.

WHITEHEAD, F. (1966) *The Disappearing Dias: A Study of the Principles and Practice of English Teaching*, London: Chatto & Windus.

19   Maxine Greene and Arts Education

Susan W. Stinson

When asked to write about the influence of Maxine Greene on arts education, I thought of all the times I had heard her speak, with images that drew me in and a message that spoke to me in a way few other theorists have done. I reviewed my collection of her books and essays, and considered how many lines from them I have quoted in my own writing, how many pages I have assigned for students to read. Her work has guided my own professional journey as dance educator, and I cannot imagine any serious scholar in arts education who is not familiar with her work. Yet in trying to put into words the influence she has had on the field of arts education, I found it rather like trying to describe Martha Graham dancing; there is no substitute for the real experience of seeing or reading a master. It was at this moment of frustration, when I realized my words could not do justice to hers, that I recognized that Maxine Greene is not only a philosopher, but an artist as well. She creates not just scholarly articles, but alternate realities, and invites us to enter them with her. Through this journey, we come to see possibilities we might not have recognized otherwise.

Greene may also be described as an advocate for arts education, although her arguments for the inclusion of the arts in education differ significantly from those of most other advocates. Advocacy is serious business for arts educators, as we are forced to continually justify our existence in the face of limited funds. The central text for arts education advocacy is a pragmatic place, following whatever trends are currently popular in education. When creativity was seen as a major goal for education, we emphasized how the arts promote creativity, even though there is still little or no evidence of transfer from creativity in the arts to that in other domains. The arts have been proclaimed for their development of necessary skills in the workplace, such as the ability to work in teams and solve problems (Hanna, 1994). With the popularity of Howard Gardner's work in multiple intelligences (Gardner, 1983), arts advocates have promoted the capacity of the arts to develop intelligences that are otherwise ignored by schools (Arts Education Partnership Working Group, 1993). Similarly, arts advocates have welcomed the increasing emphasis on multiculturalism by promoting the capacity of the arts to help students understand different cultures (Berk, 1991). In my own field of dance education, we have at times capitalized on interests in health and fitness by using these goals to justify dance in schools. Whatever schools want, it seems, the arts can provide. Greene summarizes the primary emphases on arts education advocates in the past decade as follows:

> The arts, they suggest, can contribute to the intellectual power required by this country, or to the productivity being demanded, or to the cultural literacy that is supposed to bind us together, or to the disciplinary emphases that are to enhance academic rigor and overcome shiftlessness, relativism, 'soft' electives, and the rest. (Greene, 1987, p. 13)

The central text for arts education advocacy, then, is in the pragmatic place where we live our everyday lives. In contrast, Greene tells us that the place of art is in the margins, not the central text. She quotes critic Denis Donoghue, who writes,

> Think of [life] as a page. The main text is central, it is the text of food and shelter, of daily preoccupations and jobs, keeping things going. This text is negotiated mostly by convention, routine, habit, duty, we have very little choice in it. So long as we are in this text, we merely coincide with our ordinary selves. (Donoghue cited in Greene, 1995, p. 134)

Instead of being the text of everyday life, Greene tells us, the arts belong in the margins, because they 'offer opportunities for perspective, for perceiving alternate ways of transcending and being in the world, for refusing the automatism that overwhelms choice' (1995, p. 142).

Despite the popularity of Greene's work among arts educators, I think her arguments for the arts in education are similarly on the margins of arts education advocacy. I cannot help but believe that this is where she prefers to be, a place from which she can keep challenging us beyond the taken for granted, beyond the easy answers to the questions of why the arts belong in education and what that means for what and how we should teach.

Although Greene is more concerned about 'consciousness and vitality than . . . about technical mastery and quantifiable skills' (1995, p. 178), it is not that she does not care whether children learn to read or to multiply or to use computers. It is just that she does not see these skills as ends in themselves: 'The point of acquiring learning skills and the rudiments of academic disciplines, the tricks of the educational trade, is so that they may contribute to our seeing and the naming' (1995, p. 25). Greene wants us to see and to name not only the world as it is, but 'what . . . might be . . . what should be and what is not yet' (1995, p. 19).

The story of my own relationship with Greene's work may illuminate something of the impact she has had on a generation of arts educators. When I first heard her speak (1980a), her words resonated for me in the way that a story or a poem or a dance can sometimes do. She spoke eloquently of a phenomenon that troubled me, and proposed an alternative full of hope.

Greene spoke for me when she wrote, 'I am afraid of somnolence . . . and carelessness, and impassivity, and lack of concern' (1987, p. 125). These were the qualities that I most observed in high school classrooms. I had spent my own high school and college years during the 1960s, and I remembered them as a time of passionate engagement with a variety of causes. I broke with the conservative faith of my parents to campaign for liberal causes; with the civil rights movement and the women's movement and the peace movement, I saw the world changing for the better, and believed, along with many of my peers, that I could make a difference.

I did not see this kind of passion in looking at young people from my adult vantage point. What I observed among adolescents was a pervasive sense of not-caring. In the language of dancers, they were 'marking' the movement of life, going through the motions without dancing, with little sense that the choices they made or the actions they took could make a difference in the world. Yet while I despaired of this pervasive attitude, I could find little enthusiasm for motivating students to engage in academic studies with little more relevance than the game of trivial pursuit.

The 'I don't care' phenomenon was visible not just among high school students, but throughout society. Greene described such a situation when she wrote about 'instances of people who feel themselves to be determined by outside forces or by some nameless fatality, and who feel hopelessly isolated from a world where people coming together might bring change' (1988, p. 25). In the late 1970s, an American President named the national mood as one of *malaise* and called us to our mutual responsibility to make a difference. He was widely chastised for this act; the general public, it seemed, preferred happy messages that it was already 'morning in America' rather than calls to engage in working together to create a better world.

Engagement — the opposite of malaise and not-caring — has been trivialized in current times, as simply affect (certainly not as important in education as cognition) or as motivation (a way to get students to study the things teachers think they should). Engagement, to Greene, involves not just happy involvement or a motivational trick, but rather 'arousing persons to wide-awakeness, to courageous and (I would add) resistant life' (1987, p. 15). She ponders 'ways of arousing students to choose themselves as persons who are committed, responsible, involved' (1978, p. 69) and seeks 'to enable diverse persons to break through the cotton wool of daily life and to live more consciously' (1978, p. 185).

The sensory images of wide-awakeness, of breaking through cotton wool, live not just in the intellect. Embedded in my body-consciousness, they continue to heighten my awareness of possibility and point toward the vision of education of which Greene speaks: 'Education, for me, has to do with empowering persons to move, to find new openings in experience, to make connections, to go beyond what they are taught' (1980b, p. 1). Greene's message helped to prevent me from leaving education in despair. While I see no less passivity and boredom among students today, I continue to experience the hope that Greene aroused in me.

As an arts educator, I have found especially relevant Greene's belief that the arts are a critical element in engaging and arousing students:

> It is hard for me to conceive of a better argument for the relevance of the arts in schools — if it is indeed the case, as so many people believe, that boredom and a sense of futility are among the worst obstacles to learning. To feel oneself en route, to feel oneself in a place where there are always the possibilities of clearings, of new openings, this is what we must communicate to the young if we want to awaken them to their lived situations and enable them to make sense of and to name their worlds. (Greene, 1995, pp. 149–50)

There is much that students can do in school without being engaged. One can do math, for example, without being 'into it.' Without engagement, however, one can move but not dance. Whether one is creating art, performing it, or seeing it, there can be no aesthetic experience without engagement: 'Aesthetic experiences require conscious participation in a work . . . an ability to notice what is there to be noticed' (Greene, 1995, p. 125).

The first job of the artist or arts educator, then, is to help people to attend, to notice, to enter the particular state of consciousness that is aesthetic perception. As Greene states, artists 'enable those who open themselves to what they create to see more, to hear more, to feel more, to attend to more facets of the experienced world' (1987, p. 14). This is the impact of Greene's work on those of us who open ourselves to it.

Sometimes Greene's language becomes poetic, when she uses images that let us know that she notices much that we usually miss in our everyday lives:

> Much of our involvement with things, necessarily, is instrumental. . . . Jeans are to wear; tabletops are to eat on; awls and chisels are simply tools. . . . Work has to be done, problems have to be solved, but there remain the appearances of things —

which few people know how to see. Sunflowers and blue jeans and even chisels, however, can be disconnected from their ordinary context and looked at in a new way . . . People can be asked to notice the glow of the petal of the sunflower in the half-light or the black center's stare; they can be asked to contemplate the peculiar blue of someone's jeans and to match it against the afternoon sky. They can even be invited to examine the skeletal shape of the chisel and to watch its glint against a piece of wood. More appropriately, they can be asked to articulate some of the marvelous experiences they have had by chance: the sight of a crocus on a rainy day, the choreography of a basketball game, the halo around a woman's hair in lamplight, the soft purr of voices on the street at night. (1978, p. 195)

In current times, when there is so much emphasis on abstract intellectual analysis in arts education, I find words like these particularly welcome. They remind all of us that aesthetic perception is not just about art, but about how we attend to whatever is in our presence. Perceiving the world with all of our senses is critical.

When I first read Greene's words acknowledging the power of sensory awareness, one primary effect was reassurance. I had been teaching for some years that what makes movement dance is how we attend to it; the kinesthetic sense is essential if the dancer is to make this transformation from moving to dancing. Audience members must also use the kinesthetic sense if they are to perceive dance as anything other than a 'motion picture'; they must feel in themselves the tension of the stretched arm, the risk of the balance, the release of the fall and recovery. They must not only look at the dance, but participate in it. The effect of this participation, whether on stage or in the audience, is a heightened sense of aliveness.

Without Greene's prodding to go beyond, I might have been content just to have students experience themselves dancing and find the incredible 'high' of aesthetic experience. The experience of dancing often takes us to a feel-good place inside ourselves; it is tempting to want to remain there, in 'some interiority' (Greene, 1995, p. 26), removed from the rest of the world. In such cases, aesthetic experience becomes pure escapism, a vacation from the cares of everyday life. Greene, however, reminds us that what she seeks in aesthetic experience is not just a state of being or feel-good place: 'Consciousness . . . involves the capacity to pose questions to the world, to reflect on what is presented in experience' (1988, p. 21).

One dilemma with this consciousness, of course, is that we may become aware of aspects of the world that are difficult or painful, parts that we are more likely to want to escape than to engage with. Greene warns us against the temptation to seek only beauty or solace in aesthetic experience:

We may be too likely to find occasions for shelter in the arts . . . Because we teach children whose spontaneity we want so badly to preserve, we choose too frequently to find only purity and radiance in domains that touch the depths as well as the heights of being human in the world. (1995, p. 144)

It is this understanding of consciousness as something that takes us not just within but also beyond ourselves, even to dark places, that leads Greene to recognize a link between aesthetic education and moral action:

What seems crucial is . . . the active insertion of one's perception into the lived world. Only after that does a project come to be, putting an explanation into words, fighting a plague, seeking homes for the homeless, restructuring inhumane schools. (1995, p. 74)

Greene recognizes two major connections between the arts and the moral domain. The first link is their ability to help us perceive the world through someone else's senses. As Greene tells us,

> Imagination is what makes empathy possible. It is what enables us to cross the empty spaces between ourselves and those we teachers have called 'other' over the years. If those others are willing to give us clues, we can look in some manner through strangers' eyes and hear through their ears. (1995, p. 3)

We cannot respond to injustice if it is invisible to us; we cannot respond to persons if they are invisible. One job of the arts is to make parts of the world visible, parts which we had not recognized before.

A second link that Greene helps us perceive between the arts and moral action is the capacity of the arts to awaken people to the possibility that the world can be different than it is. None of us is free until we recognize that conditions might be other than they are. As Greene notes,

> When oppression or exploitation or segregation or neglect is perceived as natural or a 'given,' there is little stirring in the name of freedom . . . When people cannot name alternatives, imagine a better state of things, share with others a project of change, they are likely to remain anchored or submerged, even as they proudly assert their autonomy. (1988, p. 9)

Certainly not all arts educators make the link between the aesthetic and moral domains. I remember one time being chastised by a well-known colleague for a presentation in which I spoke to the moral implications of several different aesthetic stances (Stinson, 1985); to that dance educator, the ethical and the aesthetic should not even be spoken of in the same conversation. Perhaps she was concerned, as is Greene, that the arts be taught not simply as morality tales or books of virtues: 'The role of imagination is not to resolve, not to point the way, not to improve. It is to awaken, to disclose the ordinarily unseen, unheard, and unexpected' (Greene, 1995, p. 28).

Although the link between the artistic and moral domains is possible, it is not guaranteed: 'For all of their emancipatory potential, the arts cannot be counted on to liberate, to ensure an education for freedom' (Greene, 1988, p. 131). Further, Greene does not suggest 'that the fostering of aesthetic experiences is the only way or even the primary way of opening critical perspectives' (1978, p. 173). She recognizes that all works of art are not equally likely to bring students 'to risk transformations to the shaping of a social vision' (1995, p. 30). As Greene writes, 'There are works of art, there are certain works in history, philosophy, and psychology, that were deliberately created to move people to critical awareness, to a sense of moral agency, and to a conscious engagement with the world' (1987, p. 162). While I am sure that Greene does not disapprove of art that is merely decorative, this is not necessarily work that she would include as a cornerstone of curriculum. Reading Greene, I have had to think about which parts of the dance curriculum seem trivial and which seem significant; she challenges us to consider what is worth learning, worth knowing.

Greene's connection between the aesthetic and the moral readily resonated with me. I wanted desperately to believe that the arts had at least the possibility to make the world a better place, probably to justify my own involvement in dance education. A more challenging part of Greene's work for me to relate to, however, has been her emphasis on the power of experiencing art works created by others, rather than on the experience of art-making. What drew me to dance was not the experience of seeing great choreographic works, but the power of experiencing myself dancing and creating dance.

Because Greene writes so much about particular art works, and so little about art-making, one might conclude that she is a supporter of Discipline Based Arts Education (DBAE). The Getty Center, as a highly visible supporter of DBAE, tells arts educators that too much time in arts education programs is spent in creating art (which they refer to as the discipline of 'production') and too little in the other arts disciplines of history, criticism, and aesthetics (Getty Center for Education in the Arts, 1985). Since few students will become artists themselves, it seems to make sense that there be more emphasis on learning about art than on making art. Greene, however, is not advocating learning art history, criticism, and aesthetics:

> Knowing 'about,' even in the most formal academic manner, is entirely different from constituting an [sic] fictive world imaginatively and entering it perceptually, affectively, and cognitively. To introduce students to the manner of such engagement is to strike a delicate balance between helping learners to pay heed — to attend to shapes, patterns . . . and helping liberate them to achieve particular works as meaningful. (1995, p. 125)

Greene does not disagree with the need for students to understand how paint on paper or movement in space become art, but she knows that this is not an end in itself:

> Of course we need to introduce students to the symbol systems associated with the various arts, but we want to do so (or so I believe) to enhance their capacity to see, to hear, to read, and to imagine — not simply to conceptualize, or to join the great 'conversation' going on over time. (1987, p. 20)

The goal of DBAE, to make the arts a part of the required core curriculum, has meshed with the contemporary movement toward 'cultural literacy.' One example of this merger may be seen in the widely cited report of the National Endowment of the Arts to Congress, *Toward Civilization* (1988), which lists great artists whose work every American should know. Although Greene acknowledges that some artistic work has more potential than other to enhance consciousness, she cannot support the idea of an artistic canon:

> What is important is that whatever is chosen is . . . attended to with care and integrity, with both critical and creative thinking, with persistence, and with a regard for what that engagement *ought* to be so it can feed into a wider knowing how and, at length, into situations where the young can teach themselves. (1995, p. 182)

Greene models this kind of engagement when she writes about her own lived experiences with art. She writes neither aesthetics, criticism, nor art history, but reveals to us what and how these works of art have helped her to see, hear, and feel, and to make meaning. Like many other readers, I went back to *Moby Dick* after reading Greene's interpretation; I realized that, in the high school class where I had been required to read this novel, no one had mentioned that the story was about *my* voyage in the world as well as that of the whaler and the creature he pursued.

Greene cites so many works of art in her writing that it is easy to feel intimidated when reading it; here is a person who is educated in the arts far beyond most of the rest of us, one who can quote a novel or a poem, or describe a painting or sculpture or ballet to illustrate or reveal any point she wishes to make. More than any justification she has written, this exemplification of what it is to know works of art serves as a profound argument for such an education. We all seek metaphors that help us make sense of our lives, to interpret our journeys. Green reminds us that art works are not just problems to be solved or a language to be spoken so we can converse with other connoisseurs of the arts, but powerful ways of making meaning of our lives and understanding what it is to be human. Her examples have convinced me that it is important to have 'one pedagogy feeding into the other; the pedagogy that empowers students to create informing the pedagogy that empowers them to attend (and, perhaps, to appreciate) and vice versa' (Greene, 1995, p. 138).

Sometimes my students, most of whom will become public school dance educators, have asked me about the 'practicality' of Greene's ideas. Admittedly it is easier to be on the margins when one is a tenured faculty member in a university, and harder as an arts educator whose job is threatened by every budget crisis, or an arts educator seeking a job in the first place. With responsibilities for teacher education, including state mandates, NCATE reviews, and other bureaucratic requirements for certification, I also live a great deal of my life in that pragmatic world. I get asked to help write national standards, create assessment tasks and scoring rubrics, judge applicants for participation in state enrichment programs. In negotiating the political dimensions of education, I sometimes find it necessary to use pragmatic arguments like those I mentioned earlier in this paper — that the arts allow for different learning styles and diverse intelligences and they may help kids learn to work together, become culturally literate and physically fit. These effects of arts education, however, are worthwhile yet still insufficient to inspire in me the kind of passion that Greene's vision ignites.

Each of us must find our own ways of dancing with the world as it is while we attempt to imagine and create a different one. As a dance educator with one foot in public education and one in the university, I have been impressed that Greene is not an 'ivory tower professor.' She has not only written and spoken about her vision of arts education, but worked to make it happen through her involvement with the Lincoln Center Institute. The institute was established in the mid-1970s by Lincoln Center for the Performing Arts, 'to foster aesthetic education as an important part of learning' (Lincoln Center Institute, 1995, p. 1). The model which has been developed, which is centered around encounters with artistic works but also includes workshops for classroom teachers as well as administrators, reveals Greene's belief that 'simply being in the presence of art forms is not sufficient to occasion an aesthetic experience or change a life' (1995, p. 125). The model had been expanded to 17 other sites around the country as of 1995.

While I am impressed with the materials I read about the Lincoln Center program, and can definitely recognize the presence of Greene's touch, I expect that it at times falls short of the vision she expresses in her work. I also expect that she does not consider the program a disappointment. Like all art, Greene's vision is not meant to be a blueprint or a direct guide for action. Her words, like the words of poetry and the movement of dance, 'mean more than they denote, evoking in those willing to pay heed other images, memories, things desired, things lost, things never entirely grasped or understood' (1995, p. 44). We may not always be able to create exactly what we imagine, but we cannot create at all without imagination, passion, and hope.

As arts educators go into the world, we need to engage in a dialectic between what is and what might be, between the texts and the margins, the pragmatic and the visionary. It is all too easy to become discouraged and give in to the 'reality' of this 'objective obsessed, product-oriented time' (Greene, 1980b, p. 2). But Greene, as an artist, knows that there is not one single reality, and that 'of all our capacities, imagination is the one that permits us to give credence to alternate realities' (1995, p. 3). As we sail in and out of the multiple realities in which we live our lives, we need a means to steer ourselves off the reefs and out of the quicksand, and a light to shine on those dark places we might otherwise fear to enter. Maxine Greene's work has served arts educators for two decades as both rudder and beacon in our journeys into schooling. Like the art we make and the art we teach, Greene's words help us to 'overcome our fear, rediscover our feelings — and, most importantly, find out who we are and what we mean' (1980a, p. 31).

References

ARTS EDUCATION PARTNERSHIP WORKING GROUP (1993) *The Power of the Arts to Transform Education: An Agenda for Action*, Washington, DC: The John F. Kennedy Center for the Performing Arts.

BERK, E. (ed.) (1991) *A Framework for Multicultural Arts Education*, New York: National Arts Education Research Center.

GARDNER, H. (1983) *Frames of Mind: The Theory of Multiple Intelligences*, New York: Basic Books.

GETTY CENTER FOR EDUCATION IN THE ARTS (1985) *Beyond Creating: The Place for Art in America's Schools*, Los Angeles: Getty Center for Education in the Arts.

GREENE, M. (1978) *Landscapes of Learning*, New York: Teachers College Press.

GREENE, M. (1980a) 'Integrations and arts spaces: Challenging the either/or,' in KIMSEY, A. (ed.), *Arts and the Child: A North Carolina Conference* (pp. 25–31), Raleigh: North Carolina Department of Cultural Resources.

GREENE, M. (1980b) *Moving Towards Possibility*, Lawther Lecture: University of North Carolina at Greensboro.

GREENE, M. (1987) 'Creating, experiencing, sense-making: Art worlds in schools,' *Journal of Aesthetic Education*, **21**, 4, pp. 11–23.

GREENE, M. (1988) *The Dialectic of Freedom*, New York: Teachers College Press.

GREENE, M. (1995) *Releasing the Imagination: Essays on Education, the Arts, and Social Change*, San Francisco: Jossey-Bass.

HANNA, J.L. (1994) 'Arts education and the transition to work,' *Arts Education Policy Review*, **96**, 2, pp. 31–6.

LINCOLN CENTER INSTITUTE (1995) *Progress Report II, 1995*, New York: Lincoln Center Institute.

NATIONAL ENDOWMENT FOR THE ARTS (1988) *Toward Civilization*, Washington, DC: US Government Printing Office, pp. 13–19.

STINSON, S.W. (1985) 'Curriculum and the morality of aesthetics,' *Journal of Curriculum Theorizing*, **6**, pp. 66–83, Fall.

20   Maxine Greene: A Religious Educator's Religious Educator

Kathleen O'Gorman

It is a privilege and a pleasure to contribute to this volume honoring and celebrating my teacher and friend Maxine Greene. I am one of perhaps thousands of educators and administrators who she has inspired, nurtured, and challenged through her example and writings, in the classroom, lecture hall, and in frequent informal meetings and conversations.

Intuition prompts me to present my tribute in narrative form. When asked to describe Maxine I most frequently find myself recounting stories about her. Thus a narrative seems to me to be the most natural and appropriate mode of relating my experience of Maxine and her influence in my life, both personally and professionally. For one thing Maxine is so natural and spontaneous, so accessible, so immediately present to us and to the world. No secretary or graduate assistant limits access to her company or her counsel. Nor is it necessary to stand on ceremony, to address her by title, to schedule appointments to see her.

A narrative seems particularly appropriate in rendering an account of a woman who created a self and a life that has made a difference in the lives of countless others. Maxine's is a story of courage and resilience in the face of personal loss and professional challenge, of creativity and generativity in the practice of her craft, of warmth and graciousness in the sharing of herself with her students and colleagues. No less is Maxine herself a rich and riveting storyteller.

Maxine's story intersects with my own most immediately and profoundly when set in the context of religious education. It is this perspective that I seek to illumine, develop, and present here as a testimony to the richness and versatility of her educational legacy to so many of us in our varied professional and academic specializations.

The Introductory Experience

Maxine Greene first came into my life through the stories related in many an after-dinner conversation by a friend and colleague at Loyola University in New Orleans. Maurice Monette was, at the time, Director of the Institute for Ministry, a graduate program offering degrees in Religious Education and Pastoral Studies. He had studied with Maxine some years earlier and talked of her stadium-size classes, her flocks of admiring students trailing her down the Teachers College corridors, her rich and engaging lectures, her stock of knowledge and stories at hand, her dry wit and somewhat eccentric charm. Through these anecdotes and vicarious experiences I not only became familiar with Maxine, I became intrigued by her as well.

I met Maxine Greene formally when I participated in several of her classes at Teachers College. After some 25 years of teaching in parochial schools and working as

Director of Religious Education in a church, I had taken a position as Program Coordinator for Loyola University's Institute for Ministry. Several years later, having been offered a sabbatical leave to complete my doctoral studies, I enrolled in the joint program in Religion and Education at Union Theological Seminary and Teachers College. This decision led to some unforeseen consequences, the most paradoxical and disarming of which was a reversal of my educational expectations. Having anticipated that the theological and spiritual dimensions of my study would be supplied by the seminary and that its more secular and pedagogical content would come from Teachers College, I was more than a bit taken aback to meet my most significant religious educators in the school of education. Maxine Greene was one of these. Through her person and her pedagogy I found new resources and fresh energy for my work at Loyola. She inspired and enabled me to, in her words, 'fund the meaning'[1] of my educational specialization, deepening and extending its relevance, contribution, and influence. All the while she remained adamantly resistant to any identification with the religious or the field of religious education.

Maxine has inspired and enabled countless others to similar ends and achievements. Given the size and composition of her classes and the number and variety of speaking invitations she accepts, it is evident that her educational appeal and contributions take many forms and find expression in diverse languages. Whatever the educational specialization, whether philosophy or aesthetics, physical or special education, administration, psychology, anthropology, health and nutrition, curriculum and instruction, adult education, literature, or religion, it finds a place within Maxine Greene's comprehensive vision and multilingual expression. Whatever the personal story and particular pedagogical orientation of her students, whether women or men, veteran or aspiring teachers, New Yorkers or visitors from other cultures and countries, each seems to derive inspiration, insight, and access to new resources through their contact and classes with Maxine.

Some Highlights of the Story

When I reflect on what I have learned from Maxine, what first comes to mind are some memorable experiences outside the classroom. One of the earliest of these occurred in a Teachers College corridor after one of the first classes I had with her. I wondered if she remembered meeting me at all, let alone the circumstances that had brought me to New York. As she passed by, she said rather matter-of-factly, 'Whatever I can do to get you back into the classroom, let me know.' I was more than a bit surprised and encouraged by such graciousness and recognition and wondered how many others she had mentored so perceptively and graciously.

A few more encounters and classes revealed Maxine's phenomenal memory. She knows many of her students by name and often what and where they teach. Over the years I find her memory remains remarkable. Keeping track of all the people, the speaking commitments, the texts. Perhaps Maxine's memory for texts is the most amazing of all. She would make many of us feel illiterate as she so easily quoted lines from plays, novels, poetry, not to mention philosophers, literary critics, even cartoons from the latest *New Yorker*. No dated, yellowed lecture notes structure her classes. More often the tools of her craft consist of an issue of *The New York Review of Books*, folded over and slipped under her arm. She wears her texts to class much like her hats, their significance derived more from their symbolic rather than practical value.

Her determination and resolve are similarly impressive. One of my most vivid memories of her relentless persistence occurred at Grand Central Station on a late winter afternoon after a snowstorm had dusted much of the Northeast. Maxine was returning from a speaking engagement in Washington when we ran into each other at the station. She told me it had taken hours to get that far because the airports had closed down and the trains were running behind schedule. She went on that she needed to get to her 6 o'clock class. Noting it was nearing 5 o'clock I said, 'You'll never make it. And anyway, the weather's so bad that your students probably won't get there either.' She looked me in the eye and said she wouldn't miss a class and before I realized it, she had disappeared into the crowd that was mobbing the next train. Not as adept at negotiating subway traffic, I caught a later train and raced to catch up with her to help her with her bags on the long six-block walk to her classroom. After checking out the possible routes she might take and not finding her along any of them, I decided to pass by her classroom on my way back to the dorm. There she was at her podium, teaching away as if she had come to class after a restful, non-eventful afternoon at home. Her students had made it to class as well, indicating they had complete confidence that their teacher would make it regardless of the weather.

Another story I find quite telling and typical also took place in a Teachers College corridor. I had asked Maxine about her daughter who was seriously ill in London. She told me that she had just gotten word that Linda's condition had deteriorated and that she found it difficult to think about preparing and delivering the talk she was scheduled to give at an upcoming conference. I suggested that she share her preoccupation with the audience. Maxine responded, 'You do that in small intimate groups; you don't do it in a crowded lecture hall.' I heard later that no one at her talk would have guessed that she was carrying such a heavy burden. From this experience I learned the importance of thinking about and discerning how much and what kind of personal experience is appropriately disclosed in the execution of our public roles and commitments.

'Funding the Meaning' of *Religious*

I am aware as I relate these stories and experiences that their selection and interpretation probably reveal as much about me as they do about Maxine Greene. They are born of the particular perspectives, aspirations, and values that have formed and guided my own story and experience and indicate perhaps as much of what I find myself looking for in Maxine as what she herself seeks to offer me. Acknowledging this inevitable tendency to project one's ideals and interpretations on another, I seek to distinguish who Maxine is and what she intends from what I envision and experience her to be. Thus I realize that it is something of an imposition to interpret Maxine's educational orientation and significance out of my immersion in the field of religious education without acknowledging its subjective bias. Interestingly Maxine has led me to this critical realization, with her insistence that unless and until we recognize what works on and within our thinking, we would not really think at all. She has likewise taught me the importance of making my own meanings and speaking in my own voice out of my own story.

With this in mind I reflect on the theological or spiritual dimensions of the education Maxine made available to me and continues albeit indirectly to offer the field of religious education. Maxine herself would never make such a claim. Indeed whenever I would refer to her in this capacity she would look at me incredulously, smile, express her appreciation for what she seemed to judge a complimentary affirmation, and then emphatically assure me that I was mistaken. Suggesting that religious can be interpreted more liberally and existentially, I explained that in my view she fulfilled Alfred North Whitehead's assertion that education was *religious* when it effected responses of duty and reverence.[2] But even the distinguished philosopher with his more implicit and less confessional interpretation of religious did not convince Maxine Greene of the religious dimension of her teaching. Try as I might to convince her otherwise, she would insist that she could not be religious because she was not affiliated with any religious community or institution. She would simply smile, shake her head, wave her hand, and dismiss the association with a remark such as, 'I don't think of myself as a religious person.' Perhaps her resistance owed more to her humility and modesty; perhaps to the rigorous standard she seemed to have set for herself. Perhaps it was due to the meaning and experience conjured up by the term in her formative years. To this day I remain unable to convince Maxine of the religious quality or dimension that I discern so clearly in her person and her teaching.

The more she resists the connection, the more valid, appropriate, and obvious it becomes for me. It is, I believe, her reluctance to describe herself as a religious person that confirms its authenticity for me. Coming from an institutionalized, explicitly religious context, I find Maxine's refusal to identify herself in this way something of a breath of fresh air. It brings to mind that familiar parable about the two individuals who went to pray in the temple. One was confident and proud and self-righteous, the other so contrite and humble and unassuming. In her resemblance to the second person, Maxine seems all the more authentically religious. It is all the more convincing when contrasted with those who make the claim to holiness so easily and readily.

Her encouragement to her students to make and fund our own meanings confirms and extends a more inclusive and less traditionally-derived interpretation of my sense of religious. For as long as I can remember I have perceived what Philip Phenix referred to as the sacred within the secular.[3] Perhaps it was the influence or experience of having a grandmother of a different faith and a mother who taught me to be sensitive to those of other faith perspectives. Whatever the source of the influence, I typically find what I consider to be sacred in unexpected, usually secular contexts. Maxine has made me even more aware of this and prompts further reflection on how and why I found more traditional and circumscribed meanings of the sacred and the religious less profound and often less authentic, and embrace instead a more implicit, existential, less prescribed, less circumscribed interpretation.

The root of religious, to 'bind back,' does not provide a ready-made explanation of its meaning; nor does it readily confirm my sense of the term. What the etymology of the descriptor does suggest is something of an effort or a tension between a fixed point or source, and an impulse away from the point of origin. As I think about what this might infer about the meaning of religious, I wonder if the binding back might describe the restraint we need to develop and exert over our tendencies toward self-indulgence, self-absorption, self-expression. Might the binding back refer to the responsibility we share to acknowledge our roots in and ties to the larger community or whole, and the necessity of submitting to its sanctions and discipline? Might religious then function as a designation for teachers who identify the creative tension between self-cultivation and self-giving? Might it describe the work of educators who promote in their students a sense of responsibility for the whole community, a sense of the tension that exists between the wisdom and blindness of traditions that we are charged to pass on, a sense of the binding force of what is right and true and just, a sense of discipline? Are not all educators religious who achieve and promote a breadth of vision and depth of concern, altruistic self-giving, personal interiority and integrity, dedication to a particular vocation, fidelity to commitments, respect for personal and cultural differences, a sense of humility, modesty, reverence, and magnanimity, and recognition of something or someone larger than ourselves and our particular place in the world? In my perspective such educators can be authentically religious whether or not they express themselves in a theological language or identify with religious institutions. These religious educators are as likely to be found teaching in homes and hospitals, barbershops and voluntary associations, libraries and museums, parks and schools and 12 step programs, theaters and therapy groups.

My inherited Christian religious orientation with its roots in Judaism enables me to perceive the religious dimension implicit within multiple forms of educational practice. The theological foundations of both traditions, with their recognition of the imminent and incarnational aspect of divine presence and activity, teach that faith and fidelity are expressed within the ordinary, within everyday life and experience. Both are characterized by a sense of historical mission that involves humanity in the effort to transform the world according to the divine plan. Both have an outer-directed orientation which leads their adherents to spread and extend the influence of their religious visions and commitments. Thus the priority and emphasis given to the community, institutions, interpersonal and social relationships, to the pursuit and practice of compassion, peace, justice, identification with the poor and oppressed, to the practice of unconditional love.

'Funding the Meaning' of Education

My experience of Maxine Greene as a religious educator is obviously drawn from a particular vision of education and a nuanced interpretation of the field. Having appealed earlier to Whitehead's religious characterization of all education, it is probably evident that my own view finds support and affirmation in his perspective. Indeed for me education is a vocation, a dedication to the pursuit of teaching and learning as an inherently valuable and meaningful, even spiritual, activity.

In this view any subject or focus of the educational process can be approached from a religious perspective. Mathematics can be taught in such a way that students grapple with and encounter the mysteries of finitude and infinity, recurring patterns and processes, randomness and predictability, the paradox of chaotic order and imaginary numbers. Music can be approached and appreciated as creative expression and mystical experience. Visual art and literature can be taught as illuminations of the problematic and the possible in the lives of individuals and societies through prophetic injunction and utopian dreams. Physics can introduce us to the wonders of the physical universe and to the comprehensive story out of which we emerge and are sustained. Economics can promote an appreciation of the Earth as our comprehensive household and effect a more equitable distribution of available goods and services. History can be interpreted as a story with sacred and salvific dimensions. Biology can introduce us to the uniqueness and contributions of our countless neighbors within the life community. Even professional education such as law and medicine can be approached in their religious dimensions as moral governance and sacramental healing. All of these subjects have a religious dimension which may or may not be explicitly identified or probed, but which is nonetheless integrated within their unique disclosures and methodologies.

This is not to imply that education is always or is even typically conceived of or enacted as a religious activity. It is rather to suggest that there is something fundamentally or inherently moral and spiritual, at least potentially, in the vocation itself, in what we teach and how we make what we teach available to our students. Such a capacity or aspect for the religious is, at least latently and tacitly, expressed in the writings of Maria Montessori in her recognition of the unlimited potential of the child, of John Dewey in his vision of education's accountability in nurturing responsible and active participants in the social order, of Paulo Freire in his assertion of education's emancipatory role and responsibility, *and* of Maxine Greene.

The Education of a Religious Educator

I expect that readers anticipate or assume that religious education is a particular and perhaps narrow form of teaching and learning, carried out primarily if not exclusively by religious institutions and groups. Most common of these forms would be Sunday School, revival meetings, catechism instruction. This is not what I mean or practice as religious education, however. The vision that animates my practice gives primacy to the more comprehensive and implicit interpretation of the field and less attention to its more particular and confessional modes. In this regard it might be helpful to think of religious education as a continuum. At one end we would find the kind of explicit and conventional instruction and socialization that is commonly practiced by religious institutions; on the other, there would be all kinds of formal and informal education through which people consciously or unconsciously develop, learn about, and respond to the spiritual or religious dimensions of their experience, of their world. The explicit end of the religious education continuum requires little elaboration or explanation. The other end, however, is more subtle and perhaps less recognized and appreciated. Here is the locus of Maxine Greene's practice.

As I reflect on what, for me, constitutes the religious dimension and impulse of Maxine's educational vision and practice, several dominant themes and emphases come to mind. The first might be identified as a profound and unwavering reverence for and confidence in the uniqueness and inherent dignity of each person. This disposition lies embedded and finds expression in the emphatic mandate she gives to education to promote consciousness, intentionality, and wide-awakeness. Again and again she charges educators and schools with the responsibility of enabling students achieve their own vantage points, to speak in their unique voices, to respect the multiplicity of forms that intelligence, creativity, language, and achievement can assume. Consistently and emphatically she stresses the necessity of confronting and resisting determinacy and the value of choosing ourselves and becoming the possibility we are. If religious visions and commitments have anything to do with how we are taught to regard and relate to each other, with providing the encouragement and resources to grow toward our full stature, with the pursuit of enlightenment, purpose, and agency, then one who gives herself to their realization can be identified as a religious educator.

Maxine's teaching and writing also manifest a prophetic aspect or quality. Her critique of formulaic, bureaucratic, prescriptive, and statistical preoccupations and distortions of educational processes and structures is reminiscent of the Hebrew prophets issuing their correctives and injunctions to the community for its failure to live up to its vision. Through her example and instruction I have learned how education might function as the critical conscience of individuals, institutions, and the social order, exposing hidden and vested interests and agendas and as Maxine would put it, 'confronting the forces that work behind our backs.'[4] Through her direction and guidance I have learned to problematize any existential situation, to approach a text, tradition, or institution through the hermeneutic of suspicion.[5] This prophetic aspect of education that is so clearly expressed and emphasized in classes with Maxine makes it uncomfortable, indeed impossible, to blindly accept and follow the dictates of bureaucratic structures and procedures. In the wake of an exposure to this capacity of educational practice, naiveté gives way to a realization that no institution is wholly beneficent, no interpretation is completely accurate or trustworthy, no tradition is exempt from the need for revision or reform.

It is Maxine's influence that helps me relate the hermeneutics of suspicion to the possibility of emancipation and transformation. It is Maxine who enables me to perceive the gap between what an institution claims to be about and what it actually accomplishes.

It is Maxine who evokes the spirit of Amos, Jeremiah and Ezechiel. It is Maxine's solidarity with the oppressed that conjures up images of Jesus chasing the moneylenders from the temple.

I discern another religious aspect of Maxine's educational vision and practice in her concern for the cultivation and expression of imagination and creativity. My association of these with the religious begins with the universe itself. Whatever else we might believe about the creator and the creative process we call the natural world, there is no denying the presence and effects of awesome imagination. So too the dreams and visions we identify with the religious realm are borne of creative imagination. These seem to spring from the soul, from the realm of the spirit.

For Maxine, creativity and imagination are the quintessential human capacities and contributions to the world. They are the means and consequence of inspiration, emancipation, and transformation. They tap and express what is under the surface, what is essential, what is missing, what is possible. Some seek the creative and imaginative in the rituals and lore of formal religion. Others like Maxine seek and find them in the arts. The religious education I encountered through Maxine was mediated through sacred texts like *To the Lighthouse* and *Moby Dick*, like Monet's impressionistic paintings and O'Keefe's sensual deserts and flowers, like Stravinski's 'Rite of Spring' and Puccini's 'Madam Butterfly,' like Wordsworth's poetry and Shakespeare's drama. Thanks to Maxine I discovered a new world of rich and versatile resources for religious education.

The Story, the Religious Education, Continues

Last summer my dream was fulfilled: I brought Maxine Greene to Loyola. For years I had tried to describe her influence and significance in my life and teaching and to convince my colleagues in theology and ministry that Maxine had something relevant and unique to offer our students. For years, too, I had tried to convince Maxine that who she was and what she taught would be appreciated by and relevant to our students.

Finally the dream and all its predictions was fulfilled. And true to form, Maxine stood at the podium assuring the crowd that had gathered to hear her that she was not religious and was not exactly sure of what she was doing there. And the students perceived the religious depths of her person and teaching and applauded and affirmed her. One of them, a religious sister, approached her after her talk and said, 'Maxine, I am not where you think I am; I am with you.' Maxine smiled her recognition that Sr. Therese and she had much in common. In fact, Maxine found and perhaps extended the common ground between herself and these ministers and religious educators, between education and education for ministry. Our Director asked if she would return to us. And I delighted in the revelation and relevance of her visit and in the anticipation of another experience and a further unfolding of the story.

Notes

1   I borrow the phrase 'funding the meaning' from Maxine who used it to describe that process through which we find and ascribe a new, richer, deeper, more integrated significance and meaning to our earlier and previous understanding of experience, events, encounters, texts, etc. We might fund the meaning of history as human story, for example, through a discovery of the history or story of the universe. The discovery enables us to understand history as a much longer process, a more comprehensive story.

2 Albert North Whitehead (1929) *The Aims of Education and Other Essays*, New York: The Free Press, p. 39.
3 Phil Phenix was a professor at Teachers College who codirected the program in Religion and Education in the 1960s and 1970s. His book (1966) *Education and the Worship of God* (Philadelphia: Westminster Press), presents an interesting vision and critique of curriculum through a matrix of interactive relationships of the sacred and the secular.
4 One of Maxine's recurring expressions denoting the presence and conduct of oppressive forces.
5 An analytical methodology which presumes that every text and subject for that matter has a shadow side that exerts a negative influence unless it is identified and confronted. One who utilizes this methodology attempts to discern and confront the flaws, distortions, unexamined assumptions and interests, mixed messages, mixed motivations, and often, negative effects in an interpretation in an effort to uncover new and deeper insights into its past and potential meaning.

21   Feeling the Teacher: A Phenomenological Reflection on Maxine Greene's Pedagogy

Nancy Lesko

I

In the Fall of 1996, several of my Indiana University colleagues asked about my recent sabbatical, especially about the semester that I spent at Teachers College working with Maxine Greene and others. After I described some aspects of Maxine's class and teaching, a woman asked, 'What did you get out of the experience?' I was oddly flustered by this 'bottom line' question, and yet some part of me accepted the provocation to get to the heart of the matter. I remember searching for something fittingly important to say; finally, I replied, 'It gave me more self-confidence.' I probably elaborated on that statement, but only that sentence remains in my memory now. My answer seemed horribly inadequate at the time; it was too insignificant, too personal, too self-revelatory. I felt that I should have been able to reel off 'important new learnings' and knowledge gathered and stored for use in writing and teaching. My answer also seemed inadequate in relation to my experience of Maxine's teaching. The grandness of Maxine's work and reputation was not lived up to, not even approached in my thin, awkward answer.

My inadequate answer has remained with me, as has the puzzle of its sources and meanings. I am utilizing that response about the influence of Maxine's teaching on my self-confidence as a signifier and this essay as one exploration of what it signifies. Understanding the signifying process involves my body, my feelings, and my mind. Thus, this essay attempts an understanding of teaching and learning as embodied practices. Although people occasionally gesture toward the body in educational discourse, generally it remains *terra incognita*, present yet unmarked. I wonder what difference it makes that our conceptions of teaching and learning are ignorant or neglectful of bodies. If we were less singly devoted to mindfulness in education, who would be affected and in what ways? In attempting to understand the phenomenology of my learning in Maxine's class, I endeavor to *materialize* the body in educational discourse. The body's entrance into educational corridors and conversations is, like my reply above, awkward and tenuous, yet strongly felt.

II

Maxine's classroom for her Spring 1996 graduate course, The Arts and American Education, on the fourth floor of Main Hall, was a small amphitheater, wider than it was deep, dimly lighted and showing wear. Some of the 15 or so long rows of wooden chair-desks were broken. A piano was stored against one wall. The 60-some students in attendance each Monday afternoon spread out over the room, with bunches of students in the front rows closest to Maxine's desk. The setting did not bespeak importance or status, as a luxurious, well-appointed classroom might. Rather, some of Maxine's students may have found that the Teachers College buildings echoed the shabbiness of many public elementary and secondary schools in and around New York City.

Maxine always arrived early, re-reading her notes or talking with students. Despite the lackluster surroundings, Maxine dressed elegantly. In the winter of 1996, she favored cowl neck sweaters, jackets, and long, heavy-linked necklaces, usually gold. Before class began, she was a speck of a woman in a large room with bad lighting. The lighting seemed to illuminate all the areas except the space she occupied, so I had to adjust and consciously focus my eyes on her slight figure at the beginning of each class. She always began promptly, talking in a familiar way with her students, in a conversational and elegant way. Once she began speaking, her intelligence, humor, questions, and connections sparkled and diminished the room's shabbiness.

She began the first class session with an elaboration of where she spoke from, her position and biases. She talked about many things under this rubric, the themes of the class, her view of American literature, and the questions for teachers in 'increasingly problematic times.' She consistently raised questions about 'how we choose ourselves,' how teachers choose their commitments in times when there is no certainty about 'the facts.' She presented herself as interested in teaching American history from multiple perspectives, which she said she was still learning. She owned that she was re-writing her book, *The Public School and the Private Vision*, in a non-canonical way. She explained that the first version excluded numerous literatures: 'This is an example of how ideology works even in a liberally educated person. I had never thought to include DuBois, Frederick Douglass, women's literature or feminism.'[1]

She explained on the first night that the literature on the syllabus was not *about* teaching and schools. Rather, 'reading literature (a work of imagination) is a way to illuminate some aspects of life.' She contended that literature helps us look at the world from multiple viewpoints. When we discuss works of art, the discussions, we will find, *do* have relevance for education and teaching. [For example,] what does it mean to intervene in someone else's world, as a teacher? . . . Literature opens perspectives, but doesn't give us truth. We need to think about that. What is the role of imagination? . . . Do we have a right, in public schools, to ask people to question their beliefs?

The literature discussed in the class included Emerson, Mann, Hawthorne, Melville, Thoreau, Douglass, Twain, Chopin, Morrison, Fitzgerald, Ellison, among others. Maxine also examined the Hudson Valley landscapes as 'moral' paintings, and she concluded her semester with a dance performance. She stated that different modalities are critical in learning and to utilize only written texts denied the human body and the senses.

The multiple perspectives that Maxine promoted were in evidence in her teaching in several ways, but it was the opening surveys of current happenings in which I best recognized Maxine's unique and powerful approach. One of the most memorable opening monologues occurred on the Monday night after Superbowl Sunday, when she humorously portrayed her husband as rabid football fan, wearing a team cap all day in the house to designate his team affiliation. The television, with the pre-game, half-time and the game itself, swallowed up the day, for Maxine as for her husband. Her sarcastic depiction of the annual male rite elicited smiles and laughter from her students. She referred to Bourdieu's class-based analysis of the making of a sports fan, thus establishing a socially-constructed view of this phenomenon. 'It's terrible when you're alienated in your own home,' she concluded.

Her representation of the masculinity and team fervor of the Superbowl was familiar to me, and to many others, who had accommodated the Superbowl and its alien alliegances in our homes. Her portrait connected directly to my own experiences and my own feelings. Her imagery — such as her husband wearing a team cap inside all day — communicated the absurdity of the event, and how unusual, cultish behavior was taken as exemplary, enacted in private and public spaces. In her narration, she was both close to it (same apartment, her husband, same New York background) and distanced (alien from sports fans, alien from sports culture). Her open sarcasm did not mince words against a sports-fetishizing culture.

Equally moving was her ironic portrait of a trip to the Grand Ole Opry. Her anecdote was occasioned by *The New Republic* (5 February 1996) lead article on the popularity of country music and its position as 'The Voice of America.' According to Bruce Feiler, 42 per cent of all radio listeners are country music devotees, which makes country the dominant music format in the United States. Feiler argues that country music speaks for the suburbs. This article on the prominence of country music sparked a story about Maxine's experience with country music. She recalled that on a visit to Nashville, Tennessee, she was taken to the Grand Ole Opry. She did not like it, and formed this opinion quite quickly, but she could not leave because the Opry building is located several miles outside of town. Thus, she portrayed herself as trapped in another alienating cultural event. Rather than endure the music, she withdrew to the lobby and spent the rest of the concert there marking papers. Again, her revulsion and refusal to participate in alien culture, and her preference for grading papers over hearing a country music concert were humorous and remarkable.

Her phenomenological eyes and ears were most acute and articulate in her opening monologues. She commented on recent articles published in *The New York Times*, *The Nation*, *The New Yorker*, or *Taboo*. She compared the rhetoric of the presidential primary to the fears at the turn of the century and the scapegoating of the poor, immigrants, and single mothers. Ralph Reed of the Christian Coalition came under regular critique that semester. In the opening monologues she ranged across topics that drew from private and public concerns, personal and political, educational and aesthetic. She also ranged across emotions; both conventional and outlaw emotions (Jaggar, 1989). She waxed eloquent on a recent art exhibit at the Guggenheim, repeated bell hooks' comments from a PBS television show, 'Black Is, Black Ain't,' remarked on the themes of a new film on Anne Frank's life, and critiqued the downsizing practices of corporations. She moved easily and quickly across emotions and connected analyses, from wonderment to excitement to aggravation to sarcasm.

Maxine's teaching involved her total body, and it evoked total response, at least from me. This small, seemingly-frail, refusing-to-retire professor called forth energy and presence to fill a large, dimly lighted classroom with sparkling ideas, moral questions, and cultural analyses. Her forays into cultural politics usually led to familiar questions — What should we teach in schools? What values does the school teach, include?

Maxine emphasized multiple perceptions of the world; often she seemed to be a dynamic mass of perceptions, observations, critique, feelings, and thoughts on the world. She read everything, it seemed, and so her perceptions were laced with references to current activities in politics and the arts. I found her discussion of *The Adventures of Huckleberry Finn* to be one of the most moving and enlightening classes, and it illustrated her use of literature to ask questions of importance to educators. In the first class, she introduced the novel as one that presents many of the most serious, ongoing questions for education. How do we educate Huck Finn? Do we detach him from everything he knows in order to educate him? What he knows is the water — he's perfectly knowledg-able on the river. Off the river, he's dumb, can't do anything.

In these ways she tacked back and forth between appreciations of the aesthetics of literature and the continuing questions that these imaginative works raised for contempor-ary educators. On that first night, she stated, 'Great American literature tends to be tragic literature,' thereby writing tragedy centrally into the syllabus. She used the tragic situa-tions in works like *The Great Gatsby* to enter into the grim aspects of human life and believes that understanding the deficiencies will act as a spur to changing the world. Her teaching about the tragic elements of the contemporary world included a commitment to move from this confrontation with tragedy to repair things.

Maxine writes that imagination in teaching can act like a good friend who, following Toni Morrison, gathers one's pieces together, makes one more whole.

> 'She is a friend of my mind. She gather me, man. The pieces I am, she gather them and give them back to me all in the right order. It's good, you know, when you got a woman who is a friend of your mind' (Morrison, 1987, pp. 272–3). This is another way to imagine imagining: it is becoming a friend of someone's mind, with the wonderful power to return to that person a sense of wholeness. Often, imagination *can* bring severed parts together, can integrate into the right order, can create wholes. (Greene, 1995, p. 38)

Her teaching, in my view, gathered my pieces: my emotions, experiences, physical tired-ness, idealist longings, sarcasm, impatience, ambivalences, and more.

III

The strongest and clearest response to being a student in Maxine's class was registered through my body. When I left her class at about 7 pm on Mondays and walked the two blocks to my temporary home in Teachers College family housing, I walked more erect, breathed more deeply, my shoulders moved easily back and down and I felt greater openness in my chest. My practice of Iyengar Yoga for numerous years helped me pinpoint these physical changes. Emotionally, I felt confident, energized, aligned. I had never experienced a teacher or class in such a way — as having a direct effect on how I stood, moved, and breathed in the world (the exception, of course, was Yoga classes). In this way, I perceived the effects of Maxine's teaching through my body.

Historically, the body has been written out of learning and teaching, and only 'mind,' distinct from and superior to the body, remains. When the body is inserted into educa-tional discourse, it is generally under the topic of 'health.' Health is the prevention of illness and the maintenance of productive, useful bodies. The body is to be controlled, made productive through 'technologies' that Michel Foucault links to education and other social institutions, such as medicine and the military.

It would appear that the body is only a vessel, a carrier of the mind and subordinate to reason. The body historically has taken up a female position — of support, invisibility, functionality — in relation to the mind, which remains the main actor, the important center, the dominant, ascendant entity. The mind demands certain behaviors and silences from the body for the greater progress of cognition. However, other traditions of teach-ing/learning, such as Iyengar Yoga proclaim that 'we think with our whole body.' If we think with our whole bodies, can this position change our view of teaching/learning?

Might such awarenesses help destabilize the gendered order of mind over body and emotions that is almost synonymous with learning and teaching?

IV

'The word Yoga has its root in the Sanskrit word "yuj" which means to merge, join, or unite' (G. Iyengar, 1983, p. 9). B.K.S. Iyengar claims that: 'Dualities like gain and loss, victory and defeat, fame and shame, body and mind, mind and soul vanish through mastery of the asanas [postures]' (B.K.S. Iyengar, 1965, pp. 42–4). I want to utilize the descriptions of and reflections on Maxine Greene's teaching to *incorporate* teaching and learning, that is, to 'bring [it] within a body' (Leder, 1990, p. 31), and to view teaching/ learning as an alignment of parts of the human body. In the way that Iyengar Yoga helps in *alignment* (a term that I prefer to integration or unity), Maxine's teaching also worked towards alignment. I see alignment as a relationship of body parts (bones, muscles, tendons in Yoga) that provides ease, strength, resilience, and connects with emotional and intellectual strength.

Although the critique of Cartesian disembodiment of thinking and knowing are widely acknowledged, nevertheless, teaching practices continue this dismemberment, a fragmentation of human knowing. Drew Leder's book, *The Absent Body*, attempts to remedy this somatic absence in philosophy. In trying to re-materialize learning, Leder describes how learning to swim or learning a new language involves initially an aware-ness of the body performing unfamiliar, difficult movements. Eventually, the separate and distinct parts of swimming (cupping hands, kicking, breathing, etc.) become known and they transform the person 'through something akin to a sedimentary process' (1990, p. 32). 'Over time, that which is acted out, rehearsed, and repeated seeps into one's organismic ground' (1990, p. 32). This sedimentation is involuntary; 'practice is what has this "spontaneous" power' (Ricoeur cited in Leder, 1990, p. 32). From my practice of Yoga, I know that my understanding and movement have changed through such a slow sedimentary process.

Being in Maxine's classroom was also a practice that affected my actions, move-ment, and breathing, my sense of being in the world, in a slow sedimentary way. Maxine's repetition of opening monologues that crossed political and private arenas, conventional and outlaw emotions, and morally ambiguous questions seemed to work on my body involuntarily.

Valerie Walkerdine emphasizes that the 'regulation of [women's] speaking and silence' in education involves a splitting off of reason from body and feelings. Reason masters emotions and denies the body in the process of becoming schooled. Walkerdine writes: 'Power became . . . the possession of the Word, of rationality, of scientific con-cepts' (1990, p. 21). That is, *the cost of women's access to academia can be seen as the splitting off of emotions and body, the irrational parts of herself.* Thus, teaching that connects or brings parts together and provides a wholeness, a solidity of knowing and self, albeit temporary, is crucial for women's education. Teaching that helps sediment a connection of otherwise alienated dimensions of women students is important feminist work. Although Belenky, Clinchy, Goldberger and Tarule (1986) have written about 'connected knowing,' they have not questioned the splitting off of reason from body and emotions, or the disembodied practice of knowing. Wendy Luttrell (1993) relates gender, race, and class in her work on women's ways of knowing, but still absents the body and emotions.

Sandra Bartky, however, pursues a phenomenology of feminine oppression, both outside and inside classrooms, and helps us perceive bodies and feelings in learning. Her chapter on 'Shame and gender' records the registering of shame on women's bodies. Bartky defines shame as involving 'the distressed apprehension of oneself as a lesser creature' (1990, p. 87). Bartky recounts her adult women students in a Chicago suburb; the students were mostly high school teachers, and the women and men in the class were of generally equal positions in terms of status and pay. Bartky observed that her women students apologized for the inadequacy of their written work, before she ever read it. They presented their papers apologetically with this physical stance: 'with head bowed, chest hollowed, and shoulders hunched slightly forward' (1990, p. 89). This physical posture was associated with the feeling of shame and the judgment of inadequacy. Bartky claims that this female subjectivity is not brought fully formed into the classroom, but that 'the classroom is also a site of its constitution' (p. 90).

My Iyengar Yoga teachers have also noted the regularity of this stance in women, 'head bowed, chest hollowed, and shoulders hunched slightly forward.' Numerous Yoga postures are deemed especially good for most women because they work to correct what Bartky identifies as a shame-ful body, which Yoga understands as a mis-alignment. Postures that open the chest, lift the head, and help the shoulders move back and down correct the shame-ful body stance. As my body learns to move in unaccustomed ways, in 'confident' ways, my thinking and feelings likewise shift, or have the opportunity to do so.

V

The power of her teaching for me was the evocation of multiple responses to everyday life situations, and her connection of these to broad philosophical and educational issues. She crossed and recrossed the borders of private/public, domestic/public, personal/political, and subjective/objective. Her critiques of everyday life connected to her critiques of corporate down-sizing and educational failure to evoke aesthetics in education. They were fueled equally, or alternately, by feelings of alienation in commonplace situations, by moral outrage, by despair, by exhilaration, by a sense of connectedness to young children in classrooms.

Thinking about Walkerdine's view of splitting in relation to Maxine's teaching, highlights not only the connection between emotions and thinking but the range of emotions expressed and acknowledged: rage, impatience, frustration, humor, pleasure [more], as well as, philosophical questions about pedagogy and education. Maxine expressed not only traditional 'feminine' emotions of compassion, optimism, but what Alison Jaggar terms 'outlaw emotions,' those outside emotional hegemony (1989, p. 160), such as revulsion, fear, irritability, or ridicule. She likewise critiqued her husband's affiliation with the Superbowl, and his inability to understand her connection with Jan Vermeer's paintings, after she visited the exhibit at the National Gallery in Washington, D.C. Maxine's teaching went places — attended to a full range of emotions — that women teachers often avoid, that I as a woman teacher often avoid. Recent essays by women over 70 years of age (*New York Times*, 9 March 1997), explained their freedom from having to be nice, from having to fix things; and they understood their ability to talk as their major source of power. Maxine's opening monologues and her honesty and emotional expressiveness might be supported by her age.

Alison Jaggar writes intriguingly of the importance of emotions, in her article, 'Love and knowledge':

Emotions, then, are wrongly seen as necessarily passive or involuntary responses to the world. Rather, they are ways in which we engage actively and even construct the world. They have both mental and physical aspects, each of which conditions the other. (1989, p. 153)

Jaggar explains her category of outlaw emotions:

[O]utlaw emotions may also enable us to perceive the world differently from its portrayal in conventional descriptions . . . [C]onventionally inexplicable emotions . . . may lead us to make subversive observations that challenge dominant conceptions of the status quo. (p. 161)

Clearly, Maxine Greene's teaching, especially her opening monologues that crossed emotional conventions and spatial locations, aligned parts of myself and worked on my body. This incorporation acknowledged outlaw emotions, critical ideas, and a moral stance on the world. As such, Maxine's teaching helped sediment the legitimacy, necessity, and power of a critical perspective on teaching and learning. Thus I stood straighter, breathed more deeply, and felt lighter and exhilarated, renewed and stronger in the world. I carry Maxine's teaching with me, the image of a small woman dwarfed by a large, anonymous room with bad lighting whose ideas and feelings could not be dwarfed or silenced.

The two terms that I have used to re-embody teaching and learning — sedimentation and alignment (with its exhilaration, lightness, and strength) — are important to consider. They begin to get at an embodied understanding of teaching for social change, and they contrast with other images of teachers: as heroes, as organic intellectuals, as revolutionaries. Maxine's teaching kept covering the same practices, but with different specifics, always asking questions with no clear moral answer; ambiguity, contradiction, multiplicity were centrally involved in the alignment for me. The repetition was necessary for its lasting effects, for its becoming part of me. Such an embodied view of social transformation gives us hope and directs us to *practice* again and again our observations, our critiques, our feelings. And to anticipate that these practices will align us, strengthen and, incongruous as it may be, lighten us. The alignment works against the dualities that we think and which limit us, constrain our imaginations. 'The right method of doing asanas [postures] brings lightness and an exhilarating feeling in the body as well as in the mind and a feeling of oneness of body, mind and soul' (B.K.S. Iyengar, 1965, p. 60).

My experience with and response to Maxine's teaching suggests that teaching in a multiple and socially contextualized way, utilizing a range of human emotions, asking questions that resonate deeply and repeatedly, like Yoga postures, can bring lightness and an exhilarating feeling in the body and a feeling of oneness of body, mind and soul.

The incongruity of her small, seemingly frail person mastering the classroom and the world with humor, criticism, sarcasm, irony, and amazement remains with me. It was her alive presence — emotional, intellectual, physical, spiritual — and her ability to communicate those different dimensions to us that displayed her pedagogical skill. The imaginative practice of her teaching gathered the pieces of myself, as she has written it can. I recall the way I walked with vigor and calmness, confident in my work, happy to be a 'colleague' in the work of education with Maxine.

VI

Recalling her recent illness and hospital stay, Maxine spoke of how, in her delirium, she came into contact with what she termed the 'demonic source' of her work. I like thinking of the demons that help produce her teaching and writing. I do not pretend to understand those demons, but in her teachers' range of feelings — outrage, sarcasm, pessimism, wonderment — and ideas on society connected with them, I learned the most. That teaching is sedimented within me, along with the elegant woman wise-cracking and talking back to corporate boardmen, and being drawn into the rooms of Vermeer and the journey of Twain. It is the complex artistic melange of ideas and emotions piled together — unexpected insights and jokes — odd passions adjacent to common passions that made me feel confident, uplifted, recommitted.

> Feminists need to be aware of how we can draw on some of our outlaw emotions in constructing feminist theory and also of how the increasing sophistication of feminist theory can contribute to the reeducation, refinement, and eventual reconstruction of our emotional constitution. (Jaggar, 1989, p. 160)

We need our demons, our unconventional feelings, our body rages, our depressions in teaching. I realize how powerful the shame-less teaching of Maxine Greene was for me. If shame is part of what many women learn in classrooms, then outlaw emotions are part of the fight against shameful education. A teacher's range of feelings and ideas and moral and aesthetic questions can combat the shame-filled education. Maxine's practice suggests that her wide-ranging emotions, thinking, and topics sedimented into my body and aligned me. I embodied her teaching in my posture, deeper breath, sense of strength and lightness. Like Yoga practice, her pedagogical practice aligned me.

I cannot yet answer my own question, What does an embodied view of teaching and learning do for us? However, from a feminist educator's perspective, a more comprehensive approach to women's education (as well as, men's education) includes outlaw emotions and related social critique. If shame is not the educational fare of women, it is terminal niceness. Outlaw emotions are a way to destabilize these effects. Our demons need to be part of our educational practice.

Note

1 This quote is from my class notes dated 22 January 1996. All subsequent quotes are likewise from my class notes.

References

BARTKY, S.L. (1990) *Femininity and Domination: Studies in the Phenomenology of Oppression*, New York and London: Routledge.

BELENKY, M.F., CLINCHY, B.M., GOLDBERGER, N.R., and TARULE, J.M. (1986) *Women's Ways of Knowing: The Development of Self, Voice, and Mind*, New York: Basic Books.

GREENE, M. (1995) *Releasing the Imagination: Essays on Education, the Arts, and Social Change*, San Francisco: Jossey-Bass Publishers.

IYENGAR, B.K.S. (1965) *Light on Yoga*, New York: Schocken Books.

IYENGAR, G.S. (1983) *Yoga: A Gem for Women*, New Delhi: Allied Publishers Private Limited.

JAGGAR, A. (1989) 'Love and knowledge: Emotion in feminist epistemology,' in JAGGAR, A. and BORDO, S. (eds) *Gender/Body/Knowledge: Feminist Reconstructions of Being and Knowing*, New Brunswick and London: Rutgers University Press, pp. 145–71.

LEDER, D. (1990) *The Absent Body*, Chicago: University of Chicago Press.

LUTTRELL, W. (1993) 'Working-class women's ways of knowing: Effects of gender, race, and class,' in CASTENELL, JR., L.A. and PINAR, W.F. (eds) *Understanding Curriculum as Racial Text*, Albany: State University of New York Press, pp. 153–78.

MORRISON, T. (1987) *Beloved*, New York: Knopf.

WALKERDINE, V. (1990) *Schoolgirl Fictions*, London and New York: Verso.

22 Thinking about Thinking: Maxine Greene on Cognition

Brent Davis and Dennis J. Sumara

We are presented with the power of the poet's vision in William Blake's 'Letter to Thomas Butts' (1977). Penned nearly two centuries ago, long before postmodernist theorists alerted us to the conceptual constraints of a scientized culture, Blake pointed to what had already faded into transparency for most: the marginalizing of diverse modes of thinking by the singular logic of a mathematized science. Blake drew on art and poetry as he sought to arouse the numbed perceptions of his contemporaries, appealing to artistic–aesthetic awarenesses that had been eclipsed by a growing devotion to a monological thinking.

Blake was well aware that the work of art has, as Gadamer (1990) has reminded us, a two-fold function: it both *represents* and *presents*. That is, the work of art simultaneously works to *remind*, to recall to our senses some phenomena that is not immediately present, and to *make mindful*, to prompt us notice our manners of perception by asking us to perceive (and, hence, to think and act) differently. The experience of the work of art, then, is an event of becoming.

The same sensibility permeates the work of Maxine Greene. Blake's words serve both to introduce the central theme of her theorizing and the pedagogic consequences of her thinking. For Greene, formal education is a complex phenomenon with tremendous transformative potential, but which all-too-often gets caught in the uncritical flow of cultural conditioning — that is, in a single (modernist and scientist) vision and in Newton's (mechanistic and reductionist) sleep. The task of schooling is thus to re-awaken the creative imagination, to effect change through efforts to have learners notice the ground of their actions.

A particular attitude toward the phenomenon of cognition is implicit in such formulations. Greene, however, rarely deals directly with the issue of cognition — and, on the occasions that she does broach the topic, she demonstrates an uncommon academic breadth by drawing on phenomenology, hermeneutics, pragmatism, feminism, critical theory, literary criticism, postmodernism, and poststructuralism, among other discourses. But this is not to say that a coherent orientation to cognition is absent in Greene's articles and books. Rather, her thinking about thinking is more enacted than announced in her writings. It is woven into her discussions of educational issues. And, unlike many of the subdisciplines of educational research, Greene does not deal with cognition as a self-contained phenomenon or a topic that is sufficient for analysis in and of itself. Cognition is not psychologized; it is not permitted to be considered apart from questions of our enculturation or as as subsidiary to our efforts to educate. For that reason, this chapter takes up the topic of cognition as the contexts of these concerns, as developed by Greene over recent decades.

Complexity: Cognition and Culture

Long before the notions of 'modernism' and 'postmodernism' were taken up in earnest by educational theorists, Maxine Greene was calling attention to the rationalistic, technocratic, foundationalizing, dichotomizing, and (largely) unconscious mindsets that underpin most of our moment-to-moment thinking and acting. And a decade before Lyotard (1984) described the 'postmodern condition' or Taylor (1991) pointed to the 'malaise of modernity,' Greene (1997) was exploring the 'ennui' and the 'quiet desperation' that are so obviously present in Western cultures, especially among school-aged children.

On the basis of these insights, Greene notes a need for embracing and fostering modes of thinking and argumentation that derive from something other than our modern, logical–rational traditions. She finds an alternative in the artistic–aesthetic experience — and, most particularly, in the experience of engaging with literary texts — which compels a questioning, a recognition, a change in perceptual possibilities.

The aesthetic experience, however, is not presented in binary opposition to the logical mode of thinking. Rather, it is offered as a means of interrupting the anaesthetizing, and largely invisible, modes of thinking and acting that give rise to our commonsensical separations of mind and body, self and other, subject and object, knower and known, rational and emotional, individual and collective, cognition and culture. For Greene, that smooth surface of reality, as jointly constituted and perceived, should be the focus of our thinking about thinking, rather than the unnoticed backdrop of such contemplations.

For Greene, then, cognition is not a subjective, inner phenomenon. Nor does she uncritically subscribe to more recent accounts of cognition that more explicitly invoke the body to circumvent the bifurcation of the mental and the physical. Conversely, she does not slip into the other extreme of dualistic thinking by regarding cognition as an externally determined, fully conditioned phenomenon. Rather, for Greene, cognition is something of a *middle way* between subjectivist–individualist and objectivist–collectivist interpretations. The individual is acknowledged to have agency, but it is an agency that is realized within the limiting conditions of a world that is largely pre-interpreted. However, rather than casting personal agency and cultural context as antagonistic forces, with the school as a third-thing that has been thrust into a mediating role, Greene sees individual and collective in complex dialogical relationship, enfolded in and unfolding from one another. The point of her discussing the influence of the collective on the psyche of the individual, then, is not to undo our enculturation; it is, rather, to enable us to recognize our part in the ongoing viability of complex social structures.

'Complex,' in this context, has a particular meaning. It is drawn from an emergent and cross-disciplinary realm of inquiry — namely 'Complexity Theory' — that Greene does not actually make use of, but which is consistent with her thinking on the inextricability of those phenomena that are normally thought of as manifestations of *culture* and those that are considered to be *cognitive*. Complexity theorists, in their investigations of those systems that tend to be described in terms of life processes (e.g. ourselves, our societies, subcultural groupings), reject the privileged language of physics and look to the organic, the dynamically evolving for a defining imagery. This repudiation of Newtonian mechanics as a foundational metaphor has prompted rethinkings of cause-effect modeling and of the Western habit of considering the whole (e.g. the classroom grouping) as the mere sum of its parts — as opposed, for example, to a form with an integrity and an emergent 'personality' of its own. In this way, scientists have found a way to think of 'culture' not as a set of prescriptive forces acting upon a citizenry, but as the ever-shifting character of shared activity — that is, as a *body* comprised of other bodies.

This is a theme that has long been present in Maxine Greene's work. Drawing principally, although not exclusively (see Greene, 1994), on the phenomenological work of Merleau-Ponty, Greene works from the premise that culture and cognition are inseparable. In saying this, however, hers seems to be a more sophisticated understanding of sociocultural theories of knowing that have recently gained a certain currency in educational discourse. As popularly taken up, these theories often lack a critical awareness of the dialogical relationship of culture and cognition. In consequence, while the fluidity of culture is acceded, the culture itself continues to be treated either as the given — that is, the taken-for-granted — in discussions of teaching and educational research, or, more critically, as an adversary that must be overcome.

Greene (1977) ascribes to neither of these positions as she announces that her 'concern is as much with persons and their lifeworlds as it is with equity in the social system.' These unfold together, and so they cannot be pried apart in some naive attempt to weigh importance or to assign priority. And it is from there that Greene (1977) arrives at the point of education: 'to enrich personal and social life even more than to train productive abilities.' In itself, the sentiment announced here might be interpreted as an enlargement of the notion of cognition, moving beyond conventional ability-focused definitions to implicate phenomena of personal identity and shared activity.

Complicity: Cognition and Schooling

For Greene, then, formal education is not seen in mere transmissive terms — that is, as the mechanism through which our society perpetuates itself. Even less does Greene perceive schooling to be at the service of the corporatist quest for 'progress.' Formal education, rather, is a critical matter.

'Critical,' of course, is a term that has been variously interpreted over the past few decades, and is often imbued with a sense of aggressive subversity. Greene's own sense of criticality is more toward the evolutionary than the revolutionary as she aligns her work with Freire's (1971) notion of *conscientization*. 'Critical' thus refers to a kind of emancipatory thinking, a criticalness that is oriented toward a freedom of perception which 'involves the capacity to assess situations in such a way that lacks can be defined, openings identified, and possibilities revealed' (Greene, 1978, p. 223). Such an education would involve 'break[ing] through, whenever possible, the persisting either/ors' (Greene, 1988) — those dichotomies and distinctions that we use uncritically to give shape to our world.

Education, so conceived, cannot be a matter of enculturation, just as it cannot be a fostering of individuality. Nor is it a balancing or a denying of the two. It must be, rather, an *entre-deux* (to borrow from Merleau-Ponty, 1962) that demands active and simultaneous interrogation of our thinking-acting and the ground of that thinking-acting. Education is thus a coincidental and inevitable transformation of individual and collective, however deliberately or accidentally such transformation is conceived.

The profound moral import of this orientation is not lost on Greene, for in calling for this manner of critical awareness, she is insisting not just that we endeavor to interpret our being-in-the-world in different ways, but that we deliberately seek to change the world through affecting our cognition: our perceptions, our thinking, our acting . . . our selves. 'Morality,' in this project, is not simply the opposite of what is conventionally understood as 'immorality'; it is more broadly understood in contradistinction to *indifference* (Greene, 1978, p. 153). It is thus that Greene sees the hope of formal education as the potential it holds for disrupting lives that are not moral (although not necessarily immoral). For her, the 'most urgent problem in education and politics . . . is to find ways of arousing such persons to active fellowship — and to active engagements with the world' (1978, p. 154).

It is not surprising, then, that Greene is profoundly critical of public schooling and the rhetoric that surrounds it. In particular, the pervasive beliefs that the project of schooling is, at best, morally upright and, at worst, morally inert, are rejected by Greene — as are those uncritical conceptions of cognition that are woven through the activities in and discussions of schooling. Greene highlights the ways that taken-for-granted beliefs about cognition are tightly entwined with the mechanical (e.g. mind as computer) and the corporatist (e.g. 'banking' knowledge) metaphors and rationales that infuse characterizations of conventional schooling. One's beliefs about cognition can never be divorced from one's rationales for formal education.

This issue is of particular relevance in the field of educational research, and Greene (1994) recently criticized the 'more or less untroubled reliance on the paradigms of mainstream science and the benign consequences that should follow from their use' (p. 423). The failure of educational researchers to attend to their own complicity in the establishment and maintenance of such troublesome structures, even while claiming to being oriented toward positive changes, was likely part of Greene's motivation for publishing a historical review of the spectrum of epistemologies and conceptions of cognition that have slipped into the taken-for-granted background of teaching and educational research (see Greene, 1994). In contrast to the corpus of literature that relies uncritically on the philosophical and theoretical work that she reviews, Greene's own educational research has been principally phenomenological in approach. Oriented toward cutting through the prejudices that enframe our thinking-acting, phenomenology seeks to enable us to recognize the world — that is, to perceive/think/act differently. In this way, it might be said that Greene's thinking about education and educational research is centrally concerned with the phenomenon of cognition.

And a theme that is recurrent in her work is clear: in matters of schooling, our thinking about thinking is never innocent. As educational researchers and as teachers, then, we are compelled to interrogate our own beliefs on the matter, along with the ways we are complicit in supporting practices that we know or that we suspect to be troublesome.

Creativity: Cognition and Learning

In the face of such complicity, Greene's work demands a particular deliberateness with regard to the educator's beliefs. Good intentions and a love of children (or of the subject matter) is not enough. This point is most clearly articulated in her discussions of the goals and processes of learning — themselves inextricable phenomena.

Greene uses the term 'learning' in a particular way, and a quick review of some of the words and phrases she uses in *Landscapes of Learning* (1978) when discussing the matter is revealing: 'moments of being,' 'extraordinary perceptual event,' 'living deliberately,' 'hermeneutical event,' 'sentiency,' 'conceptual awareness,' 'reformulation of the taken-for-granted.' Such notions stand in stark contrast to the rather mundane events that are associated with life in modern classrooms.

This contrast is perhaps best articulated through a comparison of 'intelligence' as enacted in conventional schools to Greene's formulation of the notion. Popularly understood to be an innate quality, intelligence tends to be interpreted as the capacity to solve problems that are specified within particular, narrow knowledge domains. Greene refers to the model of cognition that is associated with this conception of intelligence as 'representationist,' and the accompanying measures of intelligence as founded on 'correspondence theories' whereby the level of understanding is deemed to be the extent of match between established objective truths (the *outer*) and emerging subjective conceptions (the *inner*).

Such representationist epistemologies have been challenged in recent years by constructivist accounts of knowing. Following Piaget, these theories complexify notions of cognition by replacing the ideal of 'correspondence with external reality' with the criterion of ongoing viability — in effect, trading the desire to come upon true and universal knowledge for an acceptance that understandings are always local and particular, and hence need only fit with prevailing circumstances. Intelligence in this frame is more toward creativity; the capacity to deal with the continuously novel.

Greene also redefines intelligence in terms of creativity. (And while she too embraces anti-representationist epistemologies, it is important to note she does not align herself with constructivism — in part because of the failure of constructivists to consider the social and moral implications of their theorizing.) Drawing on the pragmatism of Dewey and Rorty (whose works draw, in turn, on Darwin's evolutionary theories), Greene refuses linearity and abstractness as necessary qualities of cognition and rejects the possibility of universal certainty. Greene (1994) also uses the work of Merleau-Ponty, whose phenomenological inquiries into perception demonstrated that 'the human being is an embodied consciousness, contextualized, situated in a landscape, an appearing world' (p. 437). Amidst such notions, the attitude toward the creation of knowledge — on both individual and collective levels — that permeates Greene's writings might be characterized as a sort of ongoing choreography of knowing agents and their circumstances. Valid knowledge, in this frame, is a matter of fitness, of adequacy that must be fluid because on the continuous co-specification of learner and setting.

The antithesis of this creative dance is at the center of conventional schooling, with its frustratingly inappropriate programs of studies consisting of 'foundational' or 'core' concepts that were chosen in very different eras under very different circumstances. Such curricula, Greene asserts, force a separation of knower(s) and knowledge as they militate against any sort of authentic engagement with the subject matter. Classroom learning, thus enacted, can never be about who we are, how we stand in the world, what we might be.

The turn toward creativity, in contrast, involves a re-focusing on precisely these issues as it compels a fusing of perception, knowledge, activity, and identity. Our sensing, knowing, doing, and being are not the ground of education for Greene, they are the figure. And so, it is not so surprising that she never takes on the issue of cognition in isolation. How might one go about disentangling our thinking about thinking from the way we are in the world, especially when engaging in conversations about education?

Within this conversation, Greene infuses a hopefulness. Against the stream of psychologized discourse that reduces cognition and learning to predeterminisitic, cause-and-effect terms, Greene suggests that we can actually choose and transform — that identity is not merely fluid and contextually dependent, but that we play a role in determining who we are. (Once again, this notion applies, simultaneously, at both the individual and the collective levels.) Identity is, in this sense, a manner of creative engagement with the world that is reflexively hinged to one's ever-shifting identifications (perceptions). Identity is thus a cognitive process, not an object to be uncovered, not a core being that unfolds naturally, but the creation of possibilities for living with the complex present.

Contingency: Cognition and Teaching

Culture, schooling, and learning in Maxine Greene's work, then, are all treated as cognitive processes — where 'cognition' is understood as a complex evolutionary dynamic that is necessitated by the need to maintain fitness within shifting circumstances. It is, simultaneously, an affecting and a being affected by.

What, then, can we say about teaching, for it is clear that conventional management-based, control-oriented, corporatist-driven classroom models do not fit with a complexified understanding of cognition? How might we effect a teaching that is deliberately transformative rather than, by default, transmissive? Greene addresses such concerns with a pedagogy that stresses two qualities: interpretation and participation.

Nowhere, however, does Greene offer a prescription for teaching. Instead she proposes a 'dialectic of freedom,' a notion intended to help us to move beyond our current selves. This dialectic implies a conversational mode of engagement, implying an attentiveness and a tentativeness of the part of the teacher. In short, it is a teaching that deeply appreciates the contingencies of existence, and rather than seeking to exorcise the indeterminate in a thrust toward controlling classroom events and learning outcomes, a dialectic of freedom relies more on a preparedness than a planning mentality.

Describing the role of the teacher with such terms as 'interrogation,' 'problematizing,' 'possibilizing,' and 'ongoing hermeneutic,' Greene focuses on the artistic experience as the location for exchanging the figure of formulated knowing for the ground of habitualized activity. She is critical of the anaesthetizing qualities of the modern school, with its repetitions, its irrelevancies, its unconsciousness — all resting on a troubling faith in the possibility of certainty. She offers instead a pedagogy that emphasizes and embraces the contingencies of existence, that does not foreclose on transformative possibilities by attempting to predetermine learning outcomes before it begins. It's not so surprising, then, that this manner of teaching relies on art and aesthetic experience, with their capacity to push past the rational — not to transcend one's enculturation, but to bring one to consciousness of constraining aspects of one's uncritical knowings.

Greene herself enacts this pedagogy in her writings. Rather than corralling her thoughts on teaching into sections on 'Pedagogical Implications,' Greene makes all her writings pedagogic, structuring them around the works of poets and novelists who have troubled common sense and who might help us to think about our thinking. It is this careful providing of opportunities, this ongoing hermeneutic that distinguishes Greene's teaching and theorizing from the hyperactive, but not necessarily educational goings-on of today's schools and 'educational' research. Greene calls for quiet spaces, for moments of slow reflection, for exploratory conversation — a sharp contrast to the sensorial bombardment of our 'high-stim' classrooms.

In all of this, the teacher is not the master or the teller. Nor is the teacher an expert guide or a facilitator. Rather, the teacher is a full participant in the learning that unfolds. Against the conventional ideal, whereby the teacher (like the learner) is not visible in the knowledge that is presented, Greene asks educators to acknowledge their complicity in what is being learned through embracing the contingencies of existence. The teacher should be present in the learning, engaging in the same sort of transformative thinking that is being asked of students while conscientiously participating in the evolution of what comes to be seen as valid and important knowledge.

Another way of saying this — again drawing on discussions of cognition that post-date much of Greene's work — is that the teacher is, at once, a vital part of the learner's and a vital part of the culture's cognitive processes. In fact, the teacher–learner coupling might be seen as a cognitive system. This sense of the relationality of teaching problematizes the traditional separation of teachers from learners. Who is teaching? and Who is learning? become academic within the aesthetic experience, as the sorts of trans-formation engendered in such an event implicate all in a dynamic evolutionary — that is to say, cognitive — process.

It is thus hardly surprising that Maxine Greene should make little direct reference to matters of cognition in her writings. It is clearly not an omission that arises from a lack of concern, nor from a lack of insight. Rather, to discuss cognition, one is compelled to make a choice: Either one goes the route of modern psychology and deliberately avoids looking beneath the surface of the definitions, the methods, and the analyses. Or one invokes the hermeneutic imagination and seeks to enlarge the notion of cognition so that it is read in all its complexity, with knowledge of our complicity, with a sense of the freeing possibilities of creativity, all amid an awareness of life's contingencies.

Of course, choosing the latter might result in the appearance that you're not talking about cognition at all, but about life. Small wonder, then, that Maxine Greene chose that route — and, in so choosing, has helped to create the conditions for today's educationists to appreciate and to participate more readily in a change of mindset that is reshaping not just our theories of cognition, but, more broadly, our senses of what it means to be educated.

References

BLAKE, W. (1977) 'Letter to Thomas Butts', in OSTRIKER, A. (ed.) *William Blake: The Complete Poems*, New York: Penguin.

FREIRE, P. (1971) *Pedagogy of the Oppressed*, New York: Seaview.

GADAMER, H.-G. (1990) *Truth and Method (2nd edition)*, New York: Continuum.

GREENE, M. (1977) 'Equality and inviolability: An approach to compensatory justice,' in BLACKSTONE, W.T. and HESLEP, R.D. (eds) *Social Justice and Preferential Treatment: Women and Racial Minorities in Education and Business*, Athens, GA: University of Georgia Press.

GREENE, M. (1978) *Landscapes of Learning*, New York: Teachers College Press.

GREENE, M. (1988) *Dialectic of Freedom*, New York: Teachers College Press.

GREENE, M. (1994) 'Epistemology and educational research: The influence of recent approaches to knowledge,' in DARLING-HAMMOND, L. (ed.) *Review of Research in Education, Volume 20*, Washington, DC: American Educational Research Association.

GREENE, M. (1997) 'The artistic–aesthetic and curriculum,' *Curriculum Inquiry* **6**, 4.

LYOTARD, J.-F. (1984) *The Postmodern Condition: A Report on Knowledge*, Minneapolis: Minnesota Press.

MERLEAU-PONTY, M. (1962) *Phenomenology of Perception*, London: Routledge.

TAYLOR, C. (1991) *The Malaise of Modernity*, Concord, ON: Anansi.

Section Five

Conclusion

Towards Beginnings

Maxine Greene

How strange! How wonderful! Here are all these people, some of them unknown to me, accounting for me somehow, saying (from their own vantage points) what I have done with my life. I am, of course, deeply moved and grateful as well, particularly to William Pinar and the rapport we have shared over the years. Because I have felt such faith in him, I have been able to rely on his judgment when it came to the contributors of these essays. While I have read only two of them I am haunted now by the existential question: Who am I? How does my becoming look to those who are strangers? What do they find in my writing, as they lend that writing some of their lives? How do their interpretations connect with my original intentions? In what ways do they relate the things I have said and felt and written to historical contexts, to my biography, to class, gender, ethnicity? Are my ideas, my enthusiasms, my commitments to be viewed as contingent on the culture as I have lived it? Where are the spaces in which I am viewed as free, with the power to choose?

These are the kinds of questions that haunt me as I ponder my own memories, as I think about past and present — and (even now) what I am not yet. Have I simply been a good student? Have I been lucky enough to be visited by inspiration — at least now and then? Saying this, I am reminded of the Nobel Lecture written by the Polish poet, Wistawa Szymborska. Exploring the meanings of inspiration, she reminded us that it is not the exclusive privilege of poets or artist. And then:

> There is, there has been, there will always be a certain group of people whom inspiration visits. It's made up of all those who've consciously chosen their calling and do their job with love and imagination. It may include doctors, teachers, gardeners — I could list a hundred more professions. Their work becomes one continuous adventure so long as they manage to keep discovering new challenges in it. Difficulties and setbacks never quell their curiosity. A swarm of new questions emerges from every problem they solve. Whatever inspiration is, it's born from a continuous 'I don't know.' (Szymborska, 1996)

Teaching, writing, speaking, looking at paintings, watching plays and dance performances, listening to music, reading (always reading), I know the challenges are always new. The questions still gather, and I relish my sense of incompleteness. I can only live, it seems to me, with a consciousness of possibility, of what might be, of what *ought* to be. Looking back, I attribute my choosing of questions to my being a woman (and a wife and mother), to my involvement with literature and the other arts, to the persisting conversations with students, to my friendships, and to my awareness of the darkness, of the silence that greets or longing for some cosmic meaning, for a 'truth.'

I surely had no philosophical 'movement' in mind when I began expressing impatience with the voice from nowhere, the voice of the anonymous (but white and male) authority. I wanted the speakers to say *who* they were and why they were saying what they were saying. I remember that the biggest compliment I received in the old days was that I was 'a woman who thought like a man.' More commonly, I was mocked for my 'soft cognition' or disposed of because I was too 'literary,' not neutral or objective enough. Again, without naming what I was doing, I was asking for an understanding of what we now call 'situatedness.' Fascinated by William James, Alfred Schutz, and Maurice Merleau-Ponty after a while, I was reaching towards some notion of 'multiple realities' (Schutz, 1967, pp. 207–57), of networks of relationships (Merleau-Ponty, 1962, p. 456). I was rejecting the model of the distanced, autonomous observer of the world, trying to work through to an image of some one participant, open to the world, *in* the world. I think that made it possible for me to reconcile my interest in social activism (particularly at the time of the Civil Rights movement and the protests against the war in Vietnam, and today with regard to land mines and homelessness) with my professional and academic concerns. But there are still land mines all over the planet; there are still neglected and homeless people on the streets; there are still violated, suffering children. And I am in no danger in my life of privilege. I am trying to nurture a Center for Social Imagination, the Arts, and Education at Teachers College; I am trying to keep writing. There are impinging silences; there are walls, and there are limits. To go back to Merleau-Ponty (1962): 'Whether it is question of things or of historical situations, philosophy has no function but to teach us once more to see them clearly . . .' And then: 'We need have no fear that our choices or actions restrict our liberty, since choice and action alone cut us loose from our anchorage'. This book will keep me working to cut loose. And I am grateful.

References

MERLEAU-PONTY, M. (1962) *Phenomenology of Perception*, London: Routledge & Kegan Paul.
SCHUTZ, A. (1967) *The Problem of Social Reality, Vol. 1. Collected Papers*:
SZYMBORSKA, W. (1996) 'Nobel lecure: *The New Republic*,' 10 December.

Notes on Contributors

Thomas E. Barone is Professor of Education at Arizona State University. His writing expresses an interest in curriculum as aesthetic, political, and institutional text. He has also theorized about and experimented with a variety of arts-based and narrative modes of educational inquiry, including literary journalism, critical biography, collaborative autobiography, and novelistic storytelling.

Alan A. Block is an Associate Professor of Education at the University of Wisconsin-Stout. He has published widely in the area of curriculum theory and practice, including three books, *Anonymous Toil*, *Occupied Reading*, and *I'm Only Bleeding: Education as the Practice of Social Violence Against Children*. His essay in this volume is to honor the healing that Maxine Greene has provided for education.

Donald Blumenfeld-Jones is Associate Professor of Curriculum and Instruction at Arizona State University. Before taking up a career in education, Blumenfeld-Jones danced professionally for 20 years, performing and choreographing modern dance. He studied and performed in New York City as well as throughout the United States and Canada. He also taught dance for many years in private studios and at Duke University and the University of North Carolina at Greensboro. As a curriculum theorist and philosopher of education, his present interests include the place and function of the arts in classrooms and in curriculum theory, classroom discipline, teacher authority, and ethics and education. He is also interested in the relationship between hermeneutics and education. Finally, Blumenfeld-Jones directs and teaches ethics, aesthetics and curriculum in a new teacher education program entitled 'Teaching for a Diverse Future.'

Jon Davies teaches curriculum and teacher education at Northern Michigan University. A graduate of Oberlin College, Jon taught high-school English in San Diego, California for many years before taking his doctoral degree at the University of San Diego. Before moving to NMU, Jon taught at Hofstra University and Louisiana State University.

Brent Davis is Assistant Professor of Education at York University, Toronto, Canada. His principal interests — cognitive theory and cultural studies — are focused in the areas of mathematics education and curriculum theory. He is the author of *Teaching Mathematics: Toward a Sound Alternative* (Garland, 1996).

David M. Dees is part-time instructor in the School of Theater and Dance at Kent State University. His research interests include the artistry of teaching, aesthetic knowing, and the incorporation of the performing arts into the curriculum. He is co-author of 'Teaching the process of aesthetic knowing and representation' in *Envisioning Process as Content: Toward a Renaissance Curriculum.*

James M. Giarelli is a Professor in Rutgers University's Graduate School of Education. He teaches courses in education and philosophy, literature, and popular culture.

Jesse Goodman is currently a Professor at Indiana University where he serves as Co-director of a masters level elementary teacher education program. Formerly, he served as chair of the doctoral program in curriculum studies. Goodman is Co-director of the Harmony Education Center, an organization committed to democratic schooling. His scholarly interests include the relationship between education and democracy, issues of school reform, teacher education/socialization, and research methodology. He has had numerous articles on these topics published in a wide variety of journals and books, and he has received five national awards for his distinguished research. His book, *Elementary Schooling for Critical Democracy*, was published in 1992 by the State University of New York Press. Currently, Goodman is collecting data for his next book on issues related to changing the culture of high-poverty schools.

Robert J. Graham is an Associate Professor in the Faculty of Education and a Senior Fellow of St. John's College at the University of Manitoba, Winnipeg, Canada. He has published widely in the area of English language arts education and on narrative approaches to teaching, learning, and research. He was the recipient of the Book of the Year Award for 1995 from the Canadian Association for Foundations in Education for his *Reading and Writing the Self: Autobiography in Education and the Curriculum* (Teachers College Press). He would like to dedicate this chapter to his wife Lori Downey and also to his daughter Rachel, currently completing Grade 2, a being of rare imagination whose stories and drawings continually amaze and delight.

Maxine Greene is William F. Russell Professor in the Foundations of Education (emerita), Teachers College, Columbia University, where she founded the Center for Arts, Social Imagination, and Education. She teaches at the Lincoln Center for the Arts and is past president of the American Educational Research Association, the American Educational Studies Association, and the Philosophy of Education Society. Among her books are *Teacher as Stranger* (1973), *Landscapes of Learning* (1978), *The Dialectic of Freedom* (1988), and *Releasing the Imagination* (1995).

James Henderson is Professor of Curriculum and Instruction at Kent State University. His research has focused on how to understand curriculum and teaching through democratically oriented curriculum studies. He is author of two texts on democratic teaching: *Reflective Teaching: Becoming an Inquiring Educator*, and *Reflective Teaching: The Study of Your Constructivist Practices*. He has also co-authored a book on democratic curriculum practice entitled *Transformative Curriculum Leadership*, and he has co-edited a text on the continuing study of this practice that is entitled *Understanding Democratic Curriculum Leadership*. He recently served as guest editor for two issues of the journal, *Teaching Education*, on the topic of transformative curriculum leadership.

Janice Hutchison coordinates Staff Development for Kent City (Ohio); she teaches a research course with high school seniors; and she serves as a Partnership Professor between the school system and Kent State University. These three professional roles are connected by a commitment to 'public displays of democracy.' Janice's recent research and publications have focused on the issue of power relations in schools.

Mary-Ellen Jacobs is an English instructor at Palo Alto College in San Antonio, Texas. She received her doctorate in curriculum theory from the University of Maryland in 1991. From 1991–95 she was Assistant Professor (secondary English education) in the

Department of Curriculum and Instruction at Louisiana State University. Her publications have appeared in *Qualitative Inquiry, Harvard Educational Review, Teaching Education,* and *Teaching and Learning.* She has also contributed a chapter to *A Light in Dark Times: Conversations in Relation to Maxine Greene,* edited by William Ayers and Janet L. Miller (Teachers College Press).

Carol S. Jeffers is Associate Professor of Art Education at California State University at Los Angeles where she works with undergraduate and graduate students in the general education, art education, and teacher education programs. Currently, she and her students are exploring metaphor, semiotics, the space between phenomenology and structuralism, and the possibility of a connective aesthetics.

Wendy Kohli is Associate Professor of Curriculum Studies at Louisiana State University. She is editor of and contributing author to *Critical Conversations in Philosophy of Education* (Routledge, 1995) and has published in a range of scholarly journals on critical hermeneutics, feminist pedagogy, multicultural democracy, as well as studies of Maxine Greene and Raymond Williams. Currently, Kohli is writing a book on the curriculum of the body.

Nancy Lesko teaches curriculum theory and history at Teachers College, Columbia University. She is currently editing *Masculinities at School* (Sage, forthcoming) and completing a manuscript examining the construction of adolescence in psychology and in policy arenas, entitled *Act Your Age! Development of the Modern Scientific Adolescent.*

Rebecca Luce-Kapler is Assistant Professor of Language and Literacy in the Faculty of Education, Queen's University, Kingston, Canada. Her current research examines the relationship among computer technologies, writing processes, and identity formation. She recently completed her doctoral dissertation, *As If Women Writing,* which explores women's relationship to the subjunctive spaces of writing. Rebecca is also a poet and fiction writer. Her most recent poetry collection, *The Grey Moon Points Back,* focuses on Canadian artist and writer, Emily Carr.

Marla Morris is a PhD candidate in curriculum theory at Louisiana State University. She has published in *The Journal of Theta Alpha Kappa/National Honor Society for Religious Studies/Theology*; *JCT: The Journal of Curriculum Theorizing; Taboo: The Journal of Culture and Education,* and *The Journal of Medical Humanities.* Currently, she is co-editing a book entitled *How We Work* (Peter Lang) which explores the creative processes of scholarship and writing. Marla's dissertation will examine the Holocaust, representation, and curriculum as memory text.

Charlene Newman teaches undergraduate education courses at Kent State University. She took the BA at Case Western Reserve University, the MA at John Carroll University, a BJS degree at the Cleveland College of Jewish Studies, and the PhD at Kent State University. Newman, and has taught Spanish grades 4 through adult; she has served in administrative positions in religious schools; she has written curriculum, taught graduate and undergraduate education courses, coordinated the field experience component of the Elementary MAT program, as well as supervised student teachers. Her interests include: constructivist teaching and supervision, professional development, autobiographical inquiry, professional collaboration, and pre-service teacher education.

Kathleen O'Gorman is Associate Professor of Religious Studies and Religious Education at the Loyola University Institute for Ministry where she has taught for the past sixteen years. She earned the EdD degree from Teachers College Columbia University in Religion and Education in 1986. There she met and studied with Maxine Greene. Her current research interests and commitments concern the integration of the arts, humanities, and sciences in a comprehensive vision of curriculum and a practice of education that is grounded in narratives of the emergent universe and our planetary home within it.

Anne E. Pautz is Visiting Assistant Professor of Education at Oklahoma State University where she teaches graduate courses in curriculum and coordinates preparation for NCATE accreditation. Her interests include gender construction and representation as well as autobiographical curriculum theory, especially as it reformulates pre-service teacher education.

William F. Pinar teaches curriculum theory at Louisiana State University, where he serves as the St. Bernard Parish Alumni Endowed Professor. He has also served as the Frank Talbott Professor at the University of Virginia and the A. Lindsay O'Connor Professor of American Institutions at Colgate University (both visiting appointments); he taught at the University of Rochester 1972–85. He is the author of *Autobiography, Politics, and Sexuality* (Peter Lang, 1994), the senior author of *Understanding Curriculum* (Peter Lang, 1995), and the editor of *Curriculum: Toward New Identities* (Garland, 1998) and *Queer Theory in Education* (Lawrence Erlbaum, 1998).

Paula M. Salvio is Associate Professor of Education at the University of New Hampshire. Through interdisciplinary studies in feminist theory, performative poetry, and literary criticism, Salvio's research aspires to conceptualize performance as a form of social inquiry in and out of school settings. She is currently writing a book on the teaching life of the Pulitzer Prize winning poet Anne Sexton.

Patrick Slattery is Associate Professor of Education at Texas A & M University where he teaches curriculum theory. He is the author of *Curriculum Development in the Postmodern Era* (Garland, 1995), co-author of *Understanding Curriculum* (Peter Lang, 1995), and co-author of *Contextualizing Teaching* (Longman, 1998). He has published articles on curriculum theory, philosophy of education, and teacher education in *JCT, Harvard Educational Review, Childhood Education, Religion and Education*, and *Curriculum Inquiry*. His research interests include the relation of education to the philosophy of time, aesthetics in the curriculum, postmodern theory, and critical cultural studies.

Susan W. Stinson is Professor of Dance at the University of North Carolina at Greensboro, where she serves as Department Head and teaches undergraduate courses in teacher preparation and graduate courses in interpretative research and curriculum. Her theoretical research concerns issues of gender, the body, and art education; her field research has focused on how young people make meaning of their experience of dance. Her scholarly work has been published in a number of journals, including *Dance Research Journal; Design for Arts in Education; Drama/Dance; Educational Theory; Impulse: The International Journal of Dance Science, Medicine, and Education; Journal of Physical Education, Recreation and Dance* as well as *JCT; Women in Performance; and the Journal of Curriculum and Supervision.*

Dennis J. Sumara is Associate Professor of Education at York University, Toronto, Canada. He has published numerous articles in curriculum theory, action research, teacher education, and language arts education. He is the author of *Private Readings in Public: Schooling the Literary Imagination* (Peter Lang, 1996).

Denise Taliaferro teaches curriculum theory at Colgate University.

Julie Teel is a graduate student at Indiana University. Her previous experience includes teaching in elementary schools and in teacher education. Ms Teel's scholarly interests include eco-feminism, curriculum studies, and elementary education. As well, she is interested in exploring the historical contributions of overlooked women educators. Ms Teel has presented several papers at the annual *JCT* (Bergamo) Conference and at AERA meetings.

Index

actions, 133
Addams, Jane, 85
The Adventures of Huckleberry Finn, 240–1
aesthetic education, 161–2, 164–5
aesthetic experience, 224, 225, 248
aesthetic literacy, 195–7
aesthetic perception, 225
aesthetic practice, 148–59
alchemical symbolization, 102–3
alienation, 69–70
alignment, 244
ambiguities, 132
American Educational Research
    Association, 11–12, 76
anthropocentric focus, 73
anxiety, 134
Appadurai, Arjun, 102
Apple, Michael, 70, 175, 206–7
Arendt, Hannah, 21, 22, 23, 116, 174, 198,
    201
Aristotle, 134, 201
Arnold, Matthew, 217–18
Aronowitz, Stanley, 2
authenticity, 69–71
autonomy, 84, 85, 87
Axtelle, George, 9, 10
Ayers, William, 31, 33, 34, 35, 140, 142, 143

Bachelard, Gaston, 110
back to basics, 30, 34
Bahktin, M.M., 112, 142, 157
Barnes, Hazel, 127
Barnes, Julian, 219
Barone, T.E., 197
Barthes, R., 2, 154
Bartky, Sandra, 243
Bauman, Zygmunt, 22
Beecher, Catherine, 198
Bell, Daniel, 3
Bender, Thomas, 4
Benjamin, Walter, 170
Berenson, Bernard, 21
Bergson, Henri, 129
Berk, E., 222

Bernstein, R.J., 193
Bernstein, Susan David, 115
Beyer, L., 197
binding back, 233
Bishop, Elizabeth, 154–5
black Americans, 89–98
Blake, William, 247
Blanchine, George, 171
Bobbitt, Franklin, 16, 191
Booth, Wayne, 219
Bordo, Susan, 117
Bowers, C.A., 35–6, 73
bracketing, 125, 132
Brameld, Theodore, 9, 10
Brecht, Bertolt, 100, 103, 104–5, 110,
    114–15
Brentano, -, 125
Brickman, William, 10
Britzman, Deborah P., 118, 194
Burrell, G., 66

Campbell, Bebe Moore, 94
Camus, Albert, 9, 19, 65, 99, 104, 124
    Sisyphus, 25–6
    The Plague, 17–18, 24, 25
Carr, David, 124–5, 126
Carr, Emily, 148
Cazden, C.B., 106
censorship, 101–2
Center for Social Imagination, the Arts, and
    Education, 12, 257
Cherryholmes, C.H., 192
Chopin, Kate, 83, 148, 197
Cioran, E.M., 21
Cixous, Helene, 82, 186
classroom pedagogy, 73
Coger, L., 110
cognition, 247–53
coherence, 51
common culture, 63
community, 42–3, 49–50, 130, 142–3
complexity theory, 248
concentration camps, 54
confinement, 81–8

confluence, 169
connectedness, 130, 194–5
connection, 81–8
connective aesthetics, 76
conscientization, 249
consciousness, 37, 78, 125–9, 133, 193, 225
  see also wide-awakeness
  Sartre, 127
  Schutz, 129
Constable, John, 163
creativity, 250–1
Creeley, Robert, 45
Cremin, Lawrence, 174
crisis of belief, 19
critical theorists, 143
cultural literacy, 227
curriculum studies, 190–212

dance, 160–73, 222
Danticat, Edwidge, 105–10, 111–16
de Beauvoir, Simone, 82–3, 130
death, 102
defamiliarization, 77, 79
dehegemonizing, 95
Deleuze, Gilles, 102
deliberation, 206
DeMitchell, T., 102
democracy, 199–201
democracy-education, 203, 204
democratic classrooms, 33
democratic community, 60–75
democratization, 190–212
Dewey, John, 35, 49, 116, 178, 234, 251
  aesthetic experience, 47–8
  democracy, 62, 64, 200, 201, 205
  educational philosophy, 191
  functionalism, 66
  imagination, 46
  social necessity, 174
  society, 60
The Dialectic of Freedom, 12, 39–45, 81,
    91–2, 175–6, 192
  democracy, 206
  emancipatory faith, 199–201
  literature, 184
  searching, 182–3
  women, 85–6
dialogic function, 112
dialogical freedom, 43, 44
dialogical nature, 93–4
dialogue, 130
Diamond, J., 73

Discipline Based Arts Education, 227
Dixon, John, 214
Dobson, Andrew, 127
Donmoyer, Robert, 110
Donnell, Alison, 109, 110, 117
Donoghue, Denis, 223
double-consciousness, 89–98
double-dipping, 113
Dreyfus, Hubert, 128
dualisms, 131
DuBois, W.E.B., 90

Educational Researcher, 11
educational salons, 12
Ellison, Ralph, 40, 94, 142
emancipation, 199–203
emancipatory thinking, 78
emotions, 243–4
empowerment, 44, 224
engagement, 224
English, 213–21
epic theatre, 103
Erhard, Werner, 41–2
EST Institute, 41
Existential Encounters for Teachers, 11, 87
existential freedom, 65–7
existential influences, 124–36
existentialism, 31, 71

Feiler, Bruce, 240
female oppression, 55
feminism, 197–8, 245
Fine, -, 69
Fisher, Bernice, 182, 184
Fisher Staples, Suzanne, 102
Flinders, D.J., 35–6
Florio-Ruane, Susan, 106
fluence, 168–9
Follesdal, Dagfinn, 127
Fornes, Maria Irene, 55
Foucault, Michel, 66, 241
Frankenna, William, 168
Frankl, V., 66
freedom, 33, 86, 89
  see also The Dialectic of Freedom
  democracy, 201–2
  dialogical, 43, 44
  double-consciousness, 91–3
  existential, 65–7
  functionalism, 66
  Greene, 130
  negative, 40, 42, 130, 202

positive, 202
Sartre, 127–8
walls, 89
women, 83–4, 86
Freire, Paulo, 175, 181, 216, 234, 249
Freud, Sigmund, 100
Frye, Northrop, 215, 216
functionalism, 66
fundamental asymmetry, 154

Gablik, Suzi, 76
Gadamer, H., 193
Gadamer, H.-G., 247
Gardner, Howard, 222
gay people, 54–5
Getty Center, 227
Giroux, Henry, 175
Gitlin, Todd, 4
Goldberg, Natalie, 31
Goodlad, J.I., 197
Goodman, J., 70
Goodman, K.S., 217
Gordon, S., 42
Gouldner, Alvin, 2
Graham, Martha, 171
Green, Thomas, 174
Grudin, Robert, 148
Grumet, M.R., 198
Guattari, Felix, 102

Habermas, Jurgen, 116
Haggadah, 25
Hall-Dennis Report, 215
Harnoy, Ofra, 148
Hawthorne, Nathaniel, 53, 76
Herzl, Theodore, 22, 23
heteroglossia, 52, 157
Hirsch, E.D., 16, 52, 175
Hoffman, Piotr, 128
Homans, George, 66
homecomer, 132
homosexuality, 101–2
hooks, bell, 95, 141, 240
Hopper, Edward, 162–3, 170
Howe, I., 3
Hunger Project, 41–2
Hurston, Zora Neale, 94, 182
Husserl, Edmund, 124–6, 132

imagery, 74
imagination, 76–80, 94–6, 104, 133, 134,
    166, 174–8, 215–17

see also Releasing the Imagination
empathy, 226
goodness, 168–9
Woolf, 150
immanence, 132, 133–4
impositional images, 93–7
Independence Day, 39–40
influence, 169
inspiration, 256
intelligence, 250–1
intentionality, 125
Iser, Wolfgang, 138, 150, 151, 154

Jacobs, Harriet, 85
Jacoby, R., 4
Jaggar, Alison, 240, 243–4, 245
Jews, 20–5
Johnson, James Weldon, 94
Jung, C., 103
Just Say No campaign, 41, 42

Kabbalists, 26
Kafka, 22
Kaplan, Mordecai, 19, 20
Kearny, William, 167
Kennedy, Liam, 2, 3, 4
Kierkegaard, Soren, 126, 166
Kohl, Herbert, 32–3
Kundera, Milan, 177

LaBoskey, V.K., 194
Lamhut, Phyllis, 171
Landscapes of Learning, 11, 30–8, 166,
    181, 250
    confinement, 81, 82
    imagination, 176, 215–16
    literature, 184
    wide-awakeness, 193
Langer, Monika, 128
Le Carré, John, 168–9
Leach, Mary, 185
Leder, Drew, 242
Levy, R.N., 25
liberalism, 84, 85–6
lifestyle enclaves, 42
lifeworld, 125, 126
limitations, 83–4
Lincoln Center Institute, 228
Lowry, Lois, 102
Luria, Isaac, 26–7
Luttrell, Wendy, 242
Lyotard, J.-F., 186, 248

Macall, Nathan, 94
McCutcheon, G., 206
Macdonald, James B., 191, 206
Macquarrie, John, 124, 125
making real, 104
making up, 104
Malamud, Bernard, 142
management-education, 203, 204
Márquez, Gabriel Garcia, 33
marginalization, 164
Marx, 20, 130
mathematics, 68–9
Mathews, David, 175
meaning, 138–9, 150, 152, 196
    culture, 35–6
    humanities, 68–9
    performing arts, 167
    religion, 234
    Schutz, 129
    Whirledge, 78–9
Mehan, H., 106
memory, 90, 131
Merleau-Ponty, Maurice, 125, 128–9, 131,
    193, 194, 249, 251, 257
Merrimack School Board, 101–2
metaphoric approach, 53
Meyer, Adolphe, 9
Mill, J.S., 130
Miller, Janet L., 195, 198, 199
Miller, Peter, 101
Miller, Sue, 85
Monet, Claude, 77, 163
Monette, Maurice, 230
montage, 110–11, 113, 114–15, 117
Montessori, Maria, 234
Moore, Marianne, 138
moral awareness, 32
moral domain, 226
moral life, 67
morality, 249
Morgan, G., 66
Morrison, Toni, 92, 94, 95, 100, 118–19,
    156–7, 241
    Beloved, 96, 158
    Jazz, 33
    memory, 90
    Playing in the Dark, 109
    The Bluest Eye, 142
Moses, 27
Mosle, Sara, 16
Mukherjee, Bharati, 142
multiculturalism, 63

multiple realities, 77, 257
multiplicity, 49
mystification, 34–5, 61

Natanson, M., 129
National Endowment of the Arts to
    Congress, 227
natural attitude, 124–5, 126
natural reflection, 132
negative freedom, 40, 42, 130, 202
Nikolais, Alwin, 171
Noddings, N., 42
not-learning, 32–3

Oberlin College, 83
Olson, D.R., 216
Olson, Robert, 124
Other, 52, 65, 91–8, 167
outlaw emotions, 243, 244, 245

Padgham, R., 197
Pagano, JoAnne, 183, 185
Paley, Grace, 83
paradigm shift, 204
Pastoriza, Andres, 107
Pateman, C., 84
pedagogical possibilities, 48–9, 52–3, 54, 55
pedagogy, 117, 118, 162, 228, 238–46, 252
perception, 128, 131, 132, 133
Percy, Walker, 51
performance, 117–18
performative consciousness, 114
performing arts, 160–73
perspectival reading, 112
Peterson, D., 73
Phenix, Philip, 233
phenomenological influences, 124–36
phenomenology, 238–46
Phi Delta Kappan, 52
Philosophy of Education Society, 10, 184–5
Piaget, 251
Picasso, Pablo, 163
Pinar, William F., 69–70, 73, 96, 190–2,
    198, 203–7, 256
Pine, N., 216
pluralism, 63–5
Polanyi, M., 193
positive freedom, 202
possibility, 76–80, 117
postmodernism, 204
potential, 79
powerlessness, 82

praxis, 32, 67, 130
  deliberative, 206
  Freire, 181
  literary, 109
  pedagogical, 48
  social, 216
  women, 83
presentational forms, 110
project, 101
promiscuous identification, 115
Prufrock, J. Alfred, 14
Prynne, Hester, 76
public education, 174–8
The Public School and the Private Vision,
  10, 139, 175–6, 239
public schools, 250
public spaces, 198–9

racism, 52, 55, 89–98
Rainer, Yvonne, 171
Rauschenberg, Robert, 171
Ravitch, Diane, 14–15, 16
Reagan, Nancy, 41
Reagan, Ronald, 41
'Real Toads and Imaginary Gardens', 138
reflective practice, 193–4
relatedness, 82
Releasing the Imagination, 12, 46–57, 91,
  134, 164, 172
religious education, 230–7
repositioning, 95
representational forms, 110
resonance, 110
responsibility, 71
reverberation, 110–11
Rich, Adrian, 63
Ricoeur, Paul, 133, 172
Rilke, Rainer Maria, 137
role models, 182
roles, 82
Rorty, Richard, 142, 177, 251
Rose, Nikolas, 101
Rosenberg, Harold, 3
Rosenberg, P., 106
Rosenblatt, Louise, 110
Roth, Philip, 21, 22
routine action, 193
Rubin, Barry, 21, 22, 23
Ruhs, Frederick, 22

Sacks, Karen, 20
Said, Edward, 2

Sartre, Jean-Paul, 60, 118, 124–8, 130,
  143–6
  dualism, 131
  freedom, 127–8
  project, 101
  responsibility, 71
Scarry, Elaine, 104
Schechtner, Richard, 114
Schloem, G., 26, 27
Schön, Donald, 194
Schubert, W.F., 190
Schutz, Alfred, 31, 125, 129–30
  actions, 133
  multiple realities, 77, 257
  wide-awakeness, 31, 65, 101, 132
Schwab, Joseph, 191, 206
science, 68–9
sedimentation, 244
segregation, 39–40, 83
Self, 52, 89–98
self-creation, 101
self-knowledge, 194–5
selfhood, 141
sex equity, 86
'Sex Equity as a Philosophical Problem', 86
sexism, 83, 84
Shange, Ntozake, 142
Sherman, Martin, 54
situatedness, 85, 95, 257
slaves, 39–40
Smith, Frank, 110
social constructs, 82
social democracy, 61–2
social responsibility, 71–2
society, 17, 19, 60
  see also community
Solomon, Robert, 124, 125
Sontag, Susan, 1–4
Spivak, Gayatri, 95
standards, 16, 30
Steven, Wallace, 172
Su, Z., 197
suicide, 102
Superbowl, 239–40
Szymborska, Wistawa, 256

Taylor, Charles, 93, 116, 248
Taylor, Paul, 171
Teacher as Stranger, 11, 14–29, 181, 184,
  215
'Teaching for Openings', 87
Temple, Francis, 99, 108, 116

Thoreau, Henry David, 19, 166
Towards a Coherent Curriculum, 51
transcendence, 32, 132
transformation, 87, 118
trickle-down theory, 41
trickster, 102
truth, 126
Twain, Mark, 46, 57
Tyler, R.W., 191
Tzimtsum, 26, 27

Vallance, E., 197
van Manen, M., 213

Walker, Alice, 92–3, 100, 182
Walker, D.F., 197
Walkerdine, Valerie, 242
walls, 89
Warnock, Mary, 157, 166
Weber, Max, 129
Weedon, C., 84
Weis, -, 69
Welsh, Sarah Lawson W., 109, 110, 117
Wexler, P., 61
Wharton, -, 83
Whirledge, Michael, 76, 78–80
White, M., 110

Whitehead, Albert North, 232–3, 234
Whitehead, Frank, 214
wide-awakeness, 100–5, 116–19, 132–3,
    193–4, 216
  existentialism, 65–7
  montage, 110–11
  performing arts, 161, 165–6
  Schutz, 31, 65, 101, 132
  sensory images, 224
  Whirledge, 80
Willard, Emma, 198
Wilson, August, 55
Winterson, Jeanette, 108
Wolf, D.P., 197
women, 55, 81–8, 183, 197–8, 243, 245
Woolf, Virginia, 46, 85, 139, 148,
    149–54
Wrangham, R., 73
Wright, Richard, 94, 144

Yennie-Donmoyer, June, 110
Yerushalmi, Yosef, 26
Young-Bruhle, Elizabeth, 183

Zeichner, K., 70, 194
Zionist movement, 23
zombie parable, 99–100